community development

COMMUNITY-BASED ALTERNATIVES IN AN AGE OF GLOBALISATION

Cover photo
The Twelve Apostles, Great Ocean Road, Victoria, Australia

The collection of sandstone structures known as the Twelve Apostles is a metaphor for the power and resilience of community. While individual structures erode over time and crumble in the face of the relentless sea that surrounds them, other structures are in the process of forming out of the cliffs, so no matter how vulnerable the individual structure is, as a group, collectively they remain strong against the elements.

community development

COMMUNITY-BASED ALTERNATIVES IN AN AGE OF GLOBALISATION

FRANK TESORIERO

PEARSON

Pearson Australia
Unit 4, Level 3
14 Aquatic Drive
Frenchs Forest NSW 2086

www.pearson.com.au

Acquisitions Editor: Joanne Stanley
Senior Project Editor: Sandra Goodall
Associate Editor: Katie Pittard
Production Administrator: Rochelle Deighton
Copy Editor: Frith Luton
Proofreader: Jo Tayler
Copyright Editor: Emma Gaulton
Indexer: Frances Paterson
Cover design by Liz Nicholson, design Bite
Cover photograph by Frank Tesoriero
Typeset by Integra, India

Printed in Malaysia (CTP - LSP)

1 2 3 4 5 14 13 12 11 10

National Library of Australia
Cataloguing-in-Publication Data

Tesoriero, Frank.

Community development : community-based alternatives in an
age of globalisation / Frank Tesoriero.

Ed. 4

ISBN 9781442518865 (pbk.)

Includes index.
Bibliography.

For tertiary students.
Community development.
Community organization.
Social service—Citizen participation.

307.14

**Pearson Australia
is a division of**

PEARSON

Contents

Acknowledgements

In undertaking to produce a fourth edition of *Community Development: Community-based Alternatives in an Age of Globalisation* I owe an enormous debt to the original author, Professor Jim Ife, who pioneered the concept and developed it over its first two editions. Jim trusted me with the task of developing a third edition and with going solo with this fourth edition. I thank him for his faith in me.

The fourth edition of *Community Development* represents contributions from many people, especially those who engaged with Jim Ife in the writing of the first two editions. I want to acknowledge the influence of the many folk who work in communities and who reflect deeply on their community work. In particular, I acknowledge the people who have worked in the Murray Mallee Communities for Children Project and in the communities in the Onkaparinga Council area in South Australia. I have been privileged to journey with them in community development.

During my 30 years of working in community development, my greatest teachers have been the people in the communities in which I have worked. Many of these people have contributed to my own practice, thinking and writing. Their work is reflected in many of the case studies. I have had the privilege of working with people who are in communities which are labelled 'disadvantaged' because of the low socioeconomic statistics and poor health indicators of those areas. However, behind the statistics there have been local people with great courage, vision, pride and commitment. They have had the capacity to act collectively to assert their rights. Many of these people have been parents of young children and adolescents, carers of sick or disabled family members and people with many heavy daily demands on them. Despite these personal burdens, they have found meaning in working together to develop their communities. I particularly pay tribute to the contributions to my learning offered by members of the Australian Indigenous communities, the Indo-Chinese refugee communities and those who lived in the 'community' of a psychiatric hospital. I have spent much time in rural south India over the past 14 years. The strong presence of community there has continually demonstrated to me the strength of community as a medium to promote social justice, human rights and a more sustainable ecology. Both the positive strength of community and the people's courage to fight the oppressive, dark sides of community have inspired me.

My colleagues and co-workers in community development over the years have also contributed indirectly, but most significantly, to this fourth edition. Their commitment and belief in community, their qualities, their strong identities as community workers and their stories continue to contribute to this text. In particular, Debbie Martin, David Gray, Mark Loughhead and Elizabeth Becker are community workers who continue to believe in community-based service.

I would like to thank the Pearson Australia team for their support and encouragement throughout the process.

Finally, I would like to express my thanks and gratitude to those around me during the writing of this edition and particularly to my partner, Sirichai Puakpoon, who continues to sustain me in body and in spirit. This support and friendship has been very important.

Frank Tesoriero

Introduction

Despite the formidable achievements of modern Western, industrialised society, it has become clear that the current social, economic and political order is unable to meet two of the most basic prerequisites for human civilisation: people living in harmony with their environment and people living peacefully with each other. If these two prerequisites cannot be met in the long term the achievements and benefits of modern society will be transitory. At the present time the achievements and benefits come at great cost to many people and for these people the achievements are but illusory.

The inability of the dominant order to meet these needs can be seen in the crises currently facing not only Western industrialised societies but all societies. The world is characterised by increasing instability—whether ecological, social, economic, political or cultural—and increasing inequities and existing institutions seem only able to provide solutions that in the long term, and even in the short term, make things worse.

Conditions continue to worsen. Neoliberal policies continue to transfer wealth from the majority world to the minority world. The concentration of increasing wealth among a few continues to exacerbate inequities and to violate human rights within countries. Continuing patriarchal regimes and the political obsession with demonising those who are different are predominant among the forces that ensure the continuation and flourishing of racism, social and political exclusion, oppression of those already oppressed, economic and political exploitation, the erosion of human rights and the degradation of the environment. These forces are becoming the norm. And war seems to be economic globalisation carried out with weapons.

In this context the need for alternative ways of doing things becomes increasingly critical. There has been increasing interest in development at the community level as an alternative way of doing things and as potentially providing a more viable and sustainable basis for achieving peaceful human relations and harmonious interaction with the environment. Among activists concerned with both environmental and human rights/social justice issues, the establishment of viable community-based structures has become a key component of strategies for change. Community development represents a vision of how things might be organised differently so that genuine ecological sustainability, human rights and social justice, which seem unachievable at a global or national level, can be realised in the experience of human community. This book represents an attempt to articulate that vision and to provide a theoretical framework for community development that will link analysis, context and action. This praxis is imperative because resistance to neoliberalism and neo-colonialism is strengthening and growing. In many areas people from local communities are joining together into global social movements, such as the World Social Forum and the People's Health Movement. The latter, at its second Assembly in July 2005, stated the movement's vision as 'a socially and economically just world in which peace prevails; a world in which all people, whatever their social condition, gender and ability, are respected, are able to claim their right to health; and the people of the world celebrate life, nature and diversity' (People's Health Movement 2005). This is a vision of an alternative world and resonates with the cry of the World Social Forum that 'another world is possible'. It is a vision shared by the analysis in this book and underpinning its theoretical framework.

The increasing interest in development at the community level has been evident in two directions. One is the embracing of community development by a wide range of occupational groups, not merely the human service professionals and community activists. The other is the existence of a much broader range of occupational and interest groups who feel that community development is important in their work, which has underscored the power of the community development perspective.

The enormous cultural variation among those who have found that this book has something valuable to say continues to be a source of energy for the author. Not only has the book been used in many different cultural and national contexts, the third edition has been translated into Indonesian.

The fourth edition of this book contains a number of important developments. The embedding of human rights in the theoretical framework is further supported by including a collectivist perspective of the idea of *strengths* as one means of translating the human rights principles into practice. Appreciative Inquiry is used as one strengths-based approach in community development to assist the reader in the translation of theory to practice. There is more discussion of ecology as the ecological crises rapidly deepen.

Chapter 1 lays the foundation for, and the context of, the remainder of the book. It describes some of the dominant and current forces that are challenging to notions of humanity and community. The chapter argues that Western societies have been inculcated with individualistic values and world views, culturally, economically and ethically. Dominant cultural values have given increasing importance to the individual. Globalisation and its accompanying economic governance perceive citizens as individual consumers. Our sense of ethics and our range of obligations have contracted down to family and perhaps our local area; meanwhile there are more widespread views that those who are strangers are to be feared and suspected. The rise of xenophobia is anathema to notions of human rights-based understandings of community. The challenging of traditional notions of collectivism and community by individualism and globalism is becoming more apparent in non-Western societies and is accompanied by increasing inequities within societies. Within this context it is argued that community is being eroded and so community must be rebuilt and forces hostile to humanity challenged; within this, community development becomes a critical response.

Chapter 2 examines the current environmental crisis and the range of responses to environmental issues. From these theoretical perspectives an ecological approach to community development is articulated, along with some core ecological principles, which need to underpin community-based alternatives in a world that is globalised and obsessed with economic growth.

Chapter 3 argues that the pursuit of social justice, working towards empowerment and the challenging of free-market paradigms, impels us to move away from a purely needs-based approach to a human rights-based approach to community development. This chapter develops an approach to human rights that is broader than the charters of civil and political rights and which builds on the developing understanding of collective rights that is more closely related to community development. It argues for the importance of having clear criteria to establish claims as human rights; of hearing the claims of marginalised, exploited and otherwise silent groups and of actively building a culture of human rights.

This chapter discusses the implications of a human rights approach by introducing the distinction between strengths and deficit approaches to development. This introduces the notion of strengths-based practice, which is developed in forthcoming chapters as one important approach within a rights-based approach.

A human rights foundation and this particular strengths based approach to human rights will continue to build a strong rationale for community development.

Chapter 4 brings together ecological and socio-political perspectives to form the basis of an integrated approach to community development.

Chapter 5 outlines the idea of change from below and the valuing of local knowledge, culture, skills, resources and processes. This is a central concern in community development as presented in this book. The rhetoric is almost self-evident; the practice is both complex and radical.

Chapter 6 explores participation as a theoretical underpinning to the preceding chapter's discussion of change from below and Appreciative Inquiry as an exemplary approach to ensuring effective participation and change from below.

Chapter 7 emphasises the importance of process in community development. Process, it is argued, will enable the community to determine its own goals and remain in control of the journey as well as the ultimate destination. This chapter seeks to establish a way of thinking where people interacting with each other is important, the quality of the collective experience is valued and it is in the experience of community processes that people are able to maximise their potential and achieve their full humanity. As well as establishing a way of thinking, it seeks also to provide the opportunity for these valued processes to become a reality for people.

Chapter 8 deals with issues of the global and the local, including globalisation, linking the global and the local, working internationally and the dangers of colonialist practice.

Chapter 9 describes an integrated and holistic approach to community development involving six components of development: social, economic, political, cultural, environmental and personal/spiritual.

Chapter 10 outlines practice principles that have emerged from previous chapters and which form the basis of a developmental approach to community development.

Chapter 11 brings together the 26 principles of community development in a way congruent with the previous chapters and discussions in the book.

Chapter 12, newly written for this fourth edition, is devoted to narrating community development stories and reflecting on those stories. This chapter highlights the way in which frameworks and practice form an iterative process that assists the community worker to make judgements in the many complex, unpredictable, puzzling and perplexing situations in communities. It finishes with a plea for passion and commitment as the hallmarks of the good community worker.

In this fourth edition, the book continues to move, in a general way, to include more practical considerations, but it is far from a simple linear development. Indeed, part of the discussion in the earlier chapters emphasises the need to reject linear thinking and so the reader is encouraged to 'jump around' and not necessarily read the book in the order in which it is presented. The book does attempt to follow a logical sequence, but there are other equally valid sequences that would have resulted in a very different ordering of the material.

The book assumes that the reader has some familiarity with basic social and political ideas, such as social class, power, the division of labour, Marxism, feminism, socialism and the like. This is not to say that detailed or expert knowledge of such topics is necessary; completion of first-year university study in sociology, anthropology, politics or some other social science discipline (or alternatively a comparable understanding gained from general reading) should provide the reader with a more than adequate background.

Frequent use is made of a number of terms that have been grossly overused and misused in recent years, such as *community*, *empowerment*, *development*, *sustainable*, *ecological*, *Green*, *social justice*, *human rights*, *community-based*, *holistic*, *participation*, *consciousness-raising*, *non-violence* and *participatory democracy*. Even though these terms have been overused, they still represent powerful ideas; indeed, their very popularity and the competing claims on their use are testaments to their power and their perceived relevance. They have an important contribution to make to the vision and the practice principles of this book and so these terms are not avoided or replaced—the aim of the book is to clarify rather than obscure the ideas behind these terms and to reinvest them with some substantive meaning for community workers.

Throughout the book the terms *community development* and *community work* have slightly different meanings. The former refers to the processes of developing community structures, while the latter refers to the actual *practice* of a person (whether paid or unpaid) who is consciously working to facilitate or achieve such development.

The terms *majority world* and *minority world* have been used throughout in favour of *the South* and *the North*, *developed* and *developing nations*, *Third World* and *First World* or other similar terms. None of these terms is wholly satisfactory. The term *Western* (or *the West*) is used in the book to refer to primarily to Western *culture*, whereas the terms *majority world* and *minority world* are used more in an economic and political context; of course the distinction is not always clear-cut, as economics and culture are themselves inextricably entwined. It should, however, be noted that there is no necessary single antithesis of *Western* in cultural terms, whereas the economic constructs of *the majority world* and *the minority world* are not only opposites, but are also in a structural relationship such that neither could exist without the other and each serves to define the other.

The term *Aotearoa* is used rather than *New Zealand* as a deliberate political and cultural statement.

Case studies appear throughout the text. These are not meant to be exhaustive stories; rather, their aim is to provide a stimulus to engage in the application of concepts and ideas to real situations and to be able to make meaning of community development activities from the point of view of ecology, social justice and human rights. Every case study is either a real process taken from practice or heavily based on practice experiences. There is a mix of Australian and international case studies as these different contexts enrich the contribution such case studies can make to community development analysis and to appreciating the way local activity is congruent with the vision of community development and the vision of an alternative world contained in this book.

At the end of chapters 1–11 there are discussion questions and reflective questions. The discussion questions aim to provide readers with the opportunity to test their understanding of the main discussion, content and concepts of the chapter. The reflective questions, on the other hand, have quite a different goal. They are generally focused on the reader, on their values, positions, ideas and approaches to community development. The focus on *self in relation to community and community development* aims to encourage and assist the development of reflective and critical community development practitioners. It is based on the belief that reflective practice is an essential ingredient to monitor the extent to which ecological, social justice and human rights principles are being adhered to and the extent to which practice promotes and progresses these principles. There are also inherent tensions among these three sets of principles. Such tensions can only be addressed through reflective practice, where community workers' questioning of each situation will lead to the regeneration of knowledge as a constant process. This book, therefore, cannot be prescriptive and claim to provide comprehensive knowledge and understanding, but rather it aims to be an important contribution to reflective workers' processes of ongoing knowledge generation and regeneration in their diverse and dynamic practice contexts – true praxis. To use Payne's (2001) terms, the book does not represent a static knowledge base in community development, but rather offers a knowledge *bias*, or a lens, through which community workers can continually build and reshape context-relevant knowledge.

Throughout the book there are a number of tables and diagrams that illustrate in summary form the ideas discussed in the text, culminating in Figure 12.1, which ambitiously attempts to summarise the entire framework. They are included with mixed feelings. While such tables and diagrams are helpful in obtaining an overview and seeing how the material fits together, this needs to be balanced against the dangers of categorisation and oversimplification. Tables and diagrams can have the effect of imposing a false sense of order on a complex and chaotic reality and, hence, of inviting simplistic solutions to complex problems. To represent complex concepts by a few words in a cell of a table is to change the very nature of the content itself and invites a dangerous reductionism. A too-rigid interpretation of such tables is antithetical to the holistic approach advocated in the early chapters and the reader is cautioned to remember that the boundaries of the tables do not represent rigid distinctions or impermeable barriers. If the tables and diagrams are regarded as an aid to comprehension, but not as rigid categorisations or definitions, they will have served their purpose.

While this book has a practical application and attempts to incorporate both theory and practice, it does not provide simple prescriptions of how to 'do' community work. A number of principles of practice are outlined, but the way in which they are translated into community development practice will vary from community to community and from worker to worker. Community work is, at heart, a creative exercise and it is impossible to prescribe creativity. Rather, one can establish theoretical understandings, a sense of vision and an examination of the nature of practice in the hope that this will stimulate a positive, informed, creative, critical and reflective approach to community work. That is the aim of this book.

A note on case studies and questions

There are discussion questions and reflective questions at the end of Chapters 1–11. Many of the chapters also contain case studies.

The case studies either describe or are based on the experiences of community workers, including the authors' experiences. They are organised to provide a short scenario to illustrate some aspects of discussion in the chapters. They are short and are not designed to tell a full and comprehensive story. Rather, they are meant be a stimulus for readers to think about some practice situations and ask questions that will enable them to reflect on the strengths and weaknesses of the practice and on issues arising from the situation. In all cases, the reader will need to make some assumptions. However, awareness of the assumptions made when working in community development is an important attribute of a community worker. Reflective practice, which is discussed in this book, is a fundamental component of practice, especially in terms of the approach taken in this book—namely a bottom-up approach based on principles of ecology, social justice and human rights.

The discussion questions are designed to allow readers to demonstrate their understanding of the important content of each chapter. They are focused on the content and some implications of the content for community development.

The reflective questions, on the other hand, are focused on the readers, their personal growth and professional identity as community workers. They are the questions that ought to form part of practice, because they are the questions that facilitate a reflective process—a process designed to understand the ways in which personal values, attitudes, experience and identity have impacts on practising community development. Reflective practice is critically analytical of the work undertaken and seeks to identify ways in which activity can be improved.

Together the case studies, discussion questions and reflective questions provide opportunities to relate the discussions in the chapters to real-life situations, understand more fully the discussions and use the content to build skills in reflective practice. In other words, these aspects of the book strengthen its applied nature and the relevance of the concepts and ideas to the activities of communities.

Beyond the welfare state: the crisis in human services, the rise of individualism and the need for community

Introduction

There is no clear agreement on the nature of the activity described as *community work*. Some see it as a profession; some see it as one aspect of some other profession or occupation, such as social work or youth work; some see it as anti-professional; some see it as people coming together to improve their neighbourhood; some see it in more ambitious terms, of righting social injustice and trying to make the world a better place; some see it in terms of social action and conflict; some see it in terms of solidarity, cohesion and consensus; some see it as inherently radical; some see it as inherently conservative; and so on (Kenny 2007). Not only do people's understandings of community work differ, but the terminology is also confused. The terms *community work*, *community development*, *community organisation*, *community action*, *community practice* and *community change* are all commonly used, often interchangeably and, although many would claim that there are important differences between some or all of these terms, there is no agreement as to what these differences are and no clear consensus as to the different shades of meaning that each implies.

There is similar confusion about the idea of community-based human services. The term *community-based* is used in a variety of contexts, and often has little substantive meaning beyond a vague indication that the service concerned is somewhat removed from the conventional bureaucratic mode. There is, however, considerable interest in the development of a community-based approach to the delivery of human services (such as health, education, housing, justice, child care, income security and personal welfare), and a belief that this represents an important improvement over the current mix of welfare state and private market. But there is still relatively little systematic thinking about what such a community-based alternative involves or its theoretical and ideological underpinnings.

This book is an attempt to make sense of community work and community-based services. It is based on the premise that the main reason for much of the confusion—and the seeming inadequacy of what passes for community work 'theory'—is that community work has not been adequately located in its social and political context, or linked to a clearly articulated social vision, in such a way that the analysis relates to action and 'real-life' practice. There are many books and articles on community work that analyse its political context, but relatively few articulate a clear and consistent theory for community work. A number of others seek to provide practical advice on 'how to do it', but it remains the case that much of the 'theory' seems unrelated to the reality of practice. Many of the stated principles of practice are fragmentary and context-free and often the goals of community work remain vague, uncharted and contradictory. Similarly, the literature on community-based services is often rhetorical rather than substantive and often does not relate specifically to relevant social and political theory.

This book attempts to remedy that deficiency. It seeks to locate community work and community-based services within a broader context of an approach to community *development*. This latter term is seen as the process of establishing or re-establishing structures of human community within which new ways of relating, organising social life, promoting human rights and meeting human needs become possible. In this context, community work is seen as the activity or practice of a person who seeks to facilitate that process of community development, whether or not that person is actually paid for filling that role. Community-based services are seen as structures and processes for meeting human needs, drawing on the resources, expertise and wisdom of the community itself.

The starting point for this exploration will be the crisis in the contemporary welfare state and the recent interest in developing some form of 'community-based' alternative. It is from examining the shortcomings of many attempts to move to a community-based model, and the identification of what is missing from these attempts, that a vision of a more viable alternative can begin to emerge.

The crisis in the welfare state

Contemporary community work must be seen within the context of the crisis in the welfare state. There has been substantial agreement among social policy writers since the early 1980s that the welfare state has entered a period of crisis, though differing theoretical explanations proposed for this crisis have resulted in a variety of prescriptions about how it should be resolved (Pierson 1991; Bryson 1992; Esping-Andersen 1990; Goodin et al. 1999; Mishra 1984, 1999; Rodger 2000). Some writers, such as Taylor-Gooby (1985) and Beilharz, Considine and Watts (1992), have questioned whether there is in fact a crisis, suggesting that uncertainty and instability are inevitable attributes of the modern welfare state and should not necessarily be seen as typical only of a specific 'crisis' period. Jamrozik (2005) argues that we are now in a *post*-welfare state, suggesting that we are beyond the welfare state, but as yet with no clear alternative to it emerging. There is almost complete agreement, however, about the inadequacy, instability and uncertainty of the welfare state and its apparent consistent inability to meet the full range of human needs.

It has become clear that the modern welfare state in Western societies has not been able to deliver all that it promised in the optimistic days of postwar consensus. The welfare state was justified by a social democratic/Fabian ideology that since the 1980s has had little legitimacy. In retrospect, the ideals of the founders of the welfare state now seem hopelessly naïve. The vision of writers such as Richard Titmuss (1968) and T.H. Marshall (1965) remains powerful, but its record of achievement, at least in English-speaking countries, is a modest one. Research has clearly indicated that the welfare state's aims of social equality, the achievement and maintenance of minimum standards of provision and the maintenance of social cohesion and collective responsibility have at best been only partially achieved (George & Wilding 1984; Le Grand 1982). The welfare state has not been an effective mechanism for bringing about a fairer society, though there is some justification for the claim that it has prevented even greater excesses of social inequality and injustice. Even in the European and Scandinavian social democracies where a welfare state has been more strongly established, there is now a modest degree of reassessment of the reliance on the welfare state as the primary institution for the meeting of human needs.

The crisis in legitimacy of the welfare state is in part due to a resource/fiscal crisis (O'Connor 1973). While high levels of economic growth could be maintained, increased social expenditure and the expansion of welfare state services were a real possibility. The slowing of economic growth placed a much heavier burden on governments and at the same time increased public demand for welfare-state services through higher levels of unemployment and poverty. This is one of the fundamental contradictions of the welfare state: that the times it is most needed are the times it can least be afforded. Writers from the so-called 'new right' in the early 1980s (e.g. Kristol 1978; Friedman & Friedman 1980) argued that this impasse was exacerbated by the phenomenon of rising expectations: democratically elected governments have to promise increasing levels of social provision in order to secure re-election and have to go beyond what can reasonably be afforded or provided by the state. It should be noted, however, that more recently government and opposition parties have been able to make a popular virtue of 'fiscal responsibility' and some have succeeded in winning elections on the promise of spending less rather than more. Interestingly they have found it difficult to maintain the same commitment once in government, and have been unable to reduce spending to the extent promised; welfare state expenditure seems to develop a momentum that is very difficult for governments to reverse (Jones 1996; Saunders 1994; Rodger 2000), despite apparently savage cuts in programs.

The other fundamental contradiction of the welfare state relates to its significance in supporting the social and political order. The welfare state plays an important role in maintaining political stability (George & Wilding 1984) or, from a Marxist point of view, as part of the structures of cultural hegemony. As Mishra (1984) and others have pointed out, the welfare state's opponents have not been able to demonstrate how democratic capitalism can be maintained without the stabilising support of the welfare state. Thus, as so clearly put by Offe (1984), governments may be unable to afford the welfare state, but they also are unable to afford to do without it.

The effects of the crisis in the welfare state are clearly visible at the level of service delivery. Continuing cutbacks in public services, lowering of the quality of service as overburdened workers are urged to 'do more with less', longer waiting lists and waiting periods, lack of access to health care (except for those who can afford private insurance), the deterioration of the public education system, poor staff morale, overcrowding and a general lack of confidence in the capacity of the public system to cope are all familiar themes in many Western societies.

The inability of governments to cope with this crisis is clearly illustrated by what passes for social policy initiatives. Often these become public relations exercises with more style than substance and there are several 'policy' techniques that have become depressingly familiar as strategies to give the impression that much is being achieved. One is the production of glossy publications full of rhetoric about 'steps forward', 'new initiatives', 'social advantage', 'social dividend', 'equity and access' and other high-minded goals. Another is an apparently perpetual succession of taskforces, working parties, summits and commissions, which can take up a good deal of time while giving the impression that 'something is being done'. A third is the repackaging of already existing programs under new, catchy titles; publications about 'family policy', for example, are notorious in this regard. Thus, if one asks a government representative about the policy on a particularly problematic issue (e.g. mental health, youth homelessness or unemployment), one is likely to be handed a slick publication full of rhetoric and to be told about a significant new taskforce that has been established to deal with the problem. Such responses have become apologies for genuine policy and represent a tacit admission that many of the problems that governments are required to deal with are in fact insoluble within the existing social, economic and political structures.

Responses to the crisis

The common responses, or proposed 'solutions', to the crisis in the welfare state can be loosely grouped into five broad approaches, though within each there are different emphases and orientations and some writers have sought to combine elements of more than one. Readers familiar with the literature on social policy will recognise that the differences between the five reflect theoretical distinctions that have been made by a number of writers, such as Wilensky and Lebeaux's institutional and residual welfare (1965), Titmuss's Model A, Model B and Model C (1974), Mishra's residual, institutional and structural models (1981), Esping-Andersen's worlds of welfare capitalism (1990) and so on. While for the purposes of this book there is not space (or need) to discuss the five approaches in detail, they can be briefly summarised as follows.

1. DEFENDING AND RE-ESTABLISHING THE WELFARE STATE

This response sees the problems of the welfare state and the withdrawal of welfare state services as essentially reversible. It argues for a reassertion of the social democratic and collectivist values that supported the development of welfare states in the postwar era and seeks to re-establish the vision of a fairer system, based on the principles of humanity, equity, progressive redistribution, caring and social justice, where strong public provision of human services is seen as the hallmark of a civilised society. This approach has been strongly argued in the United Kingdom by writers such as David Donnison (1991) and Paul Wilding (1986) and in Australia by, among others, Hugh Stretton (1987), the Evatt Research Centre (1989) and the Australian Council of Social Service (ACOSS). It has found active expression in the characteristic policy response of the so-called welfare lobby, which has argued strongly against a reduction of services, privatisation, funding cutbacks and so on as it seeks desperately to preserve as much of the existing system of public social provision as possible. While there is undoubtedly some element of self-interest in this response (as many public sector jobs depend on the success of such a strategy), it is also clear that the passion with which the welfare state's supporters fight to maintain existing services arises from a genuine commitment to the needs of service users and from a belief that the dismantling of the welfare state is both unjust and a retrograde step in terms of social progress.

2. THE 'NEW RIGHT', NEOLIBERALISM (ECONOMIC RATIONALISM) AND PRIVATISATION

The response of the political right to the crisis in the welfare state has been clearly spelled out in a number of publications (e.g. Tapper 1990; Nurick 1987) and in the political programs of several governments of the right, starting with the Thatcher and Reagan administrations in Great Britain and the United States and including the conservative governments of Canada and Aotearoa (New Zealand) in the early 1990s and Australia in the later 1990s. This approach sees the welfare state as generally undesirable and as being more likely to exacerbate than to solve social problems. It aims, therefore, to dismantle state structures for the public provision of services and replace them with market-driven, private sector activity. This is in the belief that the market, with minimal or no regulation, is the best mechanism for the provision of human services, in that it maximises efficiency, encourages competition and maximises individual choice and services' accountability to service users. The government's role is seen as minimal and policy directions include privatisation, 'user pays', private insurance, voucher systems and so on.

3. THE NEW PUBLIC MANAGEMENT

This response is based on the assumption that management in the private sector is far superior to public sector administration and so the solutions to the *inefficiencies* of the welfare state are to be sought in the methods of the private sector. This paradigm of public management, which has been dominant in the public sector since the mid- to late 1980s, is very consistent with the 'new right'. Dawson and Dargie (1999) define it as a movement and ideology and as a set of practices. It emerged from the belief that the public sector was very inefficient and in need of a major overhaul—that it did not lend itself to reasonably containing costs nor to quality improvement. As Savoie (1995) claims, 'administration' (the term traditionally used in the public sector) is significantly different from 'management'. The former term is often associated with a slow bureaucratic system and heavy hierarchy while the latter conjures up ideas of contractual relationships, efficiency, customer service, core business, risk management, performance outcomes, competition and customer-driven organisations. The new public management, with its associated privatisation of services, was also attractive in a climate of shrinking public resources. Since the introduction of the 'new right' approaches and the new public management, we are witnessing worsening health services, lower standards in education, less accessibility to affordable housing, welfare policies that are more individualised, and a blaming of the victim. Does this mean that the new public management has failed? According to Savoie (1995), the answer is a clear 'yes'; he contends that the new public management is fundamentally flawed because the public sector is *not* the private sector and practices in the private sector rarely apply to the public sector. He argues that the public and private sectors are alike, but alike in all the petty ways. The core of public administration is radically different from that of private sector management. Public administration attempts to enhance and support citizenship, which is a notion of collective identity and purpose, while private management responds to and manipulates individual, isolated consumers.

4. CORPORATISM

The corporatist approach to the crisis of the welfare state involves the establishment of structures that encourage national consensus between conflicting interests (e.g. capital and labour) and which, therefore, emphasise unity and integration. It was proposed by writers such as Mishra (1984; see also Cawson 1982), who pointed out the considerable success of countries such as Austria and Sweden, which have followed such a model. It was also characteristic of the Clinton administration in the United States and the Hawke and Keating Labor governments in Australia. The corporatist approach tends to break down the traditional barriers between public and private provision. As with the new public management, government departments are encouraged to emulate the private sector ('corporatisation') in terms of their structure, management practices, marketing of services, entrepreneurialism, employment policies and so on, but it adds an extra dimension by encouraging the private sector to take seriously its responsibility to the community in a broader sense and be concerned with social goals as well as creating profits. The two sectors become more closely integrated and the links between the two are strengthened. This approach can lead to the establishment of agencies that are not clearly definable as either public or private, relying on funding from both state and market sources, with accountability to both a government and an independent board.

5. THE SOCIALIST RESPONSE

A characteristic of the above responses is that each sees the crisis of the welfare state as essentially solvable within the existing structures of contemporary Western society. Each is fully consistent with a capitalist economic system and some writers in all three categories explicitly state that their proposed solution will strengthen rather than threaten the existing order by helping to create stability and prosperity.

Writers from a Marxist perspective (Gough 1979; Corrigan & Leonard 1978; Offe 1984; O'Connor 1973) view the crisis in the welfare state as a manifestation of the crisis in capitalism. The welfare state is seen as having grown alongside the capitalist system—as an integral part of it—and as an essential mechanism for maintaining the capitalist order. A Marxist analysis maintains that the capitalist system contains the seeds of its own destruction, through its inherent contradictions, and that the problems of advanced capitalism (of which the crisis in the welfare state is just one) can be solved only by dismantling capitalist structures and replacing them with a socialist order.

Because of the radical nature of this prescription—and also because of the 'bad press' the Marxist position has received following political change in the former Soviet Union and Eastern Europe—such socialist alternatives do not currently represent one of the mainstream policy responses to the crisis in the welfare state. Few governments or significant opposition parties currently advocate specifically socialist policies and they have largely dropped from conventional policy discourse. Nevertheless, the socialist position must be taken seriously in considering the range of possible responses to the crisis as it represents a position with a formidable theoretical and intellectual underpinning, which has been influential in shaping other radical and creative alternatives.

Specific inadequacies of the mainstream and socialist responses

It is the contention of this book that none of the above represents a convincing response to the crisis in the welfare state and that an alternative approach, built upon the concept of community-based services, has much more potential. Before moving on to explore this alternative, it is necessary to briefly outline the shortcomings of the above positions—those that represent the more orthodox policy responses and those that represent the Marxist position.

There are specific objections to each approach and one fundamental and overriding objection that applies equally to all five. Before discussing this overriding objection, the specific criticisms of each position will be briefly summarised. While these criticisms can undoubtedly be disputed by advocates of each position and they have been discussed in some detail in the theoretical literature, they nevertheless represent significant difficulties which are, at least, cause for debate.

The *defenders of the welfare state* have found it difficult to counter the criticism that large, centralised bureaucratic structures, which are an inevitable consequence of a welfare state system, are neither effective nor efficient in the delivery of human services and that they dehumanise, alienate and disempower those whom they purport to serve. In addition, the weak theoretical foundation of the social democratic approach to welfare (Taylor-Gooby & Dale 1981) has left the advocates of the welfare state open to attack from both the right and the left; it can be argued that it was only in the era of the postwar consensus that the ideological foundations of the welfare state could remain intact and this consensus has long gone.

The advocates of the *new right* approach seem unable to acknowledge what the experience of 200 years of capitalism has clearly demonstrated: while the free market may have certain advantages in terms of efficiency and competition, it has shown itself to be incapable of meeting human needs in an equitable way. It tends to exacerbate rather than reduce social and economic inequalities and in the name of competition and individualism it negates the values of caring, social solidarity, cohesion and community. The proponents of new right ideology have found it difficult to convince the general public and many 'experts' that their position is not based essentially on selfishness, greed and a lack of caring and humanity and that it does not result in significant levels of poverty, loss of community, degradation and alienation for the majority of the population.

Those who promote the *new public management* have failed to acknowledge that public administration operates within a political context. It is reasonable, if there are problems in public administration, to look to the political context and its deficiencies as a way to address public administration problems, not to blindly adopt mantras of customer empowerment, competition, outputs and performance appraisal. The new public management has resulted in solutions being grabbed without a thoughtful diagnosis of the structural problems and in an eroding of citizenship.

Corporatism is subject to significant criticism on the grounds that it represents an artificially manufactured compromise between essentially competing interests, such as capital and labour, so that at best it can be only a short-term and inevitably unstable arrangement. It can, perhaps, succeed only under certain specific economic and political conditions (e.g. relatively stable economic growth and prosperity), which cannot be expected to last indefinitely. Another criticism of the corporatist approach is that it requires trade-offs to be made at the level of peak organisations representing particular sectors of society and the economy. This militates against democratic or participatory forms of policy and decision making and serves to reinforce the power of the existing elites.

The *Marxist* alternative, while arguably resting on a much stronger theoretical and intellectual base than the other three approaches, also fails to take account of the alienating and dehumanising effects of state bureaucracies and central planning. Despite the rhetorical ideals of a truly communist society, to date communism in practice has been accompanied by extremely repressive measures. While it can be argued that this need not be the case, the experience makes it difficult for Marxists to gain significant legitimacy within contemporary social and political debate. As will be evident in the following discussion, a Marxist *analysis* has much to offer in developing an alternative response to the crisis, but the classical Marxist *solution* of state socialism does not seem a credible alternative at this time.

Specific dangers of the 'new right' and corporatism

The above very complex issues deserve more thorough treatment. The purpose of this quick, inevitably superficial discussion was simply to highlight some of the specific objections to each of the five responses to the crisis in the welfare state. Those wanting to know more should consult the substantial literature available on these issues. This book concentrates on the one overriding objection to all the above responses to the crisis. However, before discussing this fundamental objection, there are, as well as objections, very real dangers in the new right and corporatist responses. It is important for community workers to be aware of these dangers because they constitute a significant aspect of the contemporary context of community development and community-based services. In essence, the dangers lie in neoliberalism's transformation of social resources into private goods for purchase. H2O? Accompanying such practices as privatisation is the erosion of important social values. In 1987, the then prime minister of Britain, Margaret Thatcher, a major player in the introduction of neoliberalism into national and international politics and policy, unintentionally captured some of the essence of the danger in an article that appeared in *Women's Own* magazine on 3 October 1987:

> I think we've been through a period where too many people have been given to understand that if they have a problem, it's the government's job to cope with it. 'I have a problem, I'll get a grant.' 'I'm homeless, the government must house me.' They're casting their problem on society. And, you know, there is no such thing as society. There are individual men and women, and there are families. And no government can do anything except through people, and people must look to themselves first. It's our duty to look after ourselves and then, also, to look after our neighbour. People have got the entitlements too much in mind, without the obligations. There's no such thing as entitlement, unless someone has first met an obligation.

Here is the view of the new right: it proposes to respond to the failures of the welfare state by reducing society to individuals and families. In doing so, it gives responsibility to achieve and to blame for social problems, to individuals and families. Margaret Thatcher relinquishes any state role in human wellbeing. Government can have a role only if individuals are successful. This position places individuals and families who are in poverty or disadvantaged in the untenable position of not being eligible for assistance until such time as they achieve and 'succeed'. Thatcher's view soon spread in popularity among governments in the 1980s. They saw their responsibility as nurturing healthy national economies. Some made the assumption that a healthy economy would result in healthy people. To become a healthy national economy would include the ability to compete internationally. In the globalised world, a healthy economy has been considered essential and has been a top priority of governments.

From the 1980s many governments opened their countries to the global market. The accompanying deregulation of economies and the privatisation of public resources represented the dominance of economics over social concerns and, in this dominance, the world was constructed as a marketplace. Within this global marketplace, social goods were increasingly placed on the market to be bought. The expansion of the goods available to be purchased in the marketplace is evidenced by the privatisation of such resources as education, water, transport and health. This represents a transformation of public and social resources into private consumable goods.

The critiques of neoliberalism are abundant. The core of these critiques, from a social justice and human rights perspective, is that neoliberalism and the marketplace paradigm increase inequities and exclusion. The divide between the rich and the poor becomes greater. Only a few benefit from the movement of money and capital. There is no trickle-down effect that brings benefits to all. Those who can least afford to pay for services miss out. In one African country where water has been privatised and prepaid meters are used to buy water, poor families soon run out of money and are forced to search for free drinking water, which is generally unclean. Their babies contract diarrhoeal diseases and die. This is a stark example of the dangers of neoliberalism from a perspective that values meeting human needs, social justice and the promotion of human rights.

The drivers of neoliberalism, the mammoth transnational business and economic corporations, have understandably not encouraged debates on issues of social justice, human rights and social wellbeing. Many decisions that affect people's welfare are made by transnational corporations. The World Bank provides the most funding for health of any organisation on earth and so the World Health Organization has become more marginalised in determining health outcomes. Health and human wellbeing have been colonised by the economic sector and its discourses. Questions of social justice, morality and ethics are replaced by a drive for profit. Human needs continue to be met, but within a more inequitable system. It is the increasing inequity between groups within countries and between rich and poor countries that poses a significant challenge for the approach to community development that will be developed in this book. The assertion that human needs continue to be met but within structures that foster greater inequity suggests that there are problems with simply focusing on human needs. As such, this forms the basis of the argument to incorporate a *human rights-based approach* to community development, which will be developed further in Chapter 3.

Restricted visions and the rise of individualism

The erosion of community (discussed later in this chapter) and the increasing concentration of global economic power into the hands of a few have encouraged increasing individualism, particularly in Western societies. Here, value is placed on the individual and individual achievement. Failure to achieve is attributed to individual deficiencies. Valuing individual achievement strengthens competition over cooperation. Competition, furthermore, weakens social ties and tends to exclude the other. Blaming the individual renders iniquitous structures invisible and encourages hostility, fear and suspicion towards those who deviate from the norm and those against whom one competes. The other is no longer to be embraced and included, but is to be feared, suspected and excluded. Trust is eroded and replaced by increasing mistrust. The dominance of competition and its accompanying weakened social supports are evident at many levels. Not only is competition between individuals more pronounced, but also government policies, such as outsourcing and competitive tendering for services, have transformed collaborative relationships among organisations that identified as part of a service network into competitive relationships where information cannot be shared for fear of losing the competitive edge in tendering processes.

The fundamental objection

The one overriding objection to all the above responses to the crisis can be summarised as follows.

> *The crisis in the welfare state is the result of a social, economic and political system that is unsustainable and has reached a point of ecological crisis. Each conventional response to the crisis in the welfare state is itself based on the same unsustainable, growth-oriented assumptions and is therefore itself unsustainable.*

This objection to the traditional social policy responses to the crisis in the welfare state is the basis for the remainder of this book, which aims to develop an alternative approach to human services policy and practice that is more consistent with a truly sustainable society. Therefore, it is appropriate to consider this objection in more detail.

As Marxist writers have pointed out (Gough 1979), the welfare state has grown alongside industrial capitalism and it must be seen as an integral part of the existing social, economic and political order. The state provision of public services, such as health, education, housing and welfare, has not been simply the result of altruistic views of benign and caring governments, but has been necessary in order for industrial capitalism to grow and flourish and as a means of establishing and maintaining social control (Kennedy 1989). The Marxist analysis has been particularly significant in demonstrating this and it sees the welfare state as being in a symbiotic relationship with advanced capitalism: each is necessary for the other's survival. Thus modern industrial capitalism would not be possible without some form of welfare state that meets human needs, maintains stability and security and keeps the workforce healthy, happy and 'appropriately' educated so that the key processes of production and reproduction can be maintained (George & Wilding 1984).

Such an analysis means that the welfare state must be seen within the context of, and not as separate from, advanced industrial capitalism. While industrial capitalism in its present form cannot survive without some form of the welfare state, the corollary is that the welfare state in its present form cannot survive without the industrial capitalist economic order within which it has developed. There is now ample evidence that this existing order is unsustainable, as the contradictions of the system (of which the contradictions of the welfare state are only a part) become more apparent. The system is based on continued growth, which is having disastrous effects on the global environment (VanDeVeer & Pierce 1998; Gordon & Suzuki 1990). Yet the system doggedly persists despite the evidence, such that McKibbin (2007) has named it 'autistic development'. As the ecological and human costs of continuing growth and 'progress' become more evident and as the warnings that the global industrial and economic system is reaching the limits to growth are more clearly recognised

(Meadows, Meadows & Randers 1992), the urgency of the situation is highlighted. David Suzuki's (Suzuki & McConnell 1997) continual warnings underline the urgency of the current global crisis and they are now being taken seriously by increasing numbers of people. Western governments are finding it increasingly difficult to sustain economic development, appropriate standards of living and full employment (by whatever statistical artifice the latter is measured). The conventional economic solutions do not seem to work very well and are at best short term. The inequities and limits of the global economic system, to which all Western economies are now inextricably linked, are becoming more apparent (Held et al. 1999; Meyer & Geschiere 1999; Mittelman 2000; Bauman 1998; Beck 2000). Increasing numbers of economists and other commentators are reaching the conclusion that the major social and economic problems facing modern society can no longer be solved from within the existing system and that a radical change is necessary—a change, that is, to a quite different society based on different economic principles (Ekins & Max-Neef 1992; Daly & Cobb 1989; Jacobs 1991; Dauncey 1988; Doorman 1998; Henderson 1988, 1991). This change would clearly include the welfare state.

The argument thus far is in many ways consistent with a Marxist analysis; indeed, Marx and his successors have clearly identified the contradictions of capitalism and have similarly suggested the need for a radical reformulation. However, there is a fundamental difference between the Marxist position and the alternative 'Green' position on which this book is based. Marxists still assume that continuing economic growth, with a corresponding increase in productivity, wealth and personal income, is not only possible but also desirable (and, one might argue, necessary). In this they are in agreement with other ideological positions, including those of the new right and the social democrats.

It is common in elections to hear parties from many differing ideological positions, including the left, assuming that the way out of current economic problems is to step up economic growth and arguing about the best way this can be achieved. An alternative 'Green' position, however, maintains that economic growth is at best a doubtful benefit in that it causes more problems (including social, economic and environmental problems) than it solves. Indeed, in a finite world, it is clearly ludicrous to assume that growth can continue indefinitely; there is a growing body of evidence to suggest that the effective limits to growth are being reached (Meadows, Meadows & Randers 1992; Rifkin 1985).

It is thus necessary to seek a system that breaks the cycle of growth, and which is not dependent on continuing growth for its maintenance (in contrast to the existing form of industrial capitalism as well as the Marxist socialist alternative). This requires a genuinely ecological perspective incorporating a notion of sustainability; this will be explored in Chapter 2. It is worth noting, however, that in this context, *sustainability* represents a more significant departure from existing practices than is implied by many contemporary politicians and public figures, given the current trend to justify virtually any policy under the almost meaningless term 'sustainable development' or the blatantly self-contradictory 'sustainable growth'.

From this perspective, the crisis in the welfare state cannot be satisfactorily resolved using any of the five policy strategies outlined above. The existing growth-oriented social, economic and political system, within which the welfare state is located, is clearly unsustainable in anything other than a very short time span. The welfare state, certainly in the form to which we have become accustomed in the West, seems unlikely to last much longer. As the structures of society change (as, from the ecological perspective, they must), different structures and services for a more equitable meeting of human needs and the promotion of human rights will have to be developed. This should not be a surprising conclusion: the modern welfare state, though its origins can be traced back several hundred years (de Schweinitz 1943), is essentially a creature of the 20th century and of the affluent

West. Throughout all but the last hundred years or so of history the human species has been able to survive without the welfare state; even today, it's supposed benefits are enjoyed by only a minority. The welfare state is not a permanent fixture, nor is it necessarily a natural component of human civilisation.

Community-based services as an alternative

Throughout history there have been different institutions and mechanisms for the meeting of human needs. At different times the tribe, the village, the extended family, the Church, the market and the state have all been seen as playing critical roles in this process—often in combination. Each institution has had a dominant role in the meeting of needs, yet as society has changed each has proven to be by itself inadequate for the needs of the new order, though each has retained a lesser role in subsequent times. The crisis in the welfare state is simply another of these historical transitions, where the state, for which such great hopes were held, is demonstrating its inadequacy as new forms of social, economic and political structures emerge.

From this perspective it is inappropriate to put too much energy into defending or strengthening the welfare state. A more useful direction is to ask what might be an alternative form of social provision, which would be consistent with the newly emerging social and economic order. Many of the policy prescriptions that enjoy contemporary popularity represent an attempt to reinstate some of the earlier forms of the meeting of needs, principally through the market and the family. Historically, the limitations of both of these have become apparent and they are even more evident within the contemporary social and economic system, where the market is again proving its inadequacy to meet human needs equitably (Rees et al. 1993; Evatt Research Centre 1989) and where the family is under continuing pressure and is increasingly fragmented (Jamrozik & Sweeny 1996; Batten et al. 1991); there is a crisis in the institution of the contemporary family that renders it utterly incapable of meeting the demands of social care with which some seek to burden it.

Within this context, there is an increasing interest in community-based programs as an alternative mode for the delivery of human services and the equitable meeting of human needs (Shragge 1990; Ife 1993; Ewalt, Freeman & Poole 1998; Fellin 2001). After the family, the Church, the market and the state, it may now be the turn of the 'community' to carry the major responsibility for the provision of services in fields such as health, education, housing and welfare. The idea of community is a central theme in much of the Green literature (Dobson 1995) and at first sight it may seem that a community-based approach to human services is consistent with the idea of a 'post-welfare state' system based on principles of sustainability. Later chapters in this book will explore the potential of such a community-based approach as the next stage in service provision 'beyond the welfare state' and will discuss how such a system might operate and what it would mean for those 'doing' community work.

As already noted, the terms *community* and *community-based* are highly problematic and they mean different things to different people. The approach to community work and community-based services developed in this book is not necessarily consistent with the frequent usage of the terms in government policy discourse, where they have come to have as little substantive meaning as the word *sustainable*. Before outlining the community-development approach on which this book is based, it is necessary to identify some of the significant problems often associated with approaches to human services that are labelled 'community-based'. Only then will it be possible to attempt to develop a model of community development that overcomes these difficulties and has the potential to become the basis of a system of human services in a future society based on principles of sustainability.

Problems with conventional approaches to community-based services

The current interest in community-based human services, which is reflected in a good deal of government policy, has the potential for both progressive and regressive change. While it may provide an opportunity for the kind of radical developments outlined in later chapters of this book, it has also been criticised for its inherent conservatism on a number of grounds. Although this is not the place to explore these criticisms in detail, they need to be summarised and specifically acknowledged. The model developed in later chapters seeks to describe an approach that overcomes these objections to present forms of community-based social provision.

1. REDUCING THE COMMITMENT TO WELFARE

In an era in which governments are seeking to reduce expenditure on human services, community-based programs provide an excellent way for this to occur and represent a form of 'services on the cheap'. This is particularly true of the move from institutional care to community care for dependent people, where the high costs of institutional care can be reduced, but it is also true of other 'community-based' options in that they tend to rely more on the use of volunteers and staff who are paid lower wages than those in the public sector. While such cost-cutting is a frequent result of moving to community-based services, it has a tendency to become the de facto justification for such a move.

In addition, for a government intent on cost-cutting, it is often easier to reduce funding for community-based programs than funding for an equivalent service provided by the state. This is because the hard decision to reduce services is made at the community level, usually by a local management committee and so it is not as readily seen as the fault of the government, even though it flows directly from a reduction in government funding. The community management committee can in this way be easily set up as the scapegoat for the withdrawal of public services.

Thus community-based services can readily serve the political agenda of a government that is committed to reducing public expenditure and facilitate the reduction in the share of the nation's wealth going to human services.

2. COVERT PRIVATISATION

Another way in which community-based services can serve a conservative political agenda is by providing a rationale for the withdrawal of government responsibility and a corresponding move to a market-based approach. By simply withdrawing from service provision, loosely using the rhetoric of 'community responsibility', a government can allow the private market to move in to fill the gap. This could result in a community-based project being operated by a market-driven philosophy with the goal of maximisation of profit rather than the meeting of human need. Thus the terms *community* and *market* can become synonymous. This is not necessarily so; the community development model outlined in later chapters, while it does foresee a reduction in direct government activity, does not imply an increased reliance on the private market, at least in its large-scale manifestation.

3. THE FAMILY

Just as the rhetoric of 'community-based services' can be used as a justification for a return to reliance on the market to meet human need, so it can also be used to support a system where the *family* accepts a greater burden of care; as with privatisation, this is simply seeking to return to an older form of service provision, which is inappropriate for the contemporary context. Such a trend is particularly seen in the field of 'community care' for dependent people. This often does not imply that some form of local autonomous community will accept responsibility for a person's care (as would be the case with a genuinely community-based system), but rather that the person concerned will be cared for 'in the community' by members of their nuclear or extended family, usually women. It can therefore have the effect of placing extra burdens on family members, especially on women, while not acknowledging the pressures already placed on family structures and the breakdown of the traditional 'family' in contemporary society.

4. GENDER

A move to community-based services can place a disproportionate burden on women, both because of their traditional role as primary caregivers and because of the higher level of participation by women in the community sector. Within contemporary society, strongly influenced by economic rationalism, caregiving and involvement in community activities are not highly valued, as they are not seen as creating wealth or improving productivity. Hence those who do the caring are devalued, and community-based services are effectively helping to marginalise women and reinforce dominant patriarchy. As will be discussed in Chapter 3, the oppression of women is one of the fundamental forms of oppression in contemporary Western society and community-based services need to be designed in such a way that they challenge rather than reinforce this oppression.

5. THE TYRANNY OF LOCALITY

Personal mobility is a characteristic of modern Western societies and it has become accepted, even valued, that people should travel long distances to meet their needs for social interaction, entertainment, education, social services and so on. A community-based approach can be seen as restricting people to their local community when they may prefer to seek services elsewhere, because of either a belief that a better service is available in another location or a wish for anonymity and a desire to avoid gossip and intrusive neighbours.

6. LOCATIONAL INEQUALITY

Because some communities are better resourced than others, a move to a community-based approach could simply reinforce existing inequalities between communities, often based on class lines. Communities with more resources (natural, financial or human) would be able to provide higher levels of service and disadvantaged communities might be further disadvantaged by being denied support from a strong central administration.

The above criticisms of a community-based approach to human services are powerful. Taken together, they suggest that community-based services are profoundly conservative and they explain why a community-based approach has been popular, at least at the rhetorical level, with conservative governments. While the rhetoric might appear progressive, or even radical, a community-based strategy can be used to reinforce traditional conservative understandings of the family, privatisation, government cutbacks and class and gender inequalities. It is hardly surprising that some critics have demonstrated a cynicism about community-based services—at least as understood within conventional policy discourse—and have been critical of their potential to present a truly radical alternative.

The model presented in the following chapters seeks to overcome these objections and demonstrate how a community-development approach need not be conservative but could challenge such conservative ideas and help to initiate an alternative society based on social justice as well as on ecological sustainability.

The missing ingredient: community development

The criticisms above relate to a strategy of community-based services developed within the existing social, economic and political order. Such a strategy has a fundamental weakness—namely, that it assumes that there is an entity called 'community' within which human services can be based. This assumption is problematic, given the rise of individualism and the lack of strong community structures in contemporary Western society. The history of industrial society—and indeed of capitalism—has been a history of the destruction of traditional community structures, whether based on the village, the extended family or the Church. This has been necessary for the development of industrial capitalism, which has required a mobile labour force, rising levels of individual and household consumption, increased personal mobility and the dominance of an individualist ideology. While there remain some elements of traditional community structures, especially in rural areas, and while some community bonds are maintained through functional communities (e.g. ethnic communities), it is nevertheless true that community, in the traditional sense, is not a significant element of contemporary industrial society, especially in urban or suburban settings.

For this reason, the development of community-based structures seems somewhat contradictory and it is little wonder that community-based services have proven to be problematic, as suggested by the criticisms in the previous section. The central issue can best be expressed as follows: *How can there be community-based services if there is no community in which to base them?* The primary assumption of community-based services must surely be that there are community structures and processes that can take over all or some of the responsibility for the provision of human services. While traditional communities have performed these roles for centuries, more or less adequately, it is much more problematic in a society where the dominant social and economic order discourages the establishment of community, undermines community solidarity and promotes individualism.

Thus, a strategy of community-based services will not be effective unless steps are taken at the same time to reverse the trend of the destruction of community structures, which has been an integral part of capitalist industrial development. Community-based services therefore need to be accompanied by a program of *community development* that seeks to re-establish those structures. Such a program goes beyond the specifics of a particular community-based program, such as community-based child care, education or health. It needs to encompass all aspects of human activity and interaction and amounts to a radical restructuring of society. This might sound like a tall order, but, as will be demonstrated in later chapters, there are grounds for believing that we have reached a point in history where such a transformation will not only become possible but will in fact also be necessary for survival.

Is there really no community? The discussion on post-colonialism in Chapter 5 will suggest that the answer to this question is more complex than a simple yes or no.

The promise of community

Despite the problems associated with community development, and the factors working against community in modern industrial societies, the idea of community remains powerful. In 1990 the Western Australian government appointed an independent Community and Family Commission to undertake a wide-ranging inquiry into how the people of Western Australia viewed their society, what they saw as missing, and what they would like to see in the future. Significantly, one of the strongest findings that emerged from the inquiry, which incorporated a strategy of broadly based public consultations, was that people felt strongly the 'loss of community' or 'loss of identity' in modern society and that rebuilding community structures was one of their highest priorities for the future (Community and Family Commission 1992). This was seen as an important long-term solution to a number of more immediate social problems. The power of the idea of community has long been recognised; this is seen in the tendency over the years for governments to use the term liberally in titles, speeches and so on, often with little substantive meaning (Bryson & Mowbray 1981). Despite the problematic nature of the *word*, the power of the *idea* is significant as a basis for the organisation and development of alternative social and economic structures, as outlined in later chapters. It has served as a powerful vision for a number of significant writers in the field of community work (Kenny 2007; Campfens 1997; Kelly & Sewell 1988; Kuyek 1990; Nozick 1992; O'Regan & O'Connor 1989; Plant & Plant 1992; Craig 1987). It has also served as a powerful vision for communities to act and rebuild strong community.

In 1994, at the height of the Victorian government's privatisation policies, the People Together Project was established by community groups in the state of Victoria (People Together Project and Victorian Local Government Association 2000). It initially encouraged public debate and so raised the consciousness of people regarding the loss of community infrastructure and sense of cooperation resulting from competitive tendering practices under a neoliberal policy. Amid massive dismantling of community structures by government, the People Together Project facilitated many community initiatives throughout Victoria. These initiatives represented local communities regrouping and re-establishing themselves *as communities*, successfully challenging the erosion of social justice and human rights and the increasing disadvantage and inequity emerging from the new right.

The feeling of loss of community is often interpreted as nostalgia for an ideal that never really existed; advocates of community development have been accused of idealising the 'village community' whose reality was, in many instances, oppressive. This is an important criticism and it is essential that the notion of community be based on more substantial grounds than simply an ideal, even though the power of that ideal and the importance of the vision, must not be underrated. The chapters that follow seek to provide such a foundation.

Social capital and civil society

In recent years there has been increasing interest in the ideas of social capital and civil society. The idea of social capital is that one can 'invest' socially as well as economically and that, while the economic capital of a society may be increasing, if this is done at the cost of social capital it is a false gain. Social capital might be seen as the glue that holds society together—human relationships, people doing things for each other out of a sense of social obligation and reciprocity, social solidarity and community. Some commentators (Cox 1995; Winter 2000; Latham 1997) have argued that the social capital of modern Western society is eroding, as purely economic market criteria are applied to transactions between people and as individual achievement replaces community and social solidarity as the perceived priority for human action. It is argued that it has become necessary to reverse this trend, to prevent the further erosion of social capital at the expense of monetary capital and invest in programs aimed at building social capital throughout society.

Part of building social capital is the strengthening of 'civil society'. Civil society is the term used for the formal or semiformal structures that people establish voluntarily, on their own initiative, rather than as a consequence of some government program or directive. Civil society includes the non-government sector or 'third sector' (the first two sectors being the state and the private-for-profit sectors), where many varieties of non-government agencies have been established to help meet the needs of individuals, families and communities. But civil society is also broader than this. It includes service clubs—Rotary, Lions, Apex and so on—and incorporates social and recreational organisations—football clubs, tennis clubs, choral societies, walking clubs, cultural groups, amateur dramatic societies, school 'parent and citizen' associations, book clubs, youth clubs, in fact any voluntarily formed association of people with common interests or purposes. It is, in other words, the collective society that citizens have themselves chosen to form as a way to pursue their own interests. In an important research study, Robert Putnam (1993) demonstrated how the economic performance of communities was directly correlated with the extent of civil society activity: a strong civil society not only strengthens social capital, it also strengthens economic performance.

Part of the erosion of social capital in the West is the erosion of civil society. As the demands of the workplace grow, those in employment are finding they have less time and energy to participate in civil society and many community organisations are finding it increasingly difficult to recruit members and volunteers. For those who are unemployed, participation in civil society is often not valued by others; it is not seen as 'work experience' or as being relevant in the search for employment. And for those who have retired from the workforce, retirement is often constructed as a time to enjoy private 'lifestyle' pleasure and individual consumption, rather than as an opportunity to contribute skills and experience to the community. Recent soaring costs of public liability insurance premiums have been prohibitive for many community groups and civil society organisations, rendering some of them non-viable.

The erosion of social capital and of civil society represents a major problem for Western societies, and reduces the quality of life of those living in them. Community development is an obvious approach for reversing this trend, both in the wide-reaching idea of social capital and in the formalised structures of civil society, and this has been another important reason for the recent upsurge of interest in community development.

The 'needs of strangers'

With the breakdown of traditional communities and the development of modern industrial society, a fundamental change took place in the nature of human interaction, which has been described by Tönnies (1955) as the change from *Gemeinschaft* to *Gesellschaft*. While Tönnies' analysis is complex, for present purposes his distinction can be summarised (and grossly oversimplified) by saying that in *Gemeinschaft* society people interact with a relatively small number of other people, whom they know well, in many different roles; whereas in *Gesellschaft* society one has interactions with many more people, but these interactions are limited to specific instrumental activities. Thus, in *Gesellschaft* society we do not know most of the people with whom we have contact except in their specific roles of, for example, shop assistant, teacher, client, bus driver, customer, nurse or secretary. Our communication with them is limited to a discrete transaction and any knowledge of them beyond their capacity to fill the particular role is considered unnecessary, irrelevant and an intrusion into their private affairs. There is a clear understanding of what constitutes legitimate business in our dealings with another person and any attempt to cross the boundary into other aspects of human life can result in being told 'It is none of your business'. In *Gemeinschaft* society such distinctions are either not important or non-existent. People know each other well, though in smaller numbers, through a variety of different transactions. The 'public' and the 'private' are not separated, and individuals are known to each other as people rather than roles. In such a society, 'community' is a much richer, deeper and more real experience that forms the basis for all social interaction.

This distinction is critically important in considering human services and the welfare state. With the transformation from *Gemeinschaft* to *Gesellschaft*, human services, like other social interactions, have become based on instrumental relationships, with the service provider and the service user knowing each other only in those specific roles. Recently, human services has enthusiastically embraced case management as a form of service delivery. This epitomises the instrumental roles of provider and user and represents the most blatant and dramatic instrumental relationships yet seen. Even the name precludes a sense of human connection; the service becomes the control of a case. From the earlier approach of meeting the needs of one's neighbour, we have moved to a system based on meeting the 'needs of strangers', as described by a number of writers (Titmuss 1970; Wilensky & Lebeaux 1965; Watson 1980; Ignatieff 1984). This is a fundamental change that requires a different moral justification, different ethical principles and, above all, different structures. The whole apparatus of the modern welfare state has been constructed on the basis of the 'needs-of-strangers' approach, and with it have come large bureaucracies and an increasingly professionalised approach to human services. Instead of having a responsibility to meet the needs of one's neighbours, the responsibility of the citizen is to pay taxes so that somebody else (usually a professional 'expert') can be employed to do the job. Direct responsibility for human services thus moves from the citizen to a team of experts employed by the state, leaving the citizen free to pursue their private ends unencumbered by the needs of others (except in terms of financial obligation). Some people, of course, choose, for their own reasons, to become involved in helping others through voluntary activity but this is seen as a matter of individual choice rather than a responsibility of citizenship. Voluntary work is often regarded as auxiliary to the 'main' work of those employed by the welfare state to deliver human services.

It should be noted that a private market approach to human services also incorporates the needs-of-strangers model. Here the private citizen is absolved of the responsibility to meet the needs of others—even through the payment of taxes—and individuals are expected to look after themselves by purchasing services in the marketplace, possibly with the help of insurance (again purchased in a market). This form of market transaction in modern society involves limited instrumental relationships and hence it implies, in common with the welfare state, a needs-of-strangers approach.

A move to community-based services and structures, as advocated in subsequent chapters, essentially seeks to reverse the dominant trend towards the needs-of-strangers model, as epitomised by the modern welfare state. It suggests that this approach to the meeting of human needs has not worked well, and that on balance its disadvantages have outweighed its benefits. It is necessary, therefore, to examine some of the advantages claimed for the welfare state in order to see how strongly they represent objections to the development of a more community-based approach. It is the contention of this book that these benefits are more apparent than real.

The ideal of the social democratic welfare state assumed the superiority of the needs-of-strangers model for several reasons. It was argued that this would ensure an adequate *minimum standard for all*, it would help to produce a society based on *social justice*, it would be *impartial* and work 'without fear or favour', it would ensure *confidentiality* so that service users could be assured of their secrets being kept, it would ensure *anonymity* of service, thereby preventing stigma, and it would ensure proper *accountability* through the public processes of parliament and bureaucracy. Each of these claimed benefits will now be briefly considered.

1. ADEQUATE MINIMUM STANDARDS

The aim of achieving adequate minimum standards (of health, housing, education, income security, etc.) rests on two assumptions: namely, that the attainment of uniform minimum standards is possible and that it is desirable. Both of these assumptions can be questioned.

It is difficult to define minimum standards in complex modern industrial societies. In many nations, regional and cultural diversity means that what is an adequate minimum in one setting may be far from adequate in another and more than adequate in a third. In housing, for example, the definition of an *adequate* minimum is heavily influenced by both climatic and cultural factors: what will suffice in one setting will not suffice in another. Similarly, the cost of living and hence a minimum standard of income varies significantly across regions because of different costs of basic commodities, different transport needs (in some locations car ownership is a necessity, while in others it is not), differing climates (in some locations heating costs are significant) and so on. The idea of a universal minimum standard is difficult to accept and almost impossible to define in other than very basic instances, such as protection of basic human rights and dietary intake. (This exception is very important (Doyal & Gough 1991) and will be discussed in Chapter 3.) Most conventional minimum standards, such as the poverty line, are thus only approximations and are crude measures indeed of the effectiveness of social policy.

But even if such minimum standards were feasible, it could seriously be questioned whether they represented an appropriate goal for the welfare state. As will be seen in Chapter 2, an ecological perspective encourages the valuing of diversity, whereas the imposition of a universal minimum standard encourages uniformity and does not value the significance of ethnic, cultural and regional differences. Again, an exception needs to be made in areas such as basic human rights (see Chapter 3), but, at levels higher up Maslow's hierarchy of needs (Maslow 1970), the value of universal minimum standards must be questioned.

In any case, as was pointed out earlier, the research evidence suggests that the modern welfare state has been only minimally successful in meeting acceptable minimum standards of provision (George & Wilding 1984). The need for the maintenance of minimum standards is as a result a weak justification for the continuation of the welfare state and the needs-of-strangers model.

2. SOCIAL JUSTICE

The definition of *social justice* is a complex issue that is outside the scope of this chapter; it will be explored in more detail in Chapter 3. Whatever one's definition, it is not easy to make a strong case for the continuation of a needs-of-strangers approach based on social justice. There is strong evidence to suggest that the welfare state has not been successful in reducing social inequalities (Le Grand 1982), though it may have had some role in preventing inequality from becoming even greater (George & Wilding 1984). Despite the best efforts of the welfare state, structural disadvantage across class, race and gender lines is clearly maintained and numerous writers have demonstrated how the welfare state has often acted to reinforce rather than challenge these forms of structural disadvantage (e.g. Williams 1989; Gough 1979; Pascall 1986; Jamrozik 1991; Rodger 2000). As Le Grand suggests, it is a mistake to assume that the welfare state is an adequate mechanism for bringing about a fairer society; much more fundamental structural change is necessary and the welfare state can really only ameliorate the worst effects of structural disadvantage.

3. IMPARTIALITY

Partiality and discretion are present at all levels of the human services bureaucracy. Indeed, the nature of human interaction and human problems is such that some administrative discretion is required if welfare state systems are to continue to operate (Lipsky 1980). This discretion will inevitably be somewhat arbitrary, given human values and the need for the individual bureaucrat to survive in the bureaucracy. While impartiality is an ideal of the welfare state, and large volumes of rules and regulations are produced and constantly modified in pursuit of this ideal, in practice it is always necessary for workers to exercise a degree of discretion, whether officially acknowledged or not, and this results in service users not being treated with equal respect and dignity. The ideal of impartiality has not been achieved by the modern welfare state and the inevitable partiality has resulted in differing levels of access to services and varying quality of services. These differences have tended to reinforce the class, race and gender inequalities mentioned above.

The implications of this argument are significant; they will be taken up in later chapters, where the community-based alternative is spelled out in more detail. But for present purposes the point is simply that impartiality has not been a feature of the modern welfare state and that it represents a weak justification for the needs-of-strangers approach.

4. CONFIDENTIALITY

One of the advantages claimed for the needs-of-strangers model of the modern welfare state is that it is able to ensure confidentiality for service users, whereas smaller, more locally based structures could lead to private information being divulged to other people as part of a local 'gossip' network. Unfortunately, this aim of the welfare state is more apparent than real. The fact that the welfare state is, apparently of necessity, a large and complex bureaucratic structure means that information has to be shared and communicated. Reports have to be written and filed, decisions are made in teams and specific cases are discussed in meetings, consultations and professional supervision. Some are written up as case studies or used for educational purposes. As well as this large communication network, there is the tendency for workers to gossip and there are also the inevitable security breaches, misplacement of documents and coincidences of recognition. Thus, the assumption of confidentiality cannot be made in one's dealings with the welfare state, and sharing one's needs or problems (however intimate) with the welfare state is almost a guarantee that they will be known by a large number of people and recorded for posterity.

5. ANONYMITY

The service structures of *Gesellschaft* society are based in part on the assumption of a 'right' to anonymity, namely the right of a person to receive services from a stranger and to avoid sharing her/his problems with someone who is known personally. This right can be seen as an advantage of the welfare state, but it can also be seen as a manifestation of the anomie and alienation of contemporary society. Services that guarantee anonymity tend only to be depersonalised and a preference for anonymity makes sense only in a society where problems are seen as individual private concerns and where social interaction beyond fragmentary instrumental relationships is seen as deviant or dangerous. The community-based approach, discussed in later chapters, advocates the reverse: that services for people might in fact be more appropriately designed and delivered by those who know those people personally and understand their needs, culture and lifestyle. In another era such an idea would have been regarded as so obviously true as not to need stating; it is only in the context of *Gesellschaft* society, and the needs-of-strangers approach, that it is seen as a radical and almost revolutionary notion. Rather than being a reason to preserve the needs-of-strangers model, the anonymity of the welfare state can instead be regarded as a good reason for seeking a more community-based alternative.

6. ACCOUNTABILITY

Another argument put forward for the needs-of-strangers welfare state model is that, through the structures of government and the state, public accountability can be maintained. Thus service users, and society in general, have access to mechanisms by which they can question those who plan and provide the services, and can hold them accountable for their actions. The citizen has recourse to various complaints and appeals tribunals, bodies such as human rights commissions, an ombudsman and directly parliament through an elected representative.

While these accountability mechanisms may be present in theory, the experience of those who work in the welfare state is that they often do not work well, particularly for the relatively powerless and inarticulate service user. Sophisticated mechanisms have developed within bureaucracies to minimise the effects of accountability mechanisms—indeed the bureaucracy needs such mechanisms for survival.

The current climate of economic rationalism and managerialism has highlighted only one direction of accountability: accountability 'upwards' to management. More important, from the perspective of this book, is accountability 'downwards' to the service user or 'outwards' to the community. The welfare state may be moderately effective at ensuring upward accountability, but it is hard to mount a justification that it has been at all successful at supporting and encouraging accountability downwards or outwards; in fact, its very structures militate against this. It should be noted, indeed, that the common usage of the words *upwards* and *downwards* in this context simply reinforces the dominant view, which sees the manager as being in the important, superior position while the service user is kept firmly at the bottom. The model proposed in this book seeks to establish the reverse situation.

This has been a brief discussion of the objections to the needs-of-strangers approach characteristic of the modern welfare state, but it should be sufficient to demonstrate that the main arguments in support of such a model are not very strong. They should not, therefore, be seen as significant impediments to the development of a community-based model. Some of these issues will be explored in more detail in later chapters to the extent that they inform the model of policy and practice developed in this book.

The next steps

This chapter has identified, inevitably briefly, some of the problems facing the modern welfare state and has suggested that the welfare state is not sustainable in the long term. Many of the conventional policy directions proposed as a response to the crisis in the welfare state are also unlikely to be sustainable, but a community-based approach does, at first sight, seem to offer more promise. For this to occur, however, it will be necessary to base it in a much more thorough and wide-ranging analysis of change in the social, economic and political order. Community-based human services will need to be located within a broader program of social change based on a philosophy of sustainability, social justice, human rights and community development.

In order to develop such a program, and to see what community-based services might look like and how they might operate within a sustainable society, it is necessary to embark on a wider analysis. The next three chapters, therefore, will seek to develop a vision of a future society that is both ecologically feasible and based on principles of social justice and human rights. Following this, the focus will revert to community development and to the development of community-based alternatives consistent with such a vision, before moving to more specific issues of the 'practice' of community work.

>> discussion questions

1. The process of community *development*, as described in the beginning of this chapter, has some particular features that make it an alternative to current thinking and practice. The term 'community-based services' takes on a particular meaning within community development. What are the core features of these concepts?
2. Describe the five major responses to the crisis in the welfare state. What is common to all of them?
3. How do these responses serve to perpetuate the problems within the welfare state?
4. In what ways does 'individualism' erode other values that are conducive to human wellbeing and the process of community development?
5. Explain the symbiotic relationship, from a Marxist perspective, between the welfare state and capitalism.
6. There are some serious problems attached to the promotion of services labelled as 'community-based'. List and describe these problems. Explain why community-based services may be considered conservative and remain popular.
7. What may be the indications, either in support of or challenging the view, that there is no community?
8. Describe the concept 'social capital'.
9. In what ways and for what reasons may civil society have been eroded in Western societies?

>> reflective questions

1. What are some of the core values implied in the approach to community development and in community-based services? What is the fit or otherwise of these values with those of human services (both the rhetoric and the actual practice)?
2. How do the transformative qualities of the approach to community development taken in this book resonate with your own aspirations as a human service worker?
3. Which of the five responses to the crisis in the welfare state do you think are most dominant when reflecting on your experience both as a citizen and in terms of any experience or exposure you have had in the human services?
4. What might be some of the implications of the nexus between the welfare state and capitalism for human wellbeing?
5. From your personal experience of the world around you, what are your views on individualism? In what ways have you benefited or otherwise from its dominance? Who might benefit or lose from an individualistic philosophy as it drives policy and services?
6. What are your personal views about the ways in which promoting community-based services reinforce traditional views of things such as the family, class, gender and restricted government roles in health and wellbeing?
7. What are your experiences of community, both in your current life situation and in terms of your personal history from childhood?
8. Consider the various relationships you engage in, in any one week. To what extent are they indicative of either *Gemeinschaft* or *Gesellschaft* society? Explain why you mapped them where you have.

CHAPTER 2

Foundations of community development: an ecological perspective

Introduction

The approach to community work developed in this book rests on two principal foundations. The first foundation is an *ecological perspective*, which is the subject of this chapter. The second foundation, a *social justice and human rights perspective*, will be discussed in Chapter 3. Each perspective has been influential in stimulating community-based solutions to problems and in promoting community development practice, yet there have been few attempts to integrate the two. The extent to which the two perspectives are conceptually distinct is an interesting point for discussion. This will be taken up in Chapter 4, where both perspectives are considered together, leading to a vision of an alternative society in which the concept of community and the process of community development play a major role.

The ecological perspective outlined later in this chapter derives from the Green critique of the current social, economic and political order. This critique represents a powerful and fundamental challenge to many of the accepted norms of social and political discourse. It is a challenge that, in the 21st century, can no longer be ignored and which will inevitably play a major role in the shaping of a future society.

Environmental crisis

A Green analysis inevitably starts with the major environmental crises facing the world in the second decade of the 21st century. It is these crises that have led Green thinkers to seek radical alternatives and which give the Green position a sense of both urgency and inevitability. From a Green perspective, change is not a luxury that can be postponed until the time is right; the problems are urgent and immediate and failure to act could place the future of human civilisation, indeed the very survival of the human race (as well as many other species), at risk. There is no need to discuss in detail the many strands of the environmental crisis, as they are by now well known. They include pollution of air, oceans, rivers and soil; poisoning of the food chain; depletion of the earth's natural resources; ozone depletion; global warming; the extinction of species; the loss of wilderness areas; topsoil erosion; desertification; deforestation; nuclear waste and the population crisis (Brown 1994;

Ehrlich & Ehrlich 1990; Meadows, Meadows & Randers 1992; Suzuki & McConnell 1997; VanDeVeer & Pierce 1998; McKibbin 1990; Toman & Sohngen 2004; Jarman 2007; Healey 2000; Lowe 2005; Neumann 2005).

At different times, and in different places, different problems assume importance in popular consciousness. In the 1970s, for example, the resource crisis was of major public concern. From the late 1980s, problems of changing the ecological balance (specifically ozone depletion and global warming) received more attention. In places such as Tasmania and British Columbia (Canada), loss of wilderness always seems to be an issue of public significance, even though it may wax and wane elsewhere. Now, the issues of climate change and water scarcity are major public concerns. Yet despite the vagaries of public awareness and media coverage, these environmental problems are still with us and the indications are that each is getting worse. Each is sufficient to cause major concern and requires immediate and significant attention at the local, national and global level. They potentially threaten the long-term, or even medium-term, survival of the human race or, at the very least, of 'civilisation'. Taken together, they indicate an overall crisis of enormous magnitude—it is only when they are considered together that the seriousness of the environmental crisis can be fully appreciated.

Environmental responses and Green responses

In considering the responses to these crises, an important distinction needs to be made between what will here be referred to as *environmental* responses and *Green* responses. Other writers have used different terminology, such as *light green* and *dark green* (Dobson 1995), *environmental* and *ecological* (Bookchin 1991), or *deep* and *shallow ecology* (Fox 1990; Pepper 1993), but there is as yet no consistency in the literature on the wording of what is one of the most fundamental distinctions in Green thought and politics.

Environmental responses to ecological problems have two important characteristics. First, they seek to solve specific problems by finding discrete solutions (see Lowe 2005). Thus, the problem of global warming is to be solved by reducing greenhouse gases, problems of water scarcity by desalination plants, problems of pollution by anti-pollution technology, problems of population by family planning programs, problems of loss of wilderness by creating protected areas, problems of species extinction by endangered species programs and so on. Each problem is isolated and a specific solution is sought. Such an approach is characteristic of linear thinking, which has played a dominant role in the Western world view within which industrial and technological 'progress' has developed (Capra 1982; Rifkin 1985; Saul 1992; Postman 1993; Torgerson 1999). It is also informed by public choice theory and utilised by public choice analysts, who contend that those involved in environmental issues are largely motivated by self-interest (Stretton 1994).

The second characteristic of environmental responses is that they seek solutions within the existing social, economic and political order. It is not seen as necessary to change the nature of society in any fundamental way, but rather the existing order is seen as being capable of solving the problem through the application of technical expertise. This normally involves a reliance on technological solutions and, in an era in which technological progress and expertise are so highly valued, it is not surprising that sophisticated new technology should be expected, often implicitly, to solve all problems. This faith in technology and expertise is seen at its most extreme form in the reaction to the threat from nuclear waste—one of the most concerning pollution problems of the postwar era. It is still considered by many quite acceptable to continue to operate nuclear reactors producing highly toxic waste because it is assumed that eventually the problem of long-term waste disposal will be solved through some technological innovation. The possibility that such an answer may not be found because it may not exist, and the dire consequences of such an eventuality, are not seriously entertained.

By contrast, the *Green* response to environmental problems takes a more fundamental or radical approach. It sees environmental problems as being merely the symptoms of a more significant underlying problem. They are the consequence of a social, economic and political order that is patently unsustainable and thus it is the social, economic and political order that needs to be changed (Porritt 1984; Dobson 1995; Carter 1999; Neumann 2005). Conventional, linear, technological solutions to environmental problems may be adequate (and indeed essential) in the short term, but in the long term they will prove inadequate unless more fundamental social, political and economic change occurs. Thus the Green position sees environmental problems not as separate individual problems but as being related, in that they are all consequences of the major underlying problem: the unsustainability of the existing order. The Green position seeks to apply ecological principles to the solving of environmental problems, which inevitably requires a more holistic perspective than the conventional linear approach. Moran's (2006) 'Web of Life' most clearly illustrates the seamless web of interconnection and interdependence as it depicts humans as both dependent on other life forms and contributing to sustaining life. This is in stark contrast to Western capitalism's anthropocentric view of humans as dominant. Reflection on the following diagram (adapted from Moran 2006, p. 75) leads to a sound appreciation of holism. Here, in relation to food, it is clear that humans, as 'higher order consumers', are dependent on both herbivores and plants for life, as well as on the existence of their nutrients. But at the same time humans contribute, through their own decomposition and production of nutrients, to the life of plants. The

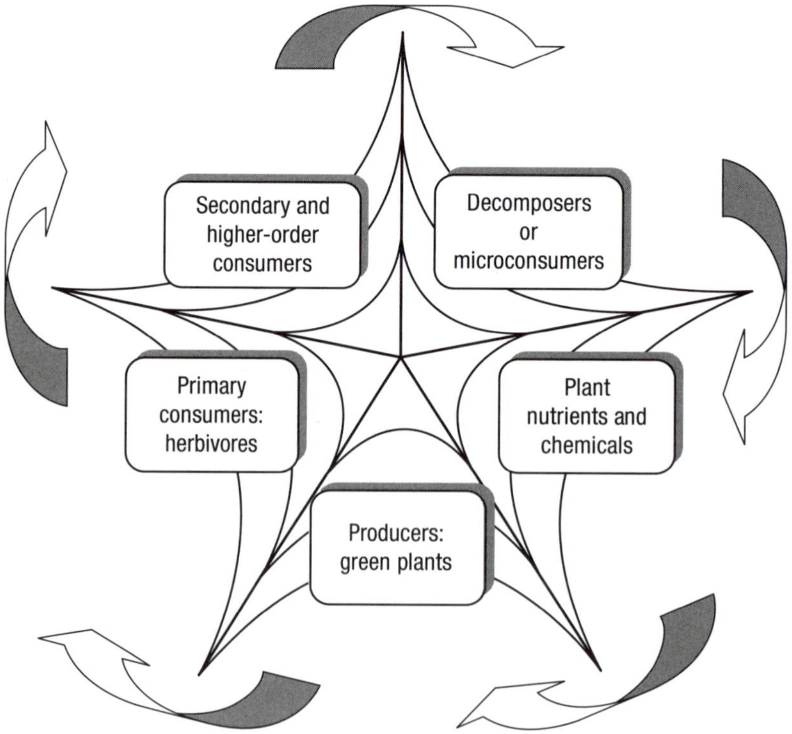

Figure 2.1 Web of Life

same interconnections and interdependencies can be mapped for any one of the actors in this web of life. If life on earth is such a web, then linear and unidimensional relations do not reflect reality and problems cannot be explained by one simple causal factor. The whole web (social, economic, political and physical) must be implicated in solutions.

If environmental problems are seen as the result of the social, economic and political system, the nature of the problem fundamentally changes. Conventional (or, in the terminology employed here, environmental) approaches to the environment see the problems as physical problems to do with water, air, pollutants, chemical reactions, soils, climate, ecosystems, temperature and so on, thus requiring essentially physical and technical solutions. Therefore, the physical sciences are seen as the major disciplinary base for dealing with these problems—the physical sciences form the basis of most courses in 'environmental science' and physical scientists are seen as the 'experts' in environmental issues. The Green perspective, in contrast, sees environmental problems as essentially social, economic and political problems. They are caused by the kind of society we have developed and to understand and deal with environmental problems we must seek wisdom and expertise from the social, economic and political sciences, rather than merely from the physical sciences and technologies that are really only able to deal with the symptoms.

The perspective of this book accepts the Green, rather than the environmental, view of ecological problems. If the ecological crisis is to be effectively resolved, it will be through social, economic and political change, rather than through scientific and technological progress. Community work is potentially one of the most effective ways to develop a more sustainable society and is thus directly relevant to a Green analysis. The expertise of community workers, in terms of both knowledge and skills, has much to contribute to the Green movement. It is therefore not surprising that the Green movement has been one of the forces behind the current upsurge of interest in community development, as illustrated in the following case.

CASE STUDY: Yasuní, Ecuador

Yasuní, a 982 000 hectare national park in the Napo Moist forest region of Ecuador, in the Amazon region, is also a UNESCO World Biosphere Reserve. Within this reserve is a zone in which the local Tagaeri and Taromenuane ethnic groups live. Yasuní also has immense oil reserves. Its history has been one of ecological and human tragedy due to unregulated oil company activity, illegal logging of cedar forests and the power and violence with which the Indigenous people's resistance efforts have been met. Introduced diseases, increasing toxicity of waterways, loss of habitat and death from violence have decreased the population of the Indigenous people in the area from 16 000 to 1000 in the last 30 years.

Successive Ecuadorian governments have wavered between violating and protecting the human inhabitants and the ecology. The Raphael Correa's government has proposed a radical plan to leave the oil under the ground of Yasuní indefinitely and for the international community to pay compensation to Ecuador. There is both strong opposition to and determined support for Correa. International, national and multinational oil companies lead the opposition; support comes from national Indigenous groups, local people and the Ecuadorian population in general.

What are the views of local people about the government proposal to keep the oil in the ground? These voices are drowned out by the more pronounced debates at international levels (Baird 2008). However, *New Internationalist* (July 2008, pp. 12–13) provided an avenue for some of these voices to be heard, as follows.

continued

Martin Santi, President of Ecuador's Indigenous organisation CONAI: . . . my main goal is to reclaim and defend our human rights which have been trampled upon . . . We have been calling for the development model to be changed so that, instead of oil, alternative ways are sought which will benefit humanity . . . Our message to the Government is that it should have a clear position on the model of development. If it only sees Mother Earth as a space that must be exploited to generate wealth, leaving those in the region destitute, then this is not a model but just a necessity of capitalism. The Government should recognise that the largest part of the territory is inhabited by Indigenous people; it must work with those who have been most excluded from the life of the country.

Manuela Ima, President of the Association of Waoraní Women: We women started to organise ourselves when we saw that the male leaders were going away to work in the city but were not bringing back money for education or health. So we decided we would get moving, empower ourselves. If we didn't do it, who was going to lead? Our work was principally to defend our territory. We had no help, no money, we just did it . . . Oil companies can destroy us. We don't like anything to do with them. And now there's talk of climate change which is going to happen in our territory as well . . . Therefore we women say: 'No more petrol companies! No more pollution!' There's a lot of contamination left in Waoraní territory. We are looking for help to get that information out, on video, in the press. In the past we women didn't talk about these things. But without animals, without food, without trees, how will we survive? . . . If anyone wants to do anything in our territory, they should speak to us first. We would like the international community to help us communicate our message that we don't want petroleum companies: we want to live in peace, in health.

Source: F. Gumán,2008, 'Speak to us First!', *New Internationalist*, no. 413, July, pp. 12–13.

Signs of community protest, Cuenca, Ecuador, 2005

- What are the views of environment held by different actors in this case study?
- What lessons can Indigenous communities teach us?
- What is the relevance of these lessons in the current ecological crisis?
- What does this case study imply about what may be barriers to moving towards a new paradigm? What interests would be threatened?
- What different uses of power are evident in this issue?

Ecuardorian Indigenous communities celebrating their relationship with Mother Earth, Cuenca, Ecuador, 2005

Themes within Green analysis

While the Green perspective accepts the fundamental social–economic–political basis for the ecological crisis, and the need for fundamental change, there is some disagreement within Green literature about the basic analysis, or exactly what it is that needs to change. Not surprisingly, Green literature reflects the divisions that can be found in broader social science writing and different perspectives that have been brought to bear on other social problems are reflected in the definition and analysis of issues raised by the ecological crisis. Some of these different perspectives are outlined briefly below, but space restrictions mean that they will inevitably be oversimplified (see Table 2.1). Readers wanting a more detailed analysis should refer to Carolyn Merchant's *Radical Ecology: the Search for a Living World* (1992).

Table 2.1 Schools of Green thought

STREAM OF GREEN THOUGHT	PERCEPTION OF MAJOR PROBLEM	PROPOSED SOLUTION	SIGNIFICANT AUTHORS
Eco-socialism	Capitalism	Socialist society	Gorz, Mellor, Ryle, Pepper, Sarker, Luke
Eco-anarchism	Hierarchy, government, bureaucracy	Decentralisation, local control, absence of central government	Bookchin, Thoreau, Marshall
Eco-feminism	Patriarchy	Feminist revolution, valuing women's attributes, ending gender oppression	Mellor, Salleh, Merchant, Shiva, Plumwood, Warren
Eco-luddism	Technology	Low-level human-scale technology, ending mindless technological 'progress'	Illich, Postman, Mander, Bowers
Anti-growth	Growth (economic, population, consumption, etc.)	No-growth society	Meadows, Suzuki, Ehrlich
Green economics	Conventional economic theory	(i) Sustainable economics, including externalities (ii) Decentralised economics	Henderson, Dauncey, Ekins, Pearce, Daly & Cobb, Jacobs
Global development	Dominance and exploitation of the majority world by the minority world, global inequity, 'development'	Global equity, appropriate development	Trainer, George, Shiva, Latouche, Norgaard
Eco-philosophy	Anthropocentric world view	Ecocentric world view	Fox, Eckersley, Naess
New paradigm thinking	Newtonian–Cartesian world view, linear thinking	Holistic, systemic paradigm	Capra, Rifkin, Henderson, Ornstein & Ehrlich

Eco-socialism

The eco-socialists argue that the ecological crisis is essentially the consequence of capitalism. In an extension of a Marxist analysis, the growth and industrialisation that have accompanied the development of capitalism are seen as having resulted in waste, overconsumption and pollution together with a lack of responsibility for the health of the planet. The environment, as well as an oppressed and alienated workforce, have paid the price for capitalism's successes. The ideology of capitalism has emphasised individualism and an exploitative relationship with the land and natural resources as well as the working class.

From this perspective, the solution to the ecological crisis lies with a form of socialism. Adequate protection for the environment and conservation of resources can be more easily achieved through a collectivist or communist system. The transition to a socialist society is, therefore, seen as being an urgent need and given added urgency by the gravity of the ecological crisis. Eco-socialism suggests that it is only through the elimination (or at least reduction) of private property and capitalist ownership of the means of production that the social and collective values inherent in a sustainable society can be realised. It is important to emphasise, however, that eco-socialism necessarily represents an extension, and to some extent a modification, of a traditional socialist view. Conventional socialists have generally accepted, and indeed often emphasised, the need for sustained economic growth as a way to enable increasing wealth to be shared more equitably. A Green position questions the viability of continued economic growth, at least in its traditional form. Similarly, traditional socialist formulations have given little attention to the environment—indeed the labour movement has often specifically opposed environmental protection on the grounds that it will 'cost jobs'. Thus eco-socialism requires an adjustment to a conventional socialist position and the formulation of a socialism that incorporates different definitions of work, different attitudes to economic growth and a more fundamental incorporation of environmental concerns.

This perspective is influential in a good deal of Green literature and many Green writers adopt some aspects of a socialist position. Writers who have attempted a deliberate synthesis of Green and socialist analyses include Sarker (1999), Luke (1999), Gorz (1980), Ryle (1988), Pepper (1993) and Mellor (1992) (the latter also incorporating feminism).

While elements of a socialist perspective are present in most Green writing (perceiving a need for social ownership and control of resources and production) the present public unpopularity of socialism has meant that this has not always been emphasised.

Eco-anarchism

A somewhat contradictory position to eco-socialism is taken by the eco-anarchists. They maintain that the ecological crisis is a result of the structures of domination and control exemplified by government, business, military forces and other forms of regulation. To anarchists these structures deny human freedom and the potential to enjoy nature. They limit genuine human interaction and human potential. They have alienated human beings from the natural world, as a result of which people have developed ecologically disastrous practices. Eco-anarchists, therefore, seek a society where there is minimal (or no) central control and decisions are taken by individuals or in small localised community groupings. Instead of hierarchical forms of social organisation, they prefer decentralised, autonomous and local forms of organisation based on ecological principles or 'social ecology', to use the words of Murray Bookchin (1990, 1991), perhaps the most influential eco-anarchist writer.

There is a long history of anarchist writers showing a concern for the natural environment, and a longing to 'get back to nature', in their quest for freedom from oppressive structures (Marshall 1992a, 1992b). For example, the work of Thoreau (1854), written in the 19th century, would not be out of place in a collection of contemporary Green writing. There is indeed an element of anarchist thinking in much of the current Green literature, specifically in the rejection of the dehumanising and alienating characteristics of large centralised government (and non-government) structures and in the advocacy of a 'small is beautiful' philosophy.

The extent to which the eco-anarchist position is incompatible with the eco-socialist analysis is an interesting issue, reflecting the uneasy and often conflicting relationship between socialists and anarchists in general political philosophy. As socialism has tended to support and encourage centralised planning, coordination and control through the state, it represents the antithesis of an anarchist position. Within the Green context, however, it can be suggested that there may not be total incompatibility between the two approaches. Just as socialism needs to be modified and extended if it is to be incorporated as eco-socialism, so anarchism needs a degree of modification if it is to become eco-anarchism. Eco-socialists will generally accept the need for some decentralised structures and favour a grassroots, decentralised form of democratic socialism rather than centralised control within a Stalinist model. Eco-anarchists, on the other hand, need to take seriously the Green view of all humanity (and other species) sharing one finite world and the ecological principle that action in any one part of the (global) system affects all others (and is thus everyone's business). This requires some degree of central coordination and control. Hence there may be some room for a common position; though eco-socialists and eco-anarchists will emphasise different components of a Green political program, both also have to accept the well-known Green maxim 'Think globally, act locally'. If there is to be a synthesis between traditional anarchists and traditional socialists, then the former will need to accept the challenge to 'think globally' and the latter to 'act locally'. Such a potential synthesis, however, is not attractive to strong advocates of either position, such as David Pepper (1993) and Murray Bookchin (1990).

Eco-feminism

While eco-socialists see the problem in terms of capitalism and eco-anarchists see it in terms of structures of domination and control, eco-feminists see the problem of an ecologically insane world primarily in terms of patriarchy and its consequences (Mellor 1992; Shiva 1989; Merchant 1980; Plumwood 1993; Salleh 1997; Warren 2000). From this point of view it is the patriarchal structures of domination, oppression and control that have resulted in a competitive, acquisitive and exploitative society. The patriarchal society has ultimately proved to be unsustainable and it is causing environmental disasters from which it is proving incapable of extricating itself.

Thus the change that eco-feminists perceive as needed is the change that is embodied in the feminist movement, where patriarchal structures are challenged, dismantled, deconstructed and replaced. Of course the feminist movement, like the other movements described in this section, is divided by different and conflicting strands and emphases (Williams 1989) and there is not space to explore these in detail here. Liberal feminists who simply argue that women should be encouraged and supported to 'compete' effectively with men within existing structures do not qualify for inclusion within the eco-feminist movement for the purposes of this analysis as they are merely reasserting the value of the existing social, economic and political order. Of greater significance is the work of structural feminist writers, who argue that a feminist analysis requires the development of a society based on different organisational principles, seeking to replace competitive structures with cooperative structures, individualism with genuine collective decision making and to value all people rather than to support the domination, oppression, control and exploitation of some by others (specifically in relation to gender). In addition, poststructural feminism emphasises discourses of oppression (the way patriarchy has dominated the discourses of power) and seeks to deconstruct such discourses and validate the voices of the marginalised. Some feminist writers also recognise the importance of characteristics traditionally ascribed to women, such as nurturing, caring, sharing, community and peace as *at least as important as* (and, for most writers, more important than) characteristics traditionally ascribed to men, such as individual competition, aggression, domination, exploitation and war.

The eco-feminist position raises two significant sets of questions for those developing a Green analysis. One is the issue of how to ensure that whatever change is initiated does not perpetuate the oppression of women or the structures and discourses of patriarchy but serves to challenge and overthrow such structures and discourses. This question will be taken up in Chapter 3 as part of the discussion of social justice and human rights principles in community development. The other issue is the extent to which women's experiences, consciousness and world views represent an alternative paradigm within which an ecologically sustainable social, economic and political order might be successfully developed. Most Green writers take both of these issues seriously (though naturally there is some variation in the extent to which they are acknowledged and discussed) and as a result there is at least some element of a feminist analysis incorporated in most of the Green literature.

Eco-luddism

Another strand within Green writing is the critique of technology, arguing that unbridled technological development, far from bringing boundless benefits for humanity, creates more problems than it solves and is largely responsible for the problems of the world today. Using the term *luddism* to describe this position is not intended to be derogatory; although the word *luddite* has become a term of abuse levelled at people who mistrust new technologies, it can also be argued that a healthy mistrust of new technologies is precisely what has been lacking during the period of industrial capitalism. The Luddites of the early 19th century, and other anti-technology movements that preceded and followed them, were in effect articulating a simple but extremely significant view—that social goals must not be subordinated to economic goals and that technological development can have negative human consequences (Harrison 1984; Hobsbawm & Rudé 1969). This strikes at the very core of the spirit of the industrial revolution and questions its fundamental assumption that technological development is for the good of all. It is small wonder that the Luddites and those in related movements were ruthlessly repressed by the authorities. Because these were essentially working-class movements, without the 'benefit' of literate and articulate spokespersons who could express their views in the respectable vocabulary of social and political philosophy, it is easy to dismiss them as ignorant and ill-informed, not deserving serious consideration. Their message, however, is profoundly relevant today and is falling at last on more sympathetic ears.

In the late 20th century the cause of the Luddites finally found its intellectual champions in writers such as Illich (1973), Postman (1993) and Mander (1991). These writers have argued that the popular view of technology as 'value-free' is a myth. Technological development carries with it certain values and particular technologies lead inevitably to particular structures, practices and abuses that cannot necessarily be foreseen but can often be of doubtful value. Certainly it is now hard to sustain an argument that technological development *per se* is always a benefit to humanity. The most extreme example, of course, is nuclear technology. There can surely be little doubt that the human experience of nuclear technology has been one where the negative consequences (including the experiences at Hiroshima, Nagasaki, Chernobyl, Mururoa, Maralinga and the threat of nuclear holocaust, and the continuing danger from radioactive wastes and 'accidents') have far outweighed the advantages (some power generation of dubious economic viability and radioisotopes for medical use).

Green writers who take this perspective see technological development as a main cause of the environmental crisis. We have developed technologies with effects we do not understand and unsustainability and uncertainty are consequences of our technological society. Such a view relies heavily on the analysis of Ivan Illich, who has argued that technologies in a number of areas have developed to the point where the disadvantages outweigh the advantages. Medical technology, he suggests, now harms more than it cures (Illich 1976) and further development no longer results in a net benefit in terms of human health. Similarly, modern transport technology has served to enslave rather than to liberate (Illich 1973). Other writers (such as Bowers 2000) have applied a comparable critique to computers and information technology, pointing out that we are so excited about the advantages that we lose sight of the negatives of computer technology: the devaluing of any human 'knowledge' or 'experience' that cannot be reduced to digital impulses, the increasing individualisation as people retreat into cyberspace and no longer interact with other human beings and the way in which information technology is redefining the dominant culture in ways that have received little critique.

From this perspective, the traditional 'environmentalist' response to ecological problems, namely, to seek a technological solution, is self-defeating. Advanced technology is seen as part of the problem rather than part of the solution.

This critique of high technology is another common theme in a good deal of Green writing. Most Green (as opposed to 'environmentalist') writers are seeking non-technological solutions to the ecological crisis and they have at least a scepticism, if not a downright mistrust, of technological development. The extent to which Green writers adopt an anti-technology position varies considerably and of course there are benefits as well as costs to most technological innovations. The problem is that the dominant culture tends to celebrate the benefits and ignore the costs: in monetary terms many businesses have failed because of a tendency to exaggerate the benefits and dismiss the costs and the planet is in similar danger if the social and environmental costs are ignored in the euphoria around new technology.

Anti-growth

Some writers in the Green movement perceive growth to be the major problem underpinning the ecological crisis. The existing order is premised on the desirability and inevitability of growth, including economic growth, population growth, the growth of urban areas, the growth of affluence and the growth of organisations. There is an equating of *bigger* with *better* and one of the major perceived criteria for success and quality is for things to be growing. Economic growth is regarded as a primary goal of economic policy and as the mechanism by which 'full employment', prosperity and community wellbeing will be maintained. It is assumed that cities will continue to grow and planners are required to determine how cities will 'cope with' growth in terms of transport, housing, land use, water, pollution and so on. The health of a business is measured by its growth in size, turnover and profit and the 'success stories' of business are of small businesses that become big businesses. The assumption of the value of growth, and of bigger being better, is so ingrained that it is barely questioned. Everything is expected (indeed required) to grow, whether it be economies, cities, businesses, community organisations, professional football leagues, universities, resource consumption or tourism.

The problem, of course, is that we live in a finite world. Growth cannot continue forever as the finite nature of the earth limits both the resources available and the extent to which the costs of growth can be borne. Writers such as David Suzuki (Suzuki & McConnell 1997) have argued that there are clear signs that the natural limits to growth are being reached and that growth cannot continue. The environmental crisis is the result of growth having outstripped the earth's capacity to cope with its consequences. The common feature of growth patterns is that they are exponential rather than linear: that is, the rate of growth itself increases rather than remaining constant and therefore plotting growth on a graph tends to produce upwardly bending curves rather than straight lines. This means that the 'day of reckoning', when the graph shoots off the top of the page and growth can no longer be sustained, tends to be closer than people realise. This was the main message of *The Limits to Growth* (Meadows, Meadows, Randers & Behrens 1972) and although the original calculations of that study have been questioned, the essential argument about the impossibility of continued growth in a finite world remains incontrovertible (Rifkin 1985; Meadows, Meadows & Randers 1992).

This critique of growth is closely related to the concept of sustainability. The existing system is seen as unsustainable and further growth only makes it more so. Hence an alternative based on principles of sustainability is advocated. This alternative would effectively limit growth and would ensure that, as much as possible, resources are used only at a rate at which they can be replaced and that output to the environment is limited to the level at which it can be absorbed. The concept of sustainability is central to a Green perspective and it will be discussed later in this chapter.

Alternative economics

Another strand of Green analysis, closely related to the 'no-growth' position, is alternative economics. This perspective sees the major problem as being the economic system that has developed within industrial capitalism, as it has encouraged overconsumption, waste, growth and the devaluing of the environment. It thus seeks to develop a new economics based on ecological principles.

There are two mainstreams within alternative 'Green' economics. The first seeks to redefine conventional economic analysis to incorporate the concerns of environmentalists. Conventional economic analysis, in calculating costs and benefits, has treated environmental factors as externalities and therefore has not included them in the comparison of costs with benefits. Thus an industry that discharges toxic waste into the environment has been able to do so without cost and the cost to the environment is not included in the calculation of the net benefit of this industry to the economy. There is, of course, a cost associated with having to clean up the environment, but this is not borne by the industry concerned so it is not considered part of its profit or loss. Indeed, environmental costs are often borne by people or governments far away from the source, as is the case with acid rain or nuclear fallout. Similarly, social costs also tend not to be included in conventional economic calculations. The social costs or benefits of a particular industry or activity, like the environmental costs, are notoriously difficult to measure (some would say impossible) and the response of conventional economics has been to treat them as externalities and therefore to leave them out of the calculation. It is this that leads, for example, to claims that nuclear power is economically viable; if the cost to humanity of having to store and monitor nuclear waste for, in some cases, hundreds of thousands of years were included, there could be no way that nuclear power would be seen as an economically viable option. That cost is certainly incurred by the decision to use nuclear power, but current economic wisdom does not include it in the calculations: it is a cost we are incurring for future generations and this apparently has little current applicability.

A related problem with conventional economics is its definition of value in terms of economic productivity or market price. That phenomena such as wilderness, native forests, peace, security and endangered species can have intrinsic value is not acknowledged in economic calculations. Thus, in an example often cited by Greens, conventional economics dictates that a standing tree has no value—it is only when it is cut down and becomes a 'resource' that it can be regarded as valuable. In this way, conventional economics can fly in the face of what, from an ecological perspective, is self-evident.

Green critics of conventional economics have therefore argued that the non-recognition of social and ecological phenomena means that economics is far from value-neutral—that in fact it serves to reinforce the existing ecologically (and socially) disastrous order. The existing system effectively acts to reduce or destroy things of value such as beauty, peace, wilderness, security, endangered species and community, while at the same time creating undesirable outcomes such as pollution, overcrowding, congestion, health problems, stress, ugliness and overconsumption. Conventional economics tends not to value such phenomena, partly because they are not readily measured, and hence decisions made on the basis of conventional economic analysis tend to reinforce policies and practices that are leading to global catastrophe. A number of Green economists are seeking to develop an alternative economics that does take account of these environmental and social factors, by developing ways in which they might be measured and incorporated in an economic analysis that more truly reflects ecological and social reality (such as Pearce, Markandya & Barbier 1989; Jacobs 1991; Daly & Cobb 1989).

The second main strand of alternative Green economics seeks a more fundamental change, beyond merely redefining the way economic equations are calculated. Hazel Henderson (1988,

1991), Paul Ekins (1986, 1992) and Manfred Max-Neef (1991) have been particularly significant writers from this perspective, arguing for a fundamental paradigm change in the way social and economic phenomena are described. Their vision of economics is embedded in a broader vision of a change of human values, incorporating many of the other perspectives described in this chapter and will be further considered below.

Another important alternative economic perspective which, like Henderson, Ekins and Max-Neef, goes further than the redefinition of economic equations, is proposed by those who seek a more decentralised and community-based economic system. For them, the main problem with conventional economic activity is that it is out of the reach of ordinary people, who are disempowered and impoverished by transnational capitalism. This transfers profits from poor areas (countries in the majority world or 'economically disadvantaged' communities in the minority world) to richer areas, thereby increasing economic inequality and inequity (George 1992; Stilwell 1993). It also contributes to ecological destruction by promoting economic activity that is not closely related to the lives and experiences of ordinary people and which takes no account of environmental sensitivities. This analysis leads to the advocacy of localised alternatives—local employment generation, community banks and credit schemes, barter systems, local currency systems (often known as LETS) and so on (Dauncey 1988). This, of course, has particular relevance for community development and will be taken up further in Chapter 9.

Throughout the literature on Green economics the perspective of E.F. Schumacher, who helped to popularise the maxim 'Small is beautiful', has been particularly important. Schumacher sought to articulate alternative, human-scale approaches to economics and technology and he was a pioneer in the alternative economics movement (Schumacher 1973; Lutz 1992). His work is also relevant in the critique of technology, described in the section on eco-luddism.

Global development

Another strand of analysis that has been significant in the development of the Green perspective has been the work done on global development by writers such as Ted Trainer (1985, 1989), Susan George (1992) and Vandana Shiva (1989, 1991). Many of the worst environmental problems occur in nations that are characterised as the 'majority world' (or developing countries, the South or the Third World) where there are high levels of pollution in urban areas, land degradation on a massive scale, high levels of population growth and where wilderness areas such as rainforests are being rapidly destroyed. Much of this environmental destruction is the result of governments of the majority world seeking to promote economic development through developing industry, more 'efficient' land use and the exploitation of natural resources. It is important to emphasise that these governments are merely seeking to emulate the economic success of the more 'developed' nations, which followed a similar route to economic prosperity through the process of industrialisation and which were often able to profit from the exploitation of their colonies (now the 'underdeveloped' nations of the majority world). Thus, they are understandably resentful of criticism from environmentalists in more affluent nations, arguing that they should not be denied the same opportunities for economic development and that it was the colonialist exploitation of the countries of the minority world that led them to be disadvantaged. The problem, of course, is that it is becoming clear that the world is unable to support the affluence of the minority world for very much longer and if the whole world were to develop to the same level as the industrialised minority world there would be a rapid escalation of the ecological crisis. The economic development of nations of the majority world, therefore, is simply hastening the coming of the ecological Armageddon.

readily accepts dominant discourses of power, ignores the important structural factors that both cause and perpetuate the dominant social, economic and political order and leads people to believe that simply by meditating, wearing crystals, reading Tarot cards or undergoing body therapy they can change the world (Bookchin 1995; Tacey 2000). This is not necessarily to deny the value of these activities in themselves—many people find them important in helping to give meaning and purpose to their lives; rather it is to emphasise that while personal growth may be desirable, and indeed necessary, it is certainly not sufficient for effective social change.

New paradigm thinking

The term *paradigm* may be becoming overused, but the concept of paradigm is particularly important in the Green literature. In this context, paradigm means the world view within which theory, practice, knowledge, science, action and so on are conceptualised. The paradigm is that set of assumptions, ideas, understandings and values (usually unstated) that sets the rules of what is to count as relevant or irrelevant—what questions should and should not be asked, what knowledge is seen as legitimate and what practices are acceptable. Acceptance of a paradigm is normally a matter of unstated, and often unconscious, consensus. For example, the dominant paradigm for scientific research and practice accepts objectively measurable and verifiable phenomena as proper objects for study and, at the same time, it rejects phenomena that cannot be thus characterised; hence astronomy is a 'proper' science while astrology is not, 'real' medicine includes drug therapy and surgery but not magic or faith healing, and so on. It is the paradigm, in other words, that defines what is 'proper' or legitimate knowledge and activity. T.S. Kuhn, who argued the importance of paradigms in *The Structure of Scientific Revolutions* (1970), described how scientific activity takes place within a certain paradigm, which, after a time, proves to be inadequate as a framework for new knowledge. As a result, there is a 'revolution' resulting in the development of a new paradigm and a reorientation of scientific thought within a new world view. The transition from Newtonian physics to the physics of relativity and quantum theory is a clear example of such a paradigm shift (or 'scientific revolution', to use Kuhn's terminology).

Although Kuhn applied the notion of paradigm to scientific endeavour, the idea has been applied much more broadly. Writers from a variety of disciplines have suggested that many of the problems currently facing the world can be understood as resulting from the inadequacy of the 'dominant paradigm', which is variously defined as *Western, industrial, Cartesian, Newtonian, mechanistic* and a number of other ways (Capra 1982; Henderson 1991; Rifkin 1985; Ornstein & Ehrlich 1989). They suggest that this particular paradigm, or world view, while it has had undoubted benefits for humanity, has now reached a point where it is increasingly dysfunctional and we will be unable to solve the pressing problems of the day unless we develop an alternative. While not all such writers would identify themselves as 'Green', new paradigm thinking has become central to the Green movement and incorporates many of the views described earlier in this chapter.

Writers from this perspective point to the origin of the dominant world view in the philosophy of 'the Enlightenment', in the physics of Newton, the philosophy and mathematics of Descartes, the scientific theory of Bacon, the utilitarianism of Bentham, the political theory of Locke and the economics of Adam Smith, among others (Capra 1982; Rifkin 1985). This dominant paradigm emphasises objective, scientific rationality and undervalues subjective experience, intuition and other forms of knowledge. The scientific method views the world as a well-ordered mechanism and the task of science is to discover the laws by which it works, through a rational and linear process (Fay 1975). To do this, it breaks up the 'machine' into its component parts and studies each in detail; these parts together make up the whole. This understanding of how the 'machine' works enables people to understand it and, hence, to dominate and exploit the natural world. Not only does 'man' have the capacity to dominate nature, 'he' is seen as having a right and, indeed, an obligation to do so, because it is such enhanced understanding and domination that makes possible 'progress' in the form of industrialisation and technological development. Such progress is regarded as a fundamental goal of human civilisation. The science of the Enlightenment was paralleled by the anthropocentrism that formed part of some of the Abrahamnic religious traditions in the Western and, later, capitalist world. Within this world view the natural environment is viewed as valuable only to the extent that it serves human welfare or is a resource for human economic endeavours (Ezzy 2004; Lowe & Paavola 2005).

Just as the whole machine is broken down into its component parts, so society is seen as made up of individuals and it is individual action and individual interests that are fundamentally important. Thus the social and economic system is seen primarily in terms of the individual and individuals acting in their own interests will result in benefits for all. This world view, based on scientific rationality, progress, individualism, domination over nature, technology, exploitation, anthropocentrism and so on, provided the context for the rise of capitalism, the industrial revolution, technological innovation, growth, the devastation of the natural world, the reinforcement of patriarchy and the development of large, alienating structures—all of which have been identified earlier in the chapter as significant causes of the current ecological crisis. Another consequence of this world view that is of particular significance for this book is the devaluing of 'community' and extended family in favour of the individual and increasingly fragmented forms of the nuclear family.

Challenges to the dominant paradigm have emerged from a number of sources. Significantly, one of the most powerful of these challenges has been from within the physical sciences, which might have been regarded as the archetype of the dominant paradigm. The impact of the Heisenberg uncertainty principle, quantum physics, relativity and chaos theory has been to question the certain, ordered and predictable world and to acknowledge the existence of unpredictability and uncertainty so the whole foundation of the dominant paradigm is called into question.

In the social sciences, the critique of positivism and empiricism has had a similar impact on the dominant paradigm. Social science built on the analogy of traditional physical sciences, with objective empirical study of social phenomena as if they are measurable objects behaving in accordance with universal laws, has been shown to be both logically inconsistent (Fay 1975) and inadequate in dealing with the complex interaction of social phenomena. The development of alternative interpretive paradigms and qualitative or naturalistic research techniques (Denzin & Lincoln 2000; Strauss & Corbin 1990; Reason 1988; Lincoln & Guba 1985) represents a seeking for an alternative to the dominant paradigm.

Arising from the humanities, postmodernism has had a major impact on social and political thought and has been an important influence for those seeking alternative formulations. It rejects the dominant paradigm as being the essence of the 'modern' and seeks different, non-linear models of cultural production and critique that reject conventional forms of logic and discourse. According to postmodernism, reality can no longer be understood in terms of the single 'meta-narrative' but is characterised by multiple discourses, fragmented meanings and continual simultaneous redefinitions; to seek a single unifying and integrating model, answer or paradigm is both futile and meaningless. As with all intellectual movements, there are various strands within postmodernism. Rosenau (1992, pp. 14ff) draws a distinction between the *sceptical* and the *affirmative* postmodernist positions and the latter, in particular, incorporating strong identification with social and political movements, has a close relationship to the Green perspective.

Within the various disciplines, other movements such as post-industrialism, feminism, post-positivism, critical theory and postcolonialism can also be regarded as part of a larger movement of questioning the validity and relevance of the dominant paradigm or Western world view and therefore as seeking to develop an alternative paradigm. Thus, the term *new paradigm thinking* encompasses a broad range of intellectual endeavour and serves to identify important linkages between analyses that have emerged in different disciplines.

Central to new paradigm thinking have been those writers who have specifically argued that what is needed is a new paradigm—in other words, a new way of thinking about the world, how it works and the place of humanity within it. Fritjof Capra has been a prominent writer in this field and his popular book *The Turning Point* (1982) represented a call for a new paradigm. From a social science point of view there are weaknesses in Capra's analysis in that he fails to deal effectively with issues of social structure, discourses of power and structural inequality (see Chapter 3). But Capra's work is significant in emphasising the importance of a holistic perspective rather than linear thinking and in seeking a paradigm that values balance rather than one which destroys it. Hazel Henderson (1988, 1995, 1996) is another important writer who has been specifically concerned with the idea of a new paradigm to replace the dominant world view of Western societies, and her approach also fits well with the analyses mentioned earlier in this chapter (e.g. eco-feminism, alternative economics, the critique of technology).

It could be argued that all the Green positions outlined in this chapter could be incorporated in the new paradigm label and that *new paradigm* may be a better term than *Green* for the overall perspective described. The alternative approach is to incorporate new paradigm thinking in a Green position as one of the many strands of thought (though perhaps the most important because of its inclusive nature) that contribute to a new Green awareness. This chapter has opted for the latter, using the term *Green* to describe a particular perspective. There are two reasons for this. One is simply that of common usage: the term *Green* is more widely used (though perhaps also more widely misused) than the term *new paradigm* and it is less intellectually pretentious. The second reason is more fundamental: *new paradigm* essentially relates to thought processes, intellectualisation, research and the way we perceive the world; *Green*, however, also contains an action perspective and implies a social movement and political process that is not necessarily present in *new paradigm*, though some new paradigm thinkers (e.g. Fay 1987) would, of course, include social and political action in their formulations.

An ecological perspective

Amid this diversity of approaches is it possible to identify a central core of Green social and political theory? The diversity itself need not present a problem as, from a Green perspective, it can be argued that there is value in diversity and that a degree of theoretical and ideological pluralism is an advantage; indeed if one were to accept a postmodern Green view, such diversity would be essential. But if the Green perspective is to provide a conceptual basis for community development, it is important to identify some core ideas that can be used as a basis for further discussion, even though these may be contested and will be contextualised in different ways. It is also important from the point of view of the Green movement itself. Many of the above strands of thought reflect familiar strands in conventional social and political discourse: socialism, feminism, anarchism, alternative economics and so on. If the Green movement is to offer something new, it is essential to focus on what makes the 'Green' forms of these intellectual positions distinctive. What is the difference between eco-socialism and conventional socialism, between eco-feminism and feminism? What does the prefix *eco-* signify, other than an attempt to appear relevant to the needs of the day? The strands of Green analysis described above are not by and large mutually exclusive, and adoption of one does not exclude the adoption of another. Indeed, some authors, such as Ehrlich, Mellor, Gorz and Shiva, were cited above in relation to more than one position. There is no logical reason why a Green position could not be developed that incorporated some elements of most, if not all, of the perspectives outlined in this chapter. Indeed, many of the perspectives reinforce rather than contradict each other.

In developing a characteristically Green position, it is difficult to define what is central to a Green perspective and what is peripheral. Many positions are claimed as part of the Green world view, some of which are quite extreme and would be rejected by many people in the Green movement. Such views can also retard the cause of the Greens by inviting negative publicity and providing ready ammunition to the Greens' political opponents. The question, then, is how to determine the core of a Green position that will be internally consistent, incorporate the central views of most people in the Green movement, provide a coherent framework for action and exclude the 'baggage' such a movement inevitably attracts.

This task has been attempted by Robert Goodin (1992), who draws a distinction between a Green 'theory of value', which he claims can be developed as a consistent and powerful philosophical position and a Green 'theory of agency', which he claims cannot be so developed. Thus his Green position includes an essentially ecocentric value analysis, but excludes many of the characteristic Green political programs and policies, such as decentralisation and community-based alternatives.

There are two problems with Goodin's approach. The first is that it does not adequately represent the reality of the Green movement, as most participants in the Green movement would insist that to develop a theory of value is not sufficient and that a program of action is necessary as well. Goodin's analysis, therefore, is only one side of the coin. A more fundamental objection arises from the epistemological base of the Green movement itself, which incorporates much of what was described above as 'new paradigm thinking'. This questions the separation of theory and action, maintaining that it is an artificial construct of the 'old paradigm'. Using the arguments of writers from critical social theory (Fay 1987; Held 1980), from the world of political practice such as Freire (1972) and from the Marxist tradition, this position insists that both theory and practice must be integrated and incorporated in a single paradigm of knowledge/action. From this perspective Goodin's distinction is inadmissible and a broader definition of what is 'essentially Green' must be developed.

For the purpose of the remaining chapters of this book and the model of community development they describe, the core of the Green position is understood in terms of some basic principles of ecology, on the grounds that it is essentially an ecological perspective that turns socialism into eco-socialism, feminism into eco-feminism and so on. Because it relies on ecological principles, this perspective will be referred to as an *ecological* perspective rather than a Green perspective, even though it is grounded in the above discussion of Green political theory.

This ecological perspective uses as unifying themes four basic principles of ecology, namely *holism*, *sustainability*, *diversity* and *equilibrium* (see Table 2.2). These are fundamental to any ecological approach and apply both to the natural world (in traditional ecological environmental studies) and to the social, economic and political order, which is the concern of this book. From these four principles, many of the analyses and prescriptions of the strands of Green writing described above emerge as natural consequences and can readily be integrated into an overall perspective broader than Goodin's 'Green theory of value', as it also incorporates a program of action. This perspective contains a degree of internal consistency because of its dependence on the

Table 2.2 An ecological perspective

ECOLOGICAL PRINCIPLE	CONSEQUENCES
1. Holism	Ecocentred philosophy Respect for life and nature Acknowledging intelligence throughout nature Rejection of linear solutions Organic change
2. Sustainability	Conservation Reduced consumption No-growth economics Constraints on technological development Anti-capitalist
3. Diversity	Valuing difference No single answer Decentralisation Networking and lateral communication Lower-level technology
4. Equilibrium	Global/local Yin/yang Gender Rights/responsibilities Peace and cooperation

four basic ecological principles. It represents a position that would probably be accepted by most Greens as legitimate and as at the core of Green philosophy, even though there would be differences of emphasis. It also incorporates most of the thinking outlined earlier in discussion of the different streams of Green thought.

Like Goodin's formulation, however, this perspective does not incorporate some elements that a number of Greens take for granted, specifically those dealing with social justice and human rights issues such as inequalities, inequities and oppression of gender, class, religion and race. These are dealt with in different ways by socialism, feminism and other approaches discussed above, but are not necessarily a part of the *ecological* framework, which is suggested here as a way to integrate the overall Green perspective. These need to be justified on different grounds, which will be the task of Chapter 3.

Ecological principle 1: holism

The principle of holism requires that every event or phenomenon must be seen as part of a whole, and that it can only properly be understood with reference to every other part of the larger system. This is opposed to linear thinking, which is a characteristic of the dominant paradigm of Western thought. Thus problems do not characteristically have simple or linear causes or solutions but must always be understood as manifestations of a wider system, as exemplified by the distinction between ecological and Green approaches outlined at the beginning of this chapter. The *interdependence* of phenomena is critical, therefore, and from this perspective is derived the classic ecological dictum 'You can never do only one thing': whatever one does will have ramifications throughout the system, often unanticipated. Therefore, everything must ideally be understood in terms of its relationship and interaction with everything else. There is no beginning or end to processes and there are no clear boundaries; instead phenomena (both physical and social) must be seen as part of a seamless web of complex interconnecting relationships. Rather than *differentiation* and *classification*, which have been characteristic of Western forms of analysis, *integration* and *synthesis* become fundamental. In 1990 Rose made a significant contribution to this understanding of interconnectedness when she examined the sophisticated approaches to change and the complexity of relationships within the concept of 'new social movements' (1990, p. 209). Her analysis of the political nature of relationships in a change process challenges the otherwise rather simplistic use of terms like 'partnerships', 'participation' and 'alliances', which can be used as mantras bearing little resemblance to human relationships. It also challenges those approaches that portray clear and distinct typologies and therefore suggest simple either/or features of relationships. These latter approaches are typified in Botes and van Rensburg's (2000) use of the familiar dichotomy between 'process' and 'outcome'. Rose's analysis departs from these binary views of change and views of change as either consensus or conflictual, towards what she refers to as 'both/and' models of change (1990, p. 209). In other words, relations are multifaceted, non-linear, integrated and synthesised.

From this principle, a number of further principles can be derived. The interconnectedness of the holistic world view leads naturally to ecocentric rather than anthropocentric perspectives, as argued by writers such as Fox (1990), Eckersley (1992), Naess (1989), Ezzy (2004), Narby (2006) and Shaw (2008). Respect for all life, the intrinsic value of the natural world, an appreciation that the capacity to know ('chai sei') exists throughout the natural world and, hence, a strong conservationist ethic follow naturally. Holism values generalist rather than specialist approaches to problems and their solutions. It also values organic change; attempts to bring about radical change to only one part of a system while ignoring the remainder are almost certain to fail and will bring about negative consequences elsewhere (a lesson yet to be learned by many conventional social and economic policy makers and critics). Change should proceed cautiously in small steps but on a broad front if it is to have any chance of success. This perspective sounds a note of caution about too strong an attachment to any of the streams of Green thought that see the ecological crisis in simplistic terms and ascribe responsibility to a single 'evil', whether it be capitalism, patriarchy, technology, growth or the work ethic. A successful Green strategy would accept the legitimacy of most or all of these analyses and seek strategies that recognised complexity and interdependence.

The holistic perspective also requires integrative links to be made between phenomena that have characteristically been regarded as distinct, such as knowledge and action, theory and practice, fact and value. Such dualisms are a part of the dominant positivist paradigm of the Western intellectual tradition (Fay 1975) and discourage the integrative approach required by the holistic perspective (Naess 1989; Plumwood 1993). This is particularly important in thinking about community development work and will be taken up again in subsequent chapters.

Ecological principle 2: sustainability

The principle of sustainability means that systems must be able to be maintained in the long term, that resources should be used only at the rate at which they can be replenished, that renewable energy sources should be utilised, that output to the environment should be limited to the level at which it can adequately be absorbed and that consumption should be minimised rather than maximised. Inevitably this would require a 'no-growth' approach to economics and social organisation, as well as the obvious environmental controls and conservation strategies. It would require a radical reformulation of economic policy and social organisation, as it would involve a system where getting bigger was discouraged rather than valued.

The concept of sustainability was emphasised by *Our Common Future*, the report of the World Commission on Environment and Development (1987), also referred to as the Brundtland Report, which is seen as a landmark document in changing environmental awareness. Unfortunately this report stopped short of explicitly developing the concept of sustainability in the above terms and sought to define it within more traditional economic parameters, allowing conventional perceptions of the desirability of growth to go unchallenged (for a fuller critique of the Brundtland Report, see Ekins 1992, pp. 30–4). Sustainability was defined in the report within the concept of *sustainable development;* as the notion of *development* is so closely linked in the public consciousness to the idea of growth (the two are often equated, at least implicitly), this has effectively diluted the meaning of *sustainability* and allowed it to be used in such a way as not to challenge the centrality of growth. Like the word *community*, *sustainable* is a word that has been so abused that it is in danger of losing its substantive meaning, to the point where the patently self-contradictory term *sustainable growth* can be unapologetically used by politicians, business leaders and commentators. Neumann discusses the 'discursive incorporation of nature as capital' (2005, p. 95) by which he means the way that nature has been capitalised, whereby nature is used by humans to produce capital and economic value. Discourse produces this state, whereby particular knowledge is articulated by those with power and thus becomes the process through which social reality comes into existence. Escobar (1996) argues from a poststructural perspective that language does not simply reflect reality, it constitutes reality. Within capitalism and its seeming embrace of ecology, such things as rainforest biodiversity are, in reality, conserved so that they can be used in the future for further capital accumulation. This is a perverse codification or construction of nature and sustainability for economic gain, which attempts to reinforce and bolster the current order.

However, if understood within its proper ecological context, the concept of sustainability is very powerful and requires a radical transformation of the existing, patently unsustainable order. Not only are unbridled growth and unnecessary consumption unacceptable, but also the concept of sustainability clearly attacks the fundamentals of traditional capitalist economics, which is predicated on growth and capital accumulation. The same is true of conventional socialist economics, which has tended to accept the desirability of continuing growth. It can, however, be argued that there are varieties of each form of economics that are not incompatible with sustainability; these tend to be the smaller-scale, decentralised versions. In the case of capitalism, this takes the form of the localised market economy; in the case of socialism, it takes the form of decentralised democratic socialism.

Thus, the ecological principle of sustainability is readily compatible with some of the arguments of the eco-socialists and the eco-anarchists. It even has a clear link with the views of the eco-luddites, as it can be suggested that unbridled technological development is also unsustainable. Such arguments would not necessarily invalidate technological development per se, but would require that such development occur for socially and environmentally determined reasons and be constrained by the need to develop sustainable rather than unsustainable technologies. This is in contrast to the perspective of technology within the dominant paradigm, which perceives technological development itself as worthwhile and which allows the technology to determine social and economic interaction (Postman 1993).

Ecological principle 3: diversity

The principle of diversity is another fundamental aspect of the ecological perspective. In nature, diverse organisms and systems evolve to meet the needs of particular circumstances and it is through diversity that natural systems are able to develop, adapt and grow. With diversity, a setback to one system or organism does not necessarily mean disaster for the whole. For example, a diversity of species of wheat means that a disease may strike one or two but is unlikely to affect all.

A diversity of cultures means that some at least will prove to be adaptable to new circumstances. Uniformity is a recipe for ecological disaster. If there are effectively only two or three species of wheat in the world, a new disease could potentially wipe out all crops. And uniformity of culture may turn out to be uniformity of a maladaptive or destructive culture, resulting in the breakdown of human civilisation; indeed it could be argued that this is the current experience of cultural globalisation (see Chapters 8 and 10).

The principle of diversity has not emerged only from a Green, or ecological, perspective. Postmodernist writers have argued that single modernist frameworks, or meta-narratives, are no longer credible or viable in an era of postmodernity and that the 'death of the meta-narrative' (Lyotard 1984) allows for, and even requires, the emergence of alternative narratives and discourses. Postmodernism both promotes and celebrates diversity. Similarly, feminism and the movement for gay and lesbian rights have emphasised the importance of diversity and have seen diversity as something to be celebrated rather than as something to be stamped out through rational planning and imposed conformity.

The principle of diversity maintains that there is not necessarily just one answer or one right way of doing things and so encourages a range of responses. Young's (1996) 'communicative democracy' provides insight into the processes that ensue from embracing diversity. Communicative democracy is concerned with the different coming together to communicate for the purpose of fair outcomes to collective problems. Giddens (1994) and Benhabib (1996) warn us that the alternative to the different engaging in this way with each other is a retreat into fundamentalisms. Young builds positively on their plea to engage by seeing difference as a positive resource in these problem-solving endeavours if the differences are each seen as partial but valuable contributions to greater collective wisdom.

Young claims that the notion of difference helps unravel the process of *transformation* of opinions and views in which there is an opportunity to learn, to understand the other by successfully expressing one's experiences and viewpoints so that others appreciate that these go far beyond the others' subjective experiences. The resource that difference represents then is a resource for learning and a resource for reaching fair and just outcomes. Conversely the presumption of unity/sameness/homogeneity as either the starting point or the goal of dialogue is, according to Young (1996), potentially exclusionary. If one is not part of the unified whole then one is excluded. Moreover if those entering into dialogue are not different, then each of the partners would simply mirror each other. There would be no change as an outcome of dialogue. These contentions both challenge more traditional linear views of social processes and suggest ways forward in the project of transforming economic, political and social structures.

Dialogue is in sharp contrast to, and much more modest than, the characteristic modernist tendency in Western societies to seek *the* right answer and then impose it on the whole system—even the whole world—whether that answer is the 'best' strain of wheat to replace all others, the 'best' form of economics, the 'best' new technology, the English language or a uniform culture. The assumption that there must be one best answer is deeply ingrained and yet it is this assumption that is questioned by the principle of diversity and the process of dialogue.

Diversity proceeds in a much more modest way—not arrogantly defining the 'best' answer and imposing it, but encouraging a variety of ways of doing things so that people can learn from the experience of others and change can proceed cautiously on the basis of a variety of accumulated wisdom. Difference, rather than uniformity, is valued. This essentially pluralist approach may be criticised as conservative in that it mistrusts 'radical' change and, indeed, a Green position inherits a good deal from a classical conservative ideology (as opposed to the radical right). Conservatives of this type value what has evolved through natural processes and warn that attempts to 'improve' on it are likely to make things worse. This is also typical of a conservationist position (it should be noted that the words *conservative* and *conservation* have the same root) and many Green causes can be justified by what is essentially conservative rhetoric: the preservation of wilderness, Indigenous land rights, the preservation of species, natural beauty, heritage buildings and so on (Goodin 1992).

The principle of diversity rather than uniformity is consistent with a major tenet of Green political thought, namely decentralisation. If diversity is valued, then people should be allowed and encouraged to find their own local solutions and ways of doing things. Centralised structures tend to create uniformity through bureaucratic control and regulation and a diverse system is much more easily achieved with maximum decentralisation of decision making, control over resources, economic activity and so on. Many Green writers (Bryant 1995; Porritt 1984; Wall 1990; Kemp & Wall 1990; Trainer 1985) have made decentralised systems a major component of their vision for a Green future. Contrary to Goodin's suggestion that this is not a *necessary* consequence of a Green position, if the ecological principle of diversity is included as a major focus, decentralisation in some form becomes inevitably part of a Green political agenda.

In a decentralised system that values diversity there need not be isolation of one decentralised community from another. Indeed, from a Green perspective it is through horizontal communication that experience can be shared and lessons can be learned far more effectively than from central bureaucratic forms of communication. Thus change emerges from below, from the day-to-day experiences of ordinary people participating through dialogue in decentralised structures and change is organic rather than centrally planned. Such a view sits comfortably with the eco-anarchist position discussed earlier.

The question of decentralisation is, however, problematic for the Greens. Unless one takes an extreme anarchist position, there is a clear need for some form of centralised coordination and perhaps even control, resulting from the interconnectedness that is emphasised by the holistic perspective. Diversity may be valued, but this does not necessarily mean that local bodies can 'go off and do their own thing', which may affect others negatively. An interconnected world requires some form of coordination. This issue will be taken up in later chapters, but it also relates directly to the final ecological principle: equilibrium.

Ecological principle 4: equilibrium

Equilibrium emphasises the importance of the relationship between systems and the need to maintain a balance between them. In the natural world, this occurs through dynamic equilibrium, where changes are naturally monitored and alterations made so that balance is maintained. Potentially conflicting systems have their interactions controlled in such a way that they are able to coexist and even become dependent on each other. This applies to animal populations, vegetation, climate, atmosphere and so on. It is essential if systems are to survive in the long term and hence be sustainable (Suzuki & McConnell 1997).

An ecological perspective, therefore, values balance, harmony, complementarity and equilibrium. Under a Green scenario, more attention would be paid to ensuring that different aspects of the social, economic and political system maintained such a balance. This naturally leads to a concern for peace and the non-violent solution of potential conflict, which will be taken up in Chapter 7. Dialogue, mediation, conflict resolution and the building of consensus, therefore, have an important place in Green thinking. The development of cooperative rather than competitive structures is valued and the assumption that competition is inherent and intrinsically valuable is seriously questioned (Kohn 1986; Argyle 1991; Craig 1993).

Another issue that is addressed by the ecological concern for equilibrium is the capacity to incorporate apparently opposing positions and accommodate dialectical relationships (Plumwood 1993). Thus dualisms—such as male and female, yin and yang, competition and cooperation, central and local, theory and practice, mind and body, personal and political, fact and value or subjective and objective—are not seen in 'all-or-nothing' terms but rather are integrated within a perspective of dynamic tension. It is the balance between them that is important and which must be maintained. Balancing tension implies diversity and difference. It is the different that must be maintained in equilibrium with each other. For a system to lose equilibrium is to risk ecological failure. Therefore one of the problems of the present order is the way in which balance has not been maintained because diversity and difference have not been positively valued or have led to oppressive relationships—for example, in terms of gender where the domination and exploitation of women by men has led to imbalance, oppression and the devaluing of women and their consciousness. Similarly, the issue of balance between conflicting cultures has not been adequately addressed—for example, the relationship between Indigenous and non-Indigenous populations, which has been one of domination and oppression rather than one of balance and mutual respect.

Thus the ecological principle of equilibrium incorporates a number of the concerns of the Green writers discussed earlier and relates to issues of gender, culture, peace, conflict and so on.

The People's Earth Charter was developed as the expression of the commitment to ecological sustainability of ordinary people across the globe after the failure of the UN and governments to produce an Earth Charter.

CASE STUDY: A People's Earth Charter

Preamble

We stand at a critical moment in Earth's history, a time when humanity must choose its future. As the world becomes increasingly interdependent and fragile, the future at once holds great peril and great promise. To move forward we must recognise that in the midst of a magnificent diversity of cultures and life forms we are one human family and one Earth community with a common destiny. We must join together to bring forth a sustainable global society founded on respect for nature, universal human rights, economic justice and a culture of peace. Towards this end, it is imperative that we, the peoples of Earth, declare our responsibility to one another, to the greater community of life and to future generations.

Earth, our home

Humanity is part of a vast evolving universe. Earth, our home, is alive with a unique community of life. The forces of nature make existence a demanding and uncertain adventure, but Earth has provided the conditions essential to life's evolution. The resilience of the community of life and the wellbeing of all its ecological systems, a rich variety of plants and animals, fertile soils, pure waters and clean air. The global environment with its finite resources is a common concern of all peoples. The protection of Earth's vitality, diversity and beauty is a sacred trust.

The global situation

The dominant patterns of production and consumption are causing environmental devastation, the depletion of resources and massive extinction of species. Communities are being undermined. The benefits of development are not shared equitably and the gap between the rich and poor is widening. Injustice, poverty, ignorance and violent conflict are widespread and the cause of great suffering. An unprecedented rise in human population has overburdened ecological and social systems. The foundations of global security are threatened. These trends are perilous—but not inevitable . . .

Universal responsibility

. . . we must decide to live with a sense of universal responsibility, identifying ourselves with the whole Earth community as well as our local communities. We are at once citizens of different nations and of one world in which the local and global are linked. Everyone shares responsibility for the present and future wellbeing of the human family and the larger living world. The spirit of human solidarity and kinship with all life is strengthened when we live with reverence for the mystery of being, gratitude for the gift of life and humility regarding the human place in nature.

We urgently need a shared vision of basic values to provide an ethical foundation for the merging world community.

Principles

I Respect and care for the community of life

- **1** Respect Earth and life in all its diversity.
- **2** Care for the community of life with understanding, compassion and love.
- **3** Build democratic societies that are just, participatory, sustainable and peaceful.
- **4** Secure Earth's bounty and beauty for present and future generations.

II Ecological integrity

- **5** Protect and restore the integrity of Earth's ecological systems, with special concern for biological diversity and the natural processes that sustain life.
- **6** Prevent harm as the best method of environmental protection and, when knowledge is limited, apply a precautionary approach.
- **7** Adopt patterns of production, consumption and reproduction that safeguard Earth's regenerative capacities, human rights and community well-being.
- **8** Advance the study of ecological sustainability and promote the open exchange and wide application of the knowledge acquired.

III Social and economic justice

- **9** Eradicate poverty as an ethical, social and environmental imperative.
- **10** Ensure that economic activities and institutions at all levels promote human development in an equitable and sustainable manner.
- **11** Affirm gender equality and equity as prerequisites to sustainable development and ensure universal access to education, health care and economic opportunity.
- **12** Uphold the right of all, without discrimination, to a natural and social environment supportive of human dignity, bodily health and spiritual wellbeing, with special attention to the rights of Indigenous peoples and minorities.

IV Democracy, non-violence and peace

- **13** Strengthen democratic institutions at all levels, and provide transparency and accountability in governance, inclusive participation in decision making and access to justice.
- **14** Integrate into formal education and life-long learning the knowledge, values and skills needed for a sustainable way of life.
- **15** Treat all living beings with respect and consideration.
- **16** Promote a culture of tolerance, non-violence, and peace.

The way forward

As never before in history, common destiny beckons us to seek a new beginning. Such renewal is the promise of these Earth Charter principles. To fulfill this promise, we must commit ourselves to adopt and promote the values and objectives of the Charter.

This requires a change of mind and heart. It requires a new sense of global interdependence and universal responsibility. We must imaginatively develop and apply the vision of a sustainable way of life locally, nationally,

continued

regionally and globally. Our cultural diversity is a precious heritage and different cultures will find their own distinctive ways to realize the vision. We must deepen and expand the global dialogue that generated the Earth Charter, for we have much to learn from the ongoing collaborative search for truth and wisdom.

Life often involves tensions between important values. This can mean difficult choices. However, we must find ways to harmonise diversity with unity, the exercise of freedom with the common good, short-term objectives with long-term goals. Every individual, family, organization and community has a vital role to play. The arts, sciences, religions, educational institutions, media, businesses, non-governmental organizations and governments are called to offer creative leadership. The partnership of government, civil society and business is essential for effective governance . . .

Let ours be a time remembered for the awakening of a new reverence for life, the firm resolve to achieve sustainability, the quickening of the struggle for justice and peace, and the joyful celebration of life.

Source: The Earth Charter Initiative, <www.earthcharterinaction.org>, accessed 1 July 2009.

- Consider the ways in which the people's Earth Charter reflects the ecological principles, holism, sustainability, diversity and equilibrium.

An ecological perspective: is it enough?

The ecological perspective outlined above—based on the four principles of holism, sustainability, diversity and equilibrium (and see Table 2.2)—incorporates most of the concerns of the different strands of Green writing discussed in the earlier part of the chapter. In addition, the emphasis on holism requires that there be some integration of the different emphases of Green writing; while there will inevitably be disagreement (which itself is valued, according to the principle of diversity), an ecological approach represented by these four principles represents a reasonable consensus position that would be accepted by the majority of writers or activists identifying themselves as Greens. It will, therefore, serve as the ecological perspective for the model of community development, which is the focus of this book.

Given the environmental crisis facing the world in the second decade of the 21st century, such a perspective is necessary in any model of community development (or of anything else). But while it is necessary, it is not thereby sufficient. The ecological position does not specifically tackle a number of issues that are fundamental to community development, including human rights, structural oppression, equity or disadvantage and discourses of power. While these concerns are not incompatible with a Green position and are to some extent implied—for example, in the commitment to balance, peace and harmony—this is a weaker implication than would be accepted by people working with disadvantaged groups who are concerned to bring about a fairer society. An ecological position may imply some degree of social equity, but this is not necessarily so. Indeed, a society based on authoritarian control and social/economic inequality could well be regarded as ecologically acceptable and as meeting the criteria of a Green political agenda. An eco-fascist system is, in theory, quite possible and might be easier to implement than the alternatives. The resort to authoritarian and divisive solutions to ecological problems is an easy policy option in societies with traditions of power, hierarchy and control and an ecological perspective could well be used to justify such measures.

For these reasons, a *social justice and human rights* perspective is also required, which deals with issues of social equity, oppression and so on. This will be the subject of Chapter 3, after which the two perspectives, ecological and social justice, will be integrated as the foundation for a community development process in Chapter 4.

The following case study is based on an actual issue and process in an Australian city. It serves to facilitate the identification of how streams of Green thought run through how issues are problematised by various interested parties.

CASE STUDY: Community action against pollution

An urban community lived for many years among various industries. Much of the industry was small-scale but polluting. An organic gardening and mulching business created constant smells, particularly from decaying oranges and other organic matter. These smells became particularly unbearable during hot summer nights when doors and windows would have to be sealed to keep out the smells. The community was a low-income community and almost none of the public housing tenants had air conditioning. Scrap metal yards created noise pollution throughout the working days and sometimes into the nights. It was almost unknown for the environmental protection agency officers to monitor pollution after hours and so noise persisted late into the night. Another industry, in the area was the leather industry, which consisted of a number of small, low-technology tanneries. These created toxins that found their way into the local waterways. A number of residents had joined together and, with the support of a local community worker, formed an environmental action group.

The group came across information that the local government authority had approved the establishment of a high-technology Korean-owned tannery and that the approval process had been fast-tracked through and around normal monitoring and consultative processes. It appeared that the approval and the fast and secretive process was designed to further the economic interests of the authority and some of the individuals on the local council, whose business interests would clearly benefit from the new tannery. This suspicion was reinforced when it was discovered that the tannery would discharge levels of toxins above the legal limits, so much so that conforming to normal processes would have resulted in the rejection of applications for setting up the tannery in the area. The action group embarked on a campaign to expose the authority decision and to fight the introduction of another tannery into their community.

The action group used the print and television media, presented a play at a national community health conference, spoke up at council meetings and challenged the decision in the courts, where it eventually won and the tannery withdrew its plans to set up in the area. The council fought the local group and claimed that the group was thwarting the economic growth and development of the area. Some other local people spoke out against the group because they believed that the new tannery would create more jobs. In fact, the new tannery would probably have forced smaller tanneries to close and its high technology meant it would have needed to employ fewer people. The decision by the company to withdraw appeared to be based on its frustration at the extended timelines forced by legal actions.

The environmental action group was indicative of a local community which was becoming less willing to tolerate the consequences of government decisions in their community, especially continuing and increasing levels of pollution. It was evident to some key community members that the more wealthy areas of the city were never subjected to industry in their communities or to decisions being imposed on them. The level of community action to fight such imposed conditions, not only in the area of pollution, was increasing with the support of the local community workers.

continued

Consider this case study in the light of the schools of Green thought outlined in Table 2.1. There are several aspects of how the problem is perceived by the different key actors that either explicitly or implicitly reflect one or several streams.

- Who are the key actors involved in this issue?
- What are the different perceptions (both explicit and implied) of the issue and to what streams of Green thought do these align?

The following case study provides an opportunity to critically view an ecological project using the lens of the four ecological principles.

CASE STUDY: Intervale Community Farm

The Intervale Community Farm is a not-for-profit, member-run, community farm that provides organic produce for 500 households in the Burlington, Vermont area of USA. Our land is located in the Intervale, a place 'between the hills' where people have farmed for many years. We are part of the global Community Supported Agriculture (CSA) movement, linking farmers and consumers together to build a sustainable food system. We are now in our 19th season.

The Intervale Community Farm (ICF) is a 35-acre community-supported agriculture (CSA) farm situated on the lower Winooski River flood plain in Burlington, Vermont. Started in 1990, we grow about 20 acres of mixed vegetables and 1 acre of berries, flowers, and herbs, with the balance in green manures, facilities, and hedgerows. At nearly 500 member households, we are one of the largest and oldest CSAs in the region.

Different from most CSAs, the membership of ICF owns the farm. Essentially a consumer cooperative, the ICF is governed by a board (the ICF Steering Committee) elected by the membership at its annual meeting. In conjunction with the Farm Manager (FM), the Steering Committee sets the overall goals of the organization and stipulates the methods that must be used to achieve them. The FM, hired by the Steering Committee, is then charged with achieving the ends using appropriate means. Overall, the system functions well, with the membership involved at the governance level, and the staff charged with all operations.

In terms of production, ICF is a typical mid-sized, diversified Vermont veggie farm. Certified organic by Vermont Organic Farmers, we employ the usual mix of crop rotation, green manures, and compost to manage the soil. We aim to do as much work as feasible with mechanized equipment. Nearly all tillage and planting is tractor-based, weed control is a mix of tractor cultivation and hand work, and most harvest is done by hand. Our primary harvest days are Monday and Thursday, prior to the CSA distributions.

All CSA distribution takes place on the farm, Monday and Thursday afternoons. Distributions can be busy, with several hundred people filing through in a 3.5-hour period. In order to engage members and give them a bit more of a sense of the farm, many of our crops are only available as pick-your-own. Members pick most of the labor-intensive crops like peas, beans, berries, flowers, and herbs, while the farm crew gathers the remainder.

Source: <www.intervalecommunityfarm.com>

- How would you critically evaluate this local/global initiative in terms of each of the ecological principles: holism, sustainability, diversity and equilibrium? What is the evidence for your evaluations?

>> discussion questions

1 What is the important distinction between *environmental* responses and *Green* responses?
2 In what ways do the themes within the Green analysis extend and/or challenge the themes found in more general social science thinking? For example, in what ways does eco-socialism extend or challenge socialism, eco-feminism extend or challenge feminism and so on?
3 What are the tensions between majority and minority world perspectives and experiences in relation to ecological issues? How might these be managed?
4 In what ways can the various Green positions outlined in this chapter be incorporated into the 'new paradigm' label?
5 What are the four ecological principles and what does each entail?
6 In what ways might an ecological perspective be both *necessary* and *insufficient* on its own as a basis for community development?

>> reflection questions

1 Environmental responses are less radical than Green responses in their demands for changes in current social, economic and political arrangements. What are your views about the two perspectives and their consequences for the type of changes they each require?
2 Would you position yourself within any or some of the streams of Green thought? If so, which ones and why? If not, why not? Identify the values you hold and how these might influence where you position yourself. What might be the implications for you, as a community worker, of the values you have identified?
3 If the world's environmental crisis demands an ecological perspective in your community work, what would this mean for your practice, the issues you work with, the ways you might problematise these issues, and the approaches you might take to addressing them within communities?
4 Read the following extract and then consider how the relationship with environment may encapsulate the sense of deep ecology, a Green analysis and the core principles of the ecological perspective as it has been developed in this chapter. How development and the market destroy relationships and long-term sustainability?

What do rivers mean to us as a society?

Indians have shared deep-rooted and multi-faceted links with their natural environment. Rivers have been a perennial source of inspiration for creativity, symbols of enlightenment and sights [sic] for a plethora of cultural activities. An intrinsic part of all rites of passage, from birth to death, Indian rivers seem to invoke both celebration and sorrow. So much a part of both the mundane and the sublime, they are almost taken for granted, and yet revered deeply.

With 'advancement', a rupture of well-established and yet vulnerable links between nature and culture has emerged, as with the evil twin of development. As India is opening up new avenues for investment, rapid construction of world class cities has become the order of the day. Every part of the country speaks the same story of 'development'.

Subjugating nature

This has stirred a massive hunger for natural resources, which now dictates the way we perceive our relationship with our environment—no longer an association of love and respect, but that of control and command, where nature turns from a source of inspiration to a commodity, a resource to be exploited before anyone else does. The world is now a reservoir of raw material, waiting to be utlised . . .

Market driven culture

The sight of poverty does not suit the idea of a city-beautiful. The riverside is meant for upper-class housing anyway! Not only is there a cultural disconnect with the river, but also a visual disconnect, as most access points to the river have been closed, walls have been built . . . In order to 'preserve' the river, the government has managed to remove the river from the imagination of people's minds . . . the river is reduced from being an awe-inspiring entity to an added feature to attract consumers . . .

. . . The essence of this argument is to re-establish people's relationships with their habitat for a more democratic and sustainable life. Rivers have, in history, belonged to the people, to communities, and not to the state authority. The people, having a sense of belonging and association with the river, took care of it and expressed concern for it.

Source: B. Ashok 2008, 'What Do Rivers Mean to us as a Society?', *The Hindu,* 21 Septemper, p. 16.

CHAPTER 3

Foundations of community development: a social justice and human rights perspective

Introduction

Chapter 2 outlined an ecological perspective, based on a Green analysis, as one of the principal foundations for a model of community development. In this chapter a social justice and human rights perspective is developed, which will serve as the second principal foundation for the model. No attempt will be made to link the two perspectives: that ambitious but necessary task will be left until Chapter 4.

It should be noted at the outset that in this chapter the discussion of social justice and human rights takes place in the context of minority world societies that have been categorised as Western (or Northern), industrial (or post-industrial) and advanced capitalist, such as the countries of North America, Europe and Australasia. This is not to deny that there are other forms of society or that the interrelationship of societies at the global level is critical to a broad understanding of social justice and human rights. Global social justice and human rights issues, and their implications for programs in the majority world, are considered further in Chapter 8.

The term *social justice* is perhaps as often used as the term *Green* and results in a similar confusion of meanings. The social justice and human rights perspective developed in this chapter, like the ecological perspective of Chapter 2, would not be universally accepted by those who use the terms. There are, inevitably, different and conflicting perspectives. As in Chapter 2, it is hoped that the perspective derived here will nevertheless represent a position consistent with that of most community workers and will therefore provide a good basis for a model of community development.

Social justice

The conventional place to start a discussion of social justice is with the theory of justice developed by John Rawls (1972, 1999). In this highly influential work, Rawls sought to determine the principles of justice that reasonable people, with no prior knowledge of their personal stake in the outcome, would seek to apply to a society in which they were to live. His argument is complex, but he concludes with three principles of justice he believes would satisfy his criteria. These are: equality in basic liberties, equality of opportunity for advancement and positive discrimination for the underprivileged in order to ensure equity.

It is hard to take issue with these principles; there would surely be broad consensus that they are highly desirable and important in any society concerned with justice, fairness or equity. The question is not whether these principles are necessary, but whether they are sufficient. A broader sociological treatment of social problems and social issues suggests that a more wide-ranging perspective than that of Rawls is required if we are to arrive at a position that will provide an adequate framework for understanding and acting on the social issues confronting community workers.

The significant point to note about Rawls' principles is that they would normally be understood as applying to individuals. But analysis from an individual perspective is only one way of understanding social issues and social injustice. In political terms the individual perspective is essentially liberal in its orientation and although this orientation has been central to mainstream Western political philosophy since Hobbes and Locke, it is a perspective that gives a limited and one-dimensional view of social phenomena and, if understood in isolation, can be criticised as being innately conservative and lacking a moral base (Bannerjee 2005).

Another serious criticism of Rawls' analysis is that he did not address the question of *why* resources need to be redistributed to the advantage of the underprivileged—*why* there is inequity. In other words, inadequate attention was paid by Rawls to exploitation and oppression as drivers of injustice. This distributional theory of social justice is limited on at least two grounds, as identified by Mullaly (1997, 2002): first, it ignores the social processes and practices that cause the maldistribution in the first place and second, it does not recognise the limits of the logic of extending the notion of distribution to non-material goods and resources (such as rights and opportunities). Rights and opportunities, unlike income and resources, are not possessions. Rights are relationships—institutionally defined rules specifying what people can do in relation to others. They refer to doing rather than having. Relationships are not equal. Relationships are imbued with power and powerlessness. They not only define what people can do, but also what they cannot do. Relationships can, therefore, be exploitative and oppressive.

If social justice is about more than distribution of resources, that is, if it is about relationships that must be free of exploitation and oppression, then power is once again implicated. Iris Marion Young provides a useful examination of social justice and oppression. Her examination of justice in *Justice and the Politics of Difference* (1990) argues for an alternative to considering justice in terms of merely the distribution of material resources. She provides a critique of two pervasive aspects of expert knowledge: positivism and reductionism. She claims that the former assumes structures and institutions as given, when they ought to undergo a normative evaluation and that the latter reduces phenomena to a unity, it values *sameness* and *commonness* over *specificity* and *difference*. In Chapter 2, the importance of diversity within an ecological perspective was discussed. Diversity is equally crucial to a social justice and human rights perspective. Young's refocus of social justice acknowledges the play of vested interests, power, domination and oppression. This, in turn, opens up an examination of the relationship between domination and oppression and thus the possibility of liberation and emancipation, and an examination of norms, trust, networks and reciprocity in communities. Reflection on these concepts is surely critical in terms of the issues confronted by community workers. Young's notion of the *unoppressive city*, which will be discussed later when exploring rights and community development, provides some useful indicators of development for communities of difference.

Approaches to disadvantage

Taylor-Gooby and Dale (1981) develop a threefold classification of 'accounts of social issues' that is useful at this point in the analysis. They describe *individual, institutional reformist* and *structural* accounts, to which can be added a *poststructural* category (see Table 3.1).

SD of H

The individual perspective

The *individual* perspective on social issues locates a social problem primarily within the individual and therefore seeks individually based solutions. For example, poverty, delinquency, suicide, depression and unemployment are seen as the result of some defect or pathology (whether psychological, biological or moral) in the individual(s) affected. Solutions are sought on the basis of individual treatment or therapy, such as counselling, moral exhortation, punishment, medical treatment or behaviour modification. While it may well be true that in many cases individual factors are significant, a purely individual account can be criticised in that it fails to take account of external factors over which the individual has little or no control. It leads readily to the phenomenon known as 'blaming the victim', where the people who suffer the consequences of an unjust society are themselves blamed for what is defined as their own inadequacies. Such an approach is inherently conservative in that it does not take account of important social, economic and political determinants such as income distribution, racism, patriarchy and market-induced inequality, leaving such exploitative structures and discourses essentially unchallenged and focusing all attention on the individual. This approach is not only conservative, but is blind to the growing evidence of the ways in which broad structural determinants affect the health and wellbeing of both individuals and communities (World Health Organization 2008).

The institutional reformist perspective

The *institutional reformist* position locates the problem within the institutional structures of the society. Thus, the inadequacies of the justice system (courts, police, prisons, etc.) are seen as contributing to the problem of crime and delinquency; poverty is seen as the result of an inadequate or

Table 3.1 Accounts of social issues

PERSPECTIVE	SOURCE OF 'BLAME'	PERCEPTION OF PROBLEM	SOLUTION
Individual	Blame the victim	Individual pathology; psychological, biological, moral or character defect	Therapy, medical treatment, behaviour modification, moral exhortation, control
Institutional reformist	Blame the rescuer	The institutions established to deal with the problem: courts, schools, welfare departments, etc.	Reorganise institutions, more resources, more services, better training, etc.
Structural	Blame the system	Structural disadvantage or oppression: class, race, gender, income distribution, power, etc.	Structural change, changing basis of oppression, liberation movements, revolution
Poststructural	Blame the discourse	Modernity, language, formation and accumulation of knowledge, shared understandings	Analysis and understanding of discourse, access to understandings, challenging the 'rules', etc.

ineffective social security system and so on. Proposed solutions to social problems, therefore, concentrate on reforming, strengthening and improving the institutions developed to deal with them, such as hospitals, schools, courts, clinics, welfare departments, charities and the employment service. Instead of 'blaming the victim', this approach might be termed 'blaming the rescuer'. Again, there is an element of conservatism as this approach concentrates on the amelioration of social problems rather than on seeking to address their underlying causes.

The structural perspective

Structural accounts of social issues see the problem as lying in oppressive and inequitable social structures. This approach might be termed 'blaming the system', as it concentrates on such issues as patriarchy, capitalism, institutional racism and income distribution and identifies oppression or structural disadvantage as the major issue to be addressed. It sees social problems as embedded in the oppressive structures of that society, whether seen in terms of class, race or gender. Therefore its prescriptions for change require major restructuring of the society, fundamental changes in power relations and the liberation of those who are oppressed (Freire 1972). It is clearly a more radical approach to the analysis of social problems, which accounts for its relative lack of popularity among mainstream governments and media commentators. Pakulski, in her discussion of refugees illegal migrants and asylum seekers as the 'new "truly disadvantaged" ' (2004, p. 206) identifies four features of disadvantage that are useful to consider within the structural perspective. First, those who are disadvantaged are economically vulnerable with high levels of income insecurity. Second, they are exposed to high-risk environments, whether these are environments of violence or industrial or other hazards. Third, they are marginalised and disempowered in terms of civil and political rights because of reduced citizenship (because of lack of opportunities to participate) and lack of access to resources. Last, they are excluded and subject to social stigma. Each of these features reflects structures that are oppressive and inequitable.

The poststructural perspective

The last category is *poststructural* accounts. At the risk of grossly oversimplifying highly complex literature, this perspective, following the work of writers such as Foucault (1972, 1973, 1979) and some postmodernists, can be characterised as being concerned with the 'discourse' associated with the particular problem. It sees the cause as lying in the use of language, the conveyance of meaning, the formation and accumulation of knowledge and the ways in which this is used to control and dominate through the definition of conformity, acceptable behaviour and so on. It is through language that we construct discourses of power and it is in the construction of such 'discursive power' that oppression and disadvantage are perpetuated. This view rejects fixed and 'objective' realities as understood by many of the advocates of structural accounts, though it is not necessarily inconsistent with some structural or quasi-structural positions, especially feminism (Clegg 1989). If 'blame' is to be applied, this perspective might be called 'blaming the discourse'. This leads to a practice involving deconstructing discourses of power and oppression and, through subsequent reconstruction, seeking understandings of shared knowledge and meanings, allowing people to help shape such alternative discourses. This approach seeks to uncover what are seen as constantly changing points of weakness within the dominant order that can be exploited for particular political ends. By validating alternative discourses, poststructuralism encourages a diversity of constructions of the 'problem' and of 'solutions'; there is no one 'right' answer. Postcolonial thinking, which is further discussed in Chapter 5, is closely aligned to the poststructural perspective.

It is important to recognise that there can be some value in all four of these perspectives or approaches. Each identifies particular aspects of social issues and social change and it is not realistic or appropriate to concentrate on one to the exclusion of some or all of the others. Conventional social policy strategies, however, tend to focus on the first two perspectives as they are relatively easy to change within the existing order and do not necessarily challenge significant interests or existing discourses of power and domination. For this reason, the critical literature, which seeks more radical alternatives, has tended to concentrate on the third and fourth perspectives, seeing the inability of social policy to take account of a structural and/or poststructural analysis as being a primary reason for its failure to address social issues and social problems adequately.

Community development, as normally practised, has been largely concerned with the second and third of these perspectives on social problems, namely the institutional reformist and structural perspectives. Most community work has focused either on ways to develop better programs, services and facilities for people at a community level or on attempting to bring about structural change towards a more just society. The individual perspective is more typically the province of the individual service worker, namely the counsellor, therapist, caseworker or psychologist. The poststructural perspective, however, has affected the thinking of community workers in more recent years. The idea of discourses of power, of deconstructing and reconstructing discourses, and of the legitimation of diversity, is seen as potentially empowering and as contributing to the 'bottom-up' perspective of community development; this will be considered in more detail in Chapter 5.

One criticism of the poststructural perspective is that, while it provides an interesting analysis of power and disadvantage, it has had relatively little to say about what one should actually do about it and so has little relevance for a community worker. However, this is a limited understanding of the potential of a poststructural approach. The importance of poststructuralism is that it allows space and legitimacy for alternative voices to be heard and validated and for alternative discourses to emerge as part of a development process; and in these terms, although it may not provide the neat prescriptions of a structural account (e.g. smash capitalism, dismantle patriarchy), it does provide a perspective on community work that can be very powerful and can strengthen the process of community empowerment.

The social justice and human rights perspective of this book, while acknowledging the usefulness of the individual and institutional approaches, is primarily located within the structural and poststructural perspectives. While changes to the individual and to organisations are important, unless changes are made to the basic structures and discourses of oppression, which create and perpetuate an unequal and inequitable society, any social justice and human rights strategy will have only limited value. Hence all programs that claim a social justice and human rights label need to be evaluated in terms of their relationship with the dominant forms of structural oppression and exclusion, particularly class, gender and race/ethnicity (but also including age, disability and sexuality) and also in terms of their role in either perpetuating or challenging dominant discourses of power. A society based on social justice and human rights principles could adequately be justified only if these forms of oppression were overcome.

The approach to community work that informs this book therefore seeks to incorporate both the structural and the poststructural perspectives. It is not necessary to see these two as inevitably in opposition: the prefix 'post-' does not necessarily imply 'anti-'. Rather, it carries the sense of 'beyond'. Thus a poststructuralist perspective can still accept the usefulness of a structural account of class, race and gender oppression, but asserts that one also needs to move beyond that to understand how those oppressions are defined and reinforced through changing discourses of power.

This position maintains that either the structural or the poststructural perspective is insufficient by itself and that each needs to be enhanced and reinforced by the other.

The question of which dimension of structural disadvantage—class, gender or race/ethnicity—is 'stronger', or more 'fundamental', can be cause for considerable disagreement and will not be pursued here. Such debate can be counterproductive, in that it can divide rather than unite potential allies in the struggle against oppression and in the promotion of social justice and of human rights. The important point, for present purposes, is not whether any one of class, gender and race/ethnicity transcends the others, but that each is a fundamental dimension of structural disadvantage and each must be addressed in any social justice and human rights strategy.

Because of the dominance of class, gender and race/ethnicity as forms of structural disadvantage, any social or political program that does not specifically question or challenge them is likely (albeit unintentionally) to reinforce these forms of oppression by accepting the dominant order that supports them. In the words of a common saying among activists, 'If you're not part of the solution, you're part of the problem'. Thus, a specific commitment to addressing the inequalities of class, gender and race/ethnicity must be a fundamental component of any social justice and human rights strategy and any existing or projected program should be evaluated in terms of its implications in this respect.

This also applies to a poststructural analysis of discourse; it is very easy unwittingly to acquiesce to, and reinforce, dominant discourses of power and oppression. One needs to be able to deconstruct dominant discourses and challenge their taken-for-granted views of 'reality' and the 'natural order of things'; again, if you are not part of the solution, you will be part of the problem. For a community worker, this amounts to being a colonist of communities, engaging in colonising activities (see Chapter 5).

Rights

Social justice implies some view of fairness or equity and the principles on which notions of fairness or equity are based generally involve some reference to rights. Hence rights are fundamental to any understanding of social justice.

Human rights represent a powerful discourse on the idea of a common humanity. They are people's attempt to define what we might all accept as the basic rights of human beings and hence are a definition of what it means to be human. The idea of human rights therefore transcends culture, class, language and other structures or discourses of difference and provides a strong moral stance from which people can argue against human rights abuses wherever they occur.

The idea of human rights is contested. There has been a strong criticism from some writers that it is essentially a Western concept, which has been used by minority world interests as an excuse to 'lecture' governments from majority world countries and is therefore an instrument of colonialism (Aziz 1999; Wronka 1992; Bauer & Bell 1999). Given the dominance of Western cultural framings of almost everything—from music to food to health to education to morality—it is not surprising that the human rights discourse has been seen to be minority world dominated, but this is no reason to abandon the idea of human rights, any more than it is a reason to abandon music, food, health, education or morality. Rather it is an argument to deconstruct the idea of human rights, to free it from its minority world domination and to allow other voices to influence the human rights discourse. Indeed, to claim that human rights is a Western concept is itself a racist claim, as it denies the fact that there is a history of human rights (though not necessarily using that name) in most, if not all, cultural and religious traditions. The earliest human rights claims were either not named or codified as 'rights' as they are today or were indirectly codified as moral codes through institutions such as culture and religion (Kingsbury 2008). Although the modern Western concept of human rights may be traced back to the Enlightenment (late 18th century), the idea has a much longer, richer and more diverse history (Ishay 1997).

Engaging in dialogue to allow other voices to contribute to the human rights discourse is not to privilege those voices simply because they are from the majority world. The so-called 'Asian values' debate illustrates the dangers in so doing. Advocates of the Asian values perspective argued that human values were not universal and so they needed to be interpreted in ways that were culturally and developmentally specific. The Bangkok Declaration of 1993 stated that the promotion of human rights ought not to be a condition of development assistance, that there should not be interference in the internal running of nations and that each nation should retain responsibility for how the human rights agenda is implemented. The dominant proponents of the Asian values stance were the powerful Asian national leaders in countries such as Singapore and Malaysia. Critiques of Asian values have focused on the way the dominant voices of the Asian values proponents served to generalise and homogenise the diversity within Asia and so did not represent the diversity of views across Asia. Moreover it was argued that their case was based on the primacy they gave to economic development and that they attempted to excuse human rights abuses in the name of economic development. Minority nations at times turned a blind eye to such abuses when it was in their own economic interests to do so. While it is beyond the scope of this book to go into depth into the Asian values debate, it is enlightening in terms of the universalism versus particularism debates on human rights. Avonius and Kingsbury's (2008) report of the 'Asian values and human rights revisited' seminar in Helsinki in 2007 provides important insights into the contested arena of universal human rights.

The traditional Western view of human rights, influenced by liberal individualism, has concentrated on *civil* and *political* rights, for example the right to free speech, freedom of assembly, freedom of religion, freedom from arbitrary detention, freedom from torture. However, human rights are about more than this. It is also important to include *social, economic* and *cultural* rights, namely the right to health care, housing, education, employment, adequate social security and so on. Also there is the so-called third generation of human rights—*collective* rights—that apply only at the level of communities or societies, such as the right to economic development and environmental rights. Taking these three groups, or generations, of human rights together, the idea of human rights becomes enlarged and includes many of the issues that are of concern to those from non-Western cultures who have criticised the minority world domination of the human rights discourse. They also clearly identify human rights issues as being of central concern to community development. Not only must community development itself satisfy the standards of human rights: it is also about helping people and communities to articulate and realise their human rights, understood in this broad sense (Ife 2001).

Like needs, human rights do not exist independently and cannot be discovered objectively. Rather they are defined, in an ongoing discursive process, by people talking about what is important about being human and how we might define our common humanity. Hence human rights are not static: they will change over time and in different contexts. Nevertheless, they can still be understood as *universal* simply because it is an ongoing discursive construction of universal themes—what we regard as universal human characteristics. The idea of human rights as discursive (i.e. defined and redefined through changing discourses) is important because it leads immediately to the question: *who is controlling the discourse* or who is defining human rights? A common criticism has been that it has been largely a minority world discourse, but this is now being addressed and the human rights literature now incorporates many majority world voices in an often vigorous debate. But the human rights discourse, though it now reflects a greater diversity of cultural experience, is still essentially a discourse of the privileged: it remains dominated by lawyers, politicians, academics, theologians and a fairly elite group of 'activists', such as the leaders of Amnesty International. It is ironic that a discourse about human rights effectively excludes those who are most affected by human rights abuse and it remains essentially *a discourse of the powerful about the powerless*.One of the major challenges for community workers is to question this domination of the human rights discourse by the voices of privilege (whether minority world or majority world) and to seek ways in which other voices, especially those of the marginalised and victims of human rights abuses, can be heard in the debates about what count as human rights.

The idea of human rights implies certain obligations on the part of the state and on the part of citizens (Holmes & Sunstein 1999). The state has an obligation to ensure that the human rights of citizens are protected and realised through the provision of legal protections, genuine equality before the law and adequate provision of health services, education, housing, income security, economic opportunity and environmental protection for all its citizens. (The fact that no nation of the world can claim such a record signals to us that we have a way to go in the realisation of human rights.) The obligations on the part of citizens are not only to respect the human rights of others but also to exercise one's own human rights and to make the most of one's opportunities. There is not much point, for example, in the right to free speech, the right to vote or the right to education if very few people in society actually claim and exercise those rights. A society that respects human rights is an active, participatory society where people understand that human rights imply responsibilities to exercise their rights. This too is a challenge for community workers and suggests that community development strategies aimed at maximising participation are important in the realisation of human rights. Participation, which is explored in detail in Chapter 6, is central and critical in community development within a human rights framework. Gandhi was an advocate for the human right of autonomy. His construction of this right beautifully captures the intertwining of rights and obligations to others through participation. For Gandhi, autonomy did not have the Western implication of individuals each doing as they please. Rather he considered autonomy as the ability to make decisions, but to make decisions that enable one to fulfil one's obligations to others. The right to autonomy, then, seemingly paradoxically, is the right to fulfil one's obligations (Terchek 1998).

There are many human rights conventions and agreements, the most significant being the Universal Declaration of Human Rights. This was drafted in 1948 and assented to by the nations of the world through the United Nations. Although it has been criticised because of the dominance of minority world views in its construction, it remains an inspiring and, in many ways, radical document. No nation could claim that all its citizens enjoy all the rights defined in the Universal Declaration. Yet it remains an important rallying point for those seeking action for a more just world. It is also important for community workers to understand other human rights conventions and their governments' responsibilities under them. Governments that are signatories to many of these conventions have certain obligations and there are mechanisms whereby governments can be called to account, especially if they are signatories to the Optional Protocol to the International Covenant on Civil and Political Rights, which gives citizens some power to appeal to the United Nations High Commission for Human Rights if they believe that their human rights have been violated. This can be an important avenue for community action; for example, a successful appeal to the UN High Commission against discriminatory laws in regard to homosexuality in the Australian state of Tasmania forced the Australian Government, under its treaty obligations, to overturn the

Tasmanian legislation, which it would have been unable to do under the Australian Constitution. A full list of human rights treaties and conventions, with complete texts, can be found on the website of the UN High Commissioner for Human Rights (www.ohchr.org), which is a valuable resource for community workers.

Human rights are universal. Human rights are also intertwined, so that addressing one human right will usually include attention to other related rights. Paragraph 5 of the Vienna Declaration and Programme of Action asserts this clearly when it states that 'All human rights are universal, indivisible and interdependent and interrelated'. The United Nation's Housing Rights Programme, jointly run by UN-HABITAT and the United Nations High Commissioner for Human Rights, is an example of a project, transcending national borders, that addresses housing from a rights-based approach. The application of a rights-based approach to housing is a major objective of this program. The interdependence of rights is starkly portrayed in a UN-HABITAT statement:

> Countless thousands of urban slum dwellers are homeless, and women and children are the first victims of violence, crime, overcrowding, and all the health hazards associated with inhuman, hazardous living conditions in our rapidly growing towns and cities. It is among slum dwellers that AIDS, malaria, and other epidemics take the heaviest toll. (2005, p. 8)

It is clear from this account that addressing housing rights necessarily entails addressing rights to safety, health, the rights of women, the rights of the child and so on. One right cannot be addressed in isolation from the others.

A rights-based approach to community development

Human rights are a vital component of community development. The fundamental principle is that community development should seek to affirm human rights and enable people to realise and exercise their human rights and be protected from human rights violations. Community development cannot be allowed to act against such human rights principles, which creates certain constraints on what is possible within community development; for example, it means that if a community worker is asked by a community to engage with it in practices of racial exclusion, that community worker is fully justified in refusing, even though this means violating the principle of community self-determination. However, it is not always as clear-cut as this. Because human rights are contested and discursively constructed, it is often necessary for a community worker to engage with the community in a discussion about human rights and about how they are constructed and understood within that community, how they are understood elsewhere and how community development might proceed in such a way that human rights are both realised and protected.

It makes sense for community development to adopt a rights approach because there are clear synergies between rights and community. Human rights imply community in several ways. Ife (2004) clearly spells these out. First, rights and responsibilities go hand in hand. Having rights implies that others have responsibilities in relation to those rights. In other words, there is an inherent reciprocity, and reciprocal relations, implied in rights. This requires the presence of others and rights cannot exist solely within an isolated individual. Therefore, some notion of a group or community of people is implied in the notion of rights. Second, if one has rights, then there is an accompanying obligation to exercise those rights and for society to encourage and support the exercise of the rights. Exercising rights, such as the right to freedom of expression, the right to be healthy or the right to education, requires some form of participation. Participation is central and vital to 'bottom-up' community development and the approach to community development taken in this book (see Chapter 6). Participation enables individuals to play citizenship roles and allows for them collectively to engage in social citizenship processes. Third, as will be argued later in this chapter, promoting human rights requires a long and complex process of building a culture of human rights. This process entails working with those who are marginalised or excluded, whose voices have not been heard, so that their claims to rights may be heard and addressed. This is an empowerment process and forms the essence of community development. It is a process that challenges dominant discourses of rights when these render invisible the rights of those who are powerless. So rights need community in order that rights can be enacted and realised. Fourth, community development needs rights. Rights provide a moral scaffolding within which community work can take place. Without this, community development is in a moral vacuum. Rights provide the moral measure to judge whether or not to support citizen participation in such things as racist activities, oppressive campaigns and so on. Finally, Ife points to a linguistic synergy between community development and human rights that vividly highlights the close relationshp between the two. He says: 'Community development sees its goal as the establishment of *human community*, while human rights emphasises the goal of achieving a *common humanity*. The two terms are both linguistically and semantically similar, if not synonymous' (2004, p. 5).

The above discussion suggests that human rights is a complex, contested and dynamic concept. If community development adopts human rights simply as they appear in the many Charters of Rights, it will be a grossly inadequate framework for community development. This is so for several reasons. First, a narrow legalistic view of human rights, while necessary, is insufficient for a realisation of human rights. Legal prescriptions of human rights will help to ensure *minimum standards* are adhered to, but will not lead to an *optimum standard* of rights. Anti-discrimination legislation, for example, will not address racism. Second, a legal framework favours those rights that are more amenable to protection in the courts and, because court processes are often expensive, such a framework may marginalise the claims for rights by the more vulnerable in society.

Many statements of human rights appear as if rights are unchanging truths. Many of these statements have been criticised for being formulated in forums which were dominated by minority world leaders and so, in their individualism, do not take account of human rights as they may be expressed in more collectivist majority world societies. The critiques of human rights declarations in the Asian values debates challenged rights as absolute truths and served to question the absolute nature of human rights claims, especially civil and political rights. If we reject the notion of rights as something objective that exists apart from human agency, then we must acknowledge that human rights are constructed by humans and that this construction is a dynamic process and must be open to scrutiny and debate. We must also acknowledge that, given the power structures and inequalities in societies, the voices of the powerful may often dominate. These powerful, dominant voices are not only in minority countries, but within majority countries as well. So, a critical element of a human rights-based approach to community development is the way in which the process of dialogue, discussion and debate to identify and construct human rights occurs. Whose voice will be heard in the debates? Whose will not? What claims will be privileged?

If community development adopts a human rights discourse, then the basis of this discourse must be much more than the lists that appear in Declarations and Charters. To embrace human rights as an effective framework for community development, we must take the responsibility to build a strong culture of human rights. This task cannot be legislated for. Building culture is a pervasive and long-term change process—in other words, the process of building a human rights culture is as complex as it is long. To replace a legalistic and somewhat static list of rights with a process of building a rights culture, we need criteria to guide the dialogue and the endeavour of articulating human rights. Ife (2001) proposes the following set of criteria:

1 That realising the claimed right is necessary for people to achieve their full humanity, in common with others.
2 That the claimed right should apply to all humanity, or at least to groups who are disadvantaged and marginalised.
3 That there is widespread support for the claimed right across cultures.
4 That all claimants can reasonably realise the right.
5 That the claimed right does not contradict other human rights.

These criteria enable judgements to be made about what claims can be considered legitimate human rights claims. Iris Marion Young's (1990) analysis of social justice provides some insight into what is required to challenge oppressive structures and work to empower those who are disadvantaged or marginalised. Her analysis brings the notions of social justice and human rights in close alignment with each other. She offers some principles to 'criticise the given, and for inspiration for imagining alternatives' (1990, p. 256) when she extracts some normative features of the *unoppressive city*, which can serve to build the ethics of social relations in the contemporary world. These features provide some guidelines about ways in which liberating participation can be supported.

- *Social differentiation without exclusion*, where those who are different can come together and intermingle, share and enrich.
- *Variety*, where structures support diversity and the relations between different groups.
- *Eroticism*, where difference excites and attracts, rather than creating fear and mistrust.
- *Publicity*, where difference can exist in communities and all people can interact with the different to listen and learn.

Young's examination, then, adds to the meaning of socially just social relations, relations that are not purely self-interested and exclusionary, but which are emancipatory and supportive of the community development approach taken in this book. Her *unoppressive city* stands in stark contrast to some of the relationships between the different that dominate the world stage today. Socially just relationships emanate from difference, but must also be supported by broader social institutions:

> Because city life is a being together of strangers, diverse and overlapping neighbors, social justice and human rights cannot issue from the institution of an Enlightenment universal public. On the contrary, social justice and human rights in the city requires the realization of a politics of difference. This politics lays down institutional and ideological means for recognizing and affirming diverse social groups by giving political representation to these groups, and celebrating their distinctive characteristics and culture. In the unoppressive city people open to unassimilated otherness. (Young 1990, pp. 240–1)

Young's analysis of social justice and the unoppressive city and Ife's human rights claims criteria together provide some clues for community development. Together they challenge the given and enable us to imagine inspiring community-based alternatives in a globalised world. But more so, Young's views give a central place to local activity and community development in realising a socially just society and building a culture of human rights.

CASE STUDY: A community project promoting human rights

The Ngarrindjeri Land and Progress Association had the goal of developing a race relations camp on the Coorong, the traditional land of the Ngarrindjeri people. Community members wanted their children to have strong Aboriginal role models and be exposed to the positive culture and heritage of their people. They wanted their children to be inculcated with pride and a sense of belonging. At the same time, the community wanted to provide cross-cultural awareness programs and training for non-Indigenous groups. In 1986 the community purchased land from the Aboriginal Lands Trust and used employment project funds to employ community members to establish the camp. Today, Camp Coorong is a robust and vibrant venture. It is a self-managed and self-supported Indigenous education and cultural facility; it provides programs that enhance appreciation of Indigenous culture and heritage to many different groups; it provides responsible adult role models for its children and youth; it engenders a sense of pride in the community and in its young people and it increases self-esteem and confidence among its community members. In its promotional material, the Ngarrindjeri Land and Progress Association states:

> At Camp Coorong we offer various activities we feel will suit any person or group wishing to learn more about Aboriginal History, Arts, Crafts and the environment within the Ngarrindjeri region.
>
> The idea of the development of Camp Coorong was a vision that we, the Ngarrindjeri people, had back in 1985. We believed that we must have a place where people can come to learn about our heritage and culture. We also believed that this would lead to non-Aboriginal people developing a better understanding of our Ngarrindjeri traditions and our relationships to the land, waters, trees, plants and animals.

The manager at Camp Coorong

At Camp Coorong, to develop better understandings, we tell of our traditions and our way of life before European invasion of our lands. We teach the ways that our ancestors lived.

We take groups out on field trips upon the land, talking about places that are important to us.

We teach our Ngarrindjeri basket-weaving techniques. We tell of our stories relating to the land, waters, trees, plants, birds and animals—people call them our dreaming stories.

Source: <http://ngarrindjeri.tvipod.com>

Camp Coorong sees itself contributing to three important issues identified by the Council for Aboriginal Reconciliation, namely a greater understanding of the land and sea in Indigenous communities, better relationships between Indigenous and non-Indigenous Australians and a greater recognition and appreciation of Indigenous culture as a valued part of Australian heritage.

(We wish to acknowledge the Ngarrindjeri people, the traditional owners of the Lower River murray, Lakes and Coorong Region in South Australia.)

- What human rights are being addressed in this community-based project?

Empowerment

The notion of empowerment is central to a social justice and human rights strategy, even though *empowerment* is another word that has been overused and is in danger of losing any substantive meaning. It is central to notions of community work and many community workers would choose to define their role in terms of an empowerment process. The idea of empowerment will receive a good deal of attention in this book. As a way of beginning the discussion in this chapter, however, a simple working definition will suffice. *Empowerment aims to increase the power of the disadvantaged*. This statement contains two important concepts, *power* and *disadvantage*, each of which needs to be considered in any discussion of empowerment as part of a social justice and human rights perspective.

Power

However one looks at empowerment, it is inevitably about power—individuals or groups having and using the opportunity to take power into their own hands, redistributing power from the 'haves' to the 'have nots' and so on. It is therefore of concern that some writers on empowerment and many practitioners who say they use an empowerment model do not give the concept of power much attention (see Rees 1991). Power is a complex and contested notion and there are varying views of power that have been identified by social and political theorists (Clegg 1989).

Political perspectives on power, which are concerned with trying to understand the nature of power in modern societies, can be divided into four categories, though each of these itself contains a number of diverging views and space limitations do not allow a detailed analysis of the varying views of the many writers who have addressed issues of power (for a detailed account, see Clegg 1989). The four categories are *pluralist* accounts, *elite* accounts, *structural* accounts and *poststructural* accounts. Each involves a different perspective on the process of empowerment.

THE PLURALIST PERSPECTIVE

The *pluralist* perspective on power is associated with the work of Dahl (1961), among others, and has been influential in a good deal of conventional political science which has sought to study power as an 'objective' phenomenon. This perspective emphasises the various individuals and groups within society that are competing for power and influence and visualises the political system as a competition between such groups (e.g. unions, pressure groups, employer bodies, non-government organisations, professions, media, consumer groups) and between individuals (e.g. business leaders, politicians, lobbyists, 'power brokers', advocates, community leaders). Power, therefore, arises from one's capacity to engage in this competing system, to know 'the rules of the game' and to be able to exert pressure and influence. The pluralist view is related to a particular perception of democracy, where everyone can have their say, all people have equal opportunity to participate and no one is all-powerful because power is spread among a number of different and competing groups. It is a perspective that is inherently conservative in that it accepts and legitimises the system as it is and simply encourages people to be better 'players' in the 'game'. Indeed the language of pluralism often relies on the metaphor of sports and games: players, stakeholders, winners and losers, the rules of the game, neutral umpire, level playing field and so on. It is in other perspectives that more emotive words like 'struggle', 'oppression', 'domination' and 'powerless' tend to be used.

From a pluralist perspective, empowerment is a process of helping disadvantaged groups and individuals to compete more effectively with other interests, by helping them to learn and to use skills in lobbying, using the media, engaging in political action, understanding how to 'work the system' and so on. The work of Alinsky (1969, 1971) in empowering African–American communities in the United States was premised on a pluralist assumption. Alinsky, one of the most influential figures in community work, did not set out to change the American political system, but simply aimed to teach African–American communities how to work more effectively within that system and to become more skilled at competing with other groups for power through social action, political pressure, covert threats, publicity and so on. Thus, although Alinsky's methods and tactics may appear radical (largely because of their novelty) and he freely used the term *radical* in his writing, his political position is basically conservative in that fundamentally it accepted the structures of American society and saw the solution for black communities as simply to help them to be more politically sophisticated.

THE ELITE PERSPECTIVE

Elite views of power acknowledge that politics is not a 'game' where all 'players' have equal opportunities to 'win'. They identify particular groups that have more than their 'share' of power, and which exercise disproportionate influence over decision making. The discussion of such elites is associated most strongly with the sociologist C. Wright Mills (1956). Elites are able to perpetuate themselves through such mechanisms as private schooling, service clubs, informal networks and contacts (the 'old boys network'), political parties and professional associations; they also have control of or access to disproportionate shares of the nation's resources. It is these elites who exercise power in a society, through their capacity to control key institutions (the media, education, political parties, public policy, the bureaucracy, parliaments, the professions). Thus, society is seen as hierarchical, with certain groups exercising power and control.

From this perspective, empowerment requires more than acquiring the ability to compete for political power by 'playing the game'; the rules of the game, after all, have been determined by the power elites and so are likely to be in their favour. As well as learning political skills, it is necessary to do something about the power elites. One way is to join them with the aim of changing or influencing them (e.g. the activist who joins a mainstream political party with a view to influencing its policies or who joins Rotary in order to have some involvement in and influence over local decisions). Another way is to seek alliances with powerful elites to pursue one's own ends, for example, by enlisting the help of the legal profession in pursuing issues of human rights or anti-discrimination legislation and practices. A third way is to seek to reduce the power of elites through more fundamental change, for example, by attempting to limit the power of professional monopolies by legal challenge.

THE STRUCTURAL PERSPECTIVE

The *structural* view of power identifies the importance of structural inequality, or oppression, as a major form of power. It draws on a range of writing, most particularly Marxist and feminist analyses (Mullaly 2002; Williams 1989; Gough 1979). While acknowledging the importance of the elites described above, the structural perspective maintains that those elites also act as representatives of dominant groups and reinforce the structural inequality that results in the unequal distribution of power. That these elites are predominantly made up of white, wealthy men is not a coincidence; it indicates the underlying importance of class, race and gender—it is these fundamental issues that have to be acknowledged in dealing with power in contemporary industrial (or post-industrial) society. From this perspective, concentrating on the elites themselves, or on individuals or groups acting in competition (the pluralist view), is to miss the point. By ignoring fundamental structural inequalities, one is reinforcing the structures that determine power relations of dominance and oppression.

From this structural perspective, empowerment is a much more challenging agenda, as it can effectively be achieved only if these forms of structural disadvantage are challenged and overcome. Empowerment, therefore, is necessarily part of a broader social change project, with a view to dismantling the dominant structures of oppression. Political education and working with elites are not sufficient (though they clearly have their place) and they are likely to be effective in bringing about a real change in power relationships only if they are part of a broader agenda specifically addressing such structural issues as class, gender and race/ethnicity.

THE POSTSTRUCTURAL PERSPECTIVE

The *poststructural* view of power, like the poststructural view of social problems, concentrates on the way in which power is understood, the use of language in defining and reinforcing relations of power and domination, the definition and accumulation of knowledge and how it is constructed and the subjective experience of power rather than its 'objective' existence. It rejects both the positivism of the pluralist theories and the mechanism of more simplistic structuralist accounts. It relies particularly on the work of Foucault (1973, 1979; Rouse 1994), who traces the ways in which ideas, language and the definition of knowledge have been used as a major mechanism of control.

From this perspective, empowerment becomes a process of challenging and changing discourses. It emphasises people's subjective understandings and the construction of their world views and points to the need for the deconstruction of these understandings and the establishment of an alternative vocabulary for empowerment. This can be achieved by validating voices other than those currently dominating the discourse and by allowing those alternative voices to be heard. The poststructural perspective thus emphasises understanding, analysis, deconstruction, education and participation in the discourse(s) of power and sees a simple concentration on action alone as inadequate.

This survey of different views of power has been necessarily brief and has glossed over major differences within these categories. Other writers (e.g. Clegg 1989) have proposed other categories and it would be wrong to assume that Table 3.2 represents the last word on the subject of power, or that there would be wide agreement on its content. It does, however, indicate some of the complexity of the concept of power and provides a useful framework for thinking about power in the context of an empowerment model of community work. From the point of view of a community worker seeking a model of empowerment, there is undoubtedly some value in each of the four

Table 3.2 Perspectives of power

PERSPECTIVE	VIEW OF SOCIETY	VIEW OF POWER	EMPOWERMENT
Pluralist groups	Competing interests; groups and individuals	Capacity to compete successfully, 'winners and losers'	Teach individuals or groups how to compete within 'the rules'
Elite	Largely controlled by self-perpetuating elites	Exercised largely by elites through ownership and control of dominant institutions	Join and influence elites, form alliances with elites, confront and seek to change elites
Structural	Stratified according to dominant forms of structural oppression: class, race and gender	Exercised by dominant groups through structures of oppression	Liberation, fundamental structural change, challenge oppressive structures
Poststructural	Defined through constructed meanings, understandings, language, knowledge accumulation and control	Exercised through control of discourse, construction of knowledge, etc.	Change the discourse, develop new subjective understandings, validate other voices, liberating education

perspectives. To the extent that pluralist and elite views are probably the dominant perspectives within the society, and shape most of the debate on power and political action, it would be counter-productive to ignore them or assume they had no value. Indeed, many of the strategies derived from these perspectives will be of considerable value to a community worker in day-to-day practice. However, the structural and poststructural perspectives, based on a more thorough conceptual foundation and with the potential for more radical and fundamental change, hold particular promise for an empowerment model that can be effectively incorporated in an overall social justice and human rights strategy. This book is premised on the assumption that it is the dismantling of the dominant structures of oppression and the reconstructing of dominant discourses of power, which must be at the centre of any progressive social change and community development project—hence strong structural and poststructural perspectives are essential.

CASE STUDY: The uses of power in local social action

A local and so-called disadvantaged community comprising 85 per cent public housing was subject to an urban renewal program. This program was devised by the government to relinquish its responsibility for ageing and decaying housing stock and transfer the land to the private housing sector. The intended outcome over ten years of development was to have a mix of housing that was 85 per cent privately owned homes. The local community was not consulted, but with the support of local community workers it lobbied to be involved in the process with the intention not of stopping the development but of ensuring that local people participated in the decisions affecting them and that these decisions would not further disadvantage people, especially those being relocated. While it may seem that government and wealthy building firms would have greater power than local people living in public housing, there were many stories emerging from the project and the people's collective action that indicated the complexity and fluidity of power and the ways in which a poststructural perspective enriches the appreciation of this complexity.

For example, threats of social action by residents potentially threatened the developer's interest in selling houses and attracting middle-class, upwardly mobile families to the area. The following statement was made by one of the residents:

> . . . and [the developer] wouldn't want the publicity, they are trying to sell houses, they don't want people chained up outside houses . . . There's been lots of discussions about what strategies people could use if we went down that track . . . We've had lots of offers over time from unions to black-ban sites . . .

The local people involved in the process were well able to influence some decisions and processes. The fluidity of power is exemplified in a statement by a government housing officer involved in the project:

> That sense of powerlessness was a powerful tool for them [the residents]. They were able to say, 'This is big government not listening to local folk, not valuing us; if we were homeowners you would not treat us like this.' So it's a fairly powerful response to social engineering and I think it's a valid one.

The view of one local person involved in the process was stated thus:

> They've [the legal partners] got everything when you look at it. But from the point of view of the community what they [the legal partners] don't like are things that are unpredictable. They don't like when people make a lot of noise, embarrass them and things like that. So you're quite powerful, because all you have to be is unpredictable and make a lot of noise, really, and then they get all wobbly . . .

- In what ways do these snippets suggest that power is broader than simply an elitist perspective?
- How may this broader view of power assist the community worker to support local people and to both maintain hope and develop effective strategies?

CITIZENSHIP AND EMPOWERMENT

Participation, which will be explored more in Chapter 6, becomes central in empowerment. The term *citizen participation,* particularly, is useful because it suggests that participation necessarily entails people fulfilling the role of citizen. At first glance, 'citizen' may appear to be too individualistic, given the promotion of collectivism in this book. However, citizenship, as used here, refers to *social citizenship processes.* This notion goes beyond a narrow view of citizenship, such as having the right to vote. Social citizenship processes involve collective action for change. These processes take on a specially important meaning in the neoliberal and individualistic context of contemporary Western society, as discussed in Chapter 1. In support of this importance, and making the connection between citizenship and community development, Shaw and Martin state:

> . . . if the space for progressive community work is to be regained, the role of community work itself must shift from that of turning citizens into consumers and customers to that of defining—and defending—democratic citizenship itself. In this sense, the essentially developmental function of traditional community work needs to be consciously re-activated as a political corrective to the managerial imperative that drives much community development. (2000, p. 408)

When citizenship and participation are measured against the seven criteria for a human rights claim (listed earlier in this chapter) both concepts meet the criteria. Empowerment becomes the process of building a culture of human rights.

Types of power

If these are the different views of how power operates in the society, there still remains the question of what sort of power is involved in the term *empowerment*; that is, what kind of power is it that we wish to enhance? This is clearly a value question. Some kinds of power, presumably, would not be sought as part of empowerment, such as the power to exploit others, the power to wage war or the power to destroy the environment. For the purposes of the model to be developed here, eight kinds of power will be considered as being involved in community-based empowerment strategies, though it must be acknowledged that these overlap and interact in often complex ways and other categories could easily be added.

1. POWER OVER PERSONAL CHOICES AND LIFE CHANCES

Many people have little power to determine the course of their own lives—to make decisions about their lifestyle, whether or not their children can remain with them, where they will live or their occupation. Also included in this category are choices about one's own body, sexuality, health and so on. These choices are commonly affected by structural factors. Thus one of the major consequences of poverty is that people have little choice or power to make decisions about their own lives. Patriarchal structures and values often restrict the power of women in making personal choices and racial oppression works to reduce this power for Indigenous people and members of ethnic minorities. Cultural norms and values, perpetuated by dominant discourses within the culture, can also restrict people's power over personal choice, irrespective of class, race and gender. An empowerment strategy, therefore, would seek to maximise people's effective choices in order to increase their power over decisions involving their personal futures.

2. POWER OVER THE ASSERTION OF HUMAN RIGHTS

While there are many declarations of human rights, these have often been established by minority world male leaders and so have tended to benefit those who proclaimed them. In the broadest sense, those who have had the power to assert human rights have by the very assertion of rights, such as freedom of speech or freedom of association, reinforced their power. They have not sought to have the voices of disadvantaged and marginalised people heard. Powerful democracies easily assert the right to safety from terrorism and have the resources to act on this assertion, often through violent means. Their power to assert rights and to act to preserve them fails to acknowledge that much terrorism is a response to oppression by powerful nations. In their action to preserve their declared rights, they choose not to appreciate the consequences of their actions, which is a violation of the safety and human life of innocent others. Because the voices of many oppressed and marginalised people remain silent, an empowerment process would ensure that these voices are heard and would engage in strategies of social and political action to demand that others' rights are asserted.

3. POWER OVER THE DEFINITION OF NEED

One of the characteristics of modern society is the 'dictatorship over needs' (Feher, Heller & Markus 1983; Marcuse 1964), in that needs are often determined and defined by people other than those who are supposedly experiencing them. In some instances, particularly in socialist regimes, it is the state that has taken on the responsibility for defining people's needs (Feher, Heller & Markus 1983).

In other cases, it is professionals such as doctors, social workers, psychologists, teachers and managers who have become the experts in the definition of need (Illich et al. 1977; Wilding 1982). In yet other cases, it is multinational corporations that convince consumers that they have particular needs. In any case, this can be seen as disempowering and an empowerment perspective would require that people be given the power of defining their own needs. Need definition also requires relevant knowledge and expertise (Ife 1980). Therefore, such an empowerment process requires that people have access to education and to information. On the other hand, such an empowerment process requires a respect and acknowledgement of the wisdom of local Indigenous knowledge and experience as relevant and legitimate.

4. POWER OVER IDEAS

Whether one takes a poststructural view of the importance of language and discourse or a Marxist view of hegemony and the control of the dominant culture, ideas are undoubtedly powerful and of critical importance in either maintaining or challenging the dominant order. An empowerment process should incorporate the power to think autonomously and not have one's world view dictated either by force or by being denied access to alternative frames of reference. It should also legitimise the expression of these ideas in a public forum, the capacity of people to enter into dialogue with each other and the ability of people's ideas to contribute to the public culture through processes of deliberative democracy where people can participate in democratic decision making as a public exercise of power (Benhabib 1996). This approach to power also emphasises the educational (in its broadest sense) aspect of empowerment.

5. POWER OVER INSTITUTIONS

A good deal of disempowerment comes from the effect of social institutions, such as the education system, the health system, the family, the Church, the social welfare system, government structures and the media. To counteract this, an empowerment strategy would aim to increase people's power over these institutions and their effects by equipping people to have an impact on them and, more fundamentally, by changing these institutions to make them more accessible, responsive and accountable to all people, not just the powerful. As indicated in Chapter 1, a community-based strategy is potentially very significant in this respect.

6. POWER OVER RESOURCES

Many people have relatively little access to resources and relatively little discretion as to how those resources will be utilised. This applies both to financial resources and to non-monetary resources such as education, opportunities for personal growth, recreation, housing, employment and cultural experiences. However, in a society where economic criteria and rewards are so significant, power over economic resources and transactions is particularly important. An empowerment strategy would seek to maximise the effective power of all people over the distribution and use of resources and to redress the evident inequality of access to resources that characterises modern society.

7. POWER OVER ECONOMIC ACTIVITY

The basic mechanisms of production, distribution and exchange are vital in any society—to have power in a society one must be able to have some control over, and access to, these mechanisms. This power is unequally distributed in modern capitalist society, which is a cause of significant disempowerment. An empowerment process would therefore seek to ensure that power over economic activity was more evenly distributed. Such increased economic power would include the development of local, alternative economic systems.

8. POWER OVER REPRODUCTION

Marx emphasised that, alongside the mechanisms of production, the mechanisms of reproduction were crucial for any society; control over the process of reproduction has been a significant issue for feminist critique. Included in the notion of reproduction is not only the process of birth but child-rearing, education and socialisation—all the mechanisms by which the social, economic and political order is reproduced in succeeding generations. Power over the process of reproduction is unequally distributed in contemporary society and, again, class, race and gender differences are critical. While this category closely relates to power over personal choice and power over ideas, as discussed above, the reproductive process is sufficiently important for it to warrant a category of its own.

The disadvantaged

If, as has been suggested, empowerment is about increasing the power of the disadvantaged, it is necessary to look not only at what constitutes power but also at the nature of disadvantage. For the purposes of the model to be developed here, we can distinguish three main categories of disadvantage, as follows.

PRIMARY STRUCTURAL DISADVANTAGE

A frequently recurring theme in the discussion in this chapter has been the importance of the three principal forms of structural disadvantage in Western societies, namely class, gender and race/ethnicity. All can be seen to be fundamental, in that they are all-pervasive and identifiable in most if not all social issues, social problems and inequities (Williams 1989). For this reason, the victims of class, gender and race/ethnicity oppression must come first in any consideration of the disadvantaged in modern society. Included among the victims of class oppression are clearly the poor and the unemployed, as it is their relationship to the means of production that has resulted in their disadvantage. The three forms of oppression obviously interact and reinforce each other; thus, to be an Indigenous woman in poverty is to be trebly disadvantaged. In any other form of disadvantage to be considered below, women, Indigenous people, members of minority ethnic groups, people in poverty, the working class and the unemployed are likely to be worse off than are men, people of Anglo-Celtic background, those with access to wealth or members of the professional/managerial class.

OTHER DISADVANTAGED GROUPS

There are other groups which can be regarded as disadvantaged while not necessarily being the victims of the primary structural disadvantage described above. These include the aged, people with disabilities (physical and intellectual), the isolated, those living in remote areas and gay and lesbian people. Not including these groups in the previous category does not imply that the disadvantage suffered by people in them is any less debilitating, painful and disempowering; this is clearly not the case. People in these groups constitute some of the most disadvantaged in society and must clearly be considered in any empowerment strategy to counter disadvantage. It is simply that these forms of disadvantage are not the result of the structural oppression of class, gender and race/ethnicity and people in these groups will almost inevitably be further disadvantaged if they also happen to be poor, Indigenous or women.

PERSONAL DISADVANTAGE

Discussing the disadvantaged purely in terms of groups can disguise the fact that people can also be disadvantaged as a result of personal circumstances. Grief, the loss of a loved one, problems with personal and family relationships, identity crisis, sexual problems, loneliness, shyness and a number of other essentially personal problems can result in disadvantage and disempowerment—sometimes for only a limited period but still important for the person concerned. While these problems can (and do) affect everybody (even the most 'advantaged' will suffer grief at the loss of a loved one), they interact with structural forms of disadvantage (class, gender and race/ethnicity), which means that some people will have access to more resources to deal with their problems than others.

Achieving empowerment

The above discussion has highlighted the complexity of both *power* and *disadvantage*, each of which is central to an understanding of empowerment. The notion of empowerment, therefore, is itself complex, as has been pointed out by writers such as Rees (1991) and Friedmann (1992). Before leaving the concept of empowerment, it is worth mentioning the various strategies that have been proposed in order to achieve the empowerment of disadvantaged groups. These can be broadly classified under the headings *policy and planning, social and political action*, and *education and consciousness raising*.

Empowerment through *policy and planning* is achieved by developing or changing structures and institutions to bring about more equitable access to resources or services and opportunities to participate in the life of the community. Policies of affirmative action or positive discrimination acknowledge the existence of disadvantaged groups (sometimes expressed specifically in structural terms) and seek to redress this disadvantage by 'changing the rules' to favour the disadvantaged. Using economic policy to reduce unemployment might also be seen as empowerment, in that it enhances people's resources, access and opportunities. Providing people with adequate and secure resources is an important empowerment strategy (Liffman 1978) and thus policies to ensure adequate income may be said to be empowering. Similarly, the development of mechanisms for service user input, locating services and facilities within easy access, establishing appropriate and accessible service user appeal mechanisms and other planning decisions can facilitate the empowerment of the disadvantaged. The concern for notions of access and equity in social policy can thus be justified on empowerment grounds.

Empowerment through *social and political action* emphasises the importance of political struggle and change in increasing effective power. How this is applied depends on one's understanding of power in the political process (pluralist, elite, structural or poststructural). But it emphasises the activist approach and seeks to enable people to increase their power through some form of direct (and often collective) action or by equipping them to be more effective in the political arena.

Empowerment through *education and consciousness raising* emphasises the importance of an educative process (broadly understood) in equipping people to increase their power. This incorporates notions of consciousness raising—helping people to understand the society and the structures of oppression, giving people the vocabulary and the skills to work towards effective change and so on.

These forms of empowerment, which are summarised in Figure 3.1, will be elaborated in later chapters, as they provide the basis for an empowerment model of community work practice. At this stage it is time to leave the notion of empowerment and consider another concept that relates to social justice and human rights perspective and which is important in community development—that of *need*.

EMPOWERMENT USES: → **TO INCREASE THE POWER OF DISADVANTAGED GROUPS:** → **OVER SUCH THINGS AS:**

policy and planning
social and political action
education

PRIMARY STRUCTURAL DISADVANTAGED GROUPS

Class
the poor
the unemployed
low-income earners
recipients of welfare

Gender
women

Race/ethnicity
Indigenous people
ethnic and cultural minorities

OTHER DISADVANTAGED GROUPS
the aged
children and youth
people with disabilities
homosexuals and transgender
the isolated (socially, geographically, etc)

THE PERSONALLY DISADVANTAGED
Those experiencing grief, loss, personal and family problems, etc.

personal choices and life chances
ideas
institutions
resources
economic activity
reproduction

Figure 3.1 Empowerment

Need

Social justice and human rights principles are often expressed in terms of need. The notion of need is fundamental in social policy, social planning and community development; it is also intimately related to the notion of rights. There are two ways in which need is seen as basic to social justice, human rights and community development: first, a belief that people or communities should have their needs 'met' and second, that people or communities should be able to define their own needs rather than have them defined by others.

Problems with conventional views of need

The notion of need is inherently complex. Traditional positivist conceptions of need discuss needs as if they have objective reality, that is, as if they exist and can be 'measured'. Thus, 'need assessment' is seen as essentially a technical exercise in methodology—measuring something which is already 'there'. The emphasis on methodology, and hence on technical expertise, leads to a situation where needs can be adequately assessed and defined only by experts who are skilled in adequate need assessment methodology. Therefore, need definition is removed from the very people who are experiencing the need and placed in the hands of professional need-definers, such as social workers, public health professionals, social researchers and psychologists. From the point of view of critics such as Illich et al. (1977), this has resulted in the rise of professional power while consequently 'disabling' the bulk of the population. Conventional professional practice, therefore, is seen as based on assumptions of disempowerment, and serves only to reinforce the powerlessness of the oppressed, by denying them the right to define and act on their own needs.

Writers such as Heller (Feher, Heller & Markus 1983) have seen totalitarian regimes as exercising a 'dictatorship over needs', where the state has taken over the role of defining people's needs, telling them what they do and do not need and hence maintaining a powerful form of control and coercion. This is the anti-democratic form of state socialism, as experienced in the postwar communist regimes of Eastern Europe, and is the equivalent at state level of Illich's views of professionalism.

Marcuse (1964) draws a distinction between 'true' and 'false' needs. The former are the needs people genuinely feel, which are required if one is to reach one's full human potential and which people will articulate if they are free to do so. 'False' needs are those we are persuaded we have, as a result of the dominant ideology, the media, advertising, the education system and so on.

Seen from these perspectives, and from the point of view of an empowerment agenda, 'need' is neither objective nor value-free. Rather it must be understood from a perspective that takes account of values and ideology and which allows for notions of liberation rather than oppression. To do this it is necessary to move away from the more conventional positivist accounts of 'needs as objects', which tend to treat 'need' as a single concept.

At this point, Bradshaw's typology of need must be mentioned, as this has become the 'conventional wisdom' on the subject of need. Bradshaw (1972) divided need into four categories: *normative need*, which is need as defined by some authority, in accordance with an accepted standard (e.g. poverty lines); *felt need*, which is need as experienced by the people concerned (e.g. assessed through social surveys); *expressed need*, which is need expressed by people seeking some form of service (e.g. assessed through looking at waiting lists or demands for services) and *comparative need*, which is need inferred from comparison of service provision with national or regional norms (e.g. comparison of a region's hospital beds per capita with the national average). An important aspect of Bradshaw's model is that one form of need does not necessarily imply another (with the exception of expressed need, which must also be felt need). This model of need is useful in that it breaks away from the view of need as a single concept, but it does not address the inherently disempowering nature of conventional need definition: all Bradshaw's categories are still 'measured' by 'experts' and his conception of need remains essentially within the positivist framework.

Need statements

An alternative approach, which does provide a framework for empowerment, can be developed around the notion of need definition. This sees the important factor not as the need itself but rather the act and process of defining need, or asserting that something is 'needed'.

A statement or definition of community need is clearly a normative, or value-laden, statement. It implies certain views of people's rights and entitlements and contains an implicit notion of what constitutes an acceptable minimum standard of personal or community wellbeing. For example, a claim that a community 'needs' a child-care centre implies some assumptions about a parent's rights to a certain lifestyle or access to the labour market, children's rights to a certain level of care and the benefits to personal and community life that a child-care centre would bring. These rights are embedded in the need definition, though they are unstated and usually unacknowledged. To the extent that people will differ over these value questions, there will be differing views on the nature or strength of the need, quite apart from any methodological issues of need assessment. This link between needs and rights is significant. It is important to note that, in the example above, reference is made to a claim without specifying who makes the claim. This question is a critical one for community development. Whether experts have made the claim or the community itself has made the claim is an important question in relation to need definition, empowerment and rights.

Using the language of needs can often obscure the political or ideological nature of an issue. Instead of focusing on a social problem, discussion of need can divert attention to the more technical (and safer) question of providing solutions. For example, a 'problem' of juvenile crime, defined as a problem of 'law and order', becomes a 'need' for more police and this draws attention away from questions about why young people are alienated and perhaps the need for structural change to address the alienation of youth in society. The problem of 'juvenile crime' focuses attention on recruiting and resourcing more police officers. A social problem can thus be depoliticised by using 'need' language and, in this way, the very act of need definition can be seen as ideological.

While a need statement is clearly normative, it also has a technical component. In the above example, the claim for a need for more police is based on an assumption that more police will in fact solve the 'problem' of juvenile crime—an assumption which is, to say the least, questionable. Such assumptions, which are implicit in statements of community need, are essentially technical, and require some knowledge of the impact and effectiveness of particular services, programs or interventions.

Need statements are also technical in that they are comparative in nature. Claiming that a community needs a particular provision can be seen as implying that this provision has a higher priority in the community than other potentially competing claims (e.g. if made within the context of a council budget committee) or that that community needs it more than other communities do (e.g. if made within the context of government decisions on the distribution of child-care funding). In such cases there is an assumption of knowledge about priorities within the community, or about the comparative situation in other communities (or both).

A model of need statements

A statement of need, then, is both a normative and a descriptive statement, reflecting both the values/ideology and knowledge/expertise of the need-definer. This means that any model of need statements must take the identity of the need-definer into account. Commonly there are five groups of people who are involved in need definition at the community level. These are: the *population* at large; *community champions/leaders; service users*, or potential service users, of the service or facility that is 'needed'; *caretakers*, namely those whose 'business' is community need, such as community workers, social workers, welfare workers, clergy, health workers and local politicians and the researchers and planners who *infer* need on the basis of statistics, survey results and other data.

As a result, one can derive a framework of need statements based on these five groups of need-definers, which is a useful way of thinking about how need is defined in communities and what meaning this may have for community development. This model is summarised in Table 3.3.

It can be seen from Table 3.3 that the five different need-definers have different perspectives, values, assumptions, interests, expertise and information on which to base their need judgements. For this reason, one would in practice expect these judgements of need to vary, which is the common experience of community workers. It does raise the important question of which form of need definition is 'better' or more legitimate. This question is of critical importance for community work.

Table 3.3 A framework of need statements

NEED-DEFINER	NEED STATEMENT	VALUES/ASSUMPTIONS	MAIN INTERESTS/ AGENDA	NATURE OF EXPERTISE	NATURE OF KNOWLEDGE/ INFORMATION BASE	POSSIBLE IMPACTS ON EMPOWERMENT, DISADVANTAGE, SOCIAL JUSTICE, HUMAN RIGHTS
Population at large	Felt need	May be consensus or conflict Homogeneity or inclusive of diversity Local perspective	Diverse interests within community	Informed by lived experiences	Lay knowledge Wisdom of lived experiences Subjective	Likely to be empowering if not vulnerable to co-option Potential to be legitimate human rights claims
Community leaders/ champions	Felt need	Collectivist, pluralist, may be consensus or conflict, may be inclusive of diversity within group or of other groups Local perspective or issue-based perspective	Perceived interests of sections of the community	Informed by leadership/ advocacy experience and broader knowledge of issues	Lay knowledge Knowledge from media Wisdom of lived experiences of others Constructed knowledge	Potentially empowering and just, if inclusive of other diverse interests and groups within community
Service users	Expressed need	May be residual welfare assumptions Local perspective	Self-interest (needs as service users)	Focused on personal lived experiences of issues and assessment of service responses	Lay knowledge Based on personal experiences and evaluation of services Constructed knowledge	May lead to more just services Not essentially human rights based or addressing broader disadvantage
Caretakers	Normative need	May be residual or universal assumptions. Program/ service/ organisation-wide perspective	Professional commitment. Self-interest (job security)	Within discipline/ professional training and professional experience	Professional theoretical models Action-oriented or reflection-based (practice wisdom) May be considered as scientific or constructed	Not empowering per se Potentially socially just if responsive to community defined needs Potentially empowering depending on processes with community
Planners, researchers	Normative/ comparative need	Values according to politics, policy environment, broad social, economic and political drivers Regional, national, global perspectives	Different, possibly competing interests/ agenda: their evidence-base; policy makers; government	Specialised expertise in research methodology	Objective, quantifiable, generalisable, scientific	Least likely to be empowering without engagement of others beyond the researchers/planners

It raises the fundamental issue of the nature of expertise and whether it is appropriate for need definition to be handed over to the experts and thus taken out of the hands of the people. There are four common approaches to this issue. One is to emphasise population-defined need and service user-defined need, asserting the primacy of people being able to define their own needs and seeing caretaker-defined need and inferred need as disempowering and reinforcing the dominance of professional power. The second is to assert (usually implicitly) the superiority of caretaker-defined need and inferred need, emphasising the technical and expert nature of need definition. The third approach is to work towards consensus among need-definers by providing service users and the general population with the expertise and resources to make more 'informed' judgements, by helping the 'professional' need-definers to be more sensitive to the perceptions and realities of the people directly concerned and by establishing genuine dialogue among the various potential definers of need. The fourth approach is a strategic use of mixed approaches. For example, needs may be identified at the community level by service users or community champions, but then translated into inferred needs so that advocacy to policy makers and decision makers can be effective.

From the perspective of this book, population definitions, community leader/champion definitions and service user definitions are the most important and should prevail as the primary forms of need definition over other forms unless basic human rights or other social justice principles are at risk. An empowerment base for community development requires that people have the capacity to define their own needs and to act to have them met—the right to participate. The role of professionals, community caretakers, researchers and planners must be to assist the community with its own need definition, possibly through helping to provide expertise where necessary and through facilitating the process or mediating the process where there are conflicts, but their role is not to assume responsibility for need definition and thereby to deny the community the right to control its own destiny. This position implies expertise within communities and a facilitating role of professionals or 'experts'. Later in this book, a closer examination of the strengths perspective of community development will provide one way in which this philosophical position can be applied in everyday community work.

Universal and relative notions of need

One of the critical debates in the literature of social need is the question of relativism and universality. The above discussion of need, by rejecting the positivist formulation and emphasising an understanding of what actually happens in the act of need definition, might be seen as implying a purely relativist understanding of human need, namely that needs vary according to the circumstances of their definition and that there is no such thing as universal human need. The universal position, on the other hand, holds that there are common needs possessed by all people and that at least some universal statements of need are valid. This position is inherent in the work of the 'classic' writers on human need, such as Abraham Maslow (1970) and Charlotte Towle (1965).

It has been strongly argued by Doyal and Gough (1991) that not only is a universal understanding of basic human need valid, but also that a relativist approach, which denies the legitimacy of such a universalist position, is both morally questionable and politically dangerous. Abandoning a universalist position on human need allows repressive governments to justify policies of oppression by invalidating any appeal to basic human rights, as has been argued in relation to the powerful proponents of the Asian values debate. It is consistent with a 'new right' ideology, which seeks to dismantle social policies based on commitment to universal principles of social justice and human rights in favour of the mechanisms of the market. A relativist model, by ignoring a structural analysis of inequality and oppression, also ignores the structural factors that perpetuate disempowerment. These factors structure people's perceived reality and lead to differences in need definition resulting from the need-definer's relationship to the structures of power and domination. Thus, many need definitions should more properly be understood as reflecting either false consciousness or cultural hegemony.

This is a very important critique and relates to other critiques of the relativism that is implied by a good deal of postmodernist or poststructuralist thought (e.g. Taylor-Gooby 1993). For this reason, it is essential that the above model of need definition be seen alongside the other social justice and human rights perspectives discussed so far in this chapter, namely empowerment and structural disadvantage. It is particularly important in this regard to link *needs* with *rights*. As suggested above, this is a necessary connection, as statements of need imply corresponding understandings of rights, even though these are usually unstated. Seeing need statements within a broader social justice perspective, which includes a commitment to universal notions of human rights, can go a long way towards satisfying the concerns of Doyal and Gough as it provides need statements with a universal moral underpinning. The way in which *needs* are defined or expressed may well be relative, because of cultural and other variations, but the human *rights* inherent in them can be claimed to be universal. One can think of need definition (particularly when defined by those in communities) as being the way in which universal rights are defined within specific social, cultural and political contexts. In this respect, local definitions of need can be seen not as dangerous relativism but rather as an extension and application of the definition of universal human rights.

Unless needs and rights are closely and explicitly linked, needs statements alone run a serious risk of contributing to greater structural inequities. On this basis, it can be argued that a commitment to human rights *must* underpin definitions and statements of human need; a needs-based approach alone is both insufficient and counterproductive to social justice and human rights aims. Traditionally, community development has engaged in the discourse of human need and 'human need' is an important concept. But if our practice is only a needs-based practice in the early 21st century, we are vulnerable to complying with those forces hostile to humane values and humanist projects. At this time in our history, human rights-based practice is critical because the for-profit sector, while it can meet needs for a price, does not have responsibility for upholding human rights; this remains the clear responsibility of a broader range of actors: the state, nations, communities and citizens.

The notion of human need refers to 'must haves', such as food, clothing, shelter, water, safety, health and so on. Needs can be met by the private for-profit sector, but, as discussed in Chapter 1, meeting needs by transforming them into commodities owned by private enterprise and to be purchased in the private marketplace makes the satisfaction of those needs possible only for those who can afford to pay for them. The privatisation of health care, for example, has meant that the health needs of the poor are not met because they are unable to pay for health services. This is an unfortunate consequence of privatisation. The main driver of the private marketplace is profit, not equity (ensuring that all people have their needs met). However, if we consider health as a human right, then the growing inequities in health status among groups are more than unfortunate. They are unfair, socially unjust and a violation of human rights.

Conclusion

This chapter has identified four key components of a social justice and human rights approach to community work: *disadvantage*, *rights*, *empowerment* and *need*. In each case, some conceptual frameworks have been identified, which will, in later chapters, be used as a basis for a model of community development. The four components are not independent. Clearly each is relevant to the others and there are obvious links between, for example, needs and rights, and empowerment and structural disadvantage. The aim of this book is to integrate the social justice and human rights perspective and the ecological perspective as a foundation for community work; the integration, then, needs to be undertaken at a higher level and this is the task of Chapter 4.

The following stories from two women's self-help groups in rural South India illustrate the close links between people's need for economic development and the rights of women to participate in their communities and to have the power to influence their living conditions and to challenge deep-seated gender oppression. While these two groups consisted of a small number of very poor women, it is estimated that there are 27 million women throughout India alone involved in local self-help groups and income-generation projects. The impact of development work with self-help groups is, then, potentially profound in terms of the needs and rights of women in the majority world.

CASE STUDY: Working for needs and rights in a development project

Anna Theresa Group, Melkavanur village

Vasantha Kumari is the leader of a group of 20 women whose major income-generating program has been a van-hire business. The whole group is involved in the scheme and all members have input into decisions and share the benefits.

In 2000 the group received a loan from Tamil Nadu Adi Dravida Housing Development Corporation (TAHDCO) of 261,317 rupees (29 rupees = A$1): 50 per cent was given as a subsidy by TAHDCO; 25 per cent is to be paid back to the bank with interest; 20 per cent is to be paid back to TAHDCO at 4 per cent interest; and 5 per cent was used upfront as a deposit.

The group originally charged 4.5 rupees per kilometre to hire the vehicle, but decided to convert the vehicle to run on gas and they now charge 3 rupees per kilometre.

By September 2003, three years after the group had received its loan, all of the income generated was used to directly pay off the debt, although there was also a component of the group's savings used to give internal loans to members, according to what the group decided. The women collectively decided that for the benefit of the group they would each save a minimum of 20 rupees per month. The women's collective income stands at 120 000 rupees a year, with expenses of around 50 500 rupees a year.

In January 2005, 2300 rupees was distributed to the members; each member received 100 rupees and the driver received 300 rupees.

Vasantha Kumari feels that the group has the confidence, knowledge and skills to be operating this business in the future, when RUHSA (the local non-government organisation/civil society organisation working with the women to support their group) withdraws its support. Before the women began this income-generating program, most of them were in a credit union and they were all doing labouring work. Now they have been educated in savings, loans and business operations and they have the skills to liaise with banks and sustain a very profitable business. The group is also advancing loans internally at two or three loans per month.

Vasantha Kumari is convinced that one of the main reasons that their income-generating program has been so successful is because the whole group has been involved instead of each individual having her own project. There are more ideas generated in the group and everyone is taking responsibility for the smooth running of the project. There are also more funds coming in and so bigger loans are available to members. She said that everyone in the group benefits and this extends to their families and the wider village, because sharing is an important part of their philosophy.

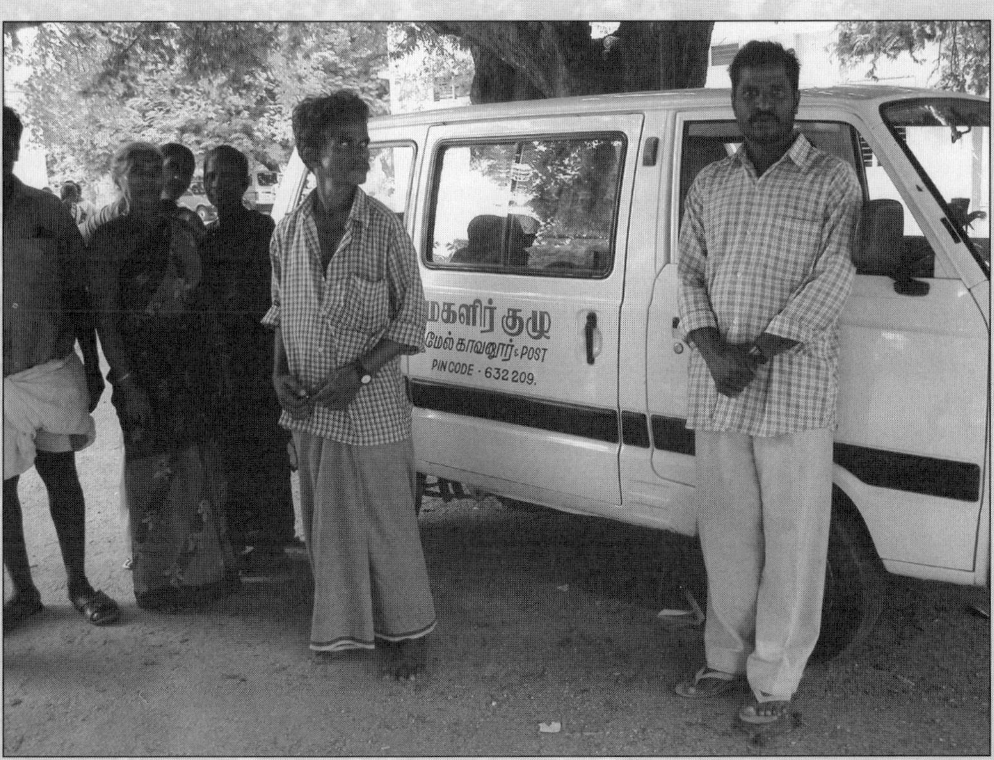

The Anna Theresa Group's hire van

The women have also learned how to go about making changes in their village. They have been successful in motivating the villagers to clean the sewerage canal, improve the quality of drinking water, install more taps throughout the village, build more houses and organise street-cleaning systems. They have also supported a disabled child to attend school by paying his fees and buying his books and have been successful in closing down illegal alcohol outlets. Their new-found confidence has enabled them to approach officials to resolve problems in the village.

The group has also been involved in some community action programs. Members worked with the panchayat (village council) officials to set up a one-day eye camp in the area. They also set up a fund for the victims of the earthquake in Gujarat, in the north-east of India, in early 2001.

Saranayalaya Group, Pasumathur village

A group of women in Pasumathur village has been involved in a number of community action programs. They also contribute to a monthly magazine called *Mutram,* which is dedicated to self-help groups and provides useful information to, and a sharing among, the self-help groups in the district. The group organised an eye camp and involved 20 other similar groups, with each group contributing 200 rupees towards the costs.

Group members make sure that they are present at every Grama Sabha (annual meeting of all people living within the panchayat) meeting and they take responsibility for representing their village needs at those meetings. The group brought attention to the water problems in the village and were successful in getting a bore well installed for drinking water, as well as increasing the number of concrete roads in and around the

continued

village. As well as regular attendance at the Grama Sabha meetings, they also approach the Block Development Officer and the local Panchayat Board president if something needs to be done. Their efforts have led to dust bins being put in every street, a thorough cleaning of the drains, separation of drainage and drinking water and the construction of concrete platforms under village taps to prevent stagnation.

When the Kargal war broke out between India and Pakistan, the women collected 1501 rupees for the wounded soldiers. The group has also taken steps towards the free construction of houses for those villagers below the poverty line.

The women say that they have learned much from the experience of organising the community action programs. They are more aware of the extent of the problems in the village. They have experienced positive encouragement and support from RUHSA, the village as a whole and the panchayat board president. They have come to feel very satisfied with the knowledge that they are making a difference in their village. The group leader, Krishnaveni, remembers the early days of the group when she and some others proposed the idea of becoming involved in community action programs. The rest of the members were very hesitant, mainly due to barriers brought about by tradition, as women were generally not supposed to come out of their homes without the permission of their husband or parents. Now, however, all 20 members are enthusiastic about the programs and they all contribute to their smooth running. The self-help group is now in the position where, if there are any problems in the village, the people go straight to it for solutions. Two of the women stood in the elections for the ward in 2002.

- What needs may these self-help groups be meeting?
- What are some of the human rights issues implied in these projects, with particular reference to gender oppression?

>> discussion questions

1. How can the relationship between social justice and exploitation/liberation be described? How is power implicated in this relationship?
2. How might the view of social justice, which goes beyond the individual perspective, be important in community development?
3. What is the value in each of the four perspectives of or approaches to disadvantage for community development?
4. It is claimed in this chapter that the idea of human rights is contested. What is problematic and limited about the view of rights that we have in the Western tradition?
5. How does the idea of rights imply obligation?
6. What are the connections between 'human rights' and 'community'?
7. What is meant by 'building a culture of human rights'?
8. What is the criticism of viewing rights as if they were unchanging truths?
9. How can each the four political perspectives of power be described?
10. What is meant by 'empowerment'?
11. How can each of the three categories of disadvantage be described?
12. What are the strategies to achieve empowerment of disadvantaged groups?

>> reflective questions

1. Think about your experience of power in your life and in your relationships. In what ways has power shown itself and what were your feelings and responses to it in different circumstances?
2. How would you approach the task of helping people and communities to articulate and realise their human rights?
3. How do you react to the close tie between rights and obligations, from your own family and cultural context? What values and assumptions can you identify that may lie behind your reactions? Where do these values and assumptions come from?
4. What personal qualities and characteristics do you have that may enable you to work, or that might be barriers to you working, with people and communities in empowering ways? List these qualities. For the conducive qualities, write a suggested strategy to strengthen them; for the barriers, write some strategies that might overcome them or at least address them.
5. Of the eight kinds of power involved in empowerment, which do you feel most comfortable with and which do you feel least comfortable with? Can you identify the reasons for your levels of comfort? What might be the implications of these for practising community work from an empowerment perspective?
6. What are your preferred approaches to needs definition, from among the five approaches outlined in Table 3.3? How do your preferences relate to your values? What assumptions do you make (about such things as rights, power, knowledge, capacity and so on) when you state a particular preference and where do these assumptions come from (your social or cultural background, family, training, reading . . .)? Do these assumptions blind you to other possibilities in relation to needs definition in community development?

CHAPTER 4

Ecology and social justice/human rights: a vision for community development

Introduction

Chapters 2 and 3 outlined the two principal bases that will be used as the foundation of a model of community work, namely an ecological perspective and a social justice and human rights perspective. Each has been important in stimulating interest in community development and community-based services. Community work has developed in part from occupations such as social work, welfare work and youth work, which adopt a specific value position of social justice. In recent years, community development has also emerged from the Green literature, as Green writers have seen it as a likely way—and perhaps the only way—to bring about a truly sustainable society. Though most community workers coming from either the ecological perspective or the social justice and human rights perspective would readily assert their support of the other position, it is important to see how both can be more fully integrated into an approach to practice. This is the task of this chapter.

The major themes that emerged out of the 1998 Conference on Governance organised by the United Nations Development Program provide a stark and chilling picture of the state of the world and a convincing rationale for the need to embrace an approach which brings together both an ecological perspective and a social justice and human rights perspective. Drawing on the conference themes Helgason describes the contemporary world thus:

> Changes in the world's economic, political and social systems have brought unprecedented improvements in human living conditions, in both developed and developing countries. However, these changes are also bringing new uncertainties and challenges as the world enters the 21st century. Signs of breakdown are everywhere: disintegration of families; destruction of indigenous societies; degradation and annihilation of plant and animal life; pollution of rivers, oceans and the atmosphere; crime, alienation and substance abuse; higher unemployment; and a widening gap in incomes and productive capabilities . . .
>
> The need for effective governance . . . has never been greater . . . Governance involves many voices and many partners, from citizens to ministers. (Helgasson 1998, pp. 21–22).

Why each perspective is insufficient without the other

Within the context of a world where both social and natural systems are in crisis, an analysis of each of the two perspectives can be used to further demonstrate why the other one, in isolation, is insufficient as a foundation for community development.

Social justice and human rights critique of the ecological perspective

The ecological perspective does not, of itself, imply social justice and human rights principles, such as empowerment, and challenging structures and discourses of oppression. There have been practice models in social work built around an ecological perspective (Germain & Gitterman 1980; Germain 1991) that have largely failed to address structural issues and have, as a result, tended to reinforce the existing order and legitimise a conservative method of practice (Pease 1991). Fundamental social justice and human rights concepts such as liberation, class, gender and race/ethnicity are often missing from a Green analysis or are dealt with only in superficial terms. Thus a number of Green prescriptions for a future society simply reinforce structures and discourses of disadvantage, unless social justice and human rights principles are also taken into account (Ife 1991). The following three examples illustrate this, in relation to class, race and gender.

The first example is the feminisation of environmental issues. Many popular publications on ways to 'change the world' or 'save the planet' concentrate on environmentally friendly ways to clean the house, control household pests, prepare meals, package shopping and so on. While such practices are undoubtedly worthwhile in themselves, the underlying message of these publications is that environmental change starts in the traditional women's domain of the home and that primary responsibility for saving the world from ecological disaster lies with women in the domestic sphere. This is a classic example of patriarchy at work, diverting attention away from the more characteristically male domains of the corporate boardroom and the cabinet room, where the most far-reaching decisions (in terms of ecological consequences) are made—where 'blame' for ecologically bad practices more properly lies and where primary responsibility for saving the planet should be located. Instead, women are made to feel vaguely guilty and somehow responsible for bringing about change; they become the 'target' for education campaigns and the focus of environmental programs. This illustrates the necessity for an adequate gender analysis within the environmental movement and, while most environmentalists pay lip service to the importance of gender issues, this is sometimes at a fairly superficial level, except, of course, among specifically eco-feminist writers.

From a social justice and human rights perspective, this is an all-too-familiar example of blaming the victim, which often occurs when a structural analysis of the issue concerned is ignored.

The second example is seen in a display at an Australian zoo about an endangered species, the numbat. The final item in the display is a large mirror with the caption 'The Greatest Threat to the Numbat', designed presumably to make the visitor reflect on their lifestyle and to engender suitable feelings of guilt. This 'gimmick' is not uncommon in zoo and museum displays dealing with environmental issues (Bookchin 1990). One can only wonder at the possible reaction of an Indigenous Australian zoo visitor, whose culture has posed no major threat to the numbat for tens of thousands of years, at having to accept the implied blame. The display has, for the Indigenous 'visitor' (for someone whose people once nurtured the land on which the zoo now stands, the term 'visitor' is itself an insult), subtly and unintentionally reinforced the marginalisation of Indigenous culture (rendering it invisible), a culture which, while certainly affecting the environment, did so in a much more ecologically sensitive way.

Not only does this example emphasise the need for a better analysis of environmental issues in race terms, it also shows the need for an empowerment perspective. Engendering feelings of guilt is of no use unless there are ways in which people can be empowered to do something about the issue concerned; feeling guilty about the possible extinction of the numbat is of little use when the zoo visitors themselves can in fact do very little about saving the numbat. The threat to the numbat comes from the social, economic and political order and the mirror display does not empower the zoo visitor towards relevant action.

The third example of the need for a social justice and human rights perspective is seen in the frequent advocacy by Greens of a carbon tax, namely a significant tax on fossil fuels to discourage the use, primarily, of the private motor vehicle. If such a tax were introduced in isolation, several readily predictable consequences would follow. Housing in inner-city areas, close to convenient public transport, would become more expensive and low-income people would be forced to live even more on the suburban fringes, where public transport is poor and where car ownership would remain a necessity. Small, fuel-efficient cars would become more expensive on the second-hand market and low-income people would only be able to afford inefficient 'gas guzzlers'. Thus low-income people would be further disadvantaged and existing inequalities would be reinforced. Evidence of this continuing and deepening social disadvantage is starkly presented in Tony Vinson's (2007) report, which maps entrenched disadvantage across Australia in urban, rural and remote communities. In addition, those living in rural areas, where there is no effective alternative form of transport, who are required to spend more of their income on fossil fuels, would be additionally burdened. While there may be value in a carbon tax from an ecological perspective, a social justice and human rights perspective requires that it be considered as only one element of a more comprehensive policy program involving housing, transport, urban planning and the promotion of viable alternatives to fossil fuels.

These three examples underline the importance of class, race and gender issues in informing the ecological perspective. The final point to be made in this section relates to the danger of eco-fascism. The seriousness of the ecological crisis results in the temptation for governments to use draconian and authoritarian measures to enforce sound ecological practices—it could be suggested that the extremely heavy penalties for littering in countries such as Singapore represent an initial step in this direction. An alarming extension of this trend is the potential for the ecological crisis to be used as an excuse for the imposition of an authoritarian regime and the denial of civil liberties by a government seeking to justify repressive measures for other purposes. The danger of eco-fascism surely underlines the importance of a strong social justice and human rights perspective to be fully integrated with environmental awareness and action.

Ecological critique of the social justice and human rights perspective

Just as the ecological perspective is seen to be inadequate without a social justice and human rights analysis, so can a social justice and human rights perspective pose significant problems unless it incorporates ecological understandings. Many traditional social justice and human rights prescriptions are not consistent with the ecological constraints of the position elaborated in Chapter 2.

The conventional economic prescription for many social problems has been economic growth. It is through growth that wealth is created—this wealth can be distributed to reduce economic disadvantage and used to fund improved social services. Thus, traditional socialist strategies have assumed continued economic growth and have concentrated on the ways the results of that growth should be distributed and used. This has enabled many socialists to avoid the difficulty of how to reduce incomes and consumption levels of the wealthy; in a growing economy with increasing prosperity, nobody need have less while the goal of equality is pursued. The ecological perspective, however, questions both the feasibility and the desirability of continued growth and sees growth as one of the major causes of the current ecological crisis. This strikes at the heart not only of the assumptions of industrial and post-industrial capitalism but also of the assumptions of socialism and communism as conventionally understood. It makes the redistribution of wealth and resources much harder to achieve; when the size of the cake is not growing, evening up the portions is going to mean that some people will have to have less. The traditional reliance on growth to provide extra resources for social justice and human rights programs is not feasible if one accepts an ecological position. Reliance then has to be on the strengths and resources within communities themselves.

Another conventional social justice and human rights strategy, again consistent with traditional socialism, is to rely on strong centralised regulation in order to protect human rights and to counter the effects of structural oppression. This has led to the support of a strong central government and bureaucratic structures as major frameworks for the delivery of human services because of the need to safeguard minimum standards and ensure equitable treatment for all. Problems with this assumption were identified in Chapter 1 and its inadequacies are further highlighted by the ecological principles discussed in Chapter 2. It runs counter to the ecological principle of diversity and organic change and has led to structures that are rigid, disempowering and unsustainable. An ecological perspective suggests that such structures create at least as many problems as they solve and that they do not represent an effective long-term solution to the meeting of human need.

Many of the ecological problems associated with social justice and human rights strategies centre on the issue of employment. Conventional social policy wisdom sees the labour market as critical for social justice and human rights and it is through work and the provision of jobs, that social justice and human rights aims can best be achieved. This reflects the primacy of the work ethic and the fundamental role played by 'jobs' in the distribution of wealth and power, the allocation of status, self-esteem and finding 'meaning' in life. From a Green perspective, the primacy of work as traditionally understood is part of the problem, rather than part of the solution and alternatives to conventional understandings of work and employment are important elements of the Green vision. From an ecological perspective the continued search for 'full employment' is unsustainable and it is essential to develop other mechanisms for the distribution of wealth and the allocation of status and worth.

Perhaps the most obvious point at which ecological and social justice/human rights strategies potentially clash is in the area of job creation. A social justice and human rights strategy without ecological awareness will support the creation of employment through the growth of industries such as logging and mining and will see the creation of jobs as taking priority over environmental concerns. An ecological perspective requires that the nature of the jobs themselves be taken into account and rejects strategies that seek to create jobs at any cost. Hence, an ecological perspective requires a significant reformulation of employment strategies as currently defined by advocates of social justice and human rights and requires a more radical redefinition than most social justice and human rights advocates have been prepared to consider. It is this clash, which is evident in the tension that can develop between conservationists and unionists, and simplistically labelled in the media as 'jobs versus the environment'. The issue, of course, is much more complex than this, and there is some encouraging work being done in the area of 'work and environment' that attempts to link the two perspectives (Conservation Council of Victoria 1993) in the realisation that each is vital to the interests of the other.

The promise of integration

From the above discussion and from the discussion in previous chapters, it can be seen that both an ecological perspective and a social justice/human rights perspective are necessary for the realisation of a society that is equitable and sustainable. Each perspective can contribute to a re-evaluation of the other and each requires the other to engage in fundamental reappraisals of some 'conventional wisdom'. The two perspectives, however, are not necessarily in competition and, for the most part, and in relation to important concepts, such as participation and empowerment, are readily compatible (Connors 2008). Points of tension between them, such as jobs versus the environment, serve to identify areas where re-evaluation and dialogue need to take place, rather than being seen as evidence of fundamental incompatibility. Indeed, the two perspectives have much in common: each is seeking a better world, each encompasses a critique of the dominant social, economic and political order and the two draw on common critical intellectual traditions, such as feminism, socialism and anarchism. The two, then, might be seen as natural allies and the possibility of developing an agenda for social change based on an integration of ecological and social justice/human rights principles has considerable potential for those who are seeking a better world. Recent writers have sought to achieve such a synthesis, from the perspective of eco-feminism, social ecology and new paradigm thinking (Hawthorne 2002; Eaton 2005; van der Ryn & Cowan 2007; Simmons 1997; Sulman 1998; Mason 1999; Bryant 1995).

From this position, it can be seen that many of the change strategies attempted by those working only from an ecological or a social justice/human rights perspective will fail, in the long term if not the short term, unless adequate account is taken of the other perspective as well. The quest for an integrated position, involving both perspectives, is therefore critical. It is also important in terms of the use of resources; experienced social justice and human rights community workers, for example, have commented on how Greens, in their enthusiastic embrace of 'community', have been 'discovering' techniques such as non-violent action and cooperative decision making that have been well known to other community workers for many years. Such 'reinventing of the wheel' represents a waste of time, energy and resources that cannot be afforded given the serious nature and urgency of the current situation, whether understood in terms of an environmental crisis, an economic crisis, a political crisis or a crisis in human and spiritual values. Development of an integrated ecological and social justice/human rights perspective and genuine dialogue between advocates of the two positions is essential.

Such an integration is also exciting. It not only provides a vision of a better society, but it also can identify new concepts that can enrich both of the perspectives and ensure that, true to the holistic paradigm, the new whole will be significantly greater than the sum of its parts. It is the identification of some of these emerging concepts, and the spelling out of that vision, which is the task of the next section.

Emerging concepts

An integration of the ecological and social justice/human rights perspectives results in some interesting formulations. It would be wrong to call them *new* as, in some instances, they reflect perceptions that have their origins in the ancient world (Marshall 1992b) or that are well understood in Indigenous cultures (Norberg-Hodge 1991); it is only recently that they have re-emerged within the Western intellectual tradition. These are identified only briefly, because to explore them in detail would require more space than is available here. They provide some interesting avenues for further development, but they are important in the present context because they have the potential to affect understandings of community and community development.

Social sustainability

The concept of sustainability—fundamental to the ecological perspective—has been developed primarily from the study of biological and physical systems. The Green analysis thus initially focused on population, species survival, pollution, energy and so on. It was subsequently applied to economic systems, the result being the original and exciting work of Green economists such as Paul Ekins (1986, 2000), Manfred Max-Neef (1991) and Hazel Henderson (1988, 1991, 1996). An integration of ecological and social justice/human rights perspectives leads naturally to a further extension of the concept to incorporate an understanding of social sustainability. This suggests that social systems and institutions, such as the family, the community, bureaucracies, educational institutions and voluntary organisations, need to be evaluated from the point of view of their sustainability. UN-HABITAT, briefly described in Chapter 3, has as its mission 'to promote socially and environmentally sustainable human settlements development and the achievement of adequate shelter for all' (UN-HABITAT 2005). This mission statement represents an attempt to integrate the ecological and human rights approaches into a concept of social sustainability.

Applying the principle of sustainability to social systems means that they must be evaluated not simply in terms of their immediate role and function but also in terms of their long-term viability, their impact on other systems, the energy they extract from their environment and their output (Dobson 1999). It can be seriously questioned whether many modern social systems, institutions and organisations meet the criterion of sustainability. Certainly many social policies are patently unsustainable, in that they demand increasing levels of resources rather than seeking more steady-state solutions. The standard social policy response to a problem is to seek ways of increasing expenditure (whether public, private or market-generated) on the assumption that this will result in the problem being solved, without a holistic understanding of the costs of such intervention or the finite nature of resources. The tendency of human service organisations to engage in almost continual organisational change and restructuring is also hardly compatible with sustainability. Thus the principle of sustainability, if applied to policy and organisations, would require a radical transformation from existing practice, in ways that have barely been considered. Social relationships are becoming increasingly unsustainable, especially in relation to marriage and the family, and this is another area where the idea of social sustainability has some potentially interesting applications—as exemplified in some forms of family therapy.

Integrating the social and the physical

The holistic approach is a fundamental principle of the ecological perspective and the Green movement has been significantly influenced by challenges to the linear, mechanistic and dualistic thinking of the 'old' paradigm. However, in the Green movement the holistic perspective has often been confined to the physical and biological sciences; an important contribution of a social justice and human rights perspective is to require the extension of holism into social and moral spheres. The case of the carbon tax, discussed above, is an example of how environmental scientists, who follow a holistic perspective within their own field, readily resort to linear thinking when it comes to policy prescriptions. A truly holistic approach would warn against the simplistic advocacy of a carbon tax in isolation and suggests that a more systemic analysis is as important in social issues as it is in biology.

Social scientists, of course, have also been concerned to develop holistic understandings, drawing heavily on systems theory, and this has affected a number of disciplines. However, they have often failed to draw on the insights of the physical sciences and frequently have as simplistic a view of the physical sciences as some physical scientists have of social issues.

The integration of these two intellectual traditions, which is implied by a truly holistic approach and by the integration of the ecological and social justice/human rights perspectives, has the promise of providing a new and more substantial intellectual rationale for action. Holism requires the transcending of dualisms (e.g. mind/body, knowledge/action, fact/value; see Plumwood 1993), including the physical/social dualism that has characterised the 'partitioning' of knowledge and understanding. It requires a broadening rather than a narrowing of the knowledge base and it emphasises the importance of activities such as community work, which draw on a broad range of knowledge and experience.

Intergenerational equity

A fundamental aspect of social justice and human rights is the notion of equity. This has been understood in terms of class, race, gender, age, disability, location and so on. The ecological perspective, with its emphasis on sustainability and long-term survival, has added to this list the concept of *intergenerational equity*, an idea that has had only limited application in mainstream social policy (except in relation to issues such as death duties). This implies that the welfare of future generations needs to be taken into account in policy decisions and that one must identify not only potential 'winners' and 'losers' within *existing* society but also whether *future* generations will 'win' or 'lose' as a result of a particular course of action. This has major implications for resource usage and represents a strong argument for conservation rather than exploitation of non-renewable resources. It also has an impact on social policies and from a specifically community development perspective it encourages the creation of community facilities and structures that will have long-term benefit and that are likely to endure. It emphasises that social responsibility extends to future generations, as well as to the disadvantaged in the present, and therefore requires policies which will, for example, not allow the development or expansion of a self-perpetuating 'underclass'.

Intergenerational equity extends not only to the future but also to the past. While we cannot change what happened in the past, we can seek to redress injustices that have occurred in the past and that affect the present. Seeking redress for past wrongs done to Indigenous people (e.g. through land rights or through apologising for the removal of children from their families, as occurred in Australia in February 2008, and compensation for such separations) is an illustration of this and shows how obligations to equity, social justice and human rights can extend back in time as well as forward.

The dominant world view has tended to lack a historical perspective. It is the present which is seen as critical; what came before is of largely 'academic' interest and the longer-term future is normally discounted in favour of immediate needs and goals. The integrated perspective developed in this chapter takes a different view: a holistic analysis requires that the past be seen as important as a framework for understanding the present and the concept of intergenerational equity forces us to confront both the past and the future and to consider the future implications of present actions.

Global justice

One of the strongest aspects of the Green movement has been its emphasis on the unity of the planet, insisting that the world must be seen as a single system and that a global perspective is essential if true sustainability is to be achieved (Deudney & Matthew 1999). This is partly because environmental problems, such as acid rain, greenhouse gases, ozone depletion and nuclear fallout, are no respecters of national boundaries and so should be the concern of all nations and all peoples. Solutions to environmental problems must be sought at a global rather than merely a national level if they are to be effective.

This global perspective has implications for social justice and human rights. Although for many years there have been groups and individuals concerned about global injustice, much of the social justice and human rights discourse takes place within national boundaries. For example, bringing about a more equitable distribution of income is seen primarily as an aim to be achieved *within* Australia, Aotearoa, Britain, the United States, Canada or wherever, through changes to wages policy, social security, taxation and so on. Traditional international studies in social policy (e.g. Esping-Andersen 1990; Evers et al. 1987) normally compare these different systems as independent entities, rather than taking a genuine international perspective by looking at issues of global injustice. Struggles for the rights of women, for fair working conditions, for freedom from discrimination or for land rights for Indigenous people are largely carried on within national boundaries. The ecological perspective insists that these issues be understood in a global context, and that the global implications of local actions be addressed (Mishra 1999; Deacon 1997).

An example is the current drive to boost minority world economies by increasing exports, which is seen as a way of increasing the nation's wealth so that social justice and human rights goals can more readily be met. While this may be justified if one takes a purely national perspective on social justice and human rights, a global perspective requires an analysis of who will 'lose' if exports are increased. The losers may well be poorer nations of the majority world that are struggling to establish viable economies and basic services. These nations may find themselves forced to spend their hard-won foreign currency on importing products because their own Indigenous-community-based industries have been dismantled on the grounds of 'inefficiency'. Such nations are finding it harder to compete in the global market with more powerful affluent nations. Hence improved living standards may be achieved in a nation like Australia at the cost of living standards in poorer nations, which, if one takes a global view of social justice and human rights, is unacceptable. Global awareness requires that all actions be understood within the global context; even a simple act such as buying a cup of coffee links the purchaser to the transnational exploitation of peasant economies, the growing of cash crops, the driving of peasants from their traditional lands and the consequent repression of human rights (Trainer 1985).

Unfortunately, 'globalisation' in the dominant discourse is usually understood only in terms of economic activity and is highly centralised and controlled. The notion of globalisation has effectively been appropriated by the ideology of free trade and neoliberalism. There is, however, an alternative literature that is exploring the possibilities of 'globalisation from below' (Falk 1993; Brecher & Costello 1994) or what Robertson refers to as 'glocalisation' (1995, p. 26), where local communities and other local sites play a mutually influential role in globalisation processes.

This attempts to integrate both a Green and a social justice and human rights perspective in developing an internationalism that is based on grassroots activism rather than the needs of transnational capital. There is also an alternative literature that identifies the resources within the major and influential world traditions (Islam, Christianity, Buddhism, Judaism, Confucianism, international law, liberalism and feminism) that can facilitate serious global dialogue about moral and ethical issues to more justly shape our world, now and into the future (Sullivan & Kymlicka 2007). These alternative formulations of globalisation have significant implications for community development work and will be explored further in Chapter 8.

The global perspective is not new, but it has often been missing in social justice and human rights work within countries of the minority world and has not been a major influence on most social-justice-based community development. The integration of ecological and social justice/human rights perspectives requires this link to be made explicit; the implications of such an approach for community work are exciting (Kelly 1992; Campfens 1997). Indeed, one of the ways in which the exploitation of poorer nations can be reduced is by richer nations becoming more self-sufficient at the local community level and hence less reliant on the spoils of the global market. In this way a community development approach in the 'developed' nations can be seen to be globally responsible and a way of contributing to global social and economic justice.

Ecocentric justice

The Green perspective has challenged the anthropocentric world view, characteristic of the Western intellectual tradition (Marshall 1992b), and Green writers such as Fox (1990), Eckersley (1992) and Narby (2006) have proposed instead an *ecocentric* perspective. This does not see the human species as dominant or deserving of special consideration, but instead emphasises the value of all living things and locates the human species as one part of the larger ecological whole, all of which has intrinsic value.

The ecocentric perspective provides a basis for the animal rights movement, vegetarianism, anti-vivisection and similar causes. It sees the issue of endangered species not simply in terms of the possible value of that species to humans, but also in terms of the 'rights' of all species to a continued existence. The interesting point for present purposes is that it extends the notion of *rights* beyond the traditional view of 'human rights' as discussed in Chapter 3 and specified in human rights conventions. If rights are seen to extend beyond humans to animals, perhaps to plants as living organisms and even to inanimate objects (as might be claimed under the Gaia hypothesis; see Lovelock 1979), the implications for a justice strategy are profound. This view would make the animal liberation movement or the debate about the genetic modification of food, for example, legitimate concerns of social justice and human rights workers and would raise ethical issues for a number of community workers, such as those working in rural communities reliant on the beef or grain growing industries.

Certainly not all writers or activists in the Green movement would accept the ecocentric position—at least not in its most uncompromising form (see Bookchin 1990; Bookchin & Foreman 1991); not all Greens, for example, are vegetarians. Nevertheless, the implications of this perspective are significant for any consideration of rights and it forces a re-evaluation of the anthropocentric nature of 'rights' as they have traditionally been understood within the social justice and human rights movement.

Environmental rights

A notion of environmental rights is incorporated in the ecocentric justice perspective outlined above, in that it implies claims of rights on behalf of non-human living beings and implies that humans do not have additional rights to other life forms. But the idea of environmental rights can also be understood from a more conventional anthropocentric perspective—even in this form it implies an extension of the more conventional understanding of 'human' rights to incorporate so-called 'third-generation' rights (Ife 2001).

In this context, the idea of environmental rights implies a right to live in an enriching rather than a blighted environment, the right to be able to experience 'nature', the right to unpolluted water and air, the right to uncontaminated food and so on. Environmental rights tend to be relative to the affluence of the community concerned; in poorer communities, especially in the majority world and in urban slums, they are likely to be linked to questions of basic survival, such as clean water and air that is fit to breathe. It is in more affluent societies that ecological rights (in terms of the right to wilderness, to an unspoiled natural environment and to freedom from visual and noise pollution) are most strongly articulated, though this is not to deny the importance of such rights for all people, regardless of where they live. The notion of environmental rights as an important aspect of human rights is another way in which an integration of ecological and social justice and human rights approaches has broadened conventional understandings. Environmental issues therefore also enter the discourse of needs and one can seek to identify definitions of environmental need, in much the same way as was done for social need in Chapter 3, by asking who defines environmental needs, from what knowledge and value perspectives, using what information base and so on. As with social need, environmental need is a contested area where there are different views on who should be defining the needs of a community.

Global and environmental obligations

In Chapter 3 the close link between rights and obligations was discussed. Departure from the Western individualistic view of human rights to one that clearly incorporates one's obligations to one's context, including other human beings and the environment, has great potential for integrating an ecological perspective and a social justice/human rights perspective. The Gandhian view of the right to autonomy discussed in Chapter 3 entwines the idea of rights with the idea of obligation to the 'other', whether the other be human or environmental. Adopting a broad view of obligation also enables the idea of obligation to transcend traditional national borders and to take a global perspective. A greater emphasis in the rights perspective on obligations and their complementarity to rights, as well as an appreciation of the close links between human rights and 'community', represents an integration of the perspectives in ways that will contribute towards a better future society.

The People's Health Movement marching in Cuenca, Ecuador, 2005

The People's Health Movement regards health as a human right and its global reach means that health issues are problematised beyond simply national health system inadequacies. The movement comprises health activists, grassroots health workers and local people across the world. Structural and poststructural perspectives inform the movement. At its first assembly in Bangladesh in 2000 and its second assembly in Ecuador in 2005, its People's Charter for Health was endorsed and strengthened. The Charter for Health provides a good case study on a movement's charter that embraces both social justice and human rights principles and an ecological perspective beyond national boundaries.

CASE STUDY: A charter to guide a people's movement

The People's Charter for Health includes, among other things, the following statements:

- Health is a social, economic and political issue and above all a fundamental human right.
- Inequality, poverty, exploitation, violence and injustice are at the root of ill-health and the deaths of poor and marginalised people.
- Health for all means that powerful interests have to be challenged, that globalisation has to be opposed, and that economic and political priorities have to be drastically changed.
- The attainment of the highest possible level of health and wellbeing is a fundamental human right.
- The principles of universal, comprehensive primary health care are the basis of all health policy.
- Governments have a fundamental responsibility to ensure universal access to quality health care.
- The participation of people and people's organisations is essential in policy formulation, implementation and evaluation.
- Health is primarily determined by the social, economic, political and physical environment and must be a top policy priority with sustainable development.
- To combat the global health crisis, we need to take action at all levels—individual, community, national, regional and global—and in all sectors. The basis for action includes: tackling the broader economic, social, political, environmental and military challenges to health; building a people-centred health system; strengthening the participation of people and people organisations, and empowering citizens.

Source: People's Health Movement 2000, *Peoples's Charter for Health*, Dhaka.

- In what ways can you identify the ideas of social justice, human rights and obligations, ecological aspects and a globalised perspective in this People's Charter for Health?

Community

The ecological and social justice/human rights perspectives, taken together, form the basis of a vision for a future society. The social justice and human rights perspective provides a vision of what is socially *desirable*: a society based on the definition and guaranteeing of rights, equity, empowerment, the overcoming of structural oppression and disadvantage, freedom to define needs and have them met and so on. The ecological perspective provides a vision of what is *feasible*, it outlines the kind of society that will be viable in the long term, namely a society based on the principles of holism, sustainability, diversity and balance. Taken together, they represent a powerful vision of the future; an important component of that vision is the concept of community, which is inevitably a fundamental concept for any 'community development' perspective. The idea of 'community' is important in both ecological and social justice/human rights perspectives and can be seen to be a natural consequence of the premises of each.

The community-based approach is reinforced by the ecological principle of diversity, as it enables different ways of doing things to be developed in different circumstances and also, by the principle of sustainability, as small-scale structures are likely to be more sensitive to their immediate environments. Community is consistent with empowerment models of change, as it provides a framework for people to take effective decisions. It is also consistent with a human rights perspective, because rights and obligations are enacted *with others*, most often on a daily basis and at the community level. Community is consistent, too, with a needs-based perspective, as it can enable people more readily to define and articulate their felt needs and aspirations.

A further justification for the incorporation of community in a vision of social change was provided in Chapter 1, namely the view that perhaps there is no alternative and that community is the institution that will succeed the family, the Church, the market and the state as the primary focus for the meeting of human needs.

Characteristics of 'community'

The definition of *community* is highly problematic and the 98 definitions that Bell & Newby (1971) found at that time had been proposed had very little in common. It is, therefore, incumbent on anyone wishing to use the word to provide some clarification of the meaning to be ascribed to it.

Before declaring the understanding of 'community', which will be used for the remainder of this book, it is important to appreciate the complexity and ambiguity of the term, because by doing so, the community worker is more able to understand with whom they are working and for what purpose—the nature of the ends or aims.

If there are at least 98 definitions of 'community', is it worth trying to arrive at one definition or is it better to abandon the concept altogether? Neither of these alternatives is very useful. Rather, deeper reflection on the concept that leads to a fuller appreciation of it, in all its complexity, is critical for community development.

Plant (1974) argues that we ought not to be searching for commonalities among the definitions of community, but rather be identifying how each of the definitions reflects different values and different agenda, different interests.

His argument implies that 'community' is not simply a description of something that exists. It is also strongly evaluative or normative. By evaluative, what is meant is it is value-laden; by normative, what are implied are norms or rules. When a word has a strong evaluative meaning, its descriptive meaning may become contested, vague and open to interpretation. Exactly this has happened with 'community'. With a complex notion like 'community', certain aspects are selected depending on different value positions that are held.

In 18th- and 19th-century German thought, 'community' was referred back to the Greek 'polis'. This was a notion of interaction, homogeneity, participation and activity that was open to all. Religion, art, politics, family life were all intertwined and closely knit. It was about 'wholeness' as opposed to fragmentation.

It is based on this background of German romantics that we often value the word 'community'.

But where do recent notions like freedom, independence, individuality, autonomy and power, status, injustice, disadvantage and oppression fit into the notion of community? Do these contemporary values simply render 'community' as a romantic notion, nostalgic for the past, or can contemporary dominant values assist us, in the human services, to define the ways in which communities and society can be transformed towards greater social justice, human rights and ecological sustainability?

These are questions that must be reflected on by community workers because in doing community development, they will be attempting to influence to develop a particular type and quality of social experience and so they need to be acutely aware of what this is—what is the purpose, what are the intended or desired outcomes?

The term 'community' can be used to render diversity within communities invisible. Those voices that are most usually made silent by more romantic references to 'community' are those of the marginalised, excluded and disadvantaged. When 'community' as descriptive and 'community' as evaluative are compared there are significant discrepancies. It is this space between the descriptive and evaluative, between what is and what ought to be and can be, between the reality and the aspirational, that is the territory for development and the space for community workers and community development.

For the remainder of this book, the term 'community' is understood as a form of social organisation with the following five related characteristics.

1. HUMAN SCALE

As a counter to large, impersonalised and centralised structures, community involves interactions on a scale that can readily be controlled and used by individuals. Thus the scale is limited to one where people will know each other or can readily get to know each other as needed and where interactions are such that they are readily accessible to all. Structures are sufficiently small that people are able to own and control them, thereby allowing for genuine empowerment. There is no 'magic number' that can be used to identify the size of such a community, though clearly it could apply to groupings of up to several thousand. This characteristic does, however, rule out particularly large groupings, such as 'the Australian community'.

2. IDENTITY AND BELONGING

To most people, the word *community* would incorporate some sense of feeling of 'belonging' or being accepted and valued within a group. It is this that leads to the use of the term *member of the community*; the concept of membership implies belonging, acceptance by others and allegiance or loyalty to the aims of the group concerned. It is therefore more than simply a group established for administrative convenience (e.g. an electorate, a school class or a workplace group), but has some of the characteristics of a club or society, to which people belong as members and where this sense of belonging is significant and positively regarded.

Thus belonging to a community gives one a sense of identity. The community can become part of a person's self-concept and is an important aspect of how one views one's place in the world. The lack of such personal identity is commonly perceived as one of the problems of modern society (Castells 1997; Community and Family Commission 1992). The decline of institutions that give people identity (e.g. the tribe, the clan, the Church or the village) can be seen as one of the reasons employment and the workplace have become so significant: they represent one of the few remaining ways in which people can legitimately achieve an identity and work has become the primary mechanism for the allocation of status. If the work ethic is to be successfully challenged, as the Green analysis proposes, it will be important to provide some other mechanism, such as community, through which people can achieve a sense of identity.

3. OBLIGATIONS

Membership of an organisation carries both rights and responsibilities, and a community also requires certain obligations from its members. There is an expectation that people will contribute to 'the life of the community' by participating actively in at least some of its activities and that they will contribute to the maintenance of the community structure. All groups need maintenance if they are to survive and the responsibility for the maintenance functions of a community rests largely with its members. Being a member of a community should not therefore be a purely passive experience, but should also involve some level of active participation.

4. *GEMEINSCHAFT*

Tönnies' distinction between *Gemeinschaft* and *Gesellschaft* (1955) was mentioned in Chapter 1. *Gemeinschaft* structures and relationships are implied by the concept of community, as opposed to the *Gesellschaft* structures and relationships of mass society. Thus a community will enable people to interact with each other in a greater variety of roles, which will be less differentiated and contractual and which will encourage interactions with others as 'whole people' rather than as limited and defined roles or categories. This is not only important in terms of self-enhancement, human contact and personal growth—it also enables individuals to contribute a wider range of talents and abilities for the benefit of others and the community as a whole.

5. CULTURE

A community provides an opportunity for an antidote to the phenomenon of 'mass culture'. The culture of modern society is produced and consumed at a mass level, resulting too often in sterile uniformity and the removal of culture from the local experiences of ordinary people (Nozick 1992). A community enables the valuing, production and expression of a local or community-based culture, which will have unique characteristics associated with that community, which will enable people to become active producers of that culture rather than passive consumers and which will thus encourage both diversity among communities and broad-based participation.

These five characteristics can be seen as forming the basis of an understanding of community as understood in the remaining chapters. They are clearly interrelated and should be seen not as necessarily distinct categories, but rather as different manifestations of the same phenomenon.

Geographical and functional communities

One critical question associated with any definition of community is whether communities must be geographically based and defined in terms of a particular locality. There is an important distinction made between *geographical* and *functional* communities, the former being based on locality and the latter on some other common element providing a sense of identity. Contemporary functional communities have been called 'post place' communities (Bradshaw 2008). Examples of functional communities that may not be locality-based are: the Italian community, the academic community, the Church community, the legal community, groups of people with specific characteristics (e.g. people with a particular disability) who get together and the many e-communities (chat rooms, MySpace, Facebook, MSN, Second Life and so on). Each of these could have the characteristics of community described above and so could legitimately be regarded as a community for the purposes of this book. Community workers, indeed, sometimes work with functional communities rather than geographical communities, a good example being those community workers who work with specific ethnic communities. Ease of personal mobility (cars, public transport) and communication technologies (email, teleconferencing) have made functional communities more possible than was the case in earlier eras and for many people they have taken the place of geographical communities as important experiences of community identity.

Both the ecological perspective and the social justice and human rights perspective, however, imply that using functional communities as a basis for community development is problematic. From an ecological perspective it can be argued that community should always be locality-based because of the importance of the whole ecosystem and the need for human communities to be integrated with the physical environment and the land. Such an argument suggests that it is humanity's artificial separation from the land, characteristic of Western societies and the anthropocentric approach, which is the cause of many current problems and that for community to be sustainable it must be integrated with a bioregional system, requiring it to be defined in terms of physical location and helping people to re-establish a connection with, and a responsibility for, their physical environment.

Another argument against functional communities is that they tend to segment rather than integrate human populations. A goal of community development, and of community-based services, is to integrate people within a community context so that they can interact with each other, nurture each other and all participate in decision making. This is harder to achieve if some groups (e.g. those with a particular ethnic background, with disabilities or with a particular profession or occupation) have a primary loyalty to a functional rather than a geographical community, rendering them less inclined to participate in locally based activities.

From a social justice and human rights perspective, there will be some people for whom a functional community is not a viable option and often these are the most disadvantaged. People without ready access to affordable transport or child care, or for whom there is not an obvious functional community for them to join, cannot be expected to have their need for community interaction met in this way. It could be argued that it is the emergence of functional communities based on work or leisure activities that has prevented some people (especially men) from spending much time in a local community setting, leaving others (typically women, older people and people with disabilities) to endure life in an impoverished and demoralising local situation, leading to loneliness, isolation, depression, drugs and suicide. If functional communities are thriving at the expense of local communities, the social justice and human rights perspective described in Chapter 3 requires that the further development of geographical communities be supported in preference to functional communities.

For these reasons, geographical communities represent a preferred option for community development and community-based services, as opposed to functional communities. Such arguments, however, can deny the legitimacy of the positive experiences some people may have in functional communities and their potential for empowerment. Given the weak structure of geographical communities, especially in urban settings, it is important that some operating functional communities be recognised and nurtured, at least until a more viable structure of geographical communities can be established. This is particularly important where functional communities represent disadvantaged or oppressed groups, such as Indigenous people, people with disabilities or newly arrived immigrants, as in these cases functional communities can be an important aspect of an empowerment process. It is less important where functional communities represent the powerful (e.g. the professions, elites and 'the business community') and there are good arguments that the maintenance of such communities could run counter to social justice and human rights aims. Geographical communities, then, may represent a more acceptable long-term goal, but the importance of some functional communities in the short and medium terms must also be recognised. In the discussion in subsequent chapters, therefore, the concept of community will generally refer to geographical communities, though the discussion can also be applied to functional communities in certain instances.

At this point mention must be made of the phenomenon of 'virtual community' or e-communities. This refers to the interaction made possible by computer-based communication technology, such as email and the range of options available through the Internet. Such technology allows significant interaction to take place between people who may never have met and this results in a new kind of community evolving in the technological age. It is, perhaps, the ultimate form of functional community, removing not only the ties of locality but also the ties of interpersonal interaction except through the computer screen. Such forms of communication as email and discussion forums can be very useful for establishing effective links *between* communities and can provide opportunities for activists and people concerned with community development to network and to form global movements for change. However, such electronic interactions imply an experience of community that is an extreme type of functional communities and so cannot be understood as being a community in the sense that the term 'community' is used in this book. To remove face-to-face personal interaction from the concept of community is the ultimate in the depersonalisation of society, which community development seeks to reverse, not reinforce. It also removes from the idea of community any sense of place or connection to the land and the physical environment and this can result in less rather than more environmental awareness and in less commitment to working towards a more sustainable environment, with potentially disastrous consequences (Bowers 2000).

Community as constructed

The earlier discussion of the meaning of the term 'community' did not result in a neat definition but rather in a set of descriptions and aspirations which the word implies. This is because community is essentially an experience, whose construction is continually generated and regenerated from the dynamic interactions and interrelationships between people and between people and their world (Crotty 1998). Such an elusive concept therefore defies objective definition. Community is elusive also because it is qualitative in the sense that community is always in a state of 'becoming'. It is felt and experienced, rather than measured and defined. Because of its constructed nature, it is not particularly helpful to think of community as something 'existing' or to 'operationalise' community in such a way that we can measure it. It is more appropriate to allow people to develop their own constructions of what community means for them, in their own context, and to help them to work towards the realisation of a form of community that meets the criteria described above.

From this perspective, community development is not about defining and establishing something called community, but it is rather an ongoing and complex process of dialogue, exchange, consciousness raising, education and action aimed at helping the people concerned to build their own version of community. This may be a very different version from that developed by another group; one of the fundamental principles of this book, which is consistent with the ecological perspective, is that there is no single 'right' formula for what constitutes community and no single 'right' way to develop it. 'Cookbook' prescriptions, while they may be intuitively appealing, are thus inappropriate and will not work most of the time (see Chapter 11). Community development is a much more complex process, full of dilemmas, problems and unpredictabilities that require unique and creative solutions. Models of community work, therefore, are valuable only if they provide frameworks within which these problems and dilemmas can be understood and creative solutions derived.

Urban, suburban and rural issues

The development of autonomous, self-reliant communities is in general a much easier task in smaller rural communities, because of the size of the community, the clear boundaries, the stable population base and existing community ties, which are likely to be stronger than in urban or suburban areas. The rural tradition of people working together in hard times is an indication of community strength and the number of community organisations and associations in country towns is a further indication of a level of community interaction that is not usually present in other locations. Thus rural towns are likely to be the areas where new alternative community structures will more readily emerge because such structures are not greatly different from people's experience. It might be argued that the characteristic conservatism of many rural communities could work against such a trend, but it is precisely this conservatism that could be a strength in community development; it would be a case of building on many of the strengths already present in many rural communities. It is also sometimes the case that the supposed conservatism of rural communities is a myth; rural communities in Saskatchewan on the Canadian prairies were historically the cradle of socialism and the cooperative movement in Canada (Melnyk 1985), and this strong radical tradition can be built on in community development; Saskatchewan today remains a province where there is considerable community-level challenge to economic rationalism and where there is a good deal of interesting activity in community-based alternatives. Even in rural communities without the radical tradition of Saskatchewan, rural recession can open up possibilities for alternative economic development on a community-based model, as is the case in Esperance in Western Australia, which has been seen as a model for alternative community-based economic development (Dauncey 1988). Alternative local currency schemes are now well established and accepted in many smaller towns, as rural communities are realising that the mainstream economy has failed them—they have set about establishing their own economies.

Similarly, human service workers in rural communities commonly find that, despite official departmental procedures, they are inevitably working on a community-based model, as opposed to a professionalised therapeutic model or a bureaucratically based state intervention model. They live in and are part of the community, meet their 'clients' in everyday social situations and use this for the clients' benefit, use their own community networks to help solve problems, find that boundaries between different agencies are extremely fluid and see people's problems and their solutions within the context of the local community. To do otherwise would be utterly inappropriate and a community-based approach is a matter of both inevitability and common sense.

It must be emphasised, however, that rural communities are not utopias; they pose their own particular problems for community workers. Conservative views on race and gender are common in many such communities and establishing a community development program based on the social justice and human rights principles of Chapter 3 presents significant challenges. Any community will present both opportunities and obstacles for community development and while rural communities have many strengths on which a community worker can build, there can be major difficulties in relation to social justice and human rights principles.

Urban and suburban areas represent a different, and potentially much more significant, set of problems for community development. Community structures are much weaker and less developed, boundaries are difficult to perceive or are non-existent and people commonly relate to groups and structures substantially removed from their local community. Many suburbs have been planned in such a way that community interaction is discouraged—far removed from common workplaces, no local employment, no obvious focal point for community activity, no local services, pedestrian traffic almost impossible and public transport minimal or non-existent. Under such circumstances, and with multiple attractions in other parts of the city, it is no wonder that people spend little time in their local neighbourhood, do not know many of their neighbours and have little identification with local community issues. Inner-city urban areas can have other problems—transient populations with little commitment to the locality, cultural conflict and concern for security and personal safety that discourages people from venturing onto the street and so on. Even with the recent and rapid increase in new inner-city apartment living in Australian cities, there is an obvious concern about security systems and a sense of a siege mentality rather than a sense of community-building.

The challenge of developing community-based structures in urban and suburban areas is a critical one as this is the context within which many people live. Finding adequate strategies for community development in such locations is, therefore, a major priority and unless this can be achieved the potential of a genuinely community-based alternative will not be recognised.

Despite the major difficulties, there are some indications that the development of community-based structures is indeed possible in such locations. This has proven easier in more disadvantaged urban or suburban communities and in urban slums: the stigmatisation of a suburb or the experience of disadvantage in a slum can act as a force to bring the community together and provide a sense of identity. The often inadequate public transport services to such suburban areas combine with poverty to render people less mobile and therefore more likely to focus on local activity. Thus, in many disadvantaged urban locations, community development work has been able to build on a strong local community identity and provide a solid foundation for the development of community-based alternatives. Also, the problems of such areas lead to the location of a variety of social services and the more progressive and community-based among them can act as a focal point for the stimulation of community development.

While such examples are far from being fully self-reliant and autonomous communities, they do represent the foundations on which such structures can be built. In more affluent neighbourhoods such structures are weaker, but nonetheless there are community-level structures that represent potential focal points for community activity—sporting clubs, church parishes, progress associations, parents and citizens associations, local action groups and so on.

The relative strength of community in more disadvantaged areas suggests an important principle for community development: it is in circumstances of adversity, or when the wider social and economic system is seen as having failed them, that people will be more likely to look to local community-based structures as an alternative. If the future is one of crisis and instability, more people are likely to find themselves in such circumstances and the potential for the community development approach is likely to grow. Today's affluent suburbs may become tomorrow's disadvantaged ghettos and community development would then become a more viable alternative.

An interesting example of this is the way in which a local, disadvantaged community used government funding for crime prevention in very different ways from other communities. In the late 1990s government funding was made available to local communities as one response to rising crime rates. Invariably communities used these funds to provide education and resources to local people, particularly elderly people, as ways to prevent such things as home invasion. Better home-security systems and so on were promoted. If anything, these strategies had the potential to erode social capital in communities, as the programs encouraged greater fear and suspicion and a siege mentality for people as they locked themselves behind deadlocks, security doors and so on. As the following case study shows, the one community that stood out in this program approached the issue in a very different way.

CASE STUDY: Building an alternative community-based structure

A socially and economically disadvantaged urban community accepted government crime-prevention funding and set up the mandatory committee, as did many other communities. This community was characterised by higher levels of unemployment and more single-parent families and was more culturally and linguistically diverse than most of the communities around it. Income and education levels were lower and the number of public-housing tenants was higher. Health indicators were generally worse than for other communities. Despite these indicators, the community had a proud history of fighting decisions that further marginalised it. For example, it strenuously fought the closure of the only high school in the area, it mounted campaigns against polluting industries and so on.

The first distinctive aspect of the crime-prevention committee was the name it gave to itself and the program—the Safety Network. This name was significant because it was the outcome of much lively discussion about the expectations of government and the aspirations of local people for their community. The committee felt very strongly that the money ought to be used to create a safe environment through strengthening community networks and encouraging increased participation in community life. This was an approach quite different to the usual one, which encouraged greater isolation behind closed doors. Over a period of several years, the Safety Network asked local people for proposals for funding. Most of these programs were not focused on the symptoms of crime. They were targeted at strengthening underlying community, to increase people's sense of ownership of and involvement in community life. In other words, in a world where crime was a reflection of meeting an individual need outside of a context of mutuality, obligation and respect for others, this program aimed to strengthen social capital, to deepen community relationships and address underlying structural factors which were conducive to increased crime rates and the erosion of community values.

The Safety Network funded many programs over a number of years. Young people showed an interest in planning and running a pop festival in the area. Funds were provided for the group and the local youth centre worked in partnership with young people to hold a very successful festival. In the process many young people developed a sense of purpose, of contributing positively to their community. Some of these young people developed important organising and leadership skills and went on to become involved in other community activities of interest to young people.

Another community group was interested in providing low-cost food to families. Realising that many of the large gardens in the area had old and unused fruit trees, they wanted to harvest and preserve the fruit and make it available to local families. Funding from the Safety Network enabled them to start the Home Harvest project. This developed into a food cooperative and the group was able to rent a shopfront premises for its activities, which became the site for many other community group meetings as well.

The Safety Network won prizes and recognition for its approach and its work. This in turn fed into the traditional sense of pride of this so-called disadvantaged community. The recognition was also an acknowledgement of the leadership role played by the community in the overall crime-prevention program.

- What would you identify as some of the strengths of this 'disadvantaged' community?
- How would you describe its approach to crime prevention?
- What might be some of the factors enabling the different approach in this community?
- What might be some of the community outcomes of this approach? Compare them with the outcomes of the more traditional approaches, such as increasing home security.

Development

The word *development* can be even more problematic than the word *community*. In some circles 'development' has become a dirty word because of the devastating consequences of the dominant form of global economic development on the nations of the majority world. Space does not permit a full analysis of these processes beyond simply noting that such a model of development has resulted in profits for transnational capital and for the elites of the majority world, while at the same time resulting in hunger and starvation for many of the poor, the breakdown of village communities, the creation of slums and urban fringe-dwellers and the decline of basic health, education and social services (Norgaard 1994; Trainer 1989; Shiva 1989; Serageldin 1995). Community development projects within this model have reinforced the process and have been part of the oppression of the most disadvantaged people. It is the responsibility of those seeking to undertake community development projects to ensure that such models are rejected and alternatives developed.

The economies of the world are subject to the forces of globalisation, an agenda basically set by the demands of transnational capital. These demands, as well as their spectacular global financial failures, are now affecting the economies of many of the so-called wealthy nations in the same direction (though not, so far, to the same extent) as those of the less wealthy. Deregulation of financial markets, the elimination of tariffs and barriers to 'free trade', privatisation, a widening gap between the rich and the poor, declining living standards, high unemployment, the cutting back of public services and the dismantling of the welfare state have become conventional economic wisdom in the countries of the English-speaking minority world (the United Kingdom, the United States, Canada, Australia and Aotearoa). This neo-conservative agenda has been pursued both by conservative governments (UK Conservatives, US Republicans, Canadian Progressive Conservatives, Australian Liberals, Aotearoa Nationals) and by governments with a more social democratic heritage (Labour in Aotearoa and the United Kingdom, Labor in Australia, Liberals in Canada, Democrats in the United States). The fact that such policies seem to be followed, irrespective of professed ideology in these five countries, indicates that the origins are not to be found within the countries themselves, or their governments, but rather in larger-scale transnational processes. The long-term consequences of such policies, if current trends continue, will be that those countries (or, in the case of the United States, large regions of them) will take on more of the characteristics of majority world nations, with wealthy elites and an increasingly powerless and underserviced group in poverty (Latouche 1991; Brecher & Costello 1994; Castells 1996). The so-called Global Financial Crisis, which started in 2008, is testimony to this.

This perspective suggests that the analysis of what has happened to the majority world should be of more than academic interest to the citizens of Australia, Aotearoa, Canada, the United Kingdom and the United States. The global economy is increasingly failing them too, and as they struggle to develop a viable alternative and regain control of their own social, economic and political affairs, the experience of the oppressed people of the world, and indeed the oppressed from within those countries, can be a source of learning and inspiration.

Alternative development

The traditional Western model of development, based on the modernisation theory (developing countries need to modernise and become like Western societies), has not been the only one applied in nations of the majority world. Alternative development models have been proposed by certain non-government aid agencies working from an explicit analysis of majority world oppression, such as Oxfam and Save the Children. These agencies have specifically aimed to develop and support community-level structures that enhance empowerment and which challenge the oppressive structures of the existing order (Campfens 1997; Ekins 1992; Serageldin 1995; Friedmann 1992; Chambers 1993; Rahman 1993; Seabrook 1993a, 1993b).

Such approaches to development characteristically involve the following: little if any reliance on government structures, local-level development, grounding in the local culture rather than imposing a model from outside, Indigenous leadership, specific addressing of the structures of disempowerment and high levels of participation by local people. They include the elimination of exploitation in development work. Further, notions of participation in development processes (Midgley 1986) give emphasis to control by people over decisions that affect their lives.

Such alternative models of development rely on the analysis of writers such as George (1992), Sachs (1992), Fanon (1961) and particularly Paulo Freire (1972). Freire's pioneering work in literacy programs in Brazil has implications way beyond his own particular experience and has been a source of inspiration to many people involved with community development (Lister 1994; Findlay 1994; Gaudiano & de Alba 1994; McLaren & Leonard 1993). For present purposes, the two important elements of Freire's work are his use of consciousness raising as a key component of development and his insistence that education and development must link the personal and the political. Thus, Freire requires that programs be grounded in the real-life experiences, sufferings and aspirations of the people as articulated by the people themselves, while at the same time these subjective experiences must be linked to an analysis of the broader social, economic and political structures that are the cause of people's oppression and disadvantage. It is only by showing how the personal and the political relate, in such a way that possibilities for action are revealed, that genuine empowerment can occur. This approach to action and development has been reflected by other writers such as Brian Fay (1975, 1987) and is a central focus of the approach to community development and community work practice described in this book.

CASE STUDY: Save the Children's child rights programming

Save the Children is one organisation that works from an alternative development paradigm, a rights-based approaches to development. Save the Children's work has a focus on children in the majority world.

Within the Save the Children approach, there are five dimensions of change, which are interrelated and mutually supporting and there are three fundamental pillars to development work.

The five dimensions of change are:

- Changes in the realisation of rights of children
- Changes in policies and practices which have an impact on children's rights
- Changes in equity and non-discrimination of children
- Changes in participation and active citizenship activity of children
- Changes in civil society's and communities' ability to support children's rights.

The three pillars of development work, which can be seen as development strategies, are:

- Direct actions taken to address violations of child rights, which will also serve to increase the credibility of any advocacy

- Strengthening the capacity of those who have a duty to uphold child rights to meet their obligations to children through improved legislation, policy, structures, institutions
- Strengthening children's understanding and capacity, as well as that of their carers and civil society, to claim their rights and to hold duty-bearers accountable.

- In what ways does the Save the Children approach to development reflect the features of an alternative model of development, as discussed in the previous paragraphs?

The wisdom of the oppressed

A fundamental principle of community development, as understood in the context of the previous chapters, is that wisdom comes from 'below' rather than from 'above'. This is emphasised in Freire's work, and in other consciousness-raising approaches, where people are assisted to articulate their own needs and to develop their own strategies of action in order to have those needs met (Kaufman & Alfonso 1997; Stiefel & Wolfe 1994; Holland & Blackburn 1998; Fals-Borda & Rahman 1991; Rahman 1993; Chambers 1993). Rather than being the source of wisdom, the 'expert' is simply a resource that may be used by the people to help them articulate and meet their own perceived needs. In the Australian context the empowerment-based poverty program of the Brotherhood of St Laurence (Liffman 1978) piloted such an approach, where the service users were given complete control of the program and the professionals, such as social workers, were answerable to them and were in a resourcing rather than a directing role. This is a reversal of the traditional professional relationship in the so-called helping professions and represents an important move towards empowerment rather than disempowerment of the users of human services.

Structures of domination and oppression have resulted in the legitimising of the 'wisdom' of the dominant groups, while the alternative wisdoms of oppressed groups go unrecognised. Thus the dominant paradigm encourages the notion that wisdom lies with senior managers, policy makers, academics, researchers, leaders of the Christian Church, respected media commentators and the authors of books. While such knowledge is undoubtedly important, it essentially becomes the wisdom of the powerful, not of the powerless, despite the best intentions of the people involved. An empowerment-based approach, such as that of Freire, will, by contrast, value the wisdom of the powerless: the victims of structural oppression who are rendered inarticulate by the dominant forms of expression and communication. An essential component of a community development approach is not only to acknowledge the wisdom of the oppressed and their right to define their own needs and aspirations in their own way, but also to facilitate the expression of that wisdom within the wider society as an essential contribution to the welfare of the human race. Thus community development must incorporate strategies of consciousness raising and of ensuring that the voices of the oppressed are heard, acknowledged and valued. This is the process of building a culture of human rights.

A particularly important component of the wisdom of the oppressed is the wisdom of Indigenous people. Indigenous people in many countries have shown how it is possible to live in harmony with the natural environment, incorporating the ecological values identified in Chapter 2, and have been able to provide for the meeting of basic human needs through essentially community-based social, economic and political structures. They have thus incorporated the major components of community development as understood in this book and so they are an important source of wisdom—not just because of their status as some of the most oppressed people in Western societies but because their values, social structures and cultural traditions clearly point the way to alternatives from which mainstream Western society has much to learn. Therefore, community development with Indigenous people must move away from being understood as something that is done *to* Indigenous people to being seen as a way in which all of humanity can *learn from* those societies which have been able to maintain their organic links with the natural environment and their social base in human community. This is increasingly being recognised within the ecological movement and it is beginning to be acknowledged that in many cases Indigenous people's spiritual and social values form a more solid basis for sustaining strong social support networks and for tackling social problems than do the conventional mechanisms of the welfare state (Knudtson & Suzuki 1992).

Another significant group that has been disadvantaged by structural oppression is women. The feminist movement has sought to develop an alternative to the characteristically male, rational, mechanistic paradigm. Patriarchal structures have not only served to dominate and oppress women, but have also devalued an alternative world view that is typically more holistic and organic. Feminist theory has become an important influence on community development as it has demonstrated effectively how to link the personal and the political within a program of consciousness raising, education and social action.

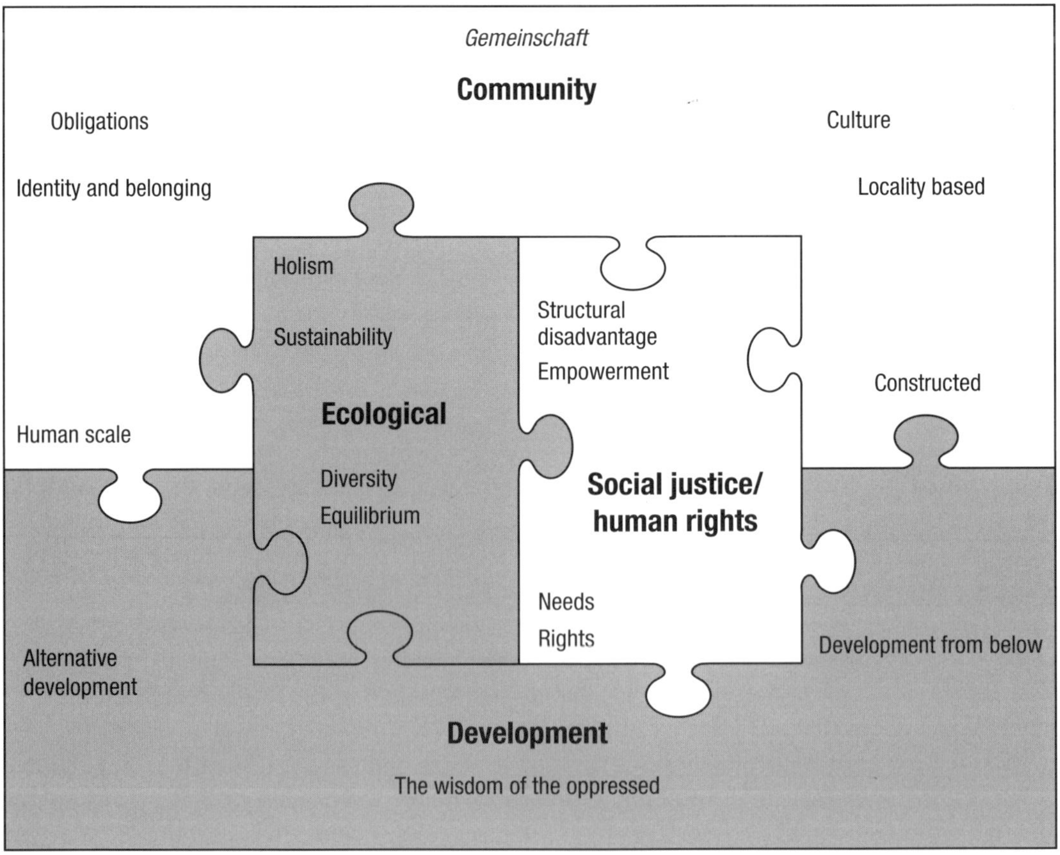

Figure 4.1 The vision of community development

The struggles of Indigenous people, women and other oppressed groups, such as ethnic and racial minorities, people with disabilities, gays and lesbians, the working class and the poor, contain many lessons for those interested in community development. The social movements that have developed from these struggles have sought to challenge the dominant structures of oppression and disadvantage. Many successful community workers have drawn heavily on the experience of labour organisers, civil rights activists, workers in the Indigenous rights movement and so on. Thus, the wisdom of the oppressed makes an important contribution, in terms of alternative values and world views, and in terms of the experience of struggle and change. This will be further developed in Chapter 5.

Figure 4.1 provides a visual representation of the discussion so far in this chapter, which has built a vision for community development by integrating ecological and social justice/human rights perspectives.

Community-based human services

It is now appropriate to revisit the idea of community-based human services. While the approach to community development outlined in this and subsequent chapters incorporates more than just human services, it is a human service perspective that particularly concerns many people working in the field of community work—the crisis in human services was an important theme in Chapter 1. Given the likely failure of the post-welfare state to continue to meet human needs and promote human rights, and the ecological unsustainability of large, centralised welfare state structures, it is important to consider how human services would look under a community-based model. If Western societies are in a period of instability and crisis, one of the most important needs will be to develop human services—such as health, education, housing, income security, law and order and care for dependent people—that are sustainable in times of crisis and which draw on the resources and expertise of the local community. In the community-based society human services will still be important, but they will be very different from human services as currently organised and experienced by both the users and the deliverers of the service.

Human services represent a particularly important aspect of community development because many community workers are employed from a human service base and expected to establish 'community-based' services in some form. Also many community workers come to community development from a background in the human services—as social workers, welfare workers, nurses, teachers, occupational therapists, psychologists, youth workers, recreation workers and so on. Thus the human services are an important focus for many community workers and a good deal of effective community development will begin from a basis in human service delivery.

Some of the ideas in the following paragraphs may seem hopelessly idealistic and naïve. Certainly they represent quite a radical departure from present practice, at least in Western societies, though they will perhaps be less remarkable to readers from other cultural traditions. However, it is important to engage in some 'visioning' of alternatives; if we do not, we have no clear idea of where we are headed. More importantly, the fact that these ideas may seem unachievable now does not mean that they will always be so. The context of practice is constantly changing and what may seem impossible today may be feasible tomorrow. In a rapidly changing world, where times of crisis create opportunities, it is very important to entertain 'unrealistic' ideas of a possible future.

Community-based solutions to social problems

One of the reasons for turning to community development as an alternative to more traditional forms of human services is that it holds a promise of a more adequate solution to many of the most pressing contemporary social problems. Problems such as unemployment, poverty, crime, loneliness, mental illness and domestic violence seem to be insoluble. Despite the best efforts of policy makers, social and behavioural scientists and human services professionals, these problems remain intractable and, if anything, are becoming more serious. As discussed in Chapter 3, this is largely due to the structural basis of such problems and from this perspective it is not surprising that they cannot be 'solved' while the basic structures of contemporary society remain intact.

The community development approach taken in this book challenges some of these structures and seeks alternatives to the taken-for-granted assumptions of the existing social, economic and political system. In so doing it holds out a hope that some of these problems might indeed be adequately addressed. For example, a community-based approach to work, together with a localised economic system, has the potential to deal with the perceived problems of unemployment and poverty in a way that is not possible in the more conventional labour market. As another example, it has become clear to many that juvenile offending is much better dealt with in its community context, rather than being removed to the artificial environment of a court (Matthews 1988). Similarly, effective community development can significantly reduce loneliness, stress and mental health problems.

The implementation of a program of community development can serve as a basis for addressing many of the social problems of contemporary society. This does not mean that there would be no need for human services in such an alternative society: there would still be a need for education, people would still fall ill, people would still need food, shelter and financial security, there would still be personal and interpersonal pain and suffering and there would still be some degree of 'antisocial' behaviour; these are part and parcel of the human condition. In a community-based system, however, services to address these issues would be organised very differently. The transformation of a local, publicly funded podiatry service illustrates the ways in which services can reorganise towards a more community-based approach, as the following case study demonstrates.

CASE STUDY: A service becomes community based

The podiatry service within a local community health service consisted of a single podiatrist. The health service was increasingly embracing more of a community development approach in many areas of its work. This included even its small medical service and its doctors. The podiatrist could see no leeway for change, as her waiting list was six months long and any distraction from seeing clients would only further lengthen the waiting list and, from her point of view, further disadvantage her clients, who were unable to afford private podiatry. She provided the only public podiatry services.

After exploration of the issues and difficulties, it became clear that many of her clients were older residents requiring only pedicure services. But what was significant was the sense from the podiatrist that these people were lonely and that their visits to the doctor and podiatrist were their only social outings. Much discussion ensued, which led to the podiatrist agreeing to trial a new approach. An advertisement was placed in the local newspaper calling for people interested in training as pedicurists. Twenty volunteers replied and were trained over four weeks. This team of pedicurists used the health services premises to provide services to the older clients. Health service volunteers used the government vehicles to transport the people to the health centre. Cups of tea and biscuits were provided. The older people sat around and chatted, both to the volunteers and to each other. The service developed into a very lively group drop-in program, dealing very effectively with issues of loneliness and isolation among the elderly, as well as foot care. When the program was fully operational, it required about two hours per week of the podiatrist's time to give support and skills training to the volunteers. After some time, the volunteers approached the health service physiotherapists for training to provide older people with basic massage. This was then added to their services.

The podiatrist was amazed that there was a way out of her seemingly intractable and worsening waiting list. She was inspired by the way in which the new program dealt with issues such as isolation, in addition to the needs traditionally satisfied by a podiatrist. She became a staunch advocate of a community-based approach and, as such, was a strategic ally in encouraging change in other parts of the health service, where overstretched health workers could not envision anything beyond long waiting lists and constant demands to react to crises.

- In what ways did the transformation of this podiatry service become more community based?
- In what ways did it more effectively deal with major social issues facing elderly people in society?
- How could the podiatrist become a change agent and catalyst for extending and developing the notion of community-based services in her agency or beyond it?

Characteristics of community-based services

As indicated in Chapter 1, the term *community-based* has been used with a variety of meanings and in some instances has been a euphemism for gender oppression, support for privatisation, erosion of public responsibility and so on. From the community development perspective, however, community-based human services are a fundamental component of an alternative society and they have the potential to replace the existing system with one that is more strongly based on principles of ecological sustainability and social justice/human rights.

The essence of this approach to human services is that the community must be responsible not only for the delivery of services but also for the identification of needs, planning of services to meet those needs, establishment of priorities within and among 'competing' services and monitoring and evaluation of programs. Under the current system many of these processes are undertaken centrally, as part of government 'policy', and this effectively disempowers local community initiative. It is only when all aspects of service delivery are controlled at community level, by the people most directly affected, that human services can be said to be genuinely community based. It is for the community itself to decide what is needed, how it should be initiated, how it should be provided and how it should be evaluated—subject, of course, to ecological, social justice and human rights constraints.

Placing primary responsibility for service delivery with the local community means that a community would utilise its own strengths in terms of human resources, expertise and so on. Services would be designed and provided by and for local community members, rather than being designed and provided by expert technicians from elsewhere. Personal experience, local knowledge, understanding and wisdom become highly valued, whereas the welfare state effectively devalues them in favour of anonymous central uniformity.

The community-based perspective requires a move away from the model of individualised and professionalised services, such as case management, which has increasingly dominated human services in industrial societies. There are three main reasons for such a change.

First, the individual/professional model reinforces individual rather than community definitions of problems and their solutions. This is inherently conservative and does not allow for the structural and poststructural factors identified in Chapter 3 to be addressed. Failure to address these issues will inevitably mean that programs and solutions will not really solve anything and will, at best, only prevent things from becoming worse.

Second, there is the very practical consideration that individualised and professionalised services are very expensive and cannot be afforded for all members of the society at a level sufficient to meet all human needs. This leads to the rationing of services and increasing inequity, where some people have to miss out or receive second-best. Given the dominance of the market, these tend to be low-income people who cannot afford to pay for services, but they can also be from other groups (e.g. rural communities, refugees, women, Indigenous people and residents of outer suburban areas).

Third, individualised and professionalised services do not empower communities or service users because knowledge and wisdom tend to be confined to the professionals and are not shared with others. Thus existing power inequalities are reinforced rather than challenged and people do not gain more control over their own lives.

An alternative community-based model would focus on skill sharing and on helping community members to use their existing skills and wisdom and further develop skills in providing services to others. Knowledge and skills would be 'owned' at the community level and shared widely among community members. Services would not, for the most part, be organised or primarily provided by outside professional experts but would be relocated in the community itself (which is where they have always been throughout human history, except for the past 200 years).

Local communities would have real authority and responsibility to manage services in the way that best suits them. The local community would establish its own priorities—for example, in the use of health resources. Service providers, including human service professionals, would be directly accountable to the local community. Professional monopolies would be dismantled and the resources of all people in the community would be used to help solve problems and provide services; thus education would become an experience in which many people, not just professional educators, contribute and where everyone learns from each other. The contribution of all community members would be valued and encouraged. Community facilities (schools, clinics, offices, halls, etc.) would be shared, rather than used for a single purpose, and various community activities would be integrated. Problems would be dealt with in their community context rather than in a removed and artificial environment. As an example, the justice system would be community based so that offending behaviour could be dealt with in its community context (Matthews 1988) rather than through the alienating formal mechanisms of the courts. Dependent people would be seen as the community's responsibility, rather than the family's or the state's, and the community itself would determine how best their needs might be met. Where people need personal or emotional support they would be able to seek it from other community members, rather than from paid counsellors or therapists, and the community would be organised in such a way that this support would be readily forthcoming. Even problems of poverty would be seen as the community's responsibility, but only as long as the community was in control of its local economy and the distribution of its own resources.

The following case study illustrates the ways in which local people can provide the support that is often considered to be the expertise of professionals.

CASE STUDY: Using local support, not professional expertise

In a part of rural south India, many local women were experiencing depression and the rate of suicide among them was somewhat alarming. This situation was consistent with World Health Organization data about mental illness and the higher prevalence among women, the role of poverty and gender oppression in these rates and so on. A lot of effort was put into talking with women in the villages. Stories were told and recorded. For the first time, the women were able to voice their concerns to health professionals who could work with them to develop responses. The women gave the workers many important messages about their experiences of depression, their views on what would help and their expectations about support. Many of the messages conveyed the women's sense of hopelessness, their belief that it was fate and their lack of expectation that they would ever receive any help or support.

In each of the villages there were at least two women's self-help groups engaged in income-generation programs. The women in these groups were also demonstrating their capacity to create positive changes in their villages by ousting illegal liquor stores, constructing concrete slabs around wells and so on. They were feeling quite powerful in many ways—and collectively so. These women were approached to see if they were interested in receiving training and ongoing support to become 'barefoot counsellors' for other women in their villages. The response was excited and enthusiastic. Thirty women were trained at the local primary health care organisation and returned to their villages ready to provide emotional support to women experiencing depression. Their social action experience as members of the self-help groups had made them aware of the structural oppressions facing women and contributing to depression and suicide and they were ready to challenge some of these.

At the same time, a group of women came to the health centre wanting to become street theatre performers after seeing a performance on the issue of female infanticide by a group that had visited their village. The health worker gave the would-be performers some of the stories from the women with depression and the group came back the next day with six small plays. The health worker worked with them to shape the plays and the performers went to many villages raising awareness about depression and its causes. Men, young people and women sat in front of their village temples in the evening to watch the performances, listen to the singing and take in some important messages.

- In what ways does this example show how local people can create structures to address important issues?
- How might the street performers be engaging in their own mental health promotion as well as helping other women with mental health issues?

Human service workers

Changing the approach to human services would require a radical reformulation of the various human service professions, including medicine, law, nursing, teaching, social work, psychology and occupational therapy. This does not mean that there would be no role for someone with specialist knowledge in these areas, but that this would be less at the level of service provision and more in terms of providing consultation for specific issues and in skilling local community members to deal effectively with particular situations. In developing such alternative models there are lessons to be learned from the experience of countries of the majority world. Basic health services, for example, can be provided at the village level by a local person who has undergone a special training program so it need not be the sole province of the medical practitioner; indeed most of the complaints people take to their GP could easily be dealt with by a community nurse or a community health worker. This would leave the highly trained medical practitioner with a very different role: to deal directly only with the more difficult or complex cases and to work to increase the skills not only of health workers but of all citizens to deal effectively with health matters. Similarly, professional teachers need not be in control of all aspects of a child's education; in fact it is a myth to assume that they are as a good deal of a person's learning (arguably the majority) takes place outside the formal education system. Those with professional qualifications in education could concentrate on skilling others to become good teachers and improving the level of education, in its broadest sense, in the community. The World Health Organization's comprehensive primary health care approach is an excellent model to radically reformulate professions and to share skills with people in communities; it is common in many majority world countries.

Within a comprehensive primary health care approach, primacy is given to community participation, local control and the accessibility, relevance, acceptability and affordability of health services and programs. A health service in south India is arranged in this way. At the local health centre the health professionals provide primary care where professional medical intervention is required. However, the health professionals also support paid workers who work in the villages (Rural Health Officers), each worker having responsibility for several villages and outcaste colonies. They, in turn, train and support health aides and family care volunteers who record the numbers of births, deaths and marriages in their villages and provide basic health education. The leaders of the village women's self-help groups also play important roles in identifying issues that require addressing to increase the health status of the village community. Much support and training is given to all these participants. Within this arrangement, health care has become deeply embedded in the community structures rather than just being provided externally by professionals.

The issue of professionalism relates to the broader range of human services professionals. A community-based model places a different perspective on the notion of professionalism. Some aspects of a professional model of practice are clearly still relevant and important, for example, practice according to a code of ethics, systematic use of knowledge and skills and so on. But there are other aspects of professionalism that work against the community-based model, namely the tendency to monopolise knowledge and skills, the 'status' aspects of professionalism and the claim to power and exclusivity on the basis of professional position. The relationship between professional

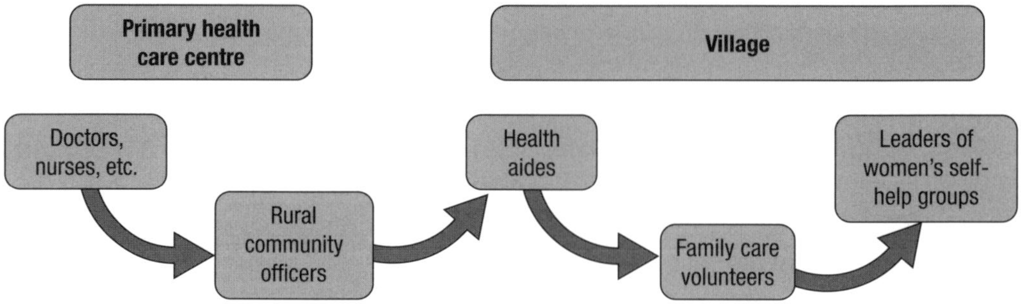

Figure 4.2 Alternative models of care in the majority world based on comprehensive primary health care

and client is, in practice, usually not one of empowerment (despite the rhetoric of some professions) but rather of disempowerment and the reinforcement of inequality.

Thus models of human service practice need to overcome these negative aspects of professionalism, whether or not the term *professional* is used. Such models would necessarily incorporate notions of sharing power, knowledge and skills with service users and teaching others how to use the knowledge and skills of the professional, rather than the professional laying exclusive claim to them. Thus education, in its broadest liberating and transformational sense, becomes a critical component of all human service work. Such a model also requires the end of professional jargon, which is used to confuse and mystify; thus, translating the insights, wisdom and knowledge of the professions into readily understood language (within each social and cultural context) is an important initiative.

Many different types of people, with different levels of training, have important roles in human services if these services are to be fully integrated into community structures. Professionals would have to accept working cooperatively (not hierarchically) with untrained people or people with lower levels of training, such as basically trained health workers providing primary health care and experienced community members with acknowledged wisdom working in the education system.

The empowerment model has been piloted in a number of settings, for example the Brotherhood of St Laurence in its work with low-income families (Liffman 1978), alternative schools, housing cooperatives and community health clinics. It requires human service workers to understand the nature of, and their position and agency in relation to, power, inequality and structural disadvantage. It also requires them to be able to enter into genuine dialogue with service users in a partnership model. This, in turn, requires the building of appropriate structures for basing human services in the local community and thus all human service workers would need some skills in community development work, as described in later chapters.

Human service workers would be primarily accountable to the local community rather than to a central bureaucracy, the 'discipline of the market' or a professional body. This would be through some form of community management committee or local government structure. The human service worker would have to be prepared to accept that 'the community knows best' what sort of service it needs and be able to communicate effectively with local community organisations.

Community-based management structures are not without their problems. Conflicts of interest, personality clashes, local politics, professional egos, traditional rivalries, ideological differences and personal agendas can all interfere with the effective and harmonious operation of community-based programs. Community-based workers need to be aware of these potential conflicts and be able to work effectively with them. Genuinely community-based programs can operate only if these tensions are adequately managed; the community-based worker needs to be politically and socially astute and able to institute appropriate conflict-resolution and consensus-building strategies.

Community-based human service workers would need to primarily be generalists. The ecological perspective suggests that the high level of specialisation is now creating more problems than it solves and that a more holistic perspective is essential. Therefore a human service worker needs be able to understand the issue with which they are working in a broad context and relate to different elements of people's reality. There would inevitably be some continuing need for specialists in particular cases. These would probably be located in larger population centres, for cases that could not be dealt with using the resources and expertise of the local community. Unlike in the present system, however, in a community-based system specialists would not be seen as having superior status to generalists but would be seen rather as a last resort for referral, to be used only if necessary.

As human service workers would be employed by their local community, ideally their services would be funded from this source using locally raised revenue. Human service workers would be contributing to, and benefiting from, a primarily local economy in the same way as other workers. They could expect some of their 'pay' to be in the form of return goods and services rather than in cash or as credit in a local trading system. Salaries might not be particularly high within such a system, but this would be true of all workers as high incomes and high-consumption lifestyles are clearly unsustainable for more than a small minority and are incompatible with a community-based society established on ecological and social justice/human rights principles.

Many human service workers would work part-time and do other work of benefit to the community the rest of the time. It would probably be difficult in this regard to define a boundary between their 'work' and their role as citizens. This would be a general characteristic of work in a community-based society and would apply to all occupations. Only an industrial capitalist system requires a clear distinction between 'work' and 'non-work'.

Human service workers would not be 'supervised' from a central point as this is a characteristic of a hierarchical and bureaucratic system. The primary accountability would be to the community. However, networking with workers from other communities (whether in person or using communication technology) would be critically important as a mechanism for the spread of knowledge and experience and for the improvement of practice.

Education for human service workers would inevitably be formulated differently. It would, of necessity incorporate skills in education, community development and working with community-level structures. A holistic approach to human service education would be essential. The human service worker would need a broad background of knowledge and skills and the capacity to integrate knowledge, understanding and wisdom from many sources, as well as the more conventional skills of their particular 'profession'. *Training* in human service work may be important, but *education* would be vital; this perspective is a direct reversal of the current competency-based instrumentalist approach to professional education. Much more of the educational curriculum would be delivered within community settings where an appreciation of how knowledge is continually generated by reflection of every new situation (Payne 2001) would be emphasised.

Finally, creativity, imagination, inspiration, initiative and enthusiasm are all attributes that would be highly desirable in a community-based human service worker. For this, education programs would need to incorporate a sense of vision and perspective as well as the more technical aspects of the job. In the community context, every work situation represents a new set of circumstances and a new challenge and a human service worker would have to respond in a new and creative way rather than applying the familiar practice formulas.

The role of government

The distinction between the *government* sector and the *non-government* sector in the provision of human services has been an important one in social policy and it has structured many debates on what have been seen as key social policy issues: the market versus the state, the role of non-government agencies, privatisation and so on. The community-based perspective renders this distinction less relevant. Community-based services would be neither government nor non-government in the conventional meanings of these terms. While having some characteristics of some non-government agencies (especially small organisations based on a self-help model), they would not be accountable merely to a limited membership-based constituency (e.g. a particular client group, an interest group, the Church), nor would they be primarily motivated by the desire for profit, as is the case with market-based services. Similarly, they would not have the normally understood characteristics of government services, such as centralised bureaucracy, primary accountability upwards and uniform regulations, though they would also, in a very real sense, be *public* services, in that they would be held publicly responsible and accountable. They would still be located within a structure of government and of public decision making, but in one based on revitalised local communities.

Conventional bureaucratic structures assign relatively little value to face-to-face contact with service users and values instead management, administration, supervision and planning. This is the consequence of organisational imperatives based on the needs of the organisation that will inevitably take precedence over the needs of service users, despite the best efforts of well-intentioned workers to make it otherwise. Much of the energy and resources of a bureaucratic organisation go to maintaining and reinforcing hierarchy, rational planning and decision making, patriarchal domination and the reinforcement of status, promotion, salary differentials and so on. The hierarchy inevitably values those at the 'top' more than those at the 'bottom' and encourages those working within it to hold similar hierarchical values. This is reflected in salary structures, other rewards (size of office, furniture, travel, allowances, cars, etc.), the way in which organisational charts are drawn, the titles of positions (especially the use of words like *manager* and *director*), the importance attached to 'promotion' or 'career advancement' and so on. Wisdom is seen as located at the top of the organisation rather than at the bottom. Decisions are made at higher levels and communicated downwards; communication in the opposite direction is seen primarily as involving data and information on which decisions can be made, rather than wisdom and understanding.

Readers could object that this is a caricature of contemporary bureaucracy and that modern management practices are different. The essential issue, however, is that whatever modern management may attempt, the basic attributes of hierarchical structures remain essentially unchanged. Modern management has not changed the value placed on 'senior' management (in terms of salary, status and mystique)—if anything, it has reinforced it. Modern management has not changed the essentially hierarchical nature of a bureaucracy, nor has it questioned the desire for 'promotion' and the assumption that the most important, interesting, enjoyable and influential work is done at the 'highest' levels. The person who is regarded as having 'done well' in their career is the one who has achieved rapid promotion and ended up as a highly paid manager, not the person who has remained at the lower levels of the organisation and continued to give high-quality service to the general public. Indeed, the main criterion for success in a career in the 'public service' is how quickly one can escape from a front-line role of actually providing a service to the public and move into the role of a supervisor, manager or policy maker.

This traditional, hierarchical view of human service organisations is based on an important assumption about power. This assumption is that the higher one's position in a hierarchy, the more one is able to achieve, the more power and influence one has and the more important and responsible are one's decisions. This means that the more skilled and competent people should be in the higher positions and that they should be paid more in recognition of the work they do. It also means that a person who wants to achieve power, whether for selfish motives or in order to bring about change, will seek to be promoted to the highest possible position as that is where their power will be maximised. Unfortunately it is often only when such people 'arrive at the top' that they find that they have been labouring under an illusion and that the assumption that power increases with organisational status is unfounded. Indeed, a common experience is that as one rises up the ladder, it is the constraints on power that increase and one finds one has increasingly less freedom and flexibility to make important decisions that affect people's lives. The decisions of senior managers and policy makers are normally so circumscribed by real or perceived political, economic and procedural constraints that they have in reality very little choice and most important decisions are not really decisions at all but merely represent the only possible response to a particular set of circumstances.

Community-based structures can represent an alternative to this hierarchical view of service organisations by relocating them on a small scale within a community context, controlled by the community itself rather than by managers and bureaucrats. This perspective is actually more consistent with the real world of the human services professional who, for the most part, will view 'the bureaucracy' as getting in the way of doing the job and who seeks to negotiate creative ways around bureaucratic regulation. The common complaint that management doesn't know what it is doing, continues to make silly decisions or doesn't understand what it is really like to work at the coalface is a further indication that the reality of bureaucratised human service work is not as it would appear to be from the organisational chart.

Simply reforming the bureaucracy and flattening or inverting the hierarchies would not bring about a genuinely community-based alternative. Even such a radically reformed bureaucracy would be inadequate because it would still be a hierarchy (although a flattened or inverted one) and would still be a large, centralised organisation. This could be only an intermediate step towards the eventual abolition of hierarchical structures, to be replaced with other forms of organisation based on collective decision making, consensus processes and so on.

In a decentralised system, there would still be some role for central government as clearly some decisions would still have to be taken centrally. That role, however, would largely be confined to the setting of minimum standards of output (e.g. in health, education, housing) rather than determining how those standards are to be met or attempting to meet them itself. Central government also would have a critical role to play in the dissemination of information and the encouragement of networking (i.e. facilitating the sharing of wisdom and experience rather than pretending to possess all wisdom itself) and in specific regulations to ensure the maintenance of fundamental human rights and freedoms. There is thus a clear distinction to be made between the *enabling* functions of central government and the actual *delivery* of human services. Under a community-based model, central government has an important and indeed vital role in the former, but a minimal role in the latter. There would inevitably be some residual role for a central government in service delivery, but only in cases where a local community was unable to provide a service because of the need for specialised expertise, technology or resources. Such services would, however, be minimised in contrast to current practice where, because of the obsession with high technology and specialisation, they are maximised (e.g. in high-tech medical treatment).

In the medium term, before a fully community-based system is instituted, central government would also have a role in the reallocation of resources because of the differing levels of resources available to communities for development. In the long term this could be reduced because of the equalising effects of local economic systems once they are properly established. However, even though economic decentralisation would reduce inequality between regions by reducing the extent to which resources were extracted from a community and transferred elsewhere, some inequality would remain because of differing levels of both the quality and the quantity of natural resources. There would still be some role for a central government, in order to maintain equity between different communities; overall, however, the role of central government in actual service delivery would be minimal and local government structures would be much more significant for all aspects of human activity. The reform and revitalisation of local government must, therefore, represent a major thrust of community development aimed at the establishment of an alternative future society.

The relocation of services at a more decentralised or community-based level does not imply that there is one level of decentralisation that is appropriate for all services. There is no single ideal size for a community base as this will vary between communities and also depend on the type of service. Some human services are better organised at an extremely localised level (e.g. child care), while others (e.g. medical care) may be better organised on a somewhat larger scale. Thus there would be a continuum of size of community base, from neighbourhood to region, but the important principle to be maintained throughout would be the fundamental principle of decentralisation—that no activity should be organised at any more centralised a level than necessary. The onus would be on those who wanted to centralise to demonstrate the benefits of such a move rather than on those who wanted to decentralise; services would always be decentralised as much as possible unless there were clearly demonstrated (and democratically agreed) reasons for doing otherwise.

An alternative vision: grounds for hope

The perspectives described thus far, taken together, represent a vision of a future society based on the principles of ecology and of social justice and human rights, achievable through an empowerment approach to the development of community, where human needs are met primarily at the community level. At this point it might be objected that such a vision is 'fine in theory' but really impossible to achieve and the vision might be dismissed as 'naïve' and 'hopelessly idealistic'. This is an important criticism levelled at most radical alternatives and it is necessary to consider its significance.

A sense of an alternative vision is not particularly fashionable at the present time yet, if creative solutions are to be found for the crisis of Western society, such thinking is essential. Positivism, modernism and the Cartesian world view have led to the de-emphasising of utopian or visionary thinking. The rationalist, pragmatic paradigm easily dismisses it as 'unrealistic' and impractical. Perhaps the ultimate expression of this is Fukuyama's (1992) argument that we have reached 'the end of history' with a convergence towards American liberal democracy (despite its blatant unsustainability and inequity).

The importance of an alternative vision—or a 'light on the hill'—is not necessarily that it will ever be achieved in full (it is this assumption that leads to criticism of its being 'unrealistic'). Rather it serves as a source of inspiration for change and as a framework for interpreting and seeking change from the perspective of medium- and long-term goals instead of being purely reactive. It allows one to seek an alternative paradigm, whereas purely reactive 'problem solving' and an insistence on being realistic mean being permanently imprisoned within the existing dominant paradigm. If we are to change the world we must be able to say, with Martin Luther King, 'I have a dream' and we must seek to share our vision of a better world.

Criticism of visionary perspectives often leads to disillusionment. The obstacles to change, in the form of institutions, structures, traditions and vested interests, are dauntingly powerful and it is easy to be overwhelmed and disempowered by the strength of the forces opposing change. However, there are some important reasons for cautious optimism and grounds for hope that change towards the kind of society envisioned in this and earlier chapters might be achievable.

One sign of hope is simply the impossibility of the existing order continuing for very much longer. As pointed out in Chapters 1 and 2, the existing social, economic and political order is blatantly unsustainable and because of this some form of fundamental change will be inevitable. The question is not whether there will be change, but rather what kind of change it will be and whether it will be towards the kind of society envisaged here.

It is clear that the world is in a period of major crisis—ecological, social, economic and political. The existing order is both unsustainable and unstable and certainty, predictability and stability will not characterise the societies of the coming decades. It has become rather hackneyed to say that times of crisis are times of opportunity, but it is true that historical periods of instability allow new alternatives to emerge that would be unthinkable in more stable and certain times. Thus the period of crisis can also be expected to allow opportunities for creative and radical change. It is important therefore that different, innovative, community-based programs be tested, evaluated and reported so that in times of instability and potential system collapse there are alternative models available to which people can turn.

Another sign of hope is that these changes are already happening, as many of the case studies throughout this book illustrate. At the grassroots level, often in unspectacular and unacknowledged ways, increasing numbers of people in different countries are experimenting with community-based alternatives, such as local economic systems, community-based education and housing cooperatives (Ekins 1992; Dauncey 1988; Seabrook 1993a). It is not something totally new and untried that is being proposed: a community-based strategy, based on principles of ecology and social justice/human rights, is already emerging as a result of the initiative of ordinary people at the grassroots level who are turning away from mainstream structures rather than as a result of any deliberate government policy.

A final source of hope and optimism is the rise of social movements such as the People's Health Movement. It has been suggested that social movements, rather than traditional political parties, may represent the politics of the future, though it must be noted that there is disagreement as to their ultimate potential for radical change (Pakulski 1991; Burgmann 1993; Mendlovitz & Walker 1987; Jennett & Stewart 1989). The women's movement, the peace movement, the Green movement, the human rights movement and black liberation movements are responsible not only for providing alternative visions but also for providing people with ways in which activism can lead to the establishment of alternative structures. Certainly the impact of social movements on mainstream politics has been significant and for many activists social movements provide a much more promising avenue for social change than do more conventional political structures.

For these reasons, while the obstacles to change are undoubtedly significant, there are strong grounds for hope and optimism. It is in this belief, and in the conviction that people have both the opportunity and the responsibility to try to make the world a better place, that the approach to community development in the remaining chapters is firmly grounded.

>> discussion questions

1 What are the ways in which each of the perspectives—the ecological perspective and the human rights/social justice perspective—is insufficient, on its own, as a basis for community development?
2 How do the following concepts integrate the ecological perspective and human rights/social justice perspective: social sustainability, social/physical integration, intergenerational equity, global justice, ecocentric justice, environmental rights?
3 Read through the discussion on 'community'. In what ways is the concept of 'community' descriptive of what is and evaluative in terms of what can or ought to be?
4 How would you describe the characteristics of 'community'?
5 What are the arguments for preferring geographical over functional community?
6 What makes rural communities easier contexts for community development?
7 What factors mean that 'development' is a problematic concept? In what ways is globalisation affecting the traditional view of development (based on the modernisation theory)?
8 How do alternative views of modernisation challenge the modernisation theory?

>> reflective questions

1 How does the description of community offered in this chapter compare with your views of community and with your experiences of community?
2 If there are some differences between your views and the description of community offered in this chapter, do those differences have any impact on what you value about community? Do they support and strengthen your values, challenge them or extend them?
3 Given your values about community and an integrated ecological and human rights/social justice perspective, are there situations in which you would challenge people constructing 'community' in ways that may contravene ecological and human rights principles?
4 What are your views about the relative merits of geographical versus functional communities? On what are your views based—your assumptions, values or experience?
5 How do the various approaches to development discussed in this chapter relate to your values and to the principles of human rights/social justice and an ecological perspective?
6 The idea of community-based services proposed in this chapter has implications for who has power in decision making about services. What is your reaction to the significant power given to local people in this idea?
7 What are your reactions to the alternative vision for a future society? Explore where these reactions may come from and their implications for work in community development. Do their implications challenge your reactions?
8 Think about the notion of 'community' as 'becoming', rather than what exists. Now explore what this may mean for your community work. Exactly what is it you would be working in if 'community' is what is unfolding as well as what exists? What may it mean for providing spaces for community development? What may it mean in terms of your purpose of doing community work?
9 The word 'strengths' has appeared quite a lot throughout this chapter. At the same time, there has been a clear focus on the crisis and social problems we face. Reflect on the ways in which a strengths perspective may shape or influence the way we construct problems and the ways in which we may relate to communities and work with them. In what ways would a strengths approach be radically different to a problem-focused approach? What may this mean for such things as social justice, human rights, empowerment and sustainability?

CHAPTER 5

Change from below

Introduction

At the heart of community development is the idea of change from below. This is a natural consequence of the ecological and social justice perspectives discussed in Chapters 2 to 4 and was referred to a number of times in those chapters. The idea that the community should be able to determine its own needs and how they should be met, that people at the local level know best what they need and that communities should be self-directing and self-reliant is attractive and it is consistent with much of the ecological and social justice writing. Hence it is easy to incorporate it into the rhetoric of community development. People are readily persuaded by statements such as 'Communities should be self-reliant', 'There should be more power at the grassroots level', or 'People should be able to determine their own future'. But while it may be easy to state the rhetoric, the idea itself when put into practice is extremely radical, and for many people requires a major change of mindset (Salleh 1997). It goes against many of the dominant and prevailing views inherent in policy making and program management, particularly in the Western tradition. This, indeed, is one of the primary reasons for the failure of many community development programs: the idea of change from below, if moved from rhetoric to actual practice, challenges a number of taken-for-granted assumptions and threatens some powerful interests. It is important, therefore, to examine in more detail the idea of change from below and what it really involves. This will be undertaken initially in relation to the ideas of *valuing local knowledge*, *valuing local culture*, *valuing local resources*, *valuing local skills* and *valuing local processes*. After this discussion, four important theoretical traditions—*anarchism*, *postcolonialism*, *postmodernism* and *feminism*—will be used to provide theoretical substance to the idea of change from below.

Valuing local knowledge

Community workers face the temptation common to all human service workers: to assume that somehow they are the 'experts' with specialist knowledge to be brought to the community and used to 'help' in some way. Special expertise, after all, is the only claim to legitimacy that community workers can have: why else would they be intruding into other people's community life? Why should community members take any notice of them, unless they have something special to 'bring' to the community? There is no doubt that community workers often do have specialist knowledge, but to privilege this knowledge, and thereby to devalue the local knowledge of the community itself, is the antithesis of community development. The valuing of local knowledge is an essential component of any community development work and this can best be summed up by the phrase 'The community knows best'. After all, it is the members of the community who have the experience of that community—of its needs and problems, its strengths and positives and its unique characteristics. If we are to engage in a community development process, it must be done on the basis of this sort of local knowledge; in this regard the community worker, unless they have been a long-term member of that community, cannot claim to be the 'expert'. It is local community members who have this knowledge, wisdom and expertise and the role of the community worker is to listen and learn from the community, not to tell the community about its problems and its needs (Holland & Blackburn 1998).

The following case study illustrates an approach to strategic planning in community development that takes account of local knowledge.

CASE STUDY: Local knowledge informing strategic planning

A local community-based service undertook a strategic planning exercise every five or so years. On these occasions workers would consult with the community about what they wanted from the service. While this seemed very reasonable as a way of including local people's views, it was invariably the case that what the people wanted from the service was not possible. When it was time once again to undertake strategic planning, the process was questioned by a new community worker. The worker argued that asking people what they wanted of the service was inviting them to comment on the *professionals'* area of knowledge and that the professionals always had answers as to why what people wanted was not possible. He proposed an alternative way of helping the service decide its future directions, one which would value the knowledge of the people and which would represent fuller participation. He devised three questions to ask the people: (1) What is it like for you living in this community? (2) What things would you like to see improved? (3) If there were other people keen to do something, would you join in? The staff embarked on a process of asking these questions on the streets, in schools, at shopping centres and other local meeting places. Where the respondent showed some enthusiasm at the first question, the subsequent questions were asked. After some time, there were clear issues identified and many people willing to engage in strategies to address them. The issues included access to quality food, isolation, security, pollution and assisting youth. This transformed process ensured that the service's activities were solidly based on the lived experience of local people. It also meant that local people were mobilised collectively and they defined the strategies to address the issues. Consequently, the strategic planning process represented a form of participation that was much deeper than the usual 'community consultation'. (Refer to Chapter 6 for more discussion on participation.)

- How did this new process value local knowledge?
- What were the consequences for the service of listening to and engaging local people in the process of planning?

Unfortunately it is not usually the local community members who are seen as having the 'expertise'. The idea of being an expert is more usually applied to people who have undertaken formal courses of education, who have degrees or diplomas or who are members of a recognised profession (Chambers 1993). Such a notion of expertise is based on a different sort of knowledge—knowledge that is removed from the local and seen as universal: it applies in all situations. The engineer understands the physical laws that affect construction—the strength of materials, stresses and strains, forces, the effect of vibrations and so on—and this expert knowledge enables them to build bridges that will not fall down. This knowledge of physical laws can apply anywhere: building a bridge that will not fall down requires the same knowledge wherever the bridge is located. Of course that knowledge must include an understanding of different soils, climatic conditions and so on and how these can affect the stability of a bridge in different locations. But although the effects will vary with locality, it is still universal knowledge: the effect of clay soil on bridge foundations will be the same wherever that clay is located. There is, to be sure, some local knowledge that has to be taken into account. The kind of traffic that will use the bridge (whether pedestrian, motorised, horse-drawn or buffalo-drawn) will vary from place to place, as will such things as the games children want to play on the bridge (i.e. what sort of protective fencing is required for safety). But this local knowledge is relatively minor compared with the extent of local knowledge needed for community development.

Community development and bridge building are alike in that they need both local and universal knowledge. But community development must rely much more on local knowledge and correspondingly less on universal knowledge than is the case with bridge building. With universal knowledge, the worker from outside—the engineer or the community worker—is the acknowledged 'expert', who is likely to have much more knowledge than the people of the local community. But with local knowledge the outsider is not the 'expert'; the outsider must listen and learn from the local people, who clearly have far more relevant local knowledge and expertise. For the bridge builder, this is a fairly minor part of the whole exercise, but for a community worker this local knowledge is what is most important. The good community worker, therefore, will seek to value and validate that local knowledge, will listen and learn and will not assume that their external expertise can provide all (or even some) of the answers.

This may seem obvious, but such local knowledge is often devalued. There are several reasons for this. One is the professional socialisation of the community worker, who will often be trained in one of the human service professions (e.g. social work, nursing, education, psychology or recreation). The very idea of having a professional qualification carries with it some idea of expertise—specialist knowledge that is applied by the professional in the interests of the people they are working with. To question the validity or relevance of that expertise is to question the validity or relevance of the qualification itself and hence the self-concept of the worker concerned. For many workers it is important to identify with their qualifications; those qualifications give the worker a sense of legitimacy and confidence. It is therefore only natural for such a worker to value highly their external, and usually universal, knowledge and hence to devalue the local knowledge of the community. Professional identity is one of the factors that contribute to the devaluing of local knowledge, which can affect many community workers.

Another factor contributing to the devaluing of local knowledge is the way in which 'knowledge' has been understood within the mainstream discourse. The positivist paradigm, which values objective, scientific, verifiable and measurable knowledge, has been dominant in many academic disciplines to such an extent that it is often not questioned, which implies knowledge that is independent of its context, universally applicable and universally valid (Fay 1975). Usually the dominant construction of 'knowledge' is associated with the things we learn at school, at college or at university or the things we may learn from books or from the Internet. This tends not to be local, contextualised knowledge, but knowledge that is seen as universal in its application. This is further reinforced by information technology where that 'knowledge' has become equated with something that can be digitally stored and retrieved. This is inevitably objective, positive, decontextualised 'knowledge'; in such a world it is easy to forget that there are other forms of knowledge that are not so readily stored or accessed electronically (Bowers 2000).

Indigenous people from all over the world have continually emphasised the importance of other forms of 'knowledge'—spirituality, magic, beauty, nature, storytelling and knowledge of the land (Knudtson & Suzuki 1992)—and this resonates with the intuitive experience of many non-Indigenous people as well who realise that music, art, theatre, poetry, mountains, oceans, forests, animals, dance, love, laughter, games and local folklore can be profound conveyors of 'knowledge' (Narby 2006). This is knowledge that cannot be reduced to electronic impulses and so in the digital age it is readily marginalised and ignored. Yet this is the very kind of local knowledge, held by members of a community, which is vitally important for any process of community development.

A third reason for the devaluing of local knowledge is the prevalence of top-down organisations. Most organisations reflect top-down assumptions: for example, those at the 'top' of the organisation are paid more, have more prestige and more authority than those at the 'bottom' (Weber 1970). Managers, who are concerned with the 'big picture' (universal knowledge) and who determine overall policy and procedures, are seen as having more wisdom and are given more authority than front-line workers who are concerned with actually doing the work at the micro-level (local knowledge). The front-line workers, especially those with experience, accumulate a great deal of specific knowledge that is vital to actually getting the job done, but this does not achieve the same recognition or reward as the knowledge of the manager, nor is it likely to be recognised through MBA degrees, salary packages, expense accounts and attendance at conferences. Thus the very organisations in which we work, and which in their structures reflect dominant values and world views, serve to reinforce the privileging of universal knowledge over local knowledge.

Thus the valuing of local knowledge—so important for community work—is made difficult by many of the taken-for-granted assumptions about the world that affect community workers no less than others. The idea that 'the community knows best' is in many ways a radical notion, given that professionals, politicians, academics, researchers, policy analysts, bureaucrats and others in positions of power have become used to the idea that *they* know best and that their proper role is to find solutions for the problems of others and, if necessary, impose them. The idea that the people themselves might know better challenges the very structures and discourses of power that are responsible for their positions of privilege and so it is an idea that will not always be warmly welcomed.

The ease with which local knowledge can be devalued is seen in the readiness of many people and communities to seek the services of consultants, almost as the first step in any modern process of problem solving. Engaging an external consultant devalues local knowledge in two ways: first, it assumes that nobody from *within* the community has the necessary knowledge to apply to the problem; second, it assumes that the expertise that is needed can be supplied by someone external to the local context, thereby necessarily defining the needed 'knowledge' as universal rather than as local. A community development approach, however, would see this as disempowering and as devaluing the wisdom and expertise of the community (Haug 2000; Campfens 1997). It would first seek the required expertise from within the community, identifying what local wisdom and experience could be brought to bear and the range of knowledge and skills of the people within the community. It is only if it can be shown that the needed knowledge is not available from within the community that a community worker should accept that external expertise is required; a consultant should be the last resort, rather than the first. And even if it *is* necessary for such external expertise to be sought, it is important for a community worker to consider the possibility of someone from the local community acquiring that expertise themselves. This may not always be possible, of course, but a community development approach, by realising the potential for empowerment or disempowerment, will apply such an analysis to knowledge and expertise and will not rely on external expertise more often than is necessary.

There are times, of course, when external knowledge, of the kind that a community worker may contribute, can be both useful and necessary. It is also important to remember that the community worker does bring their own knowledge and expertise and that valuing local knowledge does not necessarily mean that the knowledge and expertise of the worker are ignored. The important principle is the idea of *knowledge sharing*: the community worker brings certain expertise and wisdom, as do members of the community. This means that each can learn from the other, so that the expertise of both worker and community is respected and validated. If the knowledge and wisdom can be shared, both worker and community will be enriched by the process and, working together, they will be able to move forward to appropriate action.

Valuing local culture

It is not only local *knowledge* that must be valued in the 'change from below' perspective. A community's local *culture* can also be eroded by the imposition of dominant values from outside, thereby devaluing and undermining the local community experience (Kleymeyer 1994). Community workers can readily be part of this erosion of local culture. Assumptions (often unconscious) by the community worker about the right way to do things, what is important, what is fair or right, protocols in interpersonal communication, the place of women, the proper way to raise children, the role of the family, the place of older people in society and the importance of education can conflict with the values of the community. The worker must be careful not to assume the superiority of their own cultural traditions and unless the worker is able to acknowledge and work within the local culture, their attempts at community development will not be successful.

To acknowledge and work within local culture, however, is not necessarily to agree with it or accept all local values and practices. There are many instances where a community's cultural values may not only conflict with the worker's but will also conflict with human rights principles. Examples might be a worker in a community where the subjugation of women is justified as part of traditional culture, a worker seeking to engage with a community where racist values predominate and where racism is both practised and tolerated and a worker in a community where a 'culture' of excessive alcohol consumption is the direct cause of significant domestic violence and abuse of women and children. These instances amount to human rights violations and the human rights perspective, as discussed in Chapter 3, clearly suggests that such 'cultural' values and practices are unacceptable and cannot be condoned by a community worker (Tesoriero 2008b; Kleymeyer 1994).

It is important, therefore, for community workers to be clear about the human rights perspective outlined in Chapter 3, as this becomes a yardstick by which to distinguish between a case where a community's cultural values and practices amount to human rights abuse and a case where there is simply a difference in the cultural traditions of the community and the worker. In the latter, it is important for the worker to be able to remove their 'cultural blinkers' and accept and validate local community culture—this can become a major focus of community development practice and will be discussed in Chapter 9. The former case, however, where the local culture is seen to be counter to principles of human rights, represents a particular challenge. There is little to be gained by a community worker adopting an overtly confrontationist position; this would simply result in the worker being rejected by the community. Rather, the community worker needs to remember two important things about culture. The first is that a 'culture' is never static: cultural values and practices are always changing and the challenge is to help the community engage with the process of cultural change in a reflective and developmental way. The second important thing to remember about 'culture' is that no culture is monolithic. There will be people in the community who do not fully agree with the dominant 'cultural' values and who do not engage in particular 'cultural' practices (or who do so with misgivings). Cultural values and practices are contested within communities and this is one of the reasons that cultures are dynamic rather than static. This cultural pluralism also allows the community worker to engage with the community in a way that does not necessarily validate cultural values and practices that conflict with human rights, but rather facilitates the community itself engaging in a process of cultural change and development. There is a fine line between such practice and the 'imposition' of values from outside the culture; to avoid crossing that line the community worker needs a clear understanding of a human rights perspective and also must make sure that the community itself is in control of the processes of change and development, as discussed below.

The important point is that local cultural values are significant in community development, and so it is essential for community workers to seek to understand and accept such local culture and, where possible, to validate it and work with it. To seek to impose a different set of values simply because the worker is more familiar and comfortable with them, is to engage in a form of cultural imperialism that is disempowering and runs counter to community development principles. Even where a community's cultural values and practices raise significant human rights issues, community workers need to respect and accept the importance of the local culture to the people of the community and use that as a starting point for working towards change.

CASE STUDY: Local culture contravenes human rights

The community development team in a local centre in Adelaide, South Australia, worked hard to encourage and increase community participation. So when a local group of public housing tenants approached the team wanting to become an action group concerned with public housing issues, the community workers were delighted and immediately offered support to the group. Group members said that they wanted the public housing authority to act more decisively and to be much more responsive to tenant demands to ensure a better quality of life. Because the group appeared to be well formed and clear in its objectives, the centre staff asked what support was needed. The group needed some meeting space and the use of photocopying facilities. These were offered and the offer taken up. Some weeks later, when a worker passed the photocopying machine, she noticed some photos being copied and recognised one of the photos as a photo of the home of an Indigenous family she knew well. She stopped and queried this with the group members. They responded that the homes of Indigenous people were not well kept and that they were going to campaign for these families to be relocated out of the area so that the quality of the area would be improved. The action group members were all non-Indigenous.

- How would this aspect of local culture raise important human rights issues? What are these issues?
- How could the workers use this as a starting point for working towards change in the community? What changes would they be aiming for—both immediate and in the longer term?

Valuing local resources

One of the important principles of community development is the principle of *self-reliance*, which derives directly from the ecological principle of sustainability (Haque 2000; Harcourt 1994). As described in Chapter 2, sustainability requires that structures be developed that are able to be maintained in the long term, by minimising the extent to which they draw on and consume external resources and the extent to which they create polluting or harmful products or outcomes. Self-reliance means that communities are essentially reliant on their own resources, rather than being dependent on externally provided resources (Kelly 1992).

Community-based structures in majority world countries are usually far from self-reliant. Resources—especially funding—are commonly obtained from the state through its various institutions. One of the contradictions of much community development that uses 'change from below' rhetoric is that it is often highly dependent on state financing and hence on the very welfare system it is supposed to replace. This is further reinforced by the 'Let's get a grant' mentality of many community workers, whose first reaction to any problem is to identify an external funding source in order to deal with it. Murphy and Cauchi capture the influence of the state on community development when, in relation to the government community capacity-building policies of the Victorian state government, they say:

> The fundamental principles underpinning community building are based largely on approaches which emphasise self-determination and self-reliance (i.e. that communities need to be empowered to manage their own affairs, which involves formulating their own solutions and the processes involved to achieve them).
>
> The problem with this is that most of the current crop of community-building policies and programs occurs within a strong framework of government priorities, government policies and government processes, which have been imposed on communities rather than have emanated from them.
>
> With little reference to communities beforehand, governments have decided that the community-building approach, most aspects of which seem to have been imported from the United States and the United Kingdom, contains the best strategies to strengthen communities and address their problems. (Murphy & Cauchi 2004, p. 3)

While such dependence on the state may be necessary in the short term, this usually comes at a great cost to bottom-up community development because the aim of community development must ultimately be self-reliance. Here, the resources of the state or of other external funding sources (e.g. churches, foundations) have to be reduced to a bare minimum or eliminated altogether. There are two important reasons for this. One is that reliance on external resources comes at a price, namely the price of loss of autonomy and independence; genuinely autonomous communities can flourish only in the absence of such external dependency as the experiences of those who have to rely on government grants, with their corresponding 'accountability requirements', can clearly testify. The other reason is that, as suggested in Chapter 1, the post-welfare state is not itself sustainable. If community-based structures are to replace the post-welfare state they must eventually be able to exist and sustain themselves without such reliance on external resources. Hence, without substantial self-reliance, community-based structures will not be viable in the long term.

In this regard, community workers in the minority world have much to learn from their counterparts in the majority world, who have had to develop models with only limited and insecure reliance on external sources. Community development in such a context has developed models of self-reliance significantly further than most projects in the minority world (Kelly 1992; Friedmann 1992; Seabrook 1993a; Chambers 1993; Campfens 1997; Ashford & Patkar 2001), where the temptation of government grants has been strong. Such an approach to development concentrates on identifying and developing all the resources available within the community itself and seeking to maximise these locally generated resources in the interests of the community. This, in turn, enables a community to operate autonomously and to establish genuine alternatives to centralised services and programs.

Thus to achieve self-reliance community workers and community groups need to explore the possibilities of creatively developing and using their own local resources rather than those obtained externally.

While 'resources' involve a variety of things—including skills, personnel, expertise, land and buildings—it is financial resources that are undoubtedly of primary importance for community projects and it is a lack of funds, more than any other single factor, that is the major obstacle to the successful establishment and development of many community-based structures. For this reason the economic aspects of community development are critically important to enable communities to explore other ways of becoming economically viable within a model of self-reliance. (Approaches to community economic development will be discussed in more detail in Chapter 9.)

Valuing local skills

One aspect of valuing local resources which requires special mention is the valuing of local skills. Just as with other kinds of resources, local skills can easily be passed over by an eager community worker, yet the same argument applies to skills as was applied above to knowledge. Outside expertise is often valued and sought, through consultants and others, when there are perfectly adequate skills available locally. Indeed, as with knowledge, local skills can often be more appropriate because they are grounded in local experience. But the really important point about valuing local skills is that, like valuing local knowledge, it empowers rather than disempowers. A community worker can value local skills by simply finding out the range of skills of people in the community. Often this will result in a surprisingly rich and wide-ranging list of available skills acquired by people at different stages of their life, perhaps through work, spare-time interests or learned from family members. As a simple example, why pay an outside accountant to come in to help set up an accounting system if there is a retired person in the community with accounting skills who would be willing to contribute these skills to a community group? Often a community worker, and even many community members, will be unaware of the range of available skills unless they actually go looking for them and they will often, as a matter of course, seek external expertise without stopping to ask whether it is available locally. By using local skills, one is also valuing local people, providing people with an opportunity to make a meaningful contribution and strengthening the level of self-reliance and social capital within the community itself.

Skills, like knowledge, are brought to community development by a community worker and, as with knowledge, there is the additional problem that the worker, because of their own socialisation, may tend to value their own skills and devalue those held by community members. As with knowledge, it is important for a community worker to realise that many of the people in the community will have skills that the worker can never hope to acquire and that successful community development will depend on the utilisation of those skills to assist the community development process.

Again, as with knowledge, the idea of *skill-sharing* becomes important; the community worker can learn new skills from the community, just as community members may be able to learn new skills from the community worker and it is the mutual sharing of skills, and the 'skilling' of each other, that is important. (This will be discussed in more detail in Chapter 11.)

Valuing local processes

The processes that are used in community development need not be imported from outside, as there may be local community processes that are well understood and accepted by the local community (McCowan 1996). Again, however, the temptation for a community worker is to try to institute a process that they may have learned in a course, read about in a book or used successfully in a different context. As with knowledge and skills, the socialisation of worker as 'expert' can result in the worker having a need to be seen as knowing how best it should be done and thereby feeling it is necessary to introduce processes that have their origins outside the community. There may, of course, be instances where this is appropriate, but there will be other occasions where to do so is to bypass and devalue the processes of the community itself. For example, the eager community worker may want to set up a public meeting to discuss an issue of concern and may have a set idea of what constitutes such a public meeting, including the kind of location (e.g. a church hall), the time (8 pm), the day (Thursday), the format (rules for debate, resolutions, voting, etc.), the facilitation (an independent chairperson) and the seating arrangements. This may not work in the particular community concerned; there may be a very different tradition of discussion and participation, or 8 pm may be a time that many people feel is unsafe, or Thursday might be the regular night for other local activities and so on. It is important for a community worker to seek to understand local community processes—how things are usually done—and work within this tradition. Of course local processes may be exclusionary: for example, key decisions may be made in the pub by a small group of powerful men. But the process set up by the community worker may also be exclusionary, though unintentionally, by using structures and practices with which people do not feel comfortable or by limiting the capacity of people to become involved and to have meaningful input. As with culture, understanding local processes does not mean that a community worker will necessarily want to always accept and validate them, but it is nonetheless essential to understand them, if only to know where to start.

Working in solidarity

The above discussion, of valuing local knowledge, culture, resources, skills and processes, emphasises one of the most important principles of community development: that the experience of the locals must be validated and used as a starting point by any community worker (Haug 2000). Barging in as the person with the expertise, intent on 'intervening' and bringing about change from a position of 'superior' knowledge and skills, will guarantee failure and will simply perpetuate structures and discourses of disadvantage and disempowerment. Yet it is amazing how often this happens as well-meaning people from many different professional backgrounds try to work from a community-based framework. It is very difficult for professionals, and many others who would not give themselves a 'professional' label, to be comfortable with the idea that they should not be busy, active, action-focused and outcome-driven as soon as they start to work with a community.

The community worker has to learn to step back, watch, listen, ask questions rather than provide answers, learn and try to understand. The community worker needs to acknowledge that the people of the community know much more about the community—its problems, issues, strengths, needs and ways of doing things—and that any community development process must be theirs, not the worker's.

A key component of community development work is the idea of *working in solidarity* with the people of that community. This implies that a community worker is not an independent actor who is following their own agenda, but rather has taken the time and trouble to understand the nature of the local community, the aims and aspirations of the people and the ways in which that community works. As a result, a community worker is able to join the people of that community in *their* struggle and is 'going in the same direction'. By working in this way, the worker participates in what Bhattacharyya claims is a central purpose of community development, the community's 'pursuit of solidarity and agency' (2004: p. 5). The agenda is firmly under the control of the community concerned and the community worker is not doing things 'for', 'to' or 'on behalf of' the community but rather *with* the community. Such a stance can be difficult for community workers who are socialised into being 'experts' of whatever sort and who believe that they have something more important to offer as a result of that expertise. It can also be difficult if the organisation that is responsible for the community development program (e.g. the agency that pays the community worker's salary) uses a more top-down perspective, emphasising 'proper lines of accountability', 'specifying outcomes and objectives', 'proper supervision of the worker', 'efficient management' and so on. The new public management influence on agencies exacerbates the difficulties. In some organisations, community workers who attend meetings after 5 pm must complete burdensome paperwork for insurance and risk management purposes. Nevertheless these obstacles have to be addressed if a community development project is to be effective.

Ideological and theoretical foundations for change from below

The idea of change from below is not new. It draws on several different ideological and theoretical foundations and community workers will vary in the relative importance they choose to give to each. The particular schools of thought discussed below, all of which have relevance for bottom-up practice or change from below, are *pluralism*, *democratic socialism*, *anarchism*, *postcolonialism*, *postmodernism* and *feminism*.

Pluralism

In simple terms, a pluralist position recognises that there is a diversity of interests in society and that power is not concentrated in a single location but is distributed among a number of different groups. Moving beyond this essentially descriptive position, an ideological pluralist would advocate the *desirability* of a distribution of power where no single interest group would become all-powerful but where, from the interplay of different interests, compromises would emerge that were likely to be in the best interests of all. Thus the concentration of too much power in any one location—whether government, unions, business, the media or the military—is seen as dangerous and society's best interests will be served if power is shared rather than concentrated. Decentralisation, self-reliance and change from below are, therefore, fully consistent with pluralism. However, the pluralist position does not *necessarily* support a strong bottom-up perspective. The various power groups need not be democratically structured, nor need they represent the views of their constituencies. This has, indeed, been one of the principal criticisms of corporatism (Mishra 1984), a position that has been based on the principles of pluralism (see Chapter 1). Further, a purely pluralist position takes no account of structural factors such as class, gender and race/ethnicity and its insistence on treating competing interest groups as implicitly equal serves to reinforce structural inequalities and preserve the status quo (which, from both an ecological and a social justice perspective, is the last thing we should want to do). Indeed, the very notion of *competing* interest groups is inconsistent with the cooperative perspective that is implied in much ecological and social justice/human rights thinking.

Pluralism can be used to advocate diversity without necessarily advocating fundamental change in the social, economic and political order; by itself, it leaves the basic structures untouched. Pluralism can be a potentially useful position from which to articulate opposition to particular trends and policies and to legitimise the idea of diversity within mainstream discourse. It fails, however, to provide an adequate framework for the kind of social, economic and political transformation foreshadowed in earlier chapters and cannot be accepted as a *sufficient* basis for the development of a community-based alternative that addresses the ecological and social justice agenda. To the extent that it both legitimises and encourages diversity, pluralism is an important idea within community development, but from the perspective of this book something further is needed.

Democratic socialism

A stronger ideological justification comes from the stream of democratic socialist thought, which emphasises participation and bottom-up development of socialist alternatives. This decentralised form of socialism is influenced by the work of a varied group of writers such as Benello (1992), Gorz (1989), Stilwell (1993) and Lipietz (1992).

With the increasing development and strength of transnational capitalism, governments have become almost as powerless as individuals in relation to the economic forces that control our lives. Governments must effectively operate within the parameters 'defined' by transnational capital or they face a lowering of their credit rating (determined by Moody's or Standard & Poor's, rather than by any elected or publicly accountable body) and a sudden flight of capital, leaving the nation's economy in ruins. Having surrendered most of their ability to control their economies in the name of deregulation, free trade and the global market, governments are now unable to implement many of the policies they or their electorate may wish and are effectively held to ransom by the forces of transnational capital. This consequent powerlessness of governments can be clearly seen in the inability of many so-called 'socialist' governments (such as Labor governments in Australia, Labour governments in Aotearoa and the United Kingdom and provincial NDP governments in Canada) to implement even moderate socialist programs or to achieve even minor reductions in class-based inequities. These governments have effectively had no option but to adopt policies of financial deregulation, privatisation, tax cuts, free trade and cutbacks in public services, regardless of their ideological inclinations or the wishes of the electorate. (See the fuller discussion of the impact of economic globalisation in Chapter 8.)

This has important implications for democratic socialists. The election of socialist governments becomes a relatively pointless exercise; an international perspective suggests that it is not particular governments, premiers or prime ministers who are to blame for inequality, unsustainability and injustice. They, indeed, may be as much victims as villains. A more profitable direction for democratic socialists is to look to more localised political struggle. At the local level, the potential for democratic control is greater and the influence of transnational capital less intrusive. While transnational capital can hold governments to ransom, and can require them to follow certain policies, it has less direct influence on local interactions—social activities, the economic choices of individuals and households, community politics and so on. It is true that cultural hegemony is strong and that we are exhorted and persuaded (largely through the mainstream media) to live our lives in particular ways. However, it is commonly more persuasion than threat and the sanctions against rebellious individuals, households and communities are nowhere near as strong as those facing governments.

From this perspective, the development of strong community-based structures represents a more likely context for the achievement of a democratic socialist society than does the parliamentary approach (Shannon 1991). It provides for the possibility of social or communal ownership of the means of production, though this requires production to be more locally based. Hence the decentralisation and localisation of the economy, political structures and human services represent a promising direction for democratic socialists. Capitalism can be seen as more vulnerable at the local level than at the national or transnational level and it is from a bottom-up perspective, rather than a more conventional top-down approach, that socialist alternatives are more likely to develop.

Anarchism

While anarchist thinking may not be perceived as having occupied a mainstream position in 20th-century radical thought, it has a long history as a basis for opposition to the established order (Marshall 1992a). Though the popular view of anarchism often equates it with irresponsibility, a breakdown of social relations or even terrorism and refuses to accord it the standing of a legitimate and reputable political philosophy, in reality anarchist writing is far removed from this stereotype (Ward 1988; Woodcock 1977; Marshall 1992a; Carter 1999). On the contrary, anarchist theory has a solid intellectual tradition and is fully consistent with the ecological and social justice/human rights perspectives outlined in earlier chapters.

To risk gross oversimplification, an anarchist position opposes hierarchy, authority and the intervention of the state in the lives of the people. It maintains that in conditions of freedom from such domination people are more likely to cooperate voluntarily with each other, as opposed to the conventional view, which sees authority and domination as necessary to maintaining control (Kropotkin 1972). Thus the relative absence of hierarchy and centralised control is seen as a precondition for the establishment of an effective social contract (Ward 1977) and for people to be able to lead more satisfactory and fulfilling lives. This view overturns much of the conventional wisdom about the desirability of planned and coordinated central structures (whether state or private) and centralised policy making. It therefore provides an interesting framework for understanding why so many of those traditional structures and processes do not work very well most of the time.

Murray Bookchin's social ecology (1990, 2004, 2005), which has been very influential in the Green movement, draws heavily on an anarchist analysis. For Bookchin, the domination of people by hierarchical forms of organisation is at the heart of the ecological crisis. Anarchist thinking has similarly influenced other writers who have been concerned with establishing local economies (such as Dobson 1993). The idea of 'small is beautiful' is also consistent with anarchist thinking and the move to develop structures, technologies, economies, production and decision making at a more human level is a central theme of anarchist writers. Community development writers in the social justice tradition have been less influenced by anarchist thought, because socialist, Marxist and feminist perspectives have tended to dominate attempts to develop alternative frameworks. Anarchist thinking has been more influential with the cooperative movement and the cooperative projects in Spain, which led eventually to Mondragon (Whyte & Whyte 1988; Morrison 1991; Craig 1993), though socialist analysis was also important in this process (Melnyk 1985). (Mondragon, the largest employer in the Basque country, is a network of employee-owned cooperatives and an example of how capital resources can be localised and democratised.)

Anarchist thinkers support notions of decentralisation and community control and would support so-called bottom-up development, though they would be suspicious of the *up* part of that term, as it implies the desirability of more centralised structures emerging. Anarchism provides a natural basis for the support of grassroots community development as it points strongly to the desirability of local autonomy, decentralisation and development, which starts at the grassroots level. However, anarchism remains a radical and, to many, suspect ideology. It is perhaps the most radical of all ideological positions, as it challenges in a fundamental way some of the most taken-for-granted assumptions about politics and it strongly criticises the notion of political and bureaucratic power and control; it is little wonder that it has been seen as a dangerous ideology, that its advocates have been demonised and that it has been at times ruthlessly suppressed. Nevertheless it strongly resonates with the idea of community development. Community workers are, to some degree at least, anarchists at heart, with their belief in the wisdom of the local and the importance of empowering communities to articulate and realise their own destiny. Anarchism is therefore an important ideological foundation for community development, and deserves further study and recognition by community workers.

Postcolonialism

Postcolonialism is a contested concept in postcolonial theory (Mongia 1996), but, for the purposes of this discussion, it refers to the body of thinking and writing that seeks to move beyond colonialist oppression to find a voice for those who have been silenced by that oppression and to challenge the perpetuation of structures and discourses of colonialism (Larsen 2000). The 'post' in postcolonialism may suggest a break with the past and a next stage. However, postcolonialism is discursive more than it is structural; that is, it is a critical discourse that names and examines the issues that emerge from the exploitative relations of colonialist practices and colonial relations.

Colonialism is associated with the attitudes of colonising nations, which occupy the land of other peoples and subject those colonised peoples to domination in the interests of territorial expansion, financial profit, or both. But there is a more subtle form of colonising evident in the contemporary world. One does not have to march in with an invading army or unilaterally grab land through the acts of so-called 'pioneers' to colonise another people. The forces of global capital, and the globalised culture that it has created, are imposing economic and cultural colonisation on societies throughout the world. These forces have eroded the usefulness of old binaries such as 'First' and 'Third Worlds' and the clarity of nation-states and national boundaries. The First World can be found in the Third World and the Third World in the First World. Globalisation is pervasive even though it has most commonly been associated with the influence of the United States—as the most powerful country in the world—and the global economy has created a global market for American products, from clothing and food to music and film, not to mention software and technology. But global colonisation is driven by the global economy rather than the US economy and so it is not simply American colonialism to which the world is now subjected (Barber 1995).

Colonialism refers to the attitudes and ideology that accompany *colonisation* (Said 1993). It represents a belief on the part of the colonisers in the superiority of their own culture, values and political/economic system over that of others and this justifies imposing their own 'naturally' superior system on others 'for their own good'. Colonialism, and the subtle and insidious way it operates, will be discussed in detail in Chapter 8 and its implications for community development will be examined. For present purposes it is sufficient to note that colonialist attitudes are alive and well in today's world. They can be seen in the operation of many UN agencies and in the work of a number of international aid and development agencies, as well as in the aid programs of national governments (Haug 2000). Global corporations, of course, are also often guilty of colonialism in the interest of profits.

Postcolonial thought is emancipatory. It seeks to recognise the pervasiveness of colonialism, to validate the voices of the colonised and to recognise and reverse patterns of colonialist domination. It identifies how powerful the voices of the colonisers have been, to the exclusion of others, and how this has stripped the colonised of their identity and devalued their culture. Postcolonial thought in cultural studies has served to argue that the people are not simply passive recipients of powerful forces, which shape them into puppets, consumers or subjects of capitalism. The masses contribute actively to culture building. They are creative, purposeful and can even be seditious and resistant. That there can be resistance in the relationship between the powerful and the subordinated is emancipatory. The potential for this to transform the identity and sense of strength of the colonised is immense. Furthermore, when the protest of diverse groups is linked, new alliances become possible and social movements can form. The foregrounding and legitimation of diversity takes a prominent position; this is highly consistent with the discussion in Chaper 2 of an ecological perspective. As Hoogvelt (1997, p. 170) states, 'postcolonial discourse . . . engage[s] in a radical rethink and reformulation of knowledge and social identities authored and authorized by colonialism and Western domination'.

Recent postcolonialist writers in international relations have made prominent many issues otherwise neglected by international relations literature. For example, Beier (2002) examines how European colonisation of America was legitimised by gendered and racialised discourses on Indigenous people, which kept Indigenous people marginalised and kept silent their knowledge. Nair's (2002) exploration of claims of human rights abuses in Myanmar exposes the contradictions within the discourse of the powerful Western nations where seemingly authoritative claims of human rights abuses are diluted because of their overriding economic interests. Hence postcolonialism is potentially a very important perspective for the understanding of community development as an emancipatory practice and for the affirmation of a 'change from below' perspective that seeks to validate other voices and allow space for the 'colonised' to affirm their own reality rather than be dictated to by the coloniser, even if the coloniser is a well-intentioned community worker. Postcolonialism is also powerful in the way it can inform what 'community participation' should mean, which will be considered more in Chapter 6.

Postcolonial theory challenges the claim that there is no longer community in many contexts. Postcolonialism offers the possibility that community may still exist, but be rendered invisible by other dominant discourses. It may be that the voices of the masses have been smokescreened and the activities of people in communities have been subjugated and colonised. Could it be that local people may be active, creative, even subversive and engaging actively in their relationships with the powerful, but that dominant discourses leave such activity out of sight. Could it be that local people are not silent, but, on the contrary, are highly reflexive in their views of and relationships with powerful, colonising and dominant institutions? Wynne (1996) claims that people's silence has been mistaken for trust when there is evidence that it is indicative of great lay reflexivity. Behind the silence, he contends, ordinary people negotiate their identities by taking into account a complex array of factors. These include their dependency on expert systems, their experience of a lack of agency, a sense of risk, an awareness of how institutions reconstruct history to confirm their own blamelessness and an interest in the evidence upon which they are supposed to have confidence in expert knowledge. Silence is not passive; it is busily constructing identity.

The place of workers in maintaining colonialist discourses is made clear in the following two case studies.

CASE STUDY: A worker learns about her colonialist views of a community

A meeting of community workers was discussing issues in their practice. Their turf included a patch of suburbia in the outer areas of an Australian capital city. This area was designated as one of the most disadvantaged and problematic areas in urban Australia. Poverty, single-parent families, child neglect and abuse, domestic violence and mental health issues were just some among a large list of indicators of a problematic area. The area attracted the attention of many agencies, from local government to child-protection agencies and the police. One worker reported a recent incident where a young boy ran away from an after-school program and she chased him, because of her duty of care as the worker in the program. It became clear to her that the boy was intent on giving her the run-around. It was dusk and out-of-hours for human service workers. The boy lured her into the infamous patch. As she ran through the area, along streets and in front of houses, she was amazed at what she saw. There were groups of children playing on the streets and in front yards. There were adults sitting on patio steps talking (albeit in many instances drinking as well). Children were jumping fences as they chased each other. The patch was a scene of vibrant evening activity. It contrasted dramatically with the worker's own neighbourhood where there were often no humans to be seen as they remained behind closed doors in the evening. The worker commented: 'This area we have all problematised and demonised reminded me of what our suburbs were like in the 1950s, what we have lost because of fear of others and what, as 9 to 5 workers, we have no idea still exists and is alive and well.'

- What are the work practices demonstrated here that tend to, even if inadvertently, support dominant discourses about communities in poverty and render community activity invisible?

CASE STUDY: Challenging colonialist views of community issues

A local community worker (a team leader in an agency with multiple roles) is engaged in a discussion initiated by a colleague (a caseworker in the area of child protection). The child-protection worker was discussing one of the families on her caseload, within her 'strengthening families in our neighbourhood' project. The father had smacked his son on his buttocks in quite a hard manner. The caseworker explained to her team leader that the boy had been in serious trouble and had been escorted home by the police. The worker was dismayed because she felt that the incident was evidence that, after working with the family for a year on the issue of violence, she had failed. The team leader reminded the worker that a year ago the father physically abused the boy constantly. Now the father and his son communicated much more. She asked if the worker could understand the smack on the buttocks as a response to the boy getting into serious trouble. The team leader also asked the worker if she had set goals with the family, as discussed earlier on. 'Yes,' said the worker, 'but their goals were simply avoiding the real issue of violence and abuse'. 'What were the goals?' the team leader asked. The worker replied that they included such things as the mother wanting her isolated daughter to develop friendships and so on. All of these goals were not about the real issue of violence and abuse.

- Do you think issues of isolation and lack of friendships are legitimate concerns of the mother?
- In what ways do professional and dominant discourses, such as domestic violence and child protection, serve not only to protect human rights but also to render invisible the discourses of the less powerful and so continue to colonise them?
- What would a postcolonial analysis say about this scenario? What would be entailed for the worker to radicalise her practice and challenge colonisation processes?

Postmodernism

Another important source for thinking about change from below and bottom-up practice is postmodernism. Postmodernism has had a major impact in the humanities and social sciences (e.g. Rosenau 1992; Seidman 1994; Lloyd & Thacker 1997), and has caused a significant questioning of the more conventional 'modernist' way of thinking about the world. One of the most important aspects of postmodernism has been its denial of a single rationality or world view from which to understand 'reality'. The idea of the of the 'meta-narrative' (Lyotard 1984) is that attempts to understand everything within a single narrative that 'makes sense' of everything are no longer valid (if indeed they ever were). There is, for a postmodernist, no single reality; rather, different realities are constantly being defined and redefined by different people in different contexts. Any attempt to develop a universalist understanding of history, politics or, indeed, community development, based on universally applicable generalisations, is effectively an attempt to impose one particular definition of reality on people and to privilege one view over others. This is closely related to Foucault's ideas of power as being constantly defined and redefined through changing discourses, rather than as being inherent in particular structures (Foucault 1980).

Postmodernism therefore emphasises the construction, deconstruction and reconstruction of multiple 'realities' in a world characterised by fragmentation and diversity rather than by unity and uniformity. It is in such constructions that 'reality' is created, rather than 'reality' being seen as having an independent objective existence. Modernism, by contrast, is seen as being concerned with unifying discourses, trying to fit everything together in a logical way that 'makes sense'. Modernism believes in progress and rationality in a way that postmodernism denies. Modernism assumes that there is one right answer or one best way to do something (e.g. community development), whereas postmodernism explicitly rejects such a notion and accepts multiple answers' as being equally valid. Modernism values unity and integration, while postmodernism values diversity and difference.

The relevance of postmodernism for a bottom-up perspective, or change from below, is clear. It provides a strong argument for the questioning of top-down practice, which is essentially modernist, and its valuing of diversity and difference allows for community experiences to be validated and for alternative voices to be raised and legitimised. Indeed, the postmodernist advocacy of diversity resonates with the ecological principle outlined in Chapter 2, which suggested diversity as an essential component of an ecological perspective. Postmodernism has much to offer community development—the process of community development can be seen as a process of allowing people to construct their own 'realities' at community level and engage in bottom-up development.

Foucault's emphasis on discourses of power, while not strictly within a narrowly defined postmodernism (authors differ on whether Foucault can be classified as a postmodernist; the term 'poststructuralist' is generally preferred), is also relevant here. As discussed in Chapter 3, Foucault emphasised *discourses* of power and how power is defined and redefined through changing discourses (Foucault 1972, 1979). A 'change from below' perspective of community development suggests that people in communities can engage in their own discourses of power and can have a real role in the reconstruction of power relationships that have adversely affected them. Indeed, it is only with an emphasis on the local and grassroots action for change that genuine discursive 'empowerment' can take place (Kleymeyer 1994; Kaufman & Alfonso 1997).

Before leaving postmodernism it is necessary to raise an important warning about the effect of a complete embracing of a postmodernist position for community development. Because postmodernism rejects meta-narratives, it also rejects the meta-narratives that can play an important role in community development, specifically the social justice meta-narratives of Chapter 3. Ideas of social justice, human rights, class, race and gender are usually cast as meta-narratives; they have been powerful forces in the motivation of community workers and in developing models of practice. To reject such meta-narratives in an enthusiastic embracing of postmodernism may indeed be counterproductive to community development (Ife 1999).

The community worker who is interested in postmodernism, and who sees it as important in informing community development practice, therefore needs to think critically about what contribution postmodernism can make. There are several lines such a consideration might take. One is to draw the distinction (Rosenau 1992) between *sceptical* and *affirmative* postmodernism. Sceptical postmodernism accepts an extreme relativism and can lead to a paralysis because of an inability to move beyond the immediate context. Affirmative postmodernism, on the other hand, emphasises the celebration of difference and the emancipatory potential of postmodernism to liberate and validate the voices of those who have been marginalised by an oppressive modernism. It therefore sees postmodernism as essential to genuine liberation and empowerment. This, clearly, has more relevance for community development than the more introspective sceptical version of postmodernism.

Another useful direction for community workers is to value the contribution of postmodernism without necessarily accepting the complete relativism of a postmodernist position. Hence postmodernism is seen as increasing our understanding of the world in which we live and work, rather than as requiring us to accept a particular world view. This view is more usually framed in terms of some variety of critical theory. In this sense, critical theory means an approach that validates difference and varying individual constructions of reality, while at the same time locating them within a more large-scale analysis of the oppressive structures. It thus refuses to see *structure* and *construction/discourse* as dualistically in opposition; rather, it seeks a framework in which both can contribute and where they can be held together. Critical theory emphasises the importance of understanding people's reality (or realities) and also of taking action to bring about change through the dismantling of structures of power and domination as well as the deconstruction and reconstruction of discursive power and social relations, and through opening up possibilities for people to take action to meet their self-defined needs.

The issue of postmodernism, poststructuralism and critical theory is complex and there is not space to explore it further here. While the position taken in this book is more consistent with a critical theory paradigm, this is in no way to minimise the significance of postmodernism or its relevance for community development.

Feminism

Feminism is another important perspective to inform change from below. The top-down, rational, managerial approach is characteristically patriarchal; from a feminist point of view it perpetuates structures and discourses of patriarchal domination and oppression (Kaplan 1997; Harcourt 1994; Jahan 1995).

It is not surprising that both the ecological and social justice/human rights perspectives, as discussed in Chapters 2 and 3, draw heavily on feminism. From the ecological perspective, feminism identifies patriarchal domination as one of the forces that has caused environmental devastation by emphasising the place of 'man' as dominant and 'his' role as to exploit the ecosystem for 'his' own benefit. Eco-feminist writers (Plumwood 1993; Shiva 1989; Salleh 1997; Warren 2000) have emphasised the links (from an eco-feminist perspective, the *necessary* links) between working for a genuinely sustainable ecosystem and the dismantling of patriarchal structures, processes and discourses. Similarly, from a social justice and human rights perspective, feminist writers have emphasised the significance of gender as a fundamental dimension of oppression (or, for some feminists, *the* fundamental dimension of oppression) and have demonstrated that the achievement of social justice and human rights will remain an impossible dream unless the issue of gender is adequately addressed as part of any change process.

For present purposes, however, the importance of feminism is its characterisation of top-down managerial structures as patriarchal and hence its close identification with a bottom-up perspective. Postmodern feminism reinforces this argument by emphasising the validation of the voices of the marginalised and linking this to the construction of alternative discourses of power, as discussed above.

Of course there are different varieties of feminism, and considerable disagreement between advocates of the different strands of feminist thought (Tong 1989; Williams 1989). Not all expressions of feminism are readily identified with a bottom-up approach to change. Liberal feminism, indeed, runs counter to such a view, as it does not question the structures or discourses of patriarchal power, but simply seeks to help women to compete equally within those patriarchal structures. The argument that feminism is an important perspective for the understanding of change from below specifically excludes such liberal understandings of feminism and instead refers to more radical formulations, such as structural feminism, poststructural feminism, radical feminism and eco-feminism. These are all forms of feminism that seek to change basic structures or discourses of power and oppression and the dismantling of top-down patriarchy.

Conclusion

This chapter has outlined the importance of the idea of change from below—or bottom-up practice—for community development. The idea of valuing local knowledge, skills, culture, resources and processes is important, but it is also radical, given the conventional wisdom of modern societies, which accept top-down structures and practices as a matter of course. Community development represents a direct challenge to this taken-for-granted acceptance of the top-down perspective—this represents one of the greatest challenges for a community worker. First, a worker must overcome their own socialisation within institutions that accept and reinforce the top-down approach, including the family, the education system, the workplace and the helping professions. It requires a radical rethink by many people in order to become effective community workers and to move beyond the orthodoxy of top-down thinking. This is why the various perspectives outlined in the later section of the chapter are so important, as they provide frameworks within which community workers are able to reformulate their ideas. Thinking bottom-up may be a radical position to take, but a community worker is not alone in taking such a position; it can be linked to several important intellectual traditions—anarchism, postcolonialism, postmodernism and feminism—and community workers can find much in the literature of these traditions to support their grassroots, bottom-up perspective.

The other related challenge for community development work is that the uncritical acceptance of a top-down perspective is likely to be evident within the community with which the community worker is engaged. People are likely to say that they don't really have the expertise, that they should be asking the 'outside expert', that the knowledge of external professionals is what is needed and so on. Local knowledge, skills, culture and processes are likely to be devalued by the very people who own them and community workers need to be able to engage with this 'learned powerlessness' as part of empowerment-based practice. Of course it is often not appropriate simply to ask community members to read radical feminist or anarchist literature (though in some circumstances this is a possibility). What is required of a community worker is the capacity to understand the insights of these various theoretical traditions and to reframe those insights in such a way that they relate to the lived experience of the people in the community and are grounded in their reality rather than the reality of academics and professionals. Thus community work can become a genuine dialogue about power, knowledge, wisdom and change and can seek to empower local community members to validate and use their own experience, knowledge, expertise and skills to work towards change.

>> discussion questions

1 What is the importance, in community development, of valuing local knowledge? How is local knowledge easily devalued by professionals? What are many of the taken-for-granted assumptions we can make about knowledge?
2 How does valuing local culture, local resources, local skills and local processes enable a bottom-up approach to community development?
3 What is the meaning of 'working in solidarity' with a community?
4 In what ways does a pluralist position stop short of ensuring a strong bottom-up perspective? How can it also be a useful counterfoil to those who want to maintain existing oppressive power structures?
5 How would you describe democratic socialism, anarchism and feminism as strong ideological justifications for the approach to community development taken in this book?
6 Colonialism disempowered those being colonised. How and why is postcolonialism an important idea in today's world, even when colonialism has long ended?
7 What are the contributions to and limitations of postmodernism for an ecological and human rights/social justice perspective of community development?
8 What are the problems with liberal feminism in supporting an ecological and human rights/social justice perspective of community development?

>> reflective questions

1 What would be your view of local knowledge and its value if you were working in a community? Where would these values originate? What might their implications be for a bottom-up approach to community development?
2 Do you think there are situations where local culture, skills and processes may run counter to human rights and social justice? What values of yours would suggest this is the case in these situations? Where do your values come from in terms of your experience, education, family, culture and so on?
3 What is your personal position in relation to each of the ideological justifications discussed in this chapter? What values do these positions reflect? Are they compatible with an ecological and human rights/social justice perspective of community development? If so, in what ways? If not, what changes would you need to consider to practise community development?
4 Think of a situation in your experience where power was wielded oppressively and identify your reactions to this. Now apply a postcolonial analysis to that situation and identify the extent to which your reactions and your analysis are similar or different. If there are differences, what are they and what does this mean for your own personal growth as a community worker?

CHAPTER 6

Participation

Introduction

Community development must always seek to maximise participation, with the aim being for everyone in the community to be actively involved in community processes and activities and to recreate community and personal futures. Participation is therefore an important part of empowerment and consciousness raising. It also is the means by which the concept of change from below is applied. The more people who are active participants and the more fully they participate, the more the ideals of community ownership and inclusive processes will be realised. Furthermore, as discussed in Chapter 2, it is not enough to simply assert particular human rights. For people to exercise their rights, they need to engage in processes with others and to influence decisions and balances of power. The right to good health requires engagement in the health care system, whether by simply visiting a doctor or, more politically, by lobbying for health reform, being a member of a health service committee or thinking about different political parties' health policies at election time. Which of these examples of participation are 'better' than others is a contested matter. A community worker may consider lobby groups and membership of committees to be the best forms of participation, whereas a doctor or a health manager, who wants to go down the path of least resistance, may prefer a top-down approach or want compliance from patients and a community may consider that being a passive service user is the best form of participation.

It is clear that participation is heavily value-laden and can be used differently by different people for different desired outcomes. The question of 'Who benefits?' has by no means a single, clear-cut answer. Despite the contested nature of participation, at a broad level participation has been an important consideration in operationalising change from below and in understanding the roles of citizens in democracies.

Participatory democracy

Democracy is an idea that is widely—if not universally—valued, though it is significant that its achievement has been difficult despite its widespread appeal. Democracy has many different meanings (Held 1987) and has been applied to so many differing situations that it is tempting to conclude that it has lost all substantive meaning. However, like those other much abused words 'community' and 'empowerment', democracy remains a powerful ideal and represents a crucial element in any attempt to derive a vision of a future society.

Democracy basically means rule of the people, but such a definition poses many questions. The conception of who are 'the people' has differed and it has seldom, if ever, meant all the people. In classical Athenian democracy slaves were excluded from the process as a matter of course. Until at least the late 19th century women were excluded in Western 'democracies' and in a number of countries Indigenous people have had to fight for representation in the democratic process. Even in modern 'enlightened' societies, which might consider themselves above such arbitrary forms of discrimination, many people are still denied any formal democratic participation, the most notable of such groups being people under the age of 18 and those who are not deemed to be citizens of the country in which they are living (the same restriction as applied in Athenian times).

Another issue is the question of what decisions will be taken by the people and what will be left to the individual, the family or an informal group. Are there constraints that should be placed on any form of rule, as anarchists would argue? If so, how does one determine those constraints? The 'rule of the people' can easily become the dictatorship of the people and the denial of fundamental freedoms. Making such a determination usually requires some form of definition of the 'common good', 'national interest' or 'general interest', as well as some form of definition of human rights and freedoms. These highly contentious questions, then, are inextricably linked to any consideration of the meaning and application of democracy.

For present purposes, however, the most important issue in the 'rule of the people' is how that rule will be exercised. In all but the smallest and simplest societies it is impractical to expect all the people to be able to be actively involved in all the decisions that have to be made. Hence some way has to be found to delegate decision making while retaining the democratic ideal—this leads to the notion of representative democracy. Although democracy (either in theory or in practice) takes many forms, and one can develop different models of how democratic systems either do or should work (Held 1987), these can be generally classified as varieties of either *representative* or *participatory* democracy. The former is more characteristic of modern industrial and post-industrial societies. In participatory democracy 'the people' participate directly in decision making, while in representative democracy the role of 'the people' is to select (usually through elections) those who are then entrusted to make the decisions on their behalf.

Some form of representative democracy is an inevitable consequence of large, complex, centralised societies, such as modern Western societies, and this has led to its being accepted as the 'normal' form of democracy and seldom questioned. Even at the local government level, where participatory models may be feasible, the representative model predominates and there has been little serious effort to develop participatory alternatives. There have been some notable exceptions, such as Ted Mack's approach to Australian local government in North Sydney (North Sydney Municipality 1990), and the 'precinct' system in operation in a number of local government authorities where meetings of local residents can have direct input into council decisions.

There are significant problems with representative democracy, which are highlighted by the Green and social justice/human rights positions described in previous chapters (Rayner 1998). Representative democracy involves an effective transfer of power to an elite (those elected) and a consequent disempowerment of 'the people' in whose interests democracy is supposed to work. It thus reinforces pluralist and elitist forms of politics, which are far from the empowerment ideal. It also encourages such strategies as corporatism, where decisions are made by leaders rather than as a result of democratic processes. The checks on the abuse of power, such as independent media, open access to information and rights of redress through the law, do not always work particularly effectively and are themselves often criticised for being controlled by the same elites and inaccessible to all but the wealthy and powerful. In such circumstances the effective power of the individual citizen is severely curtailed and is largely limited to the often symbolic gesture of voting every few years (and unless one happens to live in a marginal electorate this too can become a meaningless ritual). The nature of representative politics is such that the voter is often not confronted with an effective choice, such as when both major parties adopt similarly conservative policies and where the media does not legitimise any alternative party, as is the norm in many minority world 'democracies'. The supposedly democratic system then becomes a recipe for disempowerment. Many critics, of course, suggest that this is no accident and see the apparently 'democratic' structures as an effective way of maintaining the power of dominant social, economic and political interests and of legitimising the existing order. This view becomes even more plausible if we consider the adoption of neoliberalism and the new public management of neoliberal policy by many minority world representative democracies. Neoliberalism and the new public management, as discussed in Chapter 1, tend to transform the identity of people from active citizens to individualised consumers of commodities, where even such social resources as water, health and education are commodified. It is the increased sense of alienation that people experience in a large, complex society driven by technical expertise that some writers (Pateman 1970; Plant 1974; Kweit & Kweit 1981; Galiher et al. 1971) claim has largely generated an increasing interest in community participation.

In order to reverse the trends of alienation, a move towards a more participatory model of democracy is an important component of a community development strategy. There are four characteristics of a participatory democracy approach that are important for community development: *decentralisation*, *accountability*, *education* and *obligation*.

Decentralisation

Participatory democracy requires decentralised decision-making structures and decentralisation is a major component of an alternative vision based on ecological and social justice/human rights principles and change from below. While recognising that for some purposes more centralised decision making, or at least coordination, is required, the principle involved is that *no decision or function should occur at a more centralised level than is necessary*. Thus the onus is on those seeking to centralise to demonstrate the necessity for such a strategy and decentralisation becomes the norm rather than the exception. Centralised functions, where they exist, should preferably be those of coordination, information and resource provision and support for decentralised activities and structures. Mechanisms need to be developed to ensure that the perspective of the periphery, rather than the centre, is given priority when disputes arise; in the conventional view, the perspective of the centre is seen as the more valid because it is able to take an overview (Bryant 1995).

It must be pointed out that decentralisation is not without its problems and, like all such policies, it solves some problems and creates others. The problems of decentralisation tend to be associated with issues of equity and the maintenance of standards. These issues can be dealt with by more effective networking, communication and coordination rather than by central control and, as was argued in Chapter 1, the claims that the centralised state ensures equity are often illusory. A strategy of decentralisation is not without its problems and challenges, but from the perspective of participatory democracy these are outweighed by its advantages.

Accountability

The conventional view of accountability has been that of accountability upward or to the centre within a traditional bureaucratic structure. From a participatory democracy perspective, accountability downward or outward to the people directly concerned is much more important. Indeed such accountability is central to the idea of participatory democracy, as not only does participatory democracy involve 'the people' in making decisions but it requires that they be responsible for ensuring that those decisions are carried out.

Education

If people are to participate in decision making, they can be expected to do so successfully only if they are well informed about the issues at stake and the likely consequences of particular decisions. Making informed decisions requires a higher level of awareness and education (in its broadest sense, including consciousness raising; Freire 1972) than is generally understood as being necessary for participation in current forms of representative democracy. Without this awareness, attempts at participatory democracy can become merely a forum for reinforcing collective prejudice, scapegoating, stereotyping and ignorance, as can be the case with citizen-initiated referendums (Ife 2001). To embark on a program of participatory democracy without an effective education process is a recipe for failure and would serve only to support the views of those who see participatory democracy as unworkable.

Obligation

As discussed in Chapter 3, rights and obligations are linked and participatory democracy can be regarded as one instance of rights, namely people's right to self-determination and the right (and responsibility) to participate. With the exercise of these rights goes a corresponding obligation to be well informed on the relevant issues. An obligation to participate in community life is not highly valued in modern minority world society, where community has been significantly eroded or backgrounded. But such an obligation is a key component of participatory democracy. One cannot force people to participate (such coercion would, in any case, be counter to a non-violence approach), but a climate can be created in which people feel a strong moral obligation or duty to participate. One way to achieve this is to ensure that people's participation is genuine rather than token, as it is the tokenistic nature of many 'participation' programs of governments that dissuades people from participating. At best, this breeds cynical community members, who are easily able to detect tokenism and are unwilling to engage in useless 'consultations' and in making decisions with little import; at worst, it further disenfranchises and alienates already powerless people.

Deliberative democracy

One way to strengthen participatory democracy is through the idea of deliberative democracy. The way in which democracy is commonly understood is largely reactive; in a democracy we are allowed to react to the decisions of government and to seek to persuade the government to change its mind (classic pluralism). Sometimes a government will ask the community to comment on a particular proposal or plan, perhaps by inviting submissions or through a referendum. But in all these cases the role of the citizens is to react to a proposal that has already been developed or to choose between two or more specified alternatives. In such a case, the government has already determined the parameters of the choice, namely what options are 'acceptable', and has effectively 'set the rules' for citizen participation; people are asked to react to what has already been proposed rather than be part of developing proposals themselves. This contains very restricted and minimal citizen control over decisions. Deliberative democracy, however, seeks to establish mechanisms that enable citizens to participate in the deliberative process so that they can be part of actually forming the plan and developing the proposal (Saward 1998; Uhr 1998). This involves government engaging in dialogue with the community before developing a plan, rather than mounting a 'community consultation' after the plan has been developed, and seeks to draw on the wisdom and experience of the community. Like community development, deliberative democracy values the community's expertise, seeks a role for the community in defining the parameters of the issue and does not place the government in a position of being the 'expert' with superior knowledge and wisdom. Here there is a far greater degree of control in the hands of the people. Programs of deliberative democracy necessarily involve community education; realising that the problems are not easily solved, it is necessary to provide people with the knowledge and the resources to engage with the problem and to share with the government the complexity and the contradictions of dealing with issues and problems in contemporary society. It also requires a government to admit that it does not have all the answers (not easy for many politicians and bureaucrats, at least in public) and to be prepared to acknowledge the wisdom of the people. The agenda of deliberative democracy is similar to the agenda of community development; it requires a more active engagement at community level with the issues and problems facing the society and active and informed participation by citizens.

What is 'participation'?

A strategy of participatory democracy, then, is far from straightforward and involves more than simply setting up different structures and expecting them to work. It cannot be achieved quickly, as it involves reversing some strong trends in contemporary society. Rather, it must be seen as the result of a longer-term developmental process and thus becomes one of the goals (achieving human rights) as well as one of the mechanisms of community development. Within community work this has been seen in the long-standing concern for *participation* and in identifying how genuine citizen participation can be encouraged and maximised.

Participation, as a concept within community development, is widely and commonly used. It is a central concept in, and foundation principle of, community development because, among other things, it is closely linked with the notion of human rights. In this sense, participation is an end in itself; that is, it activates the notion of human rights, the right to participate in democracy and to strengthen deliberative democracy. As a process in community development, participation is connected to human rights in yet another way. If human rights are more than simply statements in Declarations—that is, if they entail actively building a culture of human rights—then ensuring that processes in community development are participatory is a significant contribution to building a culture of human rights—a culture where *citizen* participation is an expected, normal process in any decision-making endeavour. In this sense, participation is a means as well as an end, because it forms part of the foundation of the culture that enables the achievement of human rights. The 'means' and 'ends' debate has been a robust one in the development literature and the distinction between means and ends is an important one to be clear about. Oakley et al. (1991) provide a comparative analysis in Table 6.1.

Table 6.1 Comparison of participation as a means and an end

PARTICIPATION AS A MEANS	PARTICIPATION AS AN END
• It implies use of participation to achieve some predetermined goal or objective.	• It attempts to empower people to participate in their own development more meaningfully.
• It is an attempt to utilise the existing resources in order to achieve the objective of programs or projects.	• It attempts to ensure the increased role of people in development initiatives.
• The stress is on achieving the objectives and not so much on the act of participation itself.	• The focus is on improving the ability of the people to participate rather than just achieving the predetermined objectives of the project.
• It is more common in government programs, where the main concern is to mobilise the community and involve them in improving the efficiency of the delivery system.	• This view finds relatively less favour with government agencies. NGOs, in principle, agree with this viewpoint.
• The participation is generally short term.	• The participation is viewed as a long-term process.
• Participation as a means, therefore, appears to be a passive form of participation.	• Participation as an end is relatively more active and dynamic.

Source: A. Oakley et al. 1991, *Projects with People: The Practice of Participation in Rural Development*, International Labour Organization, Geneva.

Exploring the question 'What is participation?' yields a myriad of meanings. Uphoff and Cohen (1979) emphasise people having a role in decision making. Pearse and Stifel (1979, quoted in Kannan 2002) focus on people who are usually excluded from having control over resources and institutions. Paul (1987, quoted in Kannan 2002) contends that it must include the ability for people to influence activities in such a way as to enhance their wellbeing. Gahi (1990, quoted in Kannan 2002) takes an unapologetic social justice and human rights stance by framing participation as an *empowerment process* undertaken by the excluded in recognition of power differentials among groups in society.

From these descriptions, it is tempting to simply accept 'participation' as a good thing. This would be both dangerous and naïve, because participation, like 'community' and other concepts, means many things. Its meaning is therefore difficult to readily understand or identify (Bryson & Mowbray 1981; Pateman 1970; Plant 1974). Its meanings are often attached to the many different interests and agendas at play in community life and in political decision making. Because different meanings are attached to different agendas, the meaning of participation becomes contentious and meanings are often in conflict and contradictory. This can be illustrated by a situation where a local government authority wants to implement a new program that it knows will be popular with some and resisted by others. Typically, the plans for the program are on view at the local government offices in the very last stages of program planning. The short time the plans are on display inhibits wide resident input and those who find it hard to get to the office site (parents of young children, disabled people, older frail people) will not have the opportunity to participate. On the other hand, a local community worker who works with a group that may be adversely affected by the program will see participation as achieving power for that group, to have their voice heard and to influence the decisions regarding the program. In this illustration, the local government sees participation as necessary but a potential barrier to its agenda—something that it must pay lip service to; the community worker sees it as having the power to influence.

Another strategy that is used under the guise of participation is when an organisation foresees resistance to its plans and, in the early stages, invites those groups that are likely to resist into the process. During the process, the organisation will attempt to co-opt the group and so dilute and minimise potential resistance. Here, participation is used to maintain power already held by the powerful! Using participation to hold power has often meant holding on to power that oppresses others. To the extent that this happens, participation has been referred to as 'the new tyranny' because it is used to wield power unjustly and illegitimately, resulting in outcomes that lead to greater disenfranchisement and so countering our intuition about participation empowering citizens (Cooke & Kothari 2001).

If participation can be a tyranny, then how can it have a positive place in community development? Should it be abandoned because it is a cliché, is often paid only lip service, is widely misunderstood and is often not wanted except to be used tyrannically? Abandonment is one option, but to have a clear understanding of the meanings and implications of participation is a far better option, for this enables community workers to have greater control over the ways they can use participation to ensure change from below, achieve human rights outcomes and challenge tyrannical uses of participation. Dinham (2006) describes the ways in which particular approaches to participation and community expectations have jarred and therefore resulted in lower wellbeing in communities. A lack of clarity about what we mean by participation can inadvertently sabotage social justice and human rights-based outcomes. While some argue the ways in which participation can be oppressive and tyrannical, there are others who argue for its transformative potential (Hickey & Mohan 2004; Cleaver 2004). It is important for community workers to have a solid basis of knowledge about and an informed approach to participation to enable maximum participation of citizens in decision making in development projects and activities.

Arnstein (1969) proposed a model of participation which makes clear the contested nature of the concept, its complexity and the different meanings it may have. The implications of these different meanings for power are also clear from her 'ladder of citizen participation' (see Figure 6.1).

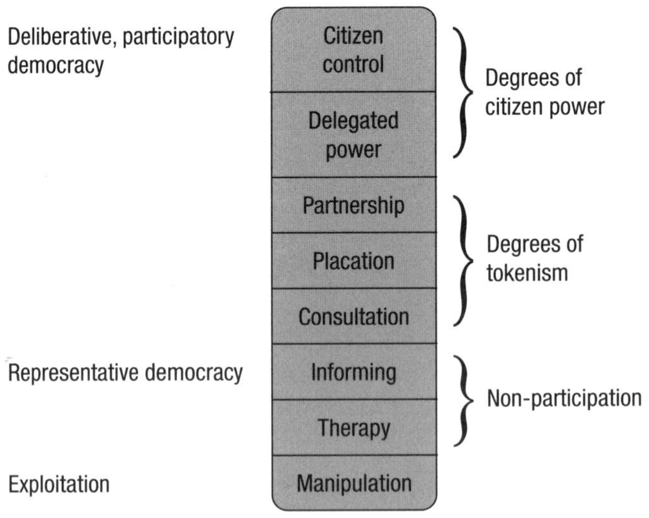

Figure 6.1 Arnstein's (1969) ladder of citizen participation

Source: Reprinted with permission from the *Journal of the American Planning Association*. Copyright American Planning Association, July 1969.

From this typology, it is clear that what may be referred to as 'participation' can range from manipulation by power holders to citizens having control over decisions that affect their lives. Across this range are corresponding degrees of control.

In 1991 the UK Health for All Network (Laris et al. 2000) developed another typology of community participation. This typology has a focus on the organisation and its relationship with its community or constituents. This is relevant for community workers who, in the main, work within organisational contexts. It is also relevant in terms of government, in the context of the earlier discussion about deliberative democracy. In this typology, the concept of power and its presence or otherwise across a range of perspectives of participation can easily be gleaned from Figure 6.2.

Participation has commonly been typecast as either genuine or token. The different perspectives on participation, which Figures 6.1 and 6.2 represent, align roughly with this more dichotomous view. These two views of participation also align with the reasons for participation that can be gleaned from the literature, which contrasts the reasons why communities support participation and the reasons why organisations and governments sponsor participation. Some of the reasons why communities may support participation centre on issues of social justice and human rights (McLean & Stutter 1993) and include the following: it is a basic right in a democracy; better decisions emerge; it is a powerful change mechanism; it builds individual and community capacity and

Deliberative, participatory democracy

High	Has control	Organisation asks community to identify the problem and make all key decisions on goals and means. Willing to help community at each step to accomplish goals.
	Has delegated	Organisation identifies and presents a problem to the community, defines the limits and asks community to make a series of decisions which can be embodied in a plan that it will accept.
	Plans jointly	Organisation presents a tentative plan subject to change and is open to advice from those affected. Subsequently expects to change plan at least slightly and perhaps more.
	Advises	Organisation presents a plan and invites questions. Prepared to modify plan only if absolutely necessary.
	Is consulted	Organisation tries to promote a plan. Seeks to develop support to facilitate acceptance or give sufficient sanction to plan so that administrative compliance can be expected.
	Receives information	Organisation makes a plan and announces it. Community is convened for information purposes. Compliance is expected.
Low	None	Community is told nothing.

Figure 6.2 UK Health for All Network continuum of community participation

Source: P. Laris, F. Verity, F. Baum & Project Team 2000, *Improving Health Services Through Consumer Participation: A Toolkit for Organisations*, Report of a consultancy for the Commonwealth Department of Health and Aged Care, Adelaide.

confidence; it challenges an alienating and bureaucratic system; it fulfils social obligations and gives a sense of contribution; it empowers people and communities; it is good as an end in itself. These reasons represent a more genuine form of participation where participants hold some power to make changes consistent with social justice and human rights. On the other hand, reasons why organisations and governments may support participation seem to meet the needs of the existing bureaucracies and include the following: it may increase effectiveness; it can build a political constituency for new programs; it can give legitimacy to existing programs and activities of organisations; it can contribute to evaluations and reviews; it is part of accountability; it is a means of sharing information; it can short-circuit opposition to the work of organisations or policy directions; it can help to ensure compliance by communities; professionals can get advice and views to assist their planning; organisations can claim they have complied with any requirements for 'community consultation'.

Problems of participation

Despite having a long and strong history (see, for example, MacPherson 1977; Brieland 1971; Strange 1972; Rostow 1971; Friere 1972; Harrison 1983; Shiva 1989; Economic Commission for Latin America 1973; Australian Government Social Welfare Commission 1973, 1974), participation is an unpopular and a problematic concept (Stiefel & Wolfe 1994). This is partly because it is contrary to the dominant individualist, consumer basis of Western society and contradicts the socialisation of many people (other than that of certain white, upwardly mobile and ambitious men, who have usually been well schooled in how to participate and to be active and effective in traditional community organisations). Overcoming this socialisation into passive consumer roles is a major challenge for community development and hence consciousness-raising becomes a critical aspect of any participation approach.

Another problem with participation is the problem of tokenism. Many apparent attempts to encourage community participation amount to varying degrees of tokenism, where people are consulted or informed about a decision but where they really have little or no power to affect it (Arnstein 1969). The history of community participation projects is riddled with examples of tokenism and people have rightly learned to look on exhortations to participate with extreme scepticism, as most people have better things to do with their time than to spend it in token participatory exercises. Any serious attempt to encourage and develop community participation must overcome this scepticism and demonstrate that it will indeed provide a genuine opportunity for people to participate meaningfully before it can hope to attract the broad involvement of the people concerned. This will inevitably take time and it must be emphasised that genuine community participation cannot be achieved quickly; it is a slow developmental process. It is sometimes possible to achieve rapid and broad-based community participation for a relatively brief period on an issue about which people feel strongly (e.g. the closure of a school or community mobilisation after a natural disaster such as recent bushfires, floods, earthquakes, mudslides), but to translate this into ongoing participation in community-based structures and decision making requires more sustained work.

Closely related to the problem of tokenism is the problem of co-option, often used by organisations and decision makers to avert threats to their existence and their stability (Selznick 1966). Participants in a process can find themselves co-opted by other forces and becoming part of the power structure that they at first thought they were opposing. This has been the fate of many representatives of citizens' groups or disempowered groups when asked to participate on government or non-government boards, committees or other bodies (Kamerman 1974). It is easy under such circumstances to lose touch with one's constituency and be seduced by the structures of power. Mowbray (1985) claims that co-option ensures that those in power are able to manage otherwise dissenting voices. Thus the radical reformer suddenly becomes 'realistic' and 'responsible' and abandons the causes for which they were elected. The consequences of co-option for Arnstein's (1969) *citizen control* can be immense. This is especially so if only a few individuals represent the interests of an affected population and those individuals shift their identification and support from their constituency to the existing power structure as the new 'in-group' (Wright & Taylor 1999), the extent of this shift being dependent on the amount of pressure exerted on the representatives by their constituencies (Bramble 1992).

Unless all people participate equally and with equal influence, *who* actually participates is another problematic issue in participation. Often the number of people from a community who participate is small and could be members of elite groups (Bracht & Tsouros 1990), that is, groups who already have the skills, knowledge, confidence and resources to participate and to influence decisions and processes. Even when there appears to be reasonable community representation on committees, working parties and so on, this does not guarantee effective community participation. There was one resident on a community centre board who prefaced most of her comments with 'the community thinks . . .' or 'the community feels . . .'. This person, a working-class, Australian Labor-voting, elderly Anglo person neither had contact with nor knew the experiences of young people, the Aboriginal families or the Vietnamese and Cambodian communities in the area. Her claim to representing the community and the credibility she had established with the existing power structures effectively increased the marginalisation of these other groups and hid the diversity within the community. Instances of representation like this are not uncommon and they occur clearly at the expense of other less organised and less visible or recognised groups (Brownlea 1987).

As noted in Chapters 2 and 4, the ecological principle of equilibrium and balance needs to be applied to the question of citizenship rights and responsibilities and one of the problems with conventional political philosophies is that they have tended to lose this balance (conservatives tend to emphasise responsibilities and ignore rights, while socialists tend to do the reverse). Essential to a community-based approach is an emphasis on both rights and responsibilities, coupled with a balance between them. Under a community-based model, membership of a community entails certain rights to receive service, support and sustenance from community structures and to take advantage of community life. But at the same time it entails responsibilities to contribute to that community and this involves participation in community processes. Unless both the rights *and* the responsibilities of community membership are acknowledged, the community is unlikely to survive in a viable form or will wither in its process of 'becoming'. Thus a community development program must encourage the recognition and promotion of both the right and the obligation to participate.

These problems with participation make it evident that, unless participation is skilfully addressed in community development, not all will benefit from it and only some interests may be served by it. These benefits will often go to those who already hold power, to the detriment of those who are marginalised and excluded. Participation must serve the interests of ecological principles and social justice and human rights, not violate them.

Encouraging and supporting participation

Despite the difficulties of achieving genuine participation, there are a number of ways in which participation can be encouraged and supported. It is important to emphasise that non-participation is not 'natural', nor is it necessarily inevitable. Many people *will* participate in community structures under the right conditions. Encouraging participation is a critical part of the community development process. While some people will not participate, a *conscious decision* not to participate is those people's right. This is very different from non-participation that results from a lack of opportunity or support to participate, which is a failure on the part of a system to realise the right to participate. Encouraging participation, then, is closely linked to realising human rights. The conditions that encourage participation are as follows.

First, *people will participate if they feel the issue or activity is important*. The way this can most effectively be achieved is if the people themselves have been able to determine the issue or action and have nominated its importance, rather than having someone from outside tell them what they should be doing. One of the keys to successful community organising has always been the selection of the issue around which to organise; the same is true in the broader domain of community development. This emphasises the importance of a community worker allowing definitions of need and priorities to arise from the community itself, rather than falling into the trap of seeking to impose them. For example, a community worker trying to mobilise a community around the issue of recreation (perhaps because this is what the worker is paid to do) will have little success if recreation is a low priority for the people of the community, who are really much more concerned about jobs and the local economy.

The second condition for participation is that *people must feel that their action will make a difference*. The community may have defined jobs as the major priority, but if people do not believe that community action can make any difference to local employment prospects, there will be little incentive to participate. It is necessary to demonstrate that the community can achieve something that will make a difference and that will result in meaningful change.

People must also feel that their actions will make a difference on an individual level. A person may believe the issue to be important and that community action could achieve something, but they may believe that other community members will be able to accomplish it and that they have no contribution to make. This implies the third condition for participation, namely that *different forms of participation must be acknowledged and valued*. Too often community participation is seen in terms of involvement in committees, formal meetings and other traditional (i.e. white, male and middle-class) procedures. While such processes can be important, many other kinds of community participation can be equally valuable. In the broad range of community development activities outlined in the following chapters, there are many different roles that community members can, and indeed must, play. These need to be recognised and valued so that activities as diverse as child-minding, bookkeeping, dance, sympathetic listening, cooking, storytelling, painting, providing basic health care, keeping records of meetings, music-making, gardening and playing football are all seen as important forms of participation and are valued. Community participation must be something for everyone and people's diverse skills, talents and interests must be taken into account.

The fourth condition for participation is that *people must be enabled to participate and be supported in their participation*. This means that issues such as the availability of transport, the provision of child care (or the inclusion of children in activities), safety, the timing and location of activities and the environment in which activities will occur are all critically important and need to be taken into account in planning community-based processes. Failure to do so will result in some sections of the community (often women or ethnic/racial minorities) being unable to participate, however much they may wish to.

The final condition for participation is that *structures and processes must not be alienating*. Traditional meeting procedures and techniques for decision making are frequently alienating for many people, particularly those who are not good at 'thinking on their feet', do not want to interrupt others, lack confidence or do not have good verbal skills. There are alternative ways of organising meetings and decision-making processes, and of structuring organisations, and these will be discussed in Chapter 9 in the context of 'political development'. The most important principle in relation to these issues of structure and process is that the community itself should control the structures and processes and should determine which forms it wants to adopt. Different styles will suit different communities and there is no one 'right' way for everyone. A style imposed from outside will almost certainly not work; while it is both useful and appropriate for a community worker to make people aware of possible alternative ways of doing things, the decision must be made by the community itself.

Questions to consider in encouraging and supporting participation

Encouraging and supporting participation is a process that requires skill and which involves continual monitoring of the effects on people of their participation in community development activities. Participation should have positive outcomes, both in terms of personal self-esteem and in terms of a sense of control over one's environment and the ability to influence decisions that affect one's life. These are not outcomes that automatically flow from participation.

CASE STUDY: Inviting participation and failing to value the local

An older woman who had been active in her community for many years was encouraged to join the Board of Management of the Community Health Service. She accepted the invitation with some pride, aware that this was yet another contribution she could make to her community. Her experience during three years on the Board was a personally destructive one, where she was left with little confidence, great confusion and feeling incompetent. The Board members, mostly professionals, spoke in an intimidating jargon. They discussed complex policy matters about which she had no knowledge. They referred in familiar terms to government officials she had not heard of. They made decisions, from her point of view, quickly and based on information she did not understand. As she voted over and over again, she felt like a token community member, somewhat used, unable to assert herself and feeling guilty that her original aspiration of making another contribution to her community had turned into an exercise of selling her fellow community members out and falsely representing them.

- Consider the idea of change from below discussed in Chapter 5 and identify the ways in which the participation in this case study failed to value the local.

The experience of the woman in the case study was the result of a lack of skilful encouragement and support so that her experience could be validated, her questions answered, her knowledge increased, her skills developed in this new area of participation and her slow but sure development affirmed and praised. There was no preparation by other Board members for this woman's membership nor was there acknowledgement of her as a new member by slowing the pace, explaining terminology and context, and so on.

Good community development is reflective practice. Reflective practice entails asking oneself questions that will avoid making the assumption that participation *per se* will lead to good community development outcomes. Asking questions will elicit answers which may indicate the need to be more appropriately responsive to the experiences of participants to ensure that participation is a positive experience. One set of questions relates to the processes in the groups in which people participate. People participate partly to meet their social and relationship needs, so it is important to ask if their relationships and networks are extending and deepening and if they have the opportunities for relationship building. The size and composition of a group is an important factor in the effectiveness of participation. Questions about the appropriateness of the size and composition of a group are important to ask. In one area, local women who had survived domestic violence formed a group with the support of a community worker and a psychologist. Over time they not only provided mutual support to each other but also set up a network of safety houses, had input into police training and spoke in many venues to raise awareness of the issues. This group was insistent that only women could be members. Another health worker in the same organisation advertised the formation of a support group for single parents in the local area. The wording of the advertisements made it clear that the invitation was extended to local *mothers*. This excluded male single parents even though the issue of the program was parenthood, one shared by both genders. When questioned about this, the worker realised that she had only worked with women and had steered towards a mothers-only group based on her own sense of comfort; she had neglected to consider the needs of a community which had a significant number of unsupported, male single parents who also had rights.

An important part of encouraging and supporting participation is ensuring that the decision to participate is, as far as possible, an easy and comfortable decision. This requires self-questioning about how easy it is for people to get to meetings, whether the time of day clashes with other scommitments like picking up children from school, whether there is child care available, whether people have transport to get to the venue and so on. For some people, participation may be something new and strange and therefore anxiety provoking. Accompanying people to the first meeting can ease tension and increase the sense of safety because the strangeness is counteracted by the presence of a familiar person. How to deal with cultural and language differences and how to ensure that these differences do not exclude are challenges in encouraging and supporting participation. How to value people and communicate that value to them is an important consideration. It is also essential to work out ways to individually negotiate each person's level of responsibility, type of participation and when they need to come and go. Engaging in these processes increases flexibility and so makes participation easier and builds people's self-esteem and their sense of making a valued contribution to their community.

Participation is positive when people feel they have some power. Power derives both from an ability to influence and from a sense of having the capacity to achieve. Reflecting, by asking questions about the power people feel they have in relation to others, about having opportunities to do things that interest them, about doing things they feel competent in, about whether their skills and abilities are being utilised and about whether there are opportunities to be and feel successful, is important if one is serious about encouraging and supporting participation.

Decision making is central to participation. There are many questions that need to be asked on a continuous basis, through the process, in relation to decision making. Are people participating in making decisions about the important issues to be addressed? Are people participating in management and decision making about directions and strategies? Are people participating in day-to-day decisions? Are their decisions implemented? Do people see their decisions being put into action? Do people see the outcomes and effects of their implemented decisions?

Barriers and factors conducive to participation

It is clear that, while it is important to work directly with local people in ways that encourage and support the participation of as many people as possible, there are broader factors in the contexts in which community workers operate that may either present barriers to participation or assist participation. It is important to be aware of these factors, to attempt to address the barriers and to capitalise on the conducive factors. Working to increase the supportiveness of the environment, as well as encouraging people to participate, is consistent with the aspirations of participatory democracy. Some problems of participation have already been discussed, namely the way participation is the antithesis of dominant individualistic values, tokenism, co-option, who participates, and an unbalanced view of rights and responsibilities. Here, further factors are identified which may hinder or help the process of participation towards its goals of empowerment and building a culture of human rights.

The extent to which barriers can be controlled will vary. It will be much easier to change the time of a meeting to suit participants than to change neoliberal ideology that casts people as isolated consumers. In this regard, Bolman (1974) suggests a useful distinction between intrinsic and extrinsic barriers to participation. Intrinsic barriers are those that are within a sponsoring organisation; extrinsic barriers are factors that lie beyond the boundaries of the organisation and which the organisation may be able to influence, but certainly not control.

Intrinsic barriers largely relate to the features of bureaucracy and professionalism. They include some of the rules and regulations of an organisation, the labyrinthine nature of its structure and the tensions between bureaucratic goals and those of the community. Organisations may not be optimally accessible to people. The language the staff use may be intimidating and alienating to local people. Local people may be very hesitant to be involved in an organisation. They may perceive a great power difference between themselves and the members of an organisation. On the other hand, an organisation may tend to depersonalise and stereotype people, and members of the organisation may appear arrogant and conceited in their dealings with local people. There may also be a great divide between what an organisation considers rational knowledge and the more 'emotive' cries of local people. Participation can sometimes threaten the sense of professionalism of members of an organisation, who may believe they have the technical training and expertise to address community issues and are far more knowledgeable, skilled and qualified than local, untrained people. Even when an organisation's attitude towards participation is positive and its members are keen to encourage and support participation, there may be a naïvity in relation to how to build effective participation. The organisation may lack support from its political or funding masters or it may be confused about the position of representatives from the community and overwhelmed by the many diverse groups in the community. Inviting local people to participate without due thought may simply encourage 'professional' volunteers. Participation may open the way for increasing conflict and there may be anxiety within the organisation about resolving and managing conflicts. If the organisation does not possess the skills and capacity to ensure that representatives and participants remain true to the mandate given by their constituencies, then the participants may increase their individual formal power and feel less obliged to liaise with their constituencies so that their participation begins to be to the detriment of the community groups they are meant to serve.

Many schools have an interest in parents becoming more involved in the life of the school. Some schools have aspirations to become 'health promoting schools', that is, to work within primary health care principles and to become an important part of community life where the community participates in the school and the school contributes to promoting the health and wellbeing of the community. However, these schools find it very difficult to encourage parent participation. Thoughtful reflection on some of the intrinsic barriers to participation would go a long way to uncovering the reasons why parents do not participate. A key intrinsic barrier is the assumption that expert professional knowledge is superior to what local people know. Valuing local knowledge is imperative and, as discussed in Chapter 5, is part of the idea of change from below, which is, in turn, at the heart of the community development approach taken in this book. However, it is often the most difficult barrier to overcome. It requires signficant changes within professionals and a seeming relinquishment of the control and power that society gives them as professionals. However, time and time again, local knowledge and wisdom have proven to be essential in resolving community issues.

Extrinsic barriers to participation are the social, economic, political and cultural contexts in which organisations operate and these can severely hamper the extent and the effectiveness of participation. The structural position of people in society can influence who participates and who does not. Kweit and Kweit (1981) note that generally people with higher-socioeconomic status are

CASE STUDY: Community participation in defining issues facilitates effective work

An Australian medical team went to a remote Cambodian village where the incidence of HIV was sharply increasing. The team applied its knowledge and skills to educate the people about the virus, its transmission, safer sex practices, the use of condoms and so on. After two weeks, one team member asked a local woman what she thought would stem the rise of HIV in the village. The woman replied, 'Rebuild our bridge'. The team member was at a loss to know how the bridge and HIV were related. He was attitudinally imprisoned by his technical medical and health knowledge. When, through the interpreter, the team member explored the woman's response, he came to appreciate the value of local knowledge and wisdom, and the limitations of his own expertise. The woman explained that before the bridge was washed out, the men would carry the produce across the bridge to sell at the market. Without the bridge, the men had a 70-kilometre journey to reach the nearest bridge that gave them access to the markets. This took three days. During the nights they were absent from home, they visited sex workers, the HIV virus was transmitted to them, they transmitted it to their wives, and babies were born HIV positive. Before the demise of the bridge, HIV was not a problem in this village.

- What impact did understanding and listening to local knowledge have on this worker and his expert knowledge of HIV prevention?

more likely to participate. Younger people generally participate less than older people. The strength of community and the social capital that is within a community are also influential in the extent and effectiveness of participation.

The literature (Brownlea 1987; Piette 1990; Bracht & Tsouros 1990; Spergel 1969; Voth & Jackson 1981; O'Neill & Trickett 1982; Ward 1992) identifies many factors that are conducive to participation and which represent positive resources for community workers. The following is a list of some of these facilitative factors:

- for Indigenous communities, full community control (See the fuller discussion of this under 'cultural development' in Chapter 9.)
- a good knowledge and clear understanding of the complexities of participation on the part of community workers
- clarity about criteria used in inviting participation to ensure exclusion is avoided
- honesty and openness to participants about any constraints and limitations of participation
- access to relevant information
- legislation, such as freedom of information legislation, which can change the expectation of participants towards participation as their right, supported by law
- training of local people in such things as lobbying and advocacy
- provision of a facilitator at community meetings
- training of chairpersons
- adequate time for local participants to perform their roles
- strong community networks and organisation
- effective participant/community communication
- multiple strategies of, and opportunities for, participation
- avoidance of professionals as community representatives
- building strong community organisations that can be community managed
- an appreciation and valuing of local knowledge, wisdom and history
- a commitment by the sponsoring organisation to a partnership approach with the community
- clear and explicitly negotiated expectations, commitments, roles, skill development opportunities and time commitment
- feedback and recognition of participants' work
- early identification and addressing of any barriers, conflicts and so on.

There is an underlying principle that should guide the community worker towards building strong, effective participation processes which take account of the barriers and conducive factors. That principle is one of building empowering relationships with local people. Empowerment, which was discussed in Chapter 3, means people having a capacity to influence the structures and decisions that affect their lives and shape the conditions in which they live. Ensuring empowering relationships calls for flexibility, feeling comfortable with ambiguity and unpredictability, having a clear social justice and rights value base, knowing how this applies to practice and sharing power in one's relationships with local people.

Partnership as participation

The notion of partnership is a currently fashionable way of constructing participation. Partnerships and collaboration are often a requirement for funding, and much recent policy and restructuring of government departments reflect a positive encouragement of the partnership concept. Today, policy makers, funders and decision makers urge the use of partnerships as a strategy. In spite of the enthusiasm with which partnership as a *modus operandi* is championed, it remains problematic. It is problematic because the complexities of the relationships that are the substance of partnerships are generally little understood (Hudson 1987; Ebers 1997; O'Neill et al. 1997; O'Riordan 1999; Roussos & Fawcett 2000; McDonald, Murphy & Payne 2001), there is little evidence of effectiveness and the little evidence there is, is inconsistent (O'Riordan 1999; Roussos & Faucett 2000; McDonald, Murphy & Payne 2001). 'Partnership' as an idea is eagerly embraced but its meaning remains nebulous.

In his classic 1949 study of the Tennessee Valley Authority, Selznick described the rationale for the partnership between the Authority and the people's institutions of the Valley as 'grass roots democracy at work' (Selznick 1966: p. 37), whereby local people would be able to influence their futures and the Authority could become committed to the interests of the Valley people. So there has been a long history of partnership proffered as a participatory mechanism critical to democracy and citizen participation in democracy. But, although partnership has been associated with particpatory democracy, the term, like 'democracy', 'community' and 'participation' itself, has multiple meanings. Most problematic is the taken-for-granted assumption of harmony and 'sameness' among partners that pervades the literature, policy and practice. This is problematic, even at the intuitive level, because much of community development is concerned with changing power structures, including the marginalised and the excluded fighting for resources and access to resources, and working in circumstances where human rights are being violated and social injustice is rampant.

The term 'partnership' has been borrowed from business literature and practice and the consensus assumptions it brings with it are about partnerships working best where goals, values and outcomes are shared by all partners (Wise & Signal 2000) and where all partners work together to achieve a common purpose (Roussos & Faucett 2000). In much of community development, there is contestation about the nature of issues, desired goals and outcomes and what is valued; and there is a power discrepancy in partners' relationships, such as between community members and organisations in the partnership. Community action aimed at stemming environmental degradation that is caused by corporations' profit-making activities is unlikely to involve relationships between local people and corporations which are of equal power and in which goals and values are shared. Where there is a pretence of sameness, the divergent goals and values of the less powerful participants are constructed as illegitimate, 'hidden agendas'. This contrasts dramatically with all that has been discussed so far about effective and genuine participation. When working with groups and partnerships it would be a mistake for the community worker to rely on traditional group work models, which assume that group processes are linear and progress neatly through forming, storming, norming and other stages. Rather, because many community development issues relate to the unequal distribution of power and resources and the attempt to redress this, how issues are defined, how strategies are identified and what goals are valued are more likely to be continually contested throughout the process and often in a chaotic fashion. Therefore, the skills required of the community developer are less about guiding groups through neat stages and more about negotiation, mediation and conflict management as ongoing demands throughout the entire process.

Acknowledging diversity among partners and their interests and agendas allows for a much richer exploration of issues, a deeper dialogue about perspectives and greater creativity in finding solutions. The arena for exploration is much wider and more expansive and so is likely to give rise to wiser decisions. Figure 6.3 depicts the difference between choosing sameness (and hiding other agendas) and choosing diversity (and including all the different partners' agendas).

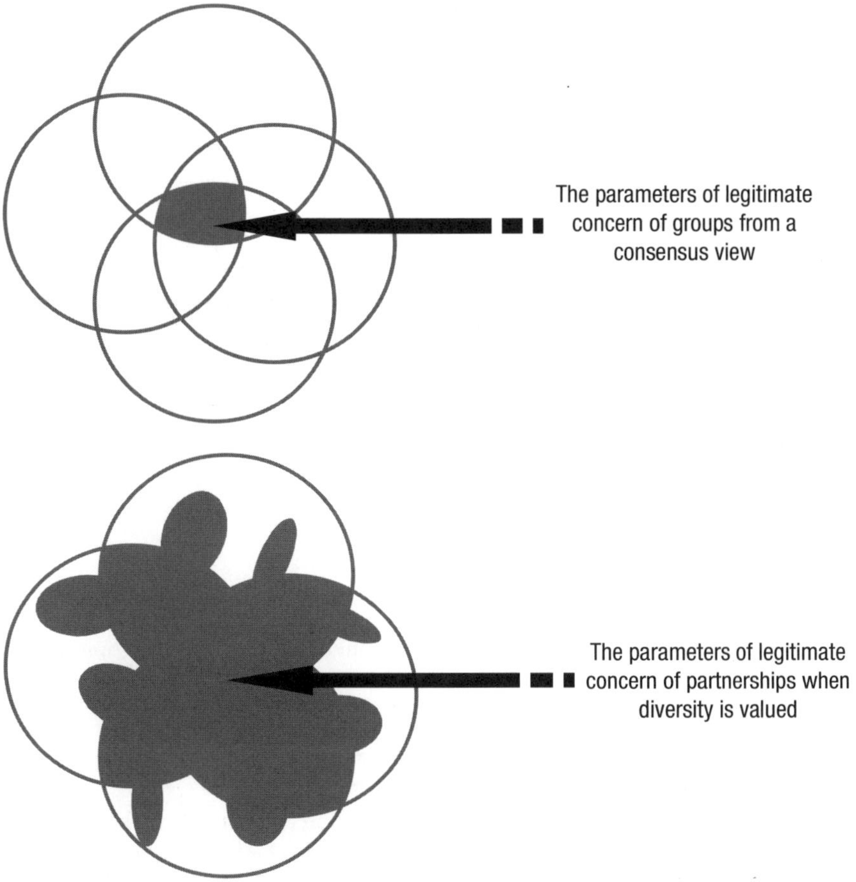

Figure 6.3 Parameters of concern of groups and partnerships

CASE STUDY: Managing mistrust in a community partnership

Let us revisit the urban renewal project in a disadvantaged public housing area described in Chapter 3. There, the focus was on the issue of power. Here, the focus is on the idea of 'partnership'. The initial social action by residents in response to the announcement of the redevelopment resulted in a partnership between the local resident action group and a number of organisations.

The resident action group had formed after the shock announcement on the radio by the government minister that the 'ghetto' (their community) was to be cleaned up by bulldozing the public housing stock and placing the redevelopment in the hands of private developers.

The local group effectively gatecrashed the partnership between the public housing authority, the local government authority and the private developer. The partnership lasted for several years during the redevelopment of the area and the relocation of the local people. At all points in the process, there was rarely consensus or high levels of trust. The local people saw the issue as the destruction of their community, which had a strong and

continued

proud history of fighting for its rights. The housing authority saw the issue as needing to manage and transfer the risk attached to decaying housing stock. The local government authority saw the issue as an opportunity to rebuild ageing infrastructure, which it could not afford to do alone. The private developer saw the issue as needing to make a profit. In thse circumstances there would never be agreement on how the issue was problematised. Instead, the process required constant negotiations and renegotiations as issue after issue was raised.

The work of the community worker in this case, rather than building trust, was to *manage mistrust* in such a way that mistrust would not immobilise the participation process. Paradoxically, the skilful management of mistrust has the potential to build trust in the longer term.

- In what ways might this partnership have deviated from one of community-shared goals and values?
- What is your reaction to the idea of managing mistrust?

Partnerships, then, require the same critical interrogation as participation more generally requires. Like participation, partnerships cannot be assumed to be a good thing. They require of the community worker the same astuteness and commitment to analysis and reflective practice to ensure that local people can participate effectively.

Measuring participation

Community workers need to know to what extent participation is effective and they need to know how to systematically reflect on or monitor participation processes in order to adjust their practice in response to ongoing learning. The evaluation and measurement of participation will be quite different from many of the dominant forms of evaluation, and community workers have to clearly recognise participation as a dynamic and ever-changing process of complex interrelationships. How participation is measured or evaluated provides challenging theoretical issues, as well as raising issues of accountability. Most data collection in organisations tends to be quantitative. Data are collected on such things as number of service users, occasions of service, length of occasions of service and types of problems. These data are rarely useful in evaluating outcomes. Rather, they measure input and the use of resources. Evaluating outcomes has been a vexed issue in many organisations. At times, funding is available to undertake more formal evaluations of programs. At these times, careful thought can be given to methodology, aims, questions and key stakeholders. Additionally, external evaluators can be employed and a formal written report produced. However, it is more often the case in the day-to-day work of community development that these resources are not available and formal evaluation processes are not in place.

Because of the qualitative and dynamic nature of participation, measuring it demands that we move beyond the more traditional evaluation frameworks. Participation is not simply a single event that happens. It is an ongoing and dynamic, interactive process that should underlie any community development activity and guide its progress. One cannot, therefore, simply take a snapshot of it, as more traditional research tends to do. The more dominant approach to evaluation has some features that do not fit with participation: it is often overly concerned with *input* of resources and *efficiency* in producing material outcomes; it *privileges* quantitative data and analysis; it is limited and static and fails to capture the more subtle, dynamic and relationship aspects of participation; it is

CASE STUDY: Participation—measuring outcomes, not statistics

One local community agency of a government organisation, which provided services to individuals and families, set up group work programs and supported community development initiatives in the local area and reported its activities on a monthly basis in statistical form. This data went to the central office of the government department each month. On one occasion, the central office asked some questions about the report. It appeared that one community worker had spent what the central office considered an inordinate amount of time with a group of 12 residents over several months. This compared unfavourably with some of the caseworkers in the agency who had statistics indicating that they had seen over 80 clients per month and many more occasions of service.

The 12 people the community worker was working with had been concerned about the number of isolated elderly people in the community. They accessed the Australian Bureau of Statistics data on households in the area with a single occupant over 60 years of age and without a private vehicle. The data threw up some collectors' districts (each district comprising about 200 households) where the prevalence of these households was high. The group of 12 members then doorknocked in these areas to make contact with the people in the households. In many cases, security doors were kept locked when members of the group called and it was clear that the older people were living in fear of home invasion and physical harm. With persistent effort and by providing consistent, clear information on who they were and what their purpose was, the group members slowly earned the trust of many of the residents. Relationships developed and members were invited into homes for chats and coffee.

A local church ran a volunteer-based coffee shop in the local shopping centre and the group asked the organisers if groups of the elderly people could meet there for coffee, in the hope that bringing people together would create new friendships. The coffee shop people agreed and groups began to meet there on a fortnightly basis. In all, 20 groups and 200 older people were meeting and many friendships formed. People discussed where each other lived and some people found they lived very close to others in the group. So they started to visit each other independently as friends. The coffee shop volunteers took on the central role in maintaining the program.

To the extent that 200 older people were less isolated and the coffee shop volunteers were involved in the program, it would be fair to say that the community had become a more supportive community. Twelve people had achieved a significant community outcome, but the government department was concerned about the community worker supporting only 12 people. The data collection system could not appreciate outcomes, yet the data were being used evaluatively to question the use of resources, taking no account of the effectiveness, in community development terms, of the activity and the support for people's participation in an issue which they identified as problematic in their community. Why only 12 people out of a population of over 40 000 participated is another, separate issue. Asking questions about encouraging and supporting participation would, no doubt, provide insight into ways in which more people might have been stimulated to take part in the social action. However, what is of interest here is the question of how participation is measured or evaluated.

- How would you measure participation and its outcomes in this case study?

often *externally driven* and *top-down*, time consuming and sometimes costly, which makes it often not affordable in community development projects. These features are at odds with the approach to community development taken in this book.

The United Nations Development Program (UNDP) identifies four principles to guide the evaluation of participation.

1 It should be qualitative as well as quantitative.
2 It should be dynamic rather than static to enable an entire process over time to be evaluated.
3 It requires continuous monitoring to capture the dynamism of the process through qualitative descriptions.
4 It must include the voice of the people, who must play an active role in the evaluation.

The UNDP sees qualitative research as a more appropriate way than quantitative research to evaluate participation, for various reasons.

- Qualitative research is naturalistic enquiry, studying processes as they occur.
- It is heuristic and iterative; that is, it evolves as it discovers understandings, which then change and reshape the questions to be asked.
- It is holistic and attempts to embrace many perspectives and avoids reducing a phenomenon to discrete categories.
- It is inductive, by starting with what is observed and discerning patterns from what is observed, rather than having predetermined concepts in mind. This is consistent with what is to be evaluated—the process of participation.

Participation is not simply about outputs. It is a process and so encompasses many levels and dimensions of change: changes in capacity of organisations, communities and individuals; changes in attitudes and behaviour; changes in access to resources; changes in power balances; changes in perceptions of stakeholders. Participation has the potential to contribute to significant changes in the political, cultural, economic and social aspects of communities and of people's lives.

What would indicate effective participation? As a rule of thumb, it is useful to identify the minimum number of indicators rather than the maximum, which would be overwhelming in time and effort. The minimum number of indicators represents the number that would adequately describe the process of participation. It is also important not to have a standard list of indicators, but to ensure that the ones used are appropriate to the specific contexts of the community development projects being evaluated. The following is a sample of indicators. They are not a model and should not be used as an exhaustive list. They are meant to give a flavour of the indicators that can be developed in evaluating participation.

Quantitative indicators of participation include:

- positive changes in local services
- numbers of meetings and attendance numbers
- proportion of different sections of the community attending
- numbers of people affected by the issue attending
- numbers of local leaders taking on roles
- numbers of local people taking on project roles
- numbers of local people involved in different aspects of the project and at different times.

Qualitative indicators of participation include:

- a community's growing capacity to organise for action
- growing support in the community and strengthening networks
- increased community knowledge about such things as finance and project management
- community desire to be involved in decision making

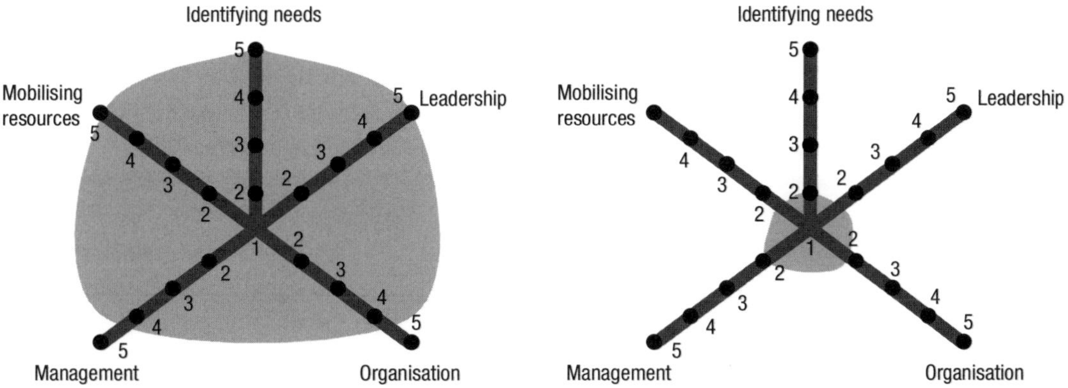

Figure 6.4 Full participation versus minimal or token participation

Source: W. Bickman, S. B. Rifkin and M. Shrestra 1989, 'Towards the Measurement of Community Participation', *World Health Forum*, vol. 10, no. 3/4, pp. 467–72, reproduced with permission of the World Health Organization.

- increasing ability of those participating to put decisions into action
- increasing reach of participants beyond the project to representing it in other organisations
- emerging leaders from the community
- increased networking with other projects, communities, organisations
- commencing influence over policy.

Bickman, Rifkin and Shrestra (1989) take these types of indicators as a basis for describing a developing methodology for measuring community participation, which focuses on processes rather than activities. The diagrams in Figure 6.4 can be used to create a community participation profile, in which the extent of participation is made visually stark. Each process is graded 1 to 5, with 1 representing minimum community participation and 5 representing maximum participation. Changes in a community development project can be measured over time or with the involvement of different planners or participants. The methodology was developed for health programs in Nepal. The indicators are descriptive and are designed as a developmental tool rather than a summative evaluation methodology. Given the difficulties and pitfalls of attempting to set objective and uniform quantitative values for indicators such as levels of community participation in management, the methodology should not be used to discriminate between programs on the basis of 'scores'. Rather it can serve as a useful guide to check if projects are aware of, and attempting to address, these vital aspects of community participation.

Conclusion

This chapter has explored the complexities of the notion of participation. An understanding of participation and the ability to incorporate it as a central component in community work is essential when approaching community work from the perspective taken in this book. Change from below is at the heart of community development and participation brings to life this notion. It enacts the value given to local knowledge, skills, culture, resources and processes. It enables working in solidarity with communities. Indeed, participation is a right and is vital in aspirations towards participatory democracy.

>> discussion questions

1 What are the limitations of representative democracy for community development?
2 Explain the four characteristics of participatory democracy important to community development.
3 How does the idea of deliberative democracy strengthen participatory democracy?
4 What are the various meanings given to the idea of 'participation'?
5 Why would it be naïve to simply assume that participation is good?
6 What are some of the problems associated with participation?
7 How might participation be encouraged?
8 What factors help or hinder participation?
9 Describe the idea of 'partnership' as a form of participation.
10 What are some important considerations in measuring participation?

>> reflective questions

1 What is your view on the concept of representative democracy, drawing on your own life experience as a citizen?
2 What are your reactions to the various meanings of participation, in particular those represented in the degrees of participation depicted in Figures 6.1 and 6.2? What values are implied in your reactions? What might this mean for a bottom-up approach to community development? In what ways might you have to re-evaluate your own position in the light of this reflection?
3 When you consider the facilitative factors for participation, which of them do you feel confident about and which might you have to focus on in terms of skill development and personal growth?
4 If you have had an experience of working in a partnership, to what extent were there differences among the partners and how were these handled? How would you handle them differently in the future if you were to fully accept diversity in partnerships and all that that entails?

CHAPTER 7

The primacy of process in community development

Introduction

The bottom-up, 'change from below' approach discussed in Chapter 5 and participation discussed in Chapter 6 are fundamental principles of community development—principles to guide how community development is implemented: the process. This chapter considers this fundamental principle, namely the importance and the integrity of process. In the current climate, so dominated by a concern for outcomes and objectives, the community development emphasis on process is as radical as the emphasis on change from below and participation. It similarly requires a major reorientation for many community workers, who have become used to outcome-based thinking; and it can be difficult to explain to those who have accepted the commonly held view that the end justifies the means and for whom 'where we end up' is more important than 'how we get there'. Participation is central to change from below and critical in maintaining a focus on process. Chapter 11 will deal more specifically with the skills and roles involved in working through the processes of community development.

Process and outcome

There are two types of journey we can take. One is the journey where the aim is to arrive at our destination as quickly and as comfortably as possible. We plan our journey, we work out the best route to take, and we estimate how long it will last, so that we know when we have to start in order to arrive on time. Everything is geared to the arrival and it is a journey on which we want no surprises. If we encounter the unexpected—a detour, an unexpected traffic jam, a breakdown, a late bus—we become annoyed, as it has prevented us from reaching our destination on time. The other sort of journey is the journey of discovery. Here we are not sure where we will end up; we may have some idea of where we would like to go, but typically it is ill-defined. We do not have detailed maps and we cannot predict what is likely to happen. Indeed, we expect the unexpected and when the unexpected happens we welcome it as a new opportunity. It is the journey itself that is important, rather than the arrival.

In a world that is dominated by outcomes, by arriving, by 'achieving your objectives', the first sort of journey is the appropriate metaphor. But community development is, essentially, a journey of the second type. The journey itself (the process) is what is important. A community worker will not really know where a community development process will lead and so will not be certain of the outcome. Indeed, the specification of outcomes, so common in the human services, is the antithesis of community development. A community worker who is clear at the beginning about the outcomes they hope to achieve is effectively disempowering the community, as this takes away from the community the control of the process and the determination of the direction of development.

The relative importance to be placed on process and outcome is determined in part by the way one understands the relationship between means and ends. One view sees means and ends as separate. We seek a particular end and then choose the best means by which to reach it. This is the traditional view in conventional planning and policy analysis; the end is seen as value-laden, where there is a consensus about a desired value, for example, a high level of education. The role of the policy analyst is then to decide the way in which that end might best (i.e. most effectively and efficiently) be realised, through programs of education, school building, teacher training and resource provision. This is a role for the expert; it can be done objectively and rationally and values do not come into play (Fay 1975). The role of the public—of democratic participation and of public debate—is confined to the identification of the desired end and the wider community then allows the policy experts to determine the best way for that end to be reached. This view is also reflected in the conventional planning process, where outcomes are specified and the planning is seen as an essentially technical exercise to determine the steps required to reach that outcome. Such an approach to means and ends leads naturally to the idea that 'the end justifies the means'—that it is the end result that is everything and we should use whatever means necessary to achieve it. Even violence and war can be readily justified if they are seen as reaching the ends of non-violence and peace. Such an argument has been used for centuries to justify wars, to excuse war crimes, justify the death penalty and legitimise torture, the denial of human rights and the scapegoating of minorities; all these may be seen as 'regrettable' but they are justified in the interests of achieving a greater good. On a less extreme scale, the same sort of thinking is seen in the reluctance to consider or consult communities about building a freeway, in Alinsky's (1971) view that in community action 'ethics' should be disregarded, and in the loss of jobs and industrial protection in the interests of 'the health of the economy', 'flexibility' and 'staying competitive'.

An alternative view rejects the separation of means and ends on three grounds (Fay 1975). The first is that ends can (and do) become means and means can (and do) become ends, so their separate identity cannot be maintained. An end, for example, might be to reduce unemployment, but if we ask why we want to reduce unemployment the answer (e.g. to increase people's sense of wellbeing) becomes an end and what we thought of earlier as an end has become a means instead. Similarly, we may identify a means (better teachers) to an end (higher levels of literacy), but then as soon as we ask how we can produce better teachers our means has become an end and we are seeking a means to achieve it. Thus means and ends do not remain separate and distinct.

The second ground for rejecting a distinction between means and ends is that the choice of means is not necessarily a technical, value-free decision. The justification of a means solely on the grounds of its efficiency and effectiveness in meeting an end can result in means that are unacceptable: shooting all unemployed people would be an extremely efficient and effective way of reducing unemployment, but it is hardly likely to be acceptable to the community. The choice of means cannot be value-free, but rather needs to be determined in the same way as the choice of ends; to imagine otherwise is to create the possibility of oppressive practices, such as the harsh imprisonment of offenders, mandatory sentencing of juveniles and denial of the rights of asylum-seekers or migrant workers, all in the name of 'decisive action' to 'stamp out' a perceived social problem.

The third ground for rejecting the means–ends dichotomy is the argument that ends and means are morally connected; far from the ends justifying the means, this argument suggests that the means can corrupt the end and therefore that it is impossible to reach an incorrupt, non-violent end through corrupt or violent means. It therefore refutes, for example, the argument that war is necessary to achieve peace, that violent revolution is necessary to achieve a non-violent society or that violent means such as corporal or capital punishment are necessary to eliminate crimes of violence. The experience of history is that such means are generally unsuccessful in achieving their ends—instead they perpetuate cycles of violence. After one war to achieve the great 'lasting' peace there is usually another one; a violent revolution to achieve a just society often results in oppression, which is then overthrown by another violent revolution. More violent forms of punishment send out the message that violent solutions to problems are acceptable and therefore institutionalise and reinforce a culture of violence. The Gandhian non-violence tradition has strongly argued that means and ends are linked in this way and that one can achieve genuinely peaceful, non-violent and morally consistent ends only by adopting peaceful, non-violent and morally consistent means.

The perspective of this book is grounded in the latter position, which rejects the separation of means and ends. It should be noted that not all approaches to community work share this view. Some community workers, most notably Alinsky (1969, 1971), have taken the opposite view and argued that the end will justify the means. This is evident in, for example, some of Alinsky's rules where he consistently refers to 'the enemy', advocates ridicule as a 'tactic' and in Rule 13 states 'Pick the target, freeze it, personalize it and polarize it.' The use of military metaphors is widespread in the community work literature—'strategic', 'tactics', 'campaign', 'target', 'alliance' and so on. These suggest at least an unconscious attachment to ways of thinking that tacitly accept violent means and a corresponding separation of the end from the means employed to get there. From the perspective of this book, such a separation of means and ends is unacceptable. It is in conflict with the ecological and social justice/human rights principles outlined in Chapters 2 and 3 and also with the process principles discussed further here. The *process* of community development (and community development is, essentially, a process of 'becoming') cannot be seen simply as a means to an end, but is an important end in itself, so the process and the outcome, or the means and the end, have become combined. To pursue the metaphor of the journey discussed above, community development is about setting out on a journey of discovery and about valuing and trusting the process. This requires the community worker to abandon the idea of knowing where they are heading and instead being prepared to have faith in the process and the wisdom and expertise of the community itself.

It is important to make the distinction between 'outcome' and 'purpose'. In this discussion we are referring to outcomes. The overarching purpose of community development and community building is something the community worker must be committed to as much as to process. This forms a 'tight/loose' structure for working. There is tightness because there is a clear and uncompromising commitment to purpose; but there is looseness (and lack of control) in relation to outcomes, which must always be community-driven. Having a tight and clear purpose means that the worker has a crucial role in processes—to ensure they are congruent with social justice and human rights principles and that they facilitate community-defined outcomes.

The integrity of process

The idea of the integrity of process arises from the discussion above. If means and ends cannot be separated, and if one accepts the view that corrupt means can corrupt the end, then the process of community development has more than purely instrumental value. In other words, it is important not just as a means of getting somewhere, but in its own right. Thus it is important to ensure that the process itself has integrity and does not contradict the ecological and social justice/human rights principles discussed in earlier chapters. It is not sufficient simply to seek the goal of sustainability, social justice and human rights; *it is just as important that the process itself reflect those principles*. This will be the assumption behind many of the community development principles discussed in the remainder of this book.

There are many temptations to cut corners about matters of process. To engage in good process can often be time consuming and it is tempting to try to bring matters to a conclusion without, for example, consulting all those who are likely to be affected by a decision or giving everyone concerned the opportunity to participate meaningfully. Sometimes a community worker has no choice: for example, when there is a tight deadline for a submission to a local government body regarding a planning matter and there is simply no time to engage in a broad participatory process within the community to determine the content of the submission and give everybody a stake in its final form. Here it may be necessary to compromise on process, but such a decision should always be taken with reluctance as it is effectively allowing the administrative processes of local government to take precedence over the decision-making processes of the community. In such a case, it is often important to take additional steps as well as simply making the submission. One approach might be to lobby the council for more time. Another might be to label the submission as a preliminary document with notice that a fuller submission will arrive after necessary processes have been undertaken. Another might be to make an issue of it with the council, seeking to ensure that adequate time is available to community groups in the future. Another response, which is necessary and ethically integral to community development, would be to work with the local community to share understandings of the constraints and to determine an acceptable way to handle such an eventuality in the future, such as a small group of people entrusted by the community to make a rapid response should such action be necessary again. This is an important principle for community workers; we learn by experience and, having been 'caught out' once where it has been necessary to compromise the integrity of the process, it is important to ensure that it does not happen again.

The most important aspect of the integrity of process is that the process must be owned by the community itself. Ownership will not be achieved without full participation. Community development process cannot be imposed from outside and cannot be dictated by a community worker, a local council or a government department. It has to be the process of the community itself, which is owned, controlled and sustained by the people themselves. This is not always easy to achieve as people are accustomed to having processes imposed and to responding to 'guidelines'. But there can be no such imposed process in community development. Each community is different; it has its unique cultural, geographical, social, political and demographic characteristics, its own leaders, its own problems and its own aspirations. What works in one community will not necessarily work in another and any attempt to impose something that worked in one community onto another not only runs the risk of failure but also disempowers the people of that community because it is not their own process. Of course one can learn from experience elsewhere and one may wish to try out something that worked somewhere else, but it must always be the community itself that is in control of the process.

This often results in a feeling of frustration for community workers. Because of the necessity for the process to be owned by the community, there is an element of 'starting from scratch' every time and of allowing the community to determine its own processes, working at its own pace. For a worker who has been through similar processes before, there is a temptation to speed up the process by telling people how to do it. This seldom works and it results in a process that is not owned by the community, thereby weakening rather than strengthening community development. As a simple example, when a community group is established, it is important that someone take the minutes of each meeting. For a group accustomed to meetings, this is relatively straightforward and someone will organise for this to happen. But with a group unaccustomed to meetings, the community worker may choose to resist the temptation to tell the group that they need a minute-taker, in order not to hijack the process. The worker instead might simply ask people how they will be able to remember decisions that were taken or remind themselves at the next meeting of what had been decided previously. This could lead to the group deciding itself how it might go about doing that. Or it may even be appropriate for the worker not to say anything, but to wait for the group itself to realise the importance of such record-keeping (say after the first two or three meetings). Either way, the community group is able to set up a form of record-keeping that is its own, designed to meet its own needs, and is not simply engaging in a prescribed process called 'taking the minutes' that has been imposed from outside. This is a small example, but the same approach can be applied to many different tasks. The role of the community worker may be to ask questions to encourage thought and discussion about process issues or it may be to provide answers when asked; in the above example, someone in the group may ask how other groups keep records of decisions and the worker can then provide an answer that provides a number of options or possibilities for the group to consider, rather than defining the 'right' way to do it. At a generalised level, there are no 'right' and 'wrong' ways to do community development, though in any particular social and cultural context there will certainly be right and wrong ways and it is for the community, not the worker, to determine the ways that are 'right' for it.

The remainder of this chapter examines a number of process principles of community development. These principles give process in community development a political dimension. Burkett (2001) highlights the political significance and brands 'process' as radical when he states that *community development* is a verb, not a noun. What he means by this is that community is not an object that is the end or an outcome of a process but rather it is a myriad of processes of change—it is becoming and unfolding. These processes are imbued with constant shifts. They are always contextualised differently in different locations. They are complex, unstable, uncertain, unpredictable and contested. Globalisation, as will be discussed further in Chapter 8, provides opportunities for many different and new relationships to develop and so allows space for a 'critical localism' where many local sites can engage in dialogue and consciousness-raising.

Consciousness-raising

The idea of consciousness-raising is central to community development and it is an important part of the process. It will also be discussed in later chapters, when different aspects of community development and different community development roles/skills are considered. The simple idea of consciousness-raising is that, because of the legitimacy of oppressive structures and discourses, people have come to accept oppression as somehow 'normal', 'natural' or 'inevitable' and will often not even be able to acknowledge or label their own oppression; the experience of oppression is therefore 'unconscious'. Hence there is a need to raise levels of 'consciousness', to allow people the opportunity to explore their own situations and the oppressive structures and discourses that frame their lives, in such a way that they can act to bring about change. This is a much more difficult and challenging process than it sounds. As Marxist (Freire 1972), feminist (de Beauvoir 1988), postcolonialist (Spivak 1994) and poststructuralist (Foucault 1972, 1973, 1979) writers have pointed out, one of the important aspects of oppression is the power of the structures and discourses that legitimise that oppression, for example, through the media, the education system, advertising and religious institutions. Indeed, such 'cultural hegemony', to use the Marxist term, can be both more powerful and more subtle than the control of the armed forces, police and security agencies and is much harder to identify and name, let alone challenge. Yet it is these very structures and discourses that prevent people from exploring oppression and disadvantage effectively and leave them powerless.

There are four aspects of consciousness-raising, though it needs to be emphasised that in any consciousness-raising process they will all happen at the same time; they are not steps in a linear progression. The first is *linking the personal and the political*. We tend not think of our personal experiences, joys, disappointments, needs, problems, sufferings or frustrations as being *political*; they are seen as purely part of our own individual experience and life space. Similarly, we tend to see the political as being about a 'politics' that is removed from everyday experience, to do with political parties, elections, legislatures, economics, the media and power exercised in the public domain rather than the private domain. Consciousness-raising requires that the two be brought together. This has perhaps best been achieved by feminist writers, who have emphasised that 'the personal is political' and that the personal experiences and oppression of women have to be understood in terms of politics, namely the structures and discourses of power and patriarchal oppression that apply across the public/private divide (Coote & Campbell 1982; Salleh 1997). The same perspective can be applied to other dimensions of oppression, such as class and race. In each case, personal experience of disadvantage needs to be seen in its broader structural context, just as broader structural issues need to be seen in terms of the impact on the lives of people (Mills 1970). Helping people to make the connection between the personal and the political is therefore central to consciousness-raising and, of course, a community worker can do this effectively only if they have an awareness of the connection and understand the way in which dominant structures and discourses of power deny the connection and make it difficult for people to make the link.

The second aspect of consciousness-raising is the establishment of a *dialogical relationship*. One of the criticisms of consciousness-raising is that it can become simply a form of ideological indoctrination by the community worker, where the worker imposes their values on other people using the language of liberation, but, in fact, in an oppressive and colonising way that betrays the idea of 'bottom-up' practice as described in Chapter 5. This is a very important criticism and it can be overcome only if the worker is able to establish a genuinely *dialogical* relationship with the members of the community. The idea of a dialogical relationship is based on the educative work of Paolo Freire (1972), who is the best-known and most influential writer about consciousness-raising. It requires that the community worker not enter into a relationship claiming to be the expert with superior knowledge, but instead they adopt the position described in Chapter 5 of valuing local knowledge and wisdom and seeking an equal dialogue with community members where each can learn from the other, so that they can together move towards collective action. This notion of collaborative reciprocal learning and deconstructing power differentials that may be inherent in the relationship between worker and community is a precondition for an effective consciousness-raising that is liberating rather than colonising and exploitative.

The third aspect of consciousness-raising is *sharing experiences of oppression*. It is by exploring each other's experiences of what oppression means, and how people understand and define it, that collective consciousness can develop. This idea of moving from individual experience to shared experience and then collective consciousness is central to consciousness-raising. It challenges the dominant individualism and privileging of the private experience that is so prevalent in modern Western societies. While this sharing is often achieved through discussion, in either formal or informal groups, it can sometimes be more powerfully portrayed by using other media. Theatre, art, film, storytelling and other forms of expression can be particularly powerful here. Augusto Boal (1979), whose book *Theatre of the Oppressed* is a classic in this regard, describes how when working with poor people in Lima he gave each person a camera and asked them to photograph what they thought was oppression. There were many different photographs and these provoked lively discussion. Two children photographed nails on a wall—they explained that they worked shining shoes and at the end of the day they had to hang their shoe-cleaning bags on the nails; they were in addition required to pay 'rent' for the nail. The photo of the nails was therefore, for them, a powerful symbol of oppression and a wonderful focus for discussion.

As another example, the Australian film director Peter Weir was once asked to produce a documentary on Green Valley, a public housing area in Sydney's western suburbs, popularly portrayed in the media at the time as a 'problem area'. Instead, he began by making a brief satirical film about media coming to 'the valley of doom' in search of sensational stories. Then he worked with several local residents helping them each to shoot, edit and produce their own films of what life in Green Valley was like for them, including the positive aspects of the community often ignored by journalists. These films were then shown at a public meeting, which allowed the people of that community to share their own experiences of Green Valley and begin to take control of the way their community was portrayed. Other community workers have used theatre, working with local people to produce plays about the experience of the community and setting it in a broader context of the global economy and economic exploitation (van Erven 1992). Seeing the story portrayed on stage can be a powerful tool for sharing experiences as part of the consciousness-raising process.

The fourth aspect of consciousness-raising is that it should *open up possibilities for action*. Consciousness-raising will be empowering only if it helps people not only to locate their own experiences within broader structures and discourses of oppression but also to move towards action for change (Boal 1979). As described in other chapters, community power over the definition of need and the claiming of rights is essential in community development, but there is not much point in people being able to define their needs and claim their rights if they cannot also identify ways in which they might act to have their needs met and their rights promoted. Thus empowerment for action is important in any consciousness-raising activity. It is not only about people understanding the structures and discourses that contribute to their oppression or disadvantage, but also about them acting, in Freire's words (1972), to 'transform the objective reality'—to act to bring about change. Ideally this will happen collectively as a result of the shared understandings that have developed from the processes outlined above. Collective action can be much more powerful and effective than individual action and the establishment of a collective activist identity can be a powerful outcome of the consciousness-raising process. For this reason, the exploration of lived reality and the identification of discourses of power and structures of oppression are only the first steps towards empowerment; though important, they need to be combined with the exploration of ways in which change might be effected. However, this may not always be possible, at least in the short term. Some people and communities live in such circumstances that, for good reasons, immediate action for change may not be an option for them. In such a situation an unrealistic emphasis on action for change may simply create false hopes and lead to disillusionment; here it is more important to realise that sometimes increased understanding may be all that will be achieved immediately and that this itself can be important. It is also important to realise that opportunities for change can come and go. Just because there may be no opportunity for action now does not mean that such an opportunity will not arise in the future. Along the way, small actions may represent changes, which, through consciousness-raising discussions, amount to experiences where the community has agency and exercises power. Consciousness-raising may also lead to change at some future date as social, economic and political circumstances change. But ultimately, as part of a community development process, it is the community itself, rather than the community worker, that must make such decisions.

CASE STUDY: Consciousness-raising to challenge oppression

A group of people from a village in south India formed a street theatre group. They worked with the local NGO to perform in villages in the district. One play they developed and performed was on the issue of female infanticide, which is still practised in rural India, where young babies are fed poisoned milk and the bodies are disposed of quickly.

For many families a female child means paying a large dowry at marriage and sometimes being harassed for more over the years by the husband's family. Acquiescing to these demands means borrowing from village moneylenders and throwing the family into debt for yet another generation. Another serious issue is dowry death, where the bride mysteriously burns to death at a kerosene stove after demands for more money have been unsuccessful.

The growth of women's self-help groups and income-generation programs in the district means that women, collectively, can lend and borrow among themselves and also earn an income independent of the men. This means they can now choose to use saved money for the education of daughters, avoiding the dowry system and providing opportunities for professional careers for their daughters.

The street theatre group's plays, while having some moralistic overtones, also raised awareness about the new options for parents and mothers and made links between these and the self-help group movement and income-generation programs spreading through the district. The plays tended to demonise the role of mothers-in-law in female infanticide and, in so doing, challenged this and other oppressions experienced by women in rural south India.

Night after night, villagers would flock to an area outside the village temple as the theatre troupe marched around the village, drums beating, announcing the plays. The audiences were young and old, men and women. Their attention was fixed on the theatre troupe and it was clear they were taking in messages that had great significance for them and impact on them.

- How are the discourses of oppression and the exploration of ways of changing them demonstrated in this case study?

The process of consciousness-raising can happen in a variety of ways; it does not have to be a formal, labelled activity. Rather, it represents a way of working that pervades much of what a community worker does. While it can be focused on a major activity, such as the film-making or drama described above, it can also be undertaken casually as part of day-to-day practice. In conversations over a cup of tea, in a car driving to a meeting or while discussing some particular community project, there can be many opportunities for reframing a problem or issue so that the personal and the political are linked, for sharing experiences of oppression and disadvantage and for dialogue. Consciousness-raising does not have to be a special program (and mostly is not), but can simply be a way of working that seeks any opportunity to engage in dialogue and to explore paths towards collective understanding, shared experience and action. In this way, consciousness-raising can give significant meaning to otherwise seemingly prosaic activities.

Cooperation

Many of the dominant institutions of modern society are based on the principle of competition. Capitalism itself assumes a competitive market and the implication is that unregulated competition will work to the ultimate benefit of all. The competitive ethic is reproduced in other institutions, most notably education, which is based on competitive examinations, individual achievement, prizes and competition for the 'best' jobs and which acts to socialise people for their roles in a competitive society. Competition pervades the workplace and is seen as a primary form of motivation for improved performance. Competitive sport and recreation further reinforce competition as the basis of society. Whether at work or at play, one cannot avoid it. The strength of the competitive ethic can be seen in its application in areas that do not intrinsically lend themselves to competition, where competition transforms the nature and basis of human activity. Thus, music-making, an essentially pleasurable and expressive activity, is made competitive by a system of graded examinations, eisteddfods, talent quests and competitions at all levels, from inter-school to international, thereby transforming the nature of music-making from a convivial, communal and participatory expression of culture to a competitive and ultimately elitist activity. Surfing, an exhilarating individual experience bringing one close to the forces of nature and requiring one to understand and harmonise with them, becomes defined as something that can be judged (inevitably subjectively) and given points so that it can become competitive, with the inevitable consequences: an international professional circuit, world rankings, superstars, 'iron men' and the transformation of the very nature of the activity itself. There are competitions for gardening, fishing, the family pet, babies, debating (an activity which itself turns discussion into competition), writing a novel and so on. While one is not forced to enter such competitions, they have become the only acceptable way to achieve 'excellence' and to have one's skill acknowledged and appreciated. Entering competitions is also necessary if one hopes to make a living from such activities.

The dominance of competition in modern society has led to the commonly held view that it is both natural and desirable but each of these contentions can be questioned. Kohn (1986; see also Craig 1993) maintains that competition is commonly justified on four bases: that it is unavoidable as part of 'human nature', that it motivates people to maximise their productivity, that it is enjoyable and that it makes people more self-confident and 'builds character'. Kohn examines the research evidence for these assumptions and determines that they are largely myths. He argues that competition is neither necessary nor desirable and that cooperative rather than competitive structures represent a more appropriate form for human society. The view that cooperation is at least as 'natural' to human beings as competition has been argued by other writers (Argyle 1991). Kropotkin, in his important work *Mutual Aid* (1972), examines animal behaviour and the evolution of human societies, making a strong case that cooperative assistance is the norm and the dynamic that has led to progress and success for both human and animal societies. For anarchists such as Kropotkin it is the imposition of hierarchy, dominance and authority that has extinguished the cooperative spirit and led to competition; dismantling that hierarchy would allow the 'natural' cooperative ethic of mutual aid to re-emerge. It can be suggested that, even in the supposedly highly competitive world of big business, it is cooperation—in the form of cartels, 'gentlemen's agreements' and joint ventures—rather than competition that ensures the continuing operation of the capitalist system (Gorz 1989). Indeed, much of the apparently necessary regulation of business is aimed at preventing such cooperation, which would otherwise threaten the competitive order on which capitalist economics depends.

Challenging the competitive ethic and basing social and economic structures on principles of cooperation is an important component of community development. There have been many experiments with such structures and the contemporary cooperative movement traces its origins back to the planned cooperative community of Robert Owen in the early 19th century and, most particularly, to the establishment of the Rochdale Society of Equitable Pioneers in 1844 (Melnyk 1985; Craig 1993). These cooperatives were essentially ways of people organising for mutual economic benefit through the pooling of production and/or consumption. The specified principles of Rochdale have become the bases of the cooperative movement: voluntary and open membership, democratic control, limited return on capital, surplus earnings to be returned to the members, education for the members and cooperation between cooperatives. Since Rochdale many cooperatives have been formed in widely differing social, economic, political and cultural contexts. While many were not successful, there have been many that have thrived and this, in the face of the dominance of the competitive ethic, demonstrates the viability and the adaptability of the cooperative concept. They include worker cooperatives, consumer cooperatives, housing cooperatives and cooperative or communal societies such as the kibbutz.

Cooperatives have not been without their problems; maintaining a cooperative ethos in the midst of a competitive society is not easy and many cooperatives have been unable to survive for more than a short time. Some cooperatives have grown so large over time that they have lost the features of democratic control and have become little more than conventional corporations or public agencies using a cooperative label; this is the case with some credit unions and farming cooperatives, which have been established for many years and have become part of the conservative business community.

Despite these difficulties, the lesson from the cooperative movement is that cooperative structures are indeed feasible in a wide variety of social, economic, political and cultural settings. The community-based alternative would most likely incorporate some, if not all, aspects of the cooperative movement and this would be more consistent with the ecological and social justice/human rights principles identified in Chapters 2 to 4 than would a decentralised form of competition. The challenge is to extend the cooperative concept beyond the economic (which has been the basis of most formal cooperatives) to incorporate social, political and cultural dimensions. This will be explored further in Chapter 9, but the important point for present purposes is that community development work should be seeking to establish and reinforce cooperative structures and discourses, rather than competitive structures and discourses, wherever possible. Without at least some level of cooperation and commitment to a cooperative ethic there can be no community.

The pace of development

One of the important aspects of the community development process is that it cannot be rushed. For the process to be a good one it is necessary to allow it to proceed at its 'natural' pace and to rush the process is to compromise it. This is a common source of frustration for a community worker and it is important to reiterate that *the process is the community's, not the worker's*. Hence it has to proceed at the community's pace, which may not be the pace the worker would want. This is a natural outcome of the idea of 'organic development' discussed in Chapter 2. The organic approach to change sees change occurring on a number of dimensions, through gradual processes of development rather than imposed radical change. The analogy of a growing plant was used in Chapter 2; one cannot really make a plant grow any faster, though some growth can be achieved through the provision of extra nutrients. Similarly, a community worker can help to create the right conditions for development and help to secure resources, but beyond that the pace of growth and development is really beyond their control. Indeed, just as fast-growing plants are likely to have less secure root systems and weaker, more fragile branches, so a strong resilient community is less likely to emerge from a 'quick fix' process. Community development, if it is to be successful, is a long-term process of organic development and cannot be rushed. This does not mean to say that some things cannot be achieved in the short term—some processes can be implemented quite quickly. But these are only part of the whole and the community worker must always be aware that the process needs to take its own time and work itself out in its own way.

This can be challenging for a community worker used to a world of deadlines, efficiency and outcomes, where good process is devalued and simply seen as a means to an end. It can also be frustrating for a worker who has seen similar processes through before and who can 'see' the likely outcome in advance, but has to sit with a long and (for the worker) tedious process. But there is really no alternative. Sometimes, as discussed above, the constraints of the external world demand that processes be compromised in order to meet deadlines and the community (not just the worker) needs to make a decision to that effect. However, it is important always to be seeking to allow the process to take as long as it needs and for development to occur at the pace with which the community itself is comfortable. The motto 'It takes as long as it takes' is an important one for a community worker to bear in mind. It is also worth remembering that the perceived need for speed in process seems to be a peculiarity of Western culture. Other cultures, and especially Indigenous cultures, have very different concepts of process and of time, where the phrase 'It takes as long as it takes' (with the implication that the 'outcome' can be postponed indefinitely if necessary) would be obvious and would go without saying. This is in sharp contrast to Western culture, where it is often seen as a threat to the very structures of society (with their associated deadlines, timetables, outcomes, schedules and general sense of rush). To be able to sit back, reflect and talk something through at length and in detail is a luxury that many Westerners cannot afford, but for people in other cultures it is seen as a necessity.

Peace and non-violence

While peace is a goal that would receive almost universal endorsement, it has proved extremely hard to achieve at both the global and the national levels, even if it is understood in terms of its most limited meaning, namely as *absence of war*. If *peace* is given a broader definition, to include more positive connotations of personal and community wellbeing as well as absence of stress and conflict, it is an even more elusive goal. Similarly, violence would be almost universally condemned and yet levels of violence continue to give cause for concern. Like peace, violence can be understood at a simplistic level (physical violence by individuals and groups) and at a more fundamental level, including both emotional violence and institutionalised violence; if conceived in this broader context, violence can be seen to be strongly entrenched in modern society.

If such universally desired objectives as peace and non-violence cannot be achieved, there are two possible conclusions that can be reached. One is that the structural constraints and vested interests opposing them are strong and entrenched and the other is that the methods that have been adopted for pursuing these goals are inadequate and inappropriate. In the case of peace and non-violence, it is clear that the interests and structures opposing them are extremely strong (e.g. nationalism, sectarianism, the protection of privilege and global inequality, patriarchy, colonialism, profit, the arms trade) and any peace and anti-violence strategy must address them. The non-violence perspective, however, also suggests that the conventional methods of pursuing peace—and indeed of pursuing other social change agendas—are themselves at fault.

This view draws on an analysis of the relationship of means and ends and on the critique of competition and competitive structures, as discussed earlier in this chapter.

Perhaps the most influential proponent of non-violence, at least in the 20th century, has been Mahatma Gandhi (1964). Gandhi used non-violent methods which emphasised building consensus and not polarising a community. His philosophy attacked ideas and structures, but did not attack people. He sought to allow his opponents to 'change sides' and join his movement while retaining their dignity and self-respect. This inclusive and consensus-oriented perspective is an important characteristic of the non-violent position. Consensus solutions are seen as preferable to conflict solutions (conflict, after all, can be seen as a form of violence) and non-violent approaches seek to unite rather than divide, to include rather than exclude and not to use or crystallise conflict. Such an approach may seem naïve within the context of modern Western society, but it is important to remember that many traditional societies have embodied these traditions (Norberg-Hodge 1991) and that these societies have been much more ecologically sustainable and community-based than the Western societies, which are the cause of so many of the critical problems facing the planet. Acceptance of such norms is achievable, though it would require fundamental changes to the structures of modern Western societies.

The non-violent position also accepts a broader definition of violence than is normally understood, in that it includes notions of institutional and structural violence and the violation of human rights. From this perspective, structures that perpetuate inequality, poverty and oppression are by their very nature violent and need to be challenged. The way in which many social institutions operate is seen as violent in that it perpetuates the structures and practices of oppression. Hence the notion of violence applies to more than individual or group 'acts of violence'; it also incorporates institutions and mechanisms of social control. The welfare system, the justice system, the education system, the financial system and large central bureaucracies may be regarded as structures of violence to the extent that they support and reinforce an unjust, disempowering and oppressive social and economic order.

The non-violent perspective is both powerful and radical, and it demands major questioning of accepted structures and practices. Its influence on community work has been significant (Kelly & Sewell 1988) and it represents an important aspect of the approach to community development described in later chapters.

Consensus

The differing perspectives of conflict and consensus have been critical in the conceptualisation of community development. Conflict is an inevitable part of society—especially of processes of change—and it is naïve for a community worker to assume that conflict can always be avoided. The capacity to deal with (and move beyond) conflict is an essential part of community work. But a consensus perspective is far more consistent with the approach to community development taken in this book and hence is, where possible, to be preferred.

Many approaches to community work, however, are based on models of conflict rather than consensus. In a conflict model, the emphasis is on winning, outmanoeuvering an opponent (who might be a local authority, a mining company, a landlord, a developer or some other 'villain'), or achieving something at the expense of something or someone else. The quasi-military language of much community work—*campaign*, *strategy*, *tactics*—suggests the tacit assumption of a conflict model. The problem with the conflict approach is that it produces losers as well as winners and the losers will be marginalised and alienated as a result. This works directly against community building, against inclusion and against a non-violent approach.

The consensus approach works with and through differences, towards agreement, and aims at reaching a solution that the whole group or community will 'own' as theirs. This may seem to contradict what was discussed in Chapter 6 in relation to partnerships and the criticism of the traditional view of them, which, it was argued, was based on a consensus model. What was being criticised in Chapter 6 was not the idea of consensus as agreement, but the idea of consensus as sameness. In fact, reaching agreement assumes there is difference rather than sameness. To reach agreement, one must acknowledge and respect diverse views and then enter into dialogue and negotiations to accommodate diversity and reach agreement. In this sense, consensus is an inevitable consequence of non-violence and inclusiveness. Consensus, as reaching agreement, also means more than simply agreeing to accept the will of the majority, which can leave up to 49 per cent of the community dissatisfied. It also means more than mere compromise, which can leave everyone dissatisfied. Rather, it implies that the group or community commits itself to a process that seeks to find a solution or course of action everyone can accept and own and where people agree that what has been decided is in the best interests of all. It requires that everyone should be able to have effective input into the decision and also that they are able to be part of the 'talking through' of the decision so that they are able to accept, and feel a sense of ownership of, the outcome. Consensus cannot usually be achieved quickly; it needs to be built. This will often take much longer than more conventional forms of decision making and can be very frustrating for those used to voting and 'getting the numbers'. However, in the long term it achieves much more satisfactory results and provides a stronger base for community development. It also implies a willingness and commitment on the part of community members to achieve a consensus and a commitment not to block the consensus being achieved.

As discussed earlier in relation to the pace of development, consensus basically means working through an issue, however long it takes, until everyone is comfortable with the outcome. While this might, to modern Western ears, sound a hopelessly naïve and impossible prospect, it is worth remembering that people in Indigenous communities have used such decision-making techniques for centuries and that to people from those societies the conventional Western forms of decision making seem utterly inappropriate. Such Indigenous communities have been able to sustain much stronger community structures and more ecologically sound lifestyles, and the wisdom of consensus decision making is one lesson the so-called 'developed' minority world societies can learn from them.

Community building

All community development should aim at community building. Community building involves building social capital, strengthening the social interactions within the community, bringing people together and helping them to communicate with each other in a way that can lead to genuine dialogue, understanding and social action. Loss of community has resulted in fragmentation, isolation and individualisation and community building seeks to reverse these effects. Community building is necessary if the establishment of viable and sustainable community-level structures and processes is to be achieved (Putnam 1993).

While community building may, in some circumstances, be the primary purpose or a specific objective of a community process, it is more often a consequence of some other activity. Indeed, people may feel uncomfortable about being brought together simply in order to interact with each other; they are generally much more comfortable about being brought together for a specific purpose. A recycling project, a local currency system, a community arts project, an environmental campaign, the establishment of a community school and housing cooperatives are all examples of community projects that can bring people together around a common activity, but where community bonds are strengthened in the process, making further development possible. In fact, when asked why they participate in a community project people will often say that it is meeting and getting to know other people that is most important; they may have joined initially because they believed in the value of the project itself, but it is often the social interaction associated with the project that keeps them involved.

Thus good community development will bring people together and ensure that all community activities can enhance community building by seeking to involve people as much as possible, to increase their mutual dependence for the accomplishment of tasks and to provide opportunities for both formal and informal interaction. Often it is the informal that is the most important—ensuring that there is time, space and opportunity for people to have a cup of tea together (or a glass of wine, a coffee or a can of beer, depending on the context), as well as to engage in the formal activity (Cox & Caldwell 2000).

Community building is about more than simply bringing people together. It involves encouraging people to work with each other, developing structures that mean people become more dependent on each other to get things done and seeking ways in which every person can contribute and be genuinely valued by others as a result. Group process, inclusiveness, building trust and developing a common sense of purpose are all critically important in community building and hence the idea of community building can and should pervade all community development processes.

Conclusion

Community development is, at heart, a process. In evaluating community development projects one must look at the process and in planning and implementing any community development program it is the process, rather than the outcome, to which the community worker must give primary consideration. Those who insist on 'outcome statements' need to realise that, for community development, good process is the most important 'outcome' that can be achieved. The process, if it is a good one, will enable the community to determine its own goals and to remain in control of the journey as well as the ultimate destination. For this reason community development does not always sit easily in the outcome-driven world of managerialism, which is why community development is so important.

It represents a significant challenge to a way of thinking and operating that has often bypassed the people most involved, that has tended to accept a philosophy of the end justifying the means and that has led to disempowerment. It seeks to establish a way of thinking where people interacting with each other is important, where the quality of the collective experience is valued and where it is in the experience of community processes that people are able to maximise their potential and achieve their full humanity. As well as establishing a way of thinking, it seeks also to provide the opportunity for these valued processes to become a reality for people.

>> discussion questions

1. In what ways can community development be described as a journey of discovery? What are the features of such a journey?
2. How are means and ends intertwined and what does this mean for working with communities?
3. If the community development process has value in its own right, in what ways can you relate this idea to the principles of 'bottom-up' community development and participation discussed in the last two chapters?
4. What is entailed in the idea of ownership by the community of process?
5. Describe the four aspects of consciousness-raising.
6. What makes a cooperative approach in community development such a radical approach in the contemporary social, economic and political climate?
7. What are the accepted structures and practices that a non-violent approach questions?
8. How does the conflict approach perpetuate marginalisation and alienation?
9. What is meant by consensus as discussed in this chapter?

>> reflective questions

1. What are your reactions to the idea of embarking on journeys allowing the destination to remain both unknown and in the hands of community members? Where do these reactions originate from in terms of your life experience? Do you think you will need to make changes to your position in relation to the community development process?
2. How do you think you would work within a consensus model? Would there be frustrations for you? If so, what would these be and what would be their consequences for community development? What changes does your reflection suggest that you may have to engage in as a community worker?

CHAPTER 8

The global and the local

Introduction

With the advent of globalisation, the global economy, electronic communication and accessible world travel, the idea that we live in one world has become important in all fields, including community development (Held et al. 1999; Meyer & Geschiere 1999; Mittelman 2000). This chapter will explore issues of the global and the local, internationalism and colonialism as they relate to the principles and practice of community development in a 'globalising' world.

Globalisation and localisation

The dominant discourse of globalisation is almost exclusively economic. It is about the integration of trade and financial markets at a global level and the breaking down of national barriers. This concentration on the economic is to the exclusion of other international agendas, which formed the earlier internationalist ideal and which suggested that the idea of living in 'one world' meant international agendas of peace, social justice, human rights, environmental protection, education, mutual understanding and cultural exchange. With the more recent manifestation of globalisation, these other agendas are seen as secondary to the needs of the global economy, with the implicit view that if the global economy can be made to work, the rest will follow. This is a global variation of economic fundamentalism, which has been the core policy assumption of many national governments—the idea that the economy comes first and that everything else can, and indeed must, take second place to the needs of the economy.

The economic domination of globalisation is important; it suggests that the experience of globalisation is one-sided and in the interests of the powerful. It represents an assertion of the rights of capital to move anywhere and do anything, in the interests of profit maximisation, but does not carry with it a corresponding assertion of the rights of people to do the same—except, of course, for the rich and powerful (Burbach et al. 1997; Bauman 1998). The wealthy are proud to call themselves 'citizens of the world', but that hardly applies to the poor, to refugees, to asylum-seekers and to migrant workers, who find that any rights they may have as 'global citizens' are very weak indeed.

The globalisation of the economy has not been accompanied by the globalisation of citizenship and there has been, if anything, a reaction against the realisation of global citizenship rights with a hardening of attitudes towards refugees, immigrants and ethnic minorities.

It is instructive to note that we are often encouraged to interfere in other nations' economies ('overseas investment opportunities') and to welcome others who want to interfere in our economy ('encouraging foreign investment and reducing trade barriers'). But when it comes to matters of human rights, national sovereignty suddenly becomes very important and we are warned not to interfere in the 'internal affairs' of another country and encouraged to be sensitive and cautious, nor do we welcome those from outside who want to criticise our own country's human rights record. This is a clear example of the unbalanced nature of globalisation and how it is in the interests of global profits and not (unless by coincidence) in the interests of the principles of ecological sustainability, social justice and human rights on which this book is based.

It is important to emphasise that governments, to a large degree, have little choice but to follow policies that support the interests and demands of global capital as expressed through 'the markets'. This is because the power of the global economy is such that if a government were to institute policies that displeased 'the markets', there would be an instant flight of capital, loss of investment and a currency crisis. Hence governments are operating with a very narrow range of policy options. This is one factor that makes the current experience of globalisation different from the older forms of world trade; there has been world trade for centuries, but it was always able to be controlled (and manipulated) by national governments. Now, however, it is national governments that are controlled and manipulated by the global economy—as the global financial crisis has so clearly evidenced. This is why it is unrealistic to expect too much of governments in terms of social expenditure. Governments may want to spend more on education, health, housing, poverty alleviation, public transport and so on, but while the orthodox view of 'the markets' is that this will erode profitability and that any increase in taxation will place an unbearable constraint on economic performance, it is impossible for a government to follow such policies. It is important to note that whether or not such assumptions are factually correct is immaterial; the *belief* that they are correct is sufficient to drive the forces of 'the markets' and hence it is in the *discourse* of economic fundamentalism that the power of globalisation lies.

A useful way to understand globalisation, with significant implications for community development, is through Manuel Castells' idea of the *network society*. Castells (1996, 1997, 1998) described the emergence of networks of power, where power resides in networks that communicate across national boundaries, linking powerful interests in different countries. These changing and diffuse networks of power therefore claim no geographical or political location. They may link, for example, interests in London, Jakarta, Tokyo, Mumbai, Toronto, Buenos Aires, Brisbane, Capetown, Cairo, Shanghai and Chicago, through electronic communication. One's power in this society is determined by one's access to these networks of power; there is a privileged minority with access to power and wealth and a majority that is excluded. In their influential book *The Global Trap*, Martin and Schumann (1997) point out that the global economy is able to get by very well by employing just 20 per cent of the world's population; the remaining 80 per cent are 'surplus to requirements', and will be marginalised and ignored. There is actually nothing new in this state of affairs—since the industrial revolution the world has effectively been the '80–20 society' described by Martin and Schumann, but until recently the lucky 20 per cent and the unlucky 80 per cent have been, in the main, separated by national boundaries: there were 'rich countries' and 'poor countries'. With the network society this is breaking down. Although there are still clearly some countries that are richer than others, there are now richer elites and poorer majorities in most countries of the world. Those who live in the West have been used to having the 'poor 80 per cent' living beyond their nation's boundaries, conveniently out of sight and out of mind. But one of the effects of globalisation and the network society is that national boundaries are becoming less important as boundaries of inequality and most Western nations are seeing the widening of inequalities within their borders. This has led to the creation of marginalised communities in the minority world as well as the majority world. These are typically communities that have relied on the 'old economy'—former industrial towns and cities, fishing and farming communities and so on—which are being bypassed by the global economy, perhaps best symbolised by the closure of bank branches in those communities (established banks being the representatives of the global economy at the local level, which now deem those communities not viable and irrelevant to the needs of globalised profit). Other typically marginalised communities are those that were previously protected within a welfare state and which still try to survive in the post-welfare period, such as people with chronic mental illness. Many of these people have experienced forced migration from safe asylums to the very risky streets and parks of the world's cities as a result of de-institutionisation policies driven by economic factors.

While the globalisation of the economy has not brought with it the globalisation of citizenship, social justice, human rights or equality, it has generated the globalisation of culture. The imposition of a global culture, sometimes referred to as 'Americanisation' or 'Disneyfication', has been noted by many commentators and can be seen in everyday life. People in different parts of the world are increasingly wearing similar clothes, eating similar food, watching the same movies, listening to the same music and playing the same games. The imposition of a culture, based on mainstream American consumer culture, is of course an important aspect of economic globalisation, in that it creates global markets (Barber 1995). It is much easier to manufacture and market a product if the whole world will buy it than it is if the product has to change according to regional and cultural variations—so the globalisation of culture is effectively the creation of a global market for the benefit of global capital. This has a devastating effect on local communities and cultural diversity and it also has a powerful controlling effect: if one wants to be part of the global economy, or benefit from the network society, it is important to eat, drink, dress, work and play in more or less the American way and, most important of all, to speak English. Because culture, and especially language, is so important to people's sense of identity, the globalisation of culture has a major impact on communities and local identity in many parts of the world. (This is further discussed below in the context of colonialism.)

There have been a number of reactions against globalisation in the form of various manifestations of localisation (Cox 1997; Hines 2000). Localisation has been driven by a sense of frustration at globalisation and its impact and the feeling that it is not meeting people's needs. One reaction has been *economic* localisation. This is where the globalised economy is seen as having ignored and marginalised local needs and where there have been attempts to establish local alternative economies. This includes community banks (as an alternative to the large impersonal globalised banks), local currency and exchange schemes, cooperatives, establishing local business, engaging in women's self-help groups' income-generation programs and boycotting multinationals. (This will be discussed further in Chapter 9 as part of the broader consideration of community economic development.) Another form of localisation is *cultural* localisation—the attempt to reinvest meaning and vitality in local cultural traditions, the use of local resources, celebrating local histories, revitalising local languages, holding village festivals and so on. (Community cultural development will be discussed in more detail in Chapter 9.) Finally, there is *political* localisation, where people seek an alternative form of politics based in the local, because of the perceived irrelevance of the traditional political structures and parties that are responsive to the imperatives of globalisation.

Members of a women's self-help group engage in an income-generation project—one response to economic globalisation's further marginalisation of women

These forms of localisation, as responses to globalisation, contain both dangers and opportunities. The danger is that they can become exclusive, narrow, reactionary and parochial, resulting in racism and intolerance (Kleymeyer 1994). The support for new political parties based on populism and exclusion, such as the One Nation party in Australia and some of the right-wing racist parties of Europe, can be attributed to a perception by many people that globalisation has resulted in traditional parties having no relevance to their local needs. Emphasising local culture can also lead to racism and exclusion and there seems to be an alarming increase in racism and intolerance in many societies. Vigilante and citizens' militia groups in the United States represent another alarming local trend against globalisation. Community workers at the local level may have to contend with such negative manifestations of localisation, which are a consequence of insecurity, fear, mistrust, uncertainty and a perception of irrelevance in the traditional structures and processes of politics and power.

However, there is also considerable positive potential in localisation, from a community development perspective (Campfens 1997; Wallace 1996; Kenny 2007). Localisation can provide the opportunity for the development of more self-reliant communities, as discussed in previous chapters. All of the reactions to globalisation described above can be, in fact, community development: the establishment of local currency schemes and cooperatives, the validating and promotion of local cultural traditions, participating in women's self-help groups, local communities seeking to empower themselves and so on. As well as threats, localisation presents opportunities for community development to occur, especially in the communities that have been excluded from the networks of power and marginalised by the new global economy. It is in Martin and Schumann's 80 per cent—those surplus to the requirements of the global economy—that there is tremendous potential for community development. And if the global economy does one day collapse, as seems quite likely given its evident instability and unsustainability, it is from community-based initiatives at the margins (among the 80 per cent) that viable sustainable alternatives are most likely to be developed. When the value of shares and investments collapses and when paid employment largely disappears, the local currency scheme that used to be marginalised can be the alternative that formerly wealthy people will turn to as a way of providing some form of economic security. When there is no money for state or private schools, the community-based school becomes the only viable option. When real estate becomes worthless, cooperative housing becomes a necessity. While such an economic crisis may not lead to these eventualities in the immediate future, simply thinking about the possibility can help people to realise that community-based structures are ultimately more sustainable and have a more solid social foundation than many of the institutions on which we have come to rely.

Thus globalisation, as well as apparently working against local community, has ironically also created space for community development to occur and flourish. In the marginal communities, excluded from the 'benefits' of globalisation, community is both needed and valued and the reaction of localisation has created a fertile ground for community workers and a resurgence of interest in community development.

Global and local practice

The impetus for globalisation and the reaction of localisation suggest that it is the local and the global that represent the important sites for change and practice (Campfens 1997; Karliner 2000). Most of the important decisions that affect people's lives and which affect communities are made at the global level: in boardrooms, stock exchanges, investment houses and at global economic forums far removed from local reality (Bauman 1998). As we have seen above, national governments have little power to affect these decisions and little autonomy to implement policies that contradict global economic interests. For example, the decision to close a manufacturing plant, rendering thousands of workers unemployed with devastating results for the local community, may be made on the other side of the world with little regard to the wishes of the national government and the government is unable to follow policies that would address the problem, such as providing tariff protection to the industry, investing significant public funds in the community or providing alternative employment for the workers. To do so would invoke the wrath of the global markets as it would require rises in taxation to meet the public expenditure involved as well as the breaking of world free-trade agreements; the consequences for the national economy, and the survival of that government, would be devastating. National governments have become, to some degree, helpless bystanders in the decisions that really matter. This is not to say that governments can do nothing; they can have some impact at the margins and they can create the space for such initiatives as community development to be implemented, but they cannot be expected to solve all the problems of modern society, however much the rhetoric of political parties and the conventional wisdom of politics might suggest otherwise.

This suggests that working towards change at the level of national government is unlikely to be very effective. With globalisation and localisation, the sites for effective change have moved to the global and the local and it is these two levels that must constitute the foci of action

(Lawson 2000). Community development is clearly a strategy that is aimed at change at the local level and, as suggested above, localisation has created significant space for community development to occur. While global capital may be able to intimidate national governments, its power to coerce local action is much weaker; a group of local people working to create a positive community in the local school, setting up a local currency trading scheme, forming a local environmental action group or organising participatory street theatre is unlikely to feel very threatened or intimidated by global markets. At the local level the perceived power of global forces is weaker and communities can do things that governments cannot. However, in the era of globalisation, to concentrate exclusively on the local is not enough. It is at the global level that key decisions are taken and if a community development program is really serious about ideas of ecological sustainability, social justice and human rights it is necessary to see how it can link to the global as well as the local. The Green motto, 'Think globally, act locally', is no longer sufficient. It is necessary to think *and* act globally, and to think *and* act locally (Wallace 1996). Analysis and action must take place at both levels and the key to creative and effective community work is to be able to *link the global and the local* in everyday practice.

The linking of the global and the local is therefore a major challenge for community development. In order to see how this might be achieved, it is useful to examine the idea of 'globalisation from below', as advocated by Falk (1993), Brecher and Costello (1994) and Robertson (1995), among others. This suggests that globalisation, as currently experienced, and as described above, can be characterised as globalisation 'from above'. It is exclusively in the interests of the powerful controllers of global capital and is not in the interests of ordinary people, communities and the vast majority of the world's population. Its emphasis on economics at the expense of social and environmental issues means that it does not take account of many things that directly affect the lives of people and communities. It is unaccountable and undemocratic; indeed, not only is it undemocratic, but also it can directly work against democratic participation in important decision making, so it is also *anti*-democratic. The idea of 'globalisation from below', however, is that globalisation does not have to be like that. This view suggests that some form of globalisation is now inevitable, given the development of information and communication technology and rapid travel, but it does not have to be the economic fundamentalist globalisation 'from above' as currently experienced. Indeed some form of global understanding, awareness and action—the idea that 'we live in one world'—is probably necessary if impending ecological disasters are to be avoided. Globalisation from below seeks to implement a form of globalisation that is democratic and participatory, which is about issues of direct concern to people—including ecological sustainability, social justice and human rights—and which seeks to empower rather than disempower local communities. The same technology that has made economic 'globalisation from above' possible can be used to establish globalisation from below, which is clearly more in accord with the principles of community development as described in this book.

Giddens (1994: p. 5) expands the notion of globalisation beyond a top-down economic process. He describes globalisation as a complex set of many processes, which are often contradictory and which have multiple and sometimes contradictory outcomes. He and other writers, such as Robertson (1995), include not only the way that large-scale changes have affected daily living, but also the ways in which local activity can be globally consequential. Local individual actions, such as buying recycled goods, have consequences for rainforests in distant parts of the world. Robertson refers to these bottom-up processes that have influences globally as 'glocalisation'. In the view of these perspectives, globalisation is not a unidirectional, single process but one that enables the local to influence the global.

CASE STUDY: Local action tackling a global crisis

The Murray River, which flows through four states in Australia and is a major waterway on the continent, is in serious trouble for many reasons, including unsustainable agricultural practices. Costly dredging is now necessary to keep the river mouth open and where fresh water once flowed into the sea, barrages have been built to keep salt water from backflowing into the river. There are two lakes near the entrance to the sea and these lakes are quickly drying up, with the exposed lake beds acidifying. The Murray River issue is just one example of a larger global problem of water and sustainability. Water issues are not just ecological. Water has social, economic and cultural significance, as well as environmental.

The River Murray Catchment Water Management Board has responsibility for managing the river and balancing the tensions between the social, economic, cultural and environmental demands on the river and its catchment. Because of the various demands by different groups, communities and users of the river, the Board places great emphasis on working to engage these diverse groups in the management process. The Board has a structure of Local Action Planning committees as a means of ensuring local involvement in achieving globally important ecological goals. Members of these committees are local people and they are supported and encouraged to collaborate with other local community groups, including local Landcare groups, to contribute to building up the sustainability of the Murray River. In funding terms, support to local groups of over $7 million has been gathered from different sources. Local Action Planning committees undertake research on the important issues facing their community and devise projects and programs to address these issues. Local participation and management of activities, as well as collaboration among community groups, ensures there

Local people collaborating to address environmental issues of global importance

is energetic work at the local level to contribute to the more global goals of water sustainability. Many local communities have won funds to employ project officers who build a participatory base to the local work. Typical issues being worked on by local communities within this program include the loss and decline of biodiversity among native vegetation; degradation of wetlands and erosion of coastal areas; watercourse degradation as a result of agricultural activities, such as the invasion of waterways by pasture grasses; the effects of water and wind erosion; poor soil fertility and water salination from deforestation and other causes. Reflection on these issues will show how human activity, often economic activity, over prolonged periods has contributed to the current crisis. Such economic activities have built strong communities over time. So addressing these issues must consider the social, economic and cultural importance of past practices. The participation of the diverse groups, with their diverse interests, is essential for effective processes and environmental outcomes.

- What global–local relationships are at play in the work of Local Action Planning committees in terms of the issues being addressed and some of the factors contributing to the current crisis?

'Glocalisation'—the process of globalisation from below—is already happening in a number of different forms. Local environmental groups have effectively used the Internet to share common experiences, seek expertise and join in global action campaigns (Taylor 1995). Until the advent of the Internet, a local environmental action group challenging a multinational oil company over a local issue was engaging in an unequal struggle and could not hope to match the resources and expertise of the company. Now, through the Internet, that group is able to call on worldwide resources and expertise, learn of experiences of other groups that have dealt with the same company and locate its local struggle as part of a worldwide struggle for environmental sustainability, calling on some very powerful allies. The People's Health Movement has utilised the Internet and emails to build worldwide momentum to challenge the erosion of health as a human right and to sustain the movement after its first People's Health Assembly in Bangladesh in 2000 and the second People's Health Assembly in Ecuador in 2005. It has developed and strengthened regional activities largely through the Internet and e-communication. However, it is not only through the Internet that globalisation from below can be achieved. Amnesty International provides a powerful model of how local people, working in their own local communities, can be brought together as part of an integrated global human rights movement; this was successfully established well before the advent of computers and the Internet. As a further example, Indigenous peoples have been able to connect with each other across the world and have seen their local struggles for justice and rights as part of a global struggle of Indigenous people against colonialist oppression. The proposed Multilateral Agreement on Investment, which would have given unprecedented power to transnational capital and further limited the power of national governments, was abandoned because of pressure from consumer and citizen groups all over the world, communicating through email, opposing such an erosion of the democratic rights of citizens and the autonomy of sovereign governments. Protests against the meetings of the masters of the global economy (e.g. in Seattle in 1999, Melbourne in 2000, Quebec in 2001, Edinburgh in 2005) were possible because of the capacity of activists to network globally.

The above examples are just some forms of globalisation from below. There is no single model and in a postmodern world it is appropriate that globalisation from below is a varied and diverse movement rather than a single, tightly organised one. Community development can use such forms

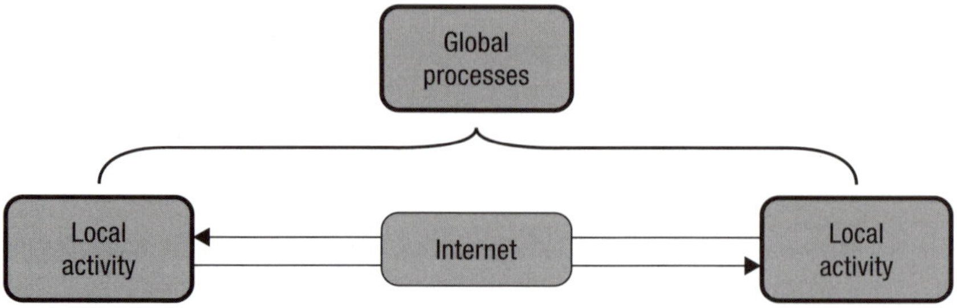

Figure 8.1 Local sites linking horizontally

of practice and, indeed, can pioneer other forms of globalisation from below. A local community will have much in common with other local communities, often geographically removed. For example, a rural community in Australia suffering the effects of rural economic decline, the collapse of traditional markets and the withdrawal of services will have more in common with similar rural communities in Canada, India, Africa, Argentina or Ireland than it will with urban or suburban communities in Australia. Such rural communities can be remarkably resilient and creative and the Internet provides a ready opportunity to share experiences, exchange stories of success and failure and dialogue about possible joint action at a global level. This form of globalisation from below, which links local sites horizontally, is represented in Figure 8.1.

The use of the Internet and the linking of local sites to each other horizontally is just one of several ways in that globalisation from below can occur. Local activity can also mediate government policy that has already been shaped by globalisation processes. This represents a more vertical form of globalisation from below. An example of this is urban renewal. This is a phenomenon occurring across many minority world nations. Decaying urban housing estates are being redeveloped with new or refurbished housing stock and a hope of community renewal. A feature of most of these projects at local sites is that public housing is being transferred to private developers and the renewed housing stock goes onto the private market for sale and rental. This reflects the pressure of national and state governments to engage in privatisation and to operate within a market paradigm, which is part of neoliberal economic globalisation. Housing, arguably a human right and once a social resource, is being commodified as a need to be met by the private sector. For one community in minority world Australia the response to the planned urban renewal was to organise to influence the process and outcomes of policy implementation so that people who were already marginalised would not be further disadvantaged by the urban renewal project. The residents realised that their community was to be dramatically changed. However, they believed that if they could use their influence to gain some policy changes, future projects and other communities might benefit. In other words, they were conscious of their ability to mediate policies that were shaped by global economic forces. They succeeded in several changes to government policy, which subsequently benefited other urban communities. This form of globalisation from below, where one local site mediates broad policy and processes, thus affecting other local sites and modifying the consequences of globalisation, is represented in Figure 8.2.

Such linking of the local and the global is now a major priority for community workers—the two should not be seen as exclusive dualistic categories. To paraphrase the feminist motto about the personal and the political, it is important to emphasise that *the local is global and the global is local*.

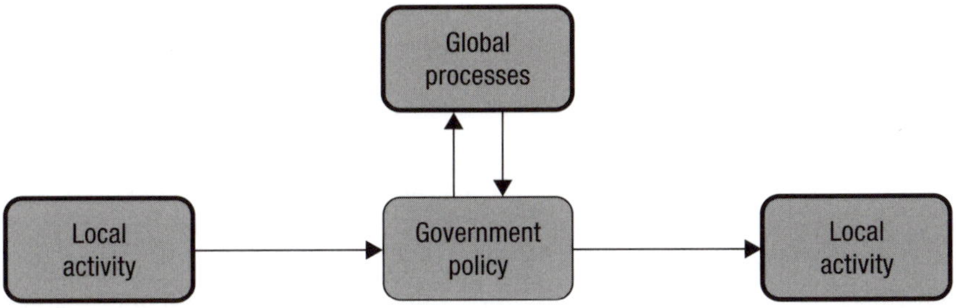

Figure 8.2 Local sites influencing broader processes

Simply engaging with community members in a dialogue about the implications of such a statement can be a significant starting point for creative global–local community development. It can be the starting point for local people to build an identity as global citizens, to identify social citizenship processes in which they can engage and then to think and act globally and locally. Landcare Australia is a movement with a global awareness of the effects of land degradation on the planet. It works to link groups of people in local sites, whether they are farmers, fisherpeople, community groups or schools. These wide-ranging local groups, in turn, engage in local projects to care for their environment. In this way, partnerships are forged and global ecological issues are addressed in numerous local sites around Australia.

Universal and contextual issues

The above discussion suggests that, in the context of the importance of globalisation and the need to link community development across national boundaries, there are common elements to community development wherever it is practised. This implies some universal principles of community development, but seems to conflict with the valuing of the local, as discussed in Chapter 5. Too much emphasis on universal principles could undermine the local essence of community work. Yet without some global understandings of what community development is and what it aims to do, community development will not be part of the important agenda of globalisation from below. For this reason, the topic of universal and contextual issues needs to be addressed.

At a general level, there are some principles of community development that apply universally and which can be seen to be necessary in any approach to community development, whatever the social, political or cultural context. These are the subjects of earlier chapters, namely:

- the idea and experience of community as being necessary for people to achieve their full humanity
- the principles of ecological sustainability, holism, balance, etc.
- the principles of social justice and human rights, including an analysis of oppression (class, gender and race/ethnicity, etc.)
- the principles of change from below, bottom-up development, valuing local knowledge and skills, etc.
- the centrality of citizen participation
- the principles of the importance and integrity of process, consciousness-raising, empowerment, cooperation, etc.

These general principles apply to all community development, whatever the context. However, they can be, and must be, contextualised very differently in different locations (Campfens 1997;

Kenny 2007). The experience of community may be important everywhere, but it will also be differently constructed and experienced in different cultural contexts; the idea of 'community' means something very different in an Inuit community in the Arctic than in an urban ghetto in Los Angeles, a township in majority world Africa, a village in Indonesia, an outer suburb of Sydney, a fishing port in Ireland and a slum in São Paolo. The experience of community—what is important about it, how it is experienced and how it can be nurtured—will be very different in those different locations. It cannot be imposed from outside and must be defined by the people themselves. The principles of ecological sustainability will also mean very different things in different communities and will imply different imperatives for community development. Structural oppression on the basis of class, gender, race and so on will be different in those different locations and the struggle against oppression will find different expressions. For example, the struggle for the liberation of women occurs in all cultural contexts, but it takes different forms, and addresses different issues in different ways, in Beijing, Jakarta, Kolkata, Kabul, Toronto, Nairobi and Riyadh. And processes such as consciousness-raising, empowerment and participation must, of necessity, take very different forms in different communities. The basic principles remain the same and provide an overall framework within which community development can be understood and dialogue can occur, but they are defined and implemented very differently.

Thus a community worker needs to have an understanding of both the local context, within which any community development experience must be grounded, and the broader picture of community development principles, which, in a general way, apply universally. If the community worker loses sight of the necessity for local contextualisation, they run the risk of adopting a colonialist approach to practice, imposing a unitary world view on all communities regardless of context. (Such colonialist practice will be discussed in some detail below.)

On the other hand, a community worker who is obsessed with the importance of local context and loses sight of universal principles and the broader global context is likely to develop a parochial practice that is irrelevant in, and has no impact upon, a globalised world. The important point to remember is that, as discussed above, the *context* of community development is both *local* and *global* and hence, when we seek to contextualise our practice, to make it grounded in the experience of people and communities, it must be contextualised both locally and globally. Hence universal principles and locally specific realities are both part of the context and must be held together. If the community worker is able to do that, it will be possible to have a locally grounded and appropriate practice, which can nevertheless be part of global movements for change within the context of globalisation from below.

This tension between local and global, or universal and specific, is a key element of the experience of community work. Community work is neither a mechanistic occupation based on universal principles that can be 'learned' from a book or by doing a course, nor a wholly localised context-specific activity where there are no principles beyond what is found within the community itself. It is rather a dynamic and often contradictory mixture of both and the worker needs to be able to live with that tension and hold both the universal and the specific together. The idea in the previous section—that the global is local and the local is global—can be applied to practice principles as well.

A purely postmodernist account of community development would reject any notion of universal principles, which would be seen as representing a modernist meta-narrative and suggest that only local constructions of community development were valid, with no uniting or universalising narrative of what community work is or should be. Similarly, a purely modernist account would seek to 'fit' all community development work into a single consistent 'model' or 'framework'. It is suggested here that neither of these is sufficient and that it is important for a community worker to hold some universal principles of community development at the same time as emphasising issues of context and diversity and the need for community development to be grounded in lived experience (Campfens 1997).

Colonialism and colonialist practice

Imperialism and colonialism are as old as human civilisations. Although the two terms are often used interchangeably, they have slightly different meanings. Colonialism (discussed briefly in Chapter 5) involves the act of colonising, invading, conquering and then taking over another people's land, resources, wealth, culture and identity. Imperialism, on the other hand, is the establishment and expansion of an empire, the administrative apparatus of ruling and maintaining control over different subject or conquered peoples. Colonisation may therefore be undertaken for the purposes of imperialism and the two are closely related, though with different emphases: imperialism emphasises expansion and glory of the dominating power, while colonialism emphasises the invasion, oppression and domination of the colonised (Said 1993). In each case, the suffix '-ism' suggests that we are dealing not with a process but with an ideology, a set of beliefs and values that belong with the process, implying a way of thinking about the world. In the following discussion, it is 'colonialism' rather than 'imperialism' that is our concern within the context of community development and the word is used with the implication of an ideology, a set of values or a world view. The *process,* as opposed to the ideology, will be referred to as 'colonising' or 'colonisation'.

The history of colonialism is the history of the domination and subjugation of one people by another. It can be seen in the colonial powers of the ancient Western world—Persia, Egypt, Greece, Rome and Byzantium—as well as in the Moghul, Ottoman, Inca and Aztec empires and the Zulu domination of other African tribal groups. The imperial adventures of the nations of Western Europe—Britain, Spain, France, Portugal, the Netherlands, Belgium—from the 17th to the 20th centuries have provided the most extensively documented stories of colonisation and have resulted directly in many of the contemporary social, political and economic problems experienced by many nations of the majority world. But it is important to remember that colonialism is not the exclusive domain of the minority world (Ferro 1997): majority world contemporary examples can be seen in Indonesia's occupation of East Timor and annexation of West Papua and in the Chinese occupation of Tibet.

Wherever colonisation occurs, the result is to the detriment of the colonised. The ideology of colonialism, however, maintains that the process is *in the interests* of the colonised. The colonising power regards itself (including its values, culture and political traditions) as superior and this justifies its colonisation of the culture and land of the colonised people; it is seen as 'for their benefit'. The ideology of the Enlightenment in Western Europe at the end of the 18th century was particularly significant in this respect: the assumption that European civilisation had reached a stage of 'enlightenment' provided a ready justification for European colonisation of other, supposedly inferior or 'unenlightened' cultures 'in their best interests'. The ideology of nationalism also justifies colonialism: if one believes that one's own nation and culture are the best in the world, there is a ready justification for imposing one's cultural values on others as this is seen as obviously in their best interests. Hence an ideology of colonialism is seductive; it flows naturally from a nationalistic valuing of one's own national identity, culture and experience. The British colonialists, for example, felt fully justified in imposing 'British' cultural values, systems of government and legal systems on their colonies; it was to them self-evident that the British system was 'the best in the world' and they were doing 'the natives' a favour by introducing them to such a superior form of civilisation (Bhabha 1994; Said 1993, 1995; Spivak 1987; Fanon 1994).

This example emphasises an important point about colonialism: colonisation is often pursued with the best of intentions, with a sincere belief that one is doing the right thing and that there are self-evident benefits for the colonised, who are being 'introduced to civilisation'. The reality of colonisation, however, is far from the rosy picture in the mind of the colonist. Whatever benefit there may be in the culture and technology of the coloniser, the result is that the colonised are stripped of their identity, their cultural heritage is denied and marginalised and they are labelled as 'primitive' second-class citizens who need to be 'educated' in the ways of the more 'advanced' civilisation of the coloniser. The colonisers would be horrified, dismayed and offended if they were to be subjected to a similar process, yet the colonised are expected, according to the ideology of colonialism, to accept—with a smile—colonisation as being 'for their own good' and to be duly grateful. If they are not, and react against colonisation, they are labelled 'unreasonable', are pathologised ('What more could you expect from people so ignorant?' or 'They resist modern methods that are proven to be more efficient') and are often coerced into acquiescing to the apparently superior culture through, if necessary, violence, imprisonment and the 'full force of law' (defined, of course, from the perspective of the coloniser).

Colonisation, of course, is motivated not only by good, if misguided, intentions. Throughout history, colonisation has brought benefits to the colonisers (usually in the form of wealth and profits) and even though it may have been implemented by well-intentioned and sometimes naïve settlers, missionaries and teachers, the underlying motives have usually been greed, profit, prestige and power. This inherent exploitation has, in most cases, been the direct result of colonisation; the nations of Africa that gained 'independence' in the postwar period were, without exception, left in a state of economic underdevelopment and with many inherited problems, while the colonising nations of Europe were able to walk away, after having exploited the people and resources of those nations for an extended period, with all the profit and bearing none of the cost. Colonisation has been a particularly brutal form of oppression, because it not only ruthlessly exploits the colonised people and appropriates their natural resources and wealth, but also it strips them of their identity, devalues their traditional culture and denies them basic human rights and even the capacity to define their humanity in their own terms. Colonisation is not only about exploitation and oppression; it also involves the invasion of the colonised people and their land, culture and institutions, the denial of their identity and the taking over of the society. The lives, culture and identity of the colonised are redefined and reshaped by the coloniser in order to fit in with the colonisers' view of the 'advantages' of their apparently 'superior civilisation', even though the very humanity of the colonised people is diminished, if not destroyed, in the process.

The impact of colonisation on the colonised is therefore both material and psychological (Fanon 1967). It leaves the colonised often with no viable identity or dignity. Typically, the culture and identity of the colonised are devalued and marginalised by the colonisers, so that the colonised in their 'natural state' are defined as less than human. But at the same time the colonised are denied full access to the apparently 'superior' culture of the colonised through systemic barriers of racism. This is the fate of many Indigenous peoples throughout the world: the dominant culture denies the legitimacy of their traditional culture and identity, but they are prevented from enjoying the full benefits of the dominant culture through racist exclusion. Effectively denied both cultural identities, it is little wonder that Indigenous communities represent some of the most oppressed people of the world and that they are experiencing a whole range of 'social problems'. This is then further compounded by the dominant ideology of individualism, which leads to the pathologising of those who have been stripped of their identity and the resultant 'blaming the victim'. Having been denied an identity and often access to their traditional land, the people concerned are labelled, victimised and, in the ultimate irony of colonialism, blamed for their own misfortune.

Colonisation is, therefore, not just a case of simple exploitation for economic benefit, though this is an important aspect of colonial domination. It is also the imposition of an ideology, or world view, which values the culture of the coloniser and devalues the culture of the colonised and thus represents a psychological and cultural assault on the victims. The ideology of colonialism is one of racial and cultural superiority, fed by the apparently benign form of nationalism and patriotism, which encourages people to believe that their nation is somehow superior to all others. The ideology of colonialism does not, however, belong only to the coloniser. A particularly insidious aspect of colonialism is that the ideology can also be adopted by the colonised. Part of the colonisation process is to impose the ideology of colonialism on the colonised, so that they too come to believe in the superiority of the colonising power. The ideology does not have to be forcibly imposed on the colonised if they will take it up of their own free will—such is the power of colonialism that this often happens. The view in many nations of the majority world that the expertise of the minority world is what is needed for social and economic development is a classic example of this. The one-way flow of 'development' wisdom, from the minority world to the majority world, or from the 'developed' to the 'developing', is perpetrated not only by development experts from the minority world but also by many in the majority world, who seek such aid rather than relying on their own economic and cultural resources (though these may already be depleted as a result of colonialist exploitation) (Haug 2000). The power of colonialism, and its capacity to perpetuate itself, rests on its remarkable ability to persuade the victims, as well as the perpetrators, of the self-evident 'benefits' of the colonial project.

It should be noted that this persuasion is never complete; there has always been some form of resistance by the colonised, even though this is often conveniently omitted from the official history as recorded by the colonisers. Similarly, not all the colonisers will totally accept the ideology of colonialism and cultural and racial superiority; there have always been objections and protests from within the colonising nations, though these too are often written out of the official history of the 'great exploits of the courageous pioneers'. In the case of the European colonisation of Australia, both of these exceptions have been well documented by, among others, Henry Reynolds (1981, 1998).

Community development has been part of the process of colonisation and it has been influenced by the ideology of colonialism. Community development programs, often sponsored by UN agencies or NGOs, have been (often unwittingly) used to further colonialist ends by helping people to accept the wisdom of conventional development aid, encouraging forms of pseudo-participation and legitimising international development projects. They also can displace pre-existing systems of local health and community care, education, justice, land use and so on, which have been established over the centuries within the local geographical and cultural context. Community development of this type can be regarded as the 'benign' or 'warm fuzzy' side of development (and can be seen as self-evidently beneficial, even when projects such as dam-building are under challenge) and can reinforce the message that development is undertaken with the best of intentions and for the benefit of the people concerned. Thus it is no coincidence that mining and oil companies, seeking legitimacy for their projects in developing nations, have instituted community development programs and funded community workers. It sends a message that the company cares and that 'development' is good for the local community, even though the actual impact can be exactly the reverse. This is not to suggest that there is no benefit in such community development programs or that the companies' motives are only profit-driven: the reality is usually more complex, with a mixture of motives, and with both social benefits and social costs resulting from the overall development. The colonialist implications of such community development programs, however, must always be identified and made explicit.

Thus far, colonialism has been discussed specifically in relation to the imposition of a colonising culture on a colonised culture, in the context of international exchanges and imperialist expansion. But the importance of the analysis, for community workers, extends well beyond this. It is not only in visiting a different culture in a foreign country that one can be affected by the ideology of colonialism. Whenever a community worker comes from a background that is in any way different from the community (e.g. through education, social class, culture, race, ethnicity or age) and can be consciously or unconsciously privileged as a result, there is the potential for colonialist practice and therefore socially unjust action and the violation of human rights. For this reason, this discussion of colonialist practice must be seen as applying to *all* community work, not only to community work across national or cultural boundaries. Every community development setting has the potential for colonialist domination, though perhaps in not so obvious a form as is the case with international work, where cultural difference and colonising processes are more evident. But this extra subtlety renders it all the more potentially dangerous. The colonising of another person, or a community, can occur across the full range of community development. All it needs is for a community worker to believe that they, in some way, have a superior world view, are more 'enlightened', have more education, more wisdom or more expertise and that their opinion counts more than those with whom they are working. Such a view may not be consciously held; it can be unconscious and formed and reinforced by education and socialisation, especially if one is a member of a dominant culture, class or profession (Illich et al. 1977; Chambers 1993). Chapter 5 discussed the importance of the worker not privileging their knowledge and expertise over those of the community, yet the worker's background will in all probability encourage them to do just that, albeit unconsciously. Any practice that does privilege the worker's knowledge and expertise becomes colonising practice; the process colonises the 'other', erodes their identity and reinforces relationships of differential power and domination. And, as we have seen, a colonialist ideology can also be held by the colonised, who thereby acquiesce in the process of colonisation and reinforce the colonising practice of the community worker. It is here that postcolonial thought (discussed in Chapter 5) becomes crucial. However, such postcolonial analysis of practice must lead to changes in practice that avoid colonialism.

The temptations of colonialist practice can be both subtle and seductive. All community workers like to feel that what they have to offer is worthwhile and that they can contribute something important to a community; why else would they be doing community development? The ideology of colonialism therefore intuitively appealing; it suggests to the worker that they can offer something worthwhile, which will benefit the community and hence it appeals to the worker's need to be wanted and to be relevant. It is very easy for a community worker, engaged in colonialist practice, to feel that they are doing a good job and working purely for the benefit of the community, while in reality that worker is reinforcing colonisation and is acquiescing in the perpetuation of colonialist oppression on class, race, ethnic or educational dimensions. Of course it is not necessarily either one or the other; more often the worker's practice will have both liberating and oppressive elements.

However, it is evident from the above discussion of colonialism and colonialist practice that such a practice is the antithesis of the approach to community development that is advocated in this book. It is therefore imperative that community workers take special care to guard against colonialist practice in their work.

Guarding against colonialist practice

How then can a community worker guard against the temptations of colonialist practice? First, it is important that a community worker have a high level of critical self-awareness and reflection. The reasons we may go into community work are complex and they are seldom purely altruistic; it is only natural for community workers to be meeting their own needs through their work and this need not be seen as problematic. But it is important for a community worker to realise this and to be aware of their own needs that may be being met in the process. As soon as a worker substitutes their own agenda for the agenda(s) of the community, colonisation is likely to take place as the autonomy and identity of the community are no longer respected. It is naïve to assume that the worker will have no such personal agenda, but it is realistic, indeed necessary, to expect that a community worker will be aware of personal agendas and needs and the dangers of colonising practice and will seek to be sensitive.

A critically aware community worker needs to be mindful of the dangers of colonialism and should try to be receptive to such a critique coming from others, whether community members, fellow workers, friends or supervisors. One way to maintain an awareness is to discuss such issues openly with other community workers or with community members themselves. Colonialists will generally frame their work as doing things 'to' or 'for' others, rather than 'with' others. They will also believe that what they are doing is 'for their [others'] own good'. They will talk about 'what this community needs' (without reference to the voices of the people themselves), about 'what I would hope to do or achieve' (not 'we') and so on. They may frame their work as their own agenda in which they want the community to participate ('How can I get people to come to my meeting?', 'How can I persuade people to cooperate?', 'How can we get people on board?', 'How can we keep them involved?' and so on). Language that separates the community worker(s) from the community itself, and which effectively privileges the worker's agenda over the community's, is a sure indication of colonialist attitudes. Whenever a community worker finds themself using such language and assuming that they know what is best for somebody else, alarm bells should ring loudly. Hence it is a good idea for workers to give close attention to the language that they, and others, use to describe community development.

More than personal self-awareness is needed, however. In reality, it is usually the case that the community worker will represent in some way the dominant or colonising culture. It is therefore important for the community worker to be able to locate themself within that culture and to see that, as a result, they represent structures and discourses of oppression and colonisation. However sensitive that worker may be to colonialist attitudes, the worker's very location within such structures and discourses means that the worker is part of the colonialist project. The very presence of the community worker can itself colonise the identity of the people with whom they are working. Hence it is not only an awareness of personal attitudes and values that is important, but also a critical awareness of the structures and discourses within which the community worker is located and the influence these have on the processes of colonisation and on the colonialist ideology of both coloniser and colonised.

For this reason it is important that a community worker allow space for the expression and validation of the culture, values and identity of the colonised and for a critique of the dominant structures and discourses of colonisation (Freire 1972). This idea of *allowing space* is critical in practice that seeks to counter colonialism. In allowing rather than colonising such space, the community worker is validating a critique of the colonialist ideology and the practice of colonisation. Characteristically, this also allows space for *resistance* to be expressed to the colonising structures and discourses, thereby questioning their legitimacy and validating an alternative. The community worker, therefore, however self-critical and well-informed about colonialism, still needs to step back and allow space for a critique, a reaction, resistance and an alternative to be articulated and validated. This can be difficult and at times painful. It may involve the community worker being on the receiving end of criticism and anger directed at the entire colonising culture, of which the worker is seen as a representative. But the expression of this anger is often a necessary precondition for moving forward in a spirit of dialogue. It is part of the recognition and the naming of structures and discourses of oppression that is a necessary part of consciousness-raising. With the acknowledgement of the oppression, it is only natural for there to be anger, resentment and, at times, violence. The important thing is to be able to move on from this stage, towards dialogue and counter-oppressive community development practice.

To avoid colonialist practice, a community worker must first *listen* and *learn*, to allow the people with whom they are working to claim the process as their own and to set the agenda (Freire 1972). It is only by stepping back, not rushing in with plans and intervention strategies, but allowing time and space for a process to be established that is truly owned by the community, that community development that is genuinely anti-colonialist can be initiated. This is easy to say, but much harder to do. As discussed in Chapter 7, it runs counter to the dominant modernist world view of certainty, plans, objectives and the need to be busy. It requires instead patience, a capacity to live with uncertainty, a readiness to trust the process and the people and an admission that the community worker is neither all-knowing nor all powerful. This is far from the world of assertiveness, self-promotion, goal-setting, achievement and competitiveness that is so dominant throughout the Western world and that has served the ends of colonialism only too well.

Following the creation of space for dialogue and action, the next important principle of anti-colonialist practice is the idea of *working in solidarity* with the community. Working in solidarity implies working with, not for, the people concerned, and that there is a real sense of a shared vision. It means that the community worker has been able to listen to and understand the agenda of the community and is able to work *alongside* the people of the community in the process of community development. Working in solidarity implies that there is no conflict of agendas between community and worker and that the two are working together in a dialogical praxis relationship (as described in Chapters 10 and 11).

The perspective of working in solidarity can be a challenge for many community workers, as it is another way of moving beyond the colonising consequences of the dominant ideologies of practice. It suggests that the struggle is for worker and community to work together to critique and deconstruct the ideology of colonialism, which, as we have seen, can affect coloniser and colonised alike. This has been a particular concern of liberation theology, deriving from the experience of priests, nuns and lay missionaries working from an empowerment perspective (Rowland 1999). The analysis of colonialism becomes, from this perspective, a framework for consciousness-raising and dialogue.

Closely related to the notion of solidarity is that of *working with* the community. This is consistent with the bottom-up approach to community development, with valuing the local and, in particular, local knowledge and wisdom. Working with the community implies a relationship that does not have colonising consequences because the community worker becomes a resource for the aims and aspirations of the community. The community worker who works with the community is 'on tap, not on top'. The discussion of participation in Chapter 6 provided insight into ways of achieving both working in solidarity and working with communities.

A final guard against the dangers of colonialism for a community worker is what can be called a 'test of reciprocity'. Simply put, this requires the worker to ask 'How would I feel if the situation were reversed?' The worker needs to imagine themself in the place of the people with whom they are working, and to ask how they would feel about the process. Put another way, it requires the worker to ask whether they are prepared to experience 'development' in the same way as it is being practised on the people of the community. This is an important test of colonialism. With international development work, for example, one might ask whether human rights activists in Australia would welcome visiting delegations from China and Indonesia criticising the Australian treatment of Indigenous people. Resistance to the idea of community development 'experts' from the majority world coming to provide expertise on development in the minority world is an indication of the extent to which colonialist ideology has been internalised. Whether we can imagine, let alone accept, the validity of such role reversals is a good measure of the influence of colonialism; community workers can guard against colonialism by applying such a test to their everyday work, in whatever setting. Often, on reflection, it will become clear that the worker may be expecting far more of a community, group or individual than that worker would be prepared to give should the roles be reversed; this should be cause for that worker to ask serious questions about colonialist ideology.

Working internationally

The issue of colonialism, while it applies to community work in any location, is obviously of particular relevance for people working in international community development. Many international aid and development agencies see community development as an important aspect of their work and a number of people who decide to take up a career in community development have a particular interest in working in another country.

The problems of colonialism and colonialist practice sound a clear warning for international community development (Leys 1996), but this does not mean that international work is not worthwhile. Indeed, in a globalising world, where we are all connected with each other, community development, like any other work, needs an international focus. Further, it must not be assumed that all aid/development agencies and their work are colonialist, as this is not the case. Many (though far from all) international development agencies are well aware of the issues and dangers of colonialist practice and work from an analysis that seeks to address the structures and discourses of colonialism. There is much of value that can be accomplished by international community development from such a perspective. Indeed the significance of globalisation requires the kind of global/local practice described earlier in this chapter so that communities can begin to address the issues of globalisation and work towards the ideal of globalisation from below. Thus, in a real sense, all community development is international community development. It is international forces that cause many of the problems faced by communities and that shape their destinies and it is international solutions that are required. International community development is no longer confined to those who choose to work in another country and a different culture; it is part of the work of all community workers.

Global inequity is one of the major problems facing the planet. Community development has much to contribute in addressing global inequities, through the strengthening and empowerment of communities, self-reliance and change from below. It is simply insufficient for community workers to withdraw from international practice because of the challenges and dangers of colonialism; rather it is important for them to work out ways of practising internationally that will help to confront colonialist practice and further the cause of globalisation from below.

In order to achieve this, it is perhaps more appropriate to talk about *internationalist* community development than about international community development. As we saw with colonialism, the adding of the suffix '-ist' or '-ism' suggests more than simply a description of a process; it suggests also values and ideology. *Internationalist* community development involves not only working internationally, but also working from the perspective of *internationalism*, which implies ideas of international solidarity, the realisation that we live in one world and the need for all people to work together in peace and harmony. Internationalism does not, however, imply a world of uniformity. It allows for—and indeed encourages and celebrates—cultural diversity, in accordance with the principle of diversity discussed in Chapter 2. Indeed it is through diversity rather than uniformity that we can learn from each other, experience important cultural exchanges and develop together. Internationalism is a movement with a long history—far longer than that of globalisation. Its agenda has not been one of economic fundamentalism or of imposing cultural uniformity. Rather it has sought to address issues of world peace, human rights, international understanding, care for the global environment and so on. It was the motivation behind many international agencies, including the League of Nations and the United Nations, though many aspects of the United Nations have been used for the imposition of more colonialist agendas by powerful minority world interests. It also resulted in the formation of many international NGOs—from the Red Cross and the Women's International League for Peace and Freedom to Amnesty International and Greenpeace. This represents the embryonic formation of a 'global civil society'—another important manifestation of a globalised world that needs to be placed alongside the economic fundamentalism of conventional globalisation.

One important way in which internationalist community development can be advanced is by requiring the flow of expertise to be two-way. It is still the case that the majority of international aid and development workers are from the minority world and are working in countries of the majority world. While the flow of expertise is thus one-way, it is inevitable that it will be affected by colonialist ideology and practice. An internationalist perspective maintains that people and communities in the minority world have as much need of consciousness-raising and community development as do people and communities in the majority world.

Reasserting the importance of an internationalist agenda and seeing it as a basis for international community development requires understandings of international solidarity that rise above colonialism. It sees dimensions of oppression, such as class, race and gender, as extending across international boundaries, requiring the people of the world, while respecting each other's differences, to work together in seeking collective solutions. International community workers can address their task from this perspective of internationalism, which does not privilege the culture of the West or the economic power of the minority world, but which seeks to link people on the basis of their common humanity and to find a framework for people to work together.

>> discussion questions

1 What are the implications of the *discourse* of economic fundamentalism, in terms of giving power to globalisation and in relation to the power of nation-states?
2 What is meant by the imposition of a global culture and what does this mean for local identity?
3 How has globalisation created space for community development to occur?
4 How does the idea of 'globalisation from below', or 'glocalisation', help community work to be effective by linking the global and the local in everyday practice?
5 What is the importance of holding some universal principles of community development?
6 How can universal principles be applied at the same time as valuing the local and appreciating diversity?
7 In what ways is colonialism inherently oppressive and exploitative?
8 How has community development been complicit in colonialism?
9 What is required for the community worker to avoid colonialist practice?
10 What is implied in the idea of 'international*ism*'?

>> reflective questions

1 Think about the tensions in linking the global and the local in community development practice. How can you manage these tensions and make the links in your practice?
2 How would you contextualise the universal principles of community development in particular situations? How would you make judgements about applying the principles and respecting the local?
3 What is the language you use in relation to community development and working with communities? What might this language indicate about your approach to the communities you might work with? Does your language indicate aspects of colonial practice or is it guarding against such aspects?
4 How do you react to the idea of allowing space to counter colonial practice, especially when allowing that space may also enable resistance to be expressed? How will you deal with personal feelings of threat in your community worker role?

CHAPTER 9

Integrated community development

Introduction

The purpose of community development is to re-establish the community as the location of significant human experience, the meeting of human needs and the experience of exercising human rights, rather than to rely on the larger, more inhuman and less accessible structures of the welfare system, the global economy, bureaucracy, professional elites and so on.

The nature of that human experience and interaction, however, is complex. Many programs of community development seek to establish a stronger community base for a single aspect of human existence, while ignoring others. Often community development, with its roots in conventional social work, will concentrate on the provision of community-based human services (such as health, housing, a women's refuge, recreation or day care) while ignoring the community's economic base. On the other hand, many projects of community economic development proceed on the assumption that from economic development all else will follow and so they ignore social needs. Indigenous people have consistently reminded non-Indigenous community workers that they ignore the spiritual dimension of human interaction and community, which Indigenous people regard as central.

Such one-dimensional community development is highly likely to fail. It derives from linear thinking rather than adopting the holistic approach that is at the basis of the ecological perspective and which is congruent with the notion of the interdependency of all human rights. By concentrating on one dimension, it ignores the richness and complexity of human life and the experience of community.

In this chapter six dimensions of community development are identified and seen as critically important. Relevant case studies are presented at the end of this chapter to enable you to explore the relationships among, and integration of, all six dimensions. This chapter is an important watershed in the development of the ideas promoted by the book, because we move from a more theoretical analysis to the practice of community development.

The six dimensions are not always distinct and they interact with each other in often complex ways. It might also be argued that some are more fundamental than others; for example, many people (particularly Indigenous people) would argue that personal/spiritual development is the basis of all the other dimensions. But for the purposes of building a model of community development, and of thinking clearly about the role of the community worker, it is useful to consider all six as fundamentally important. The six dimensions are:

- social development
- economic development

- political development
- cultural development
- environmental development
- personal/spiritual development.

In a particular situation not all of these will have equal priority or focus. Any community will have developed the six dimensions to differing levels; for example, one community might have a strong economic base, healthy political participation and a strong cultural identity, but also have poor human services, a degraded physical environment, low self-esteem and a high level of alienation. In such a community, therefore, social, environmental and personal/spiritual development will be the highest priorities in a community development program. Another community, however, will reflect a different picture and call for different priorities within a development process.

The critical point is that all six aspects of community development are important—to have a truly healthy and functioning community it is necessary to achieve high levels of development in all six dimensions. Any community worker or anyone connected with a community development program must take all six into account and the aim must be the maximising of development on all these dimensions. By adding these six components we can develop another stage of the model previously summarised in Chapter 4 (Figure 4.1). This is illustrated in Figure 9.1.

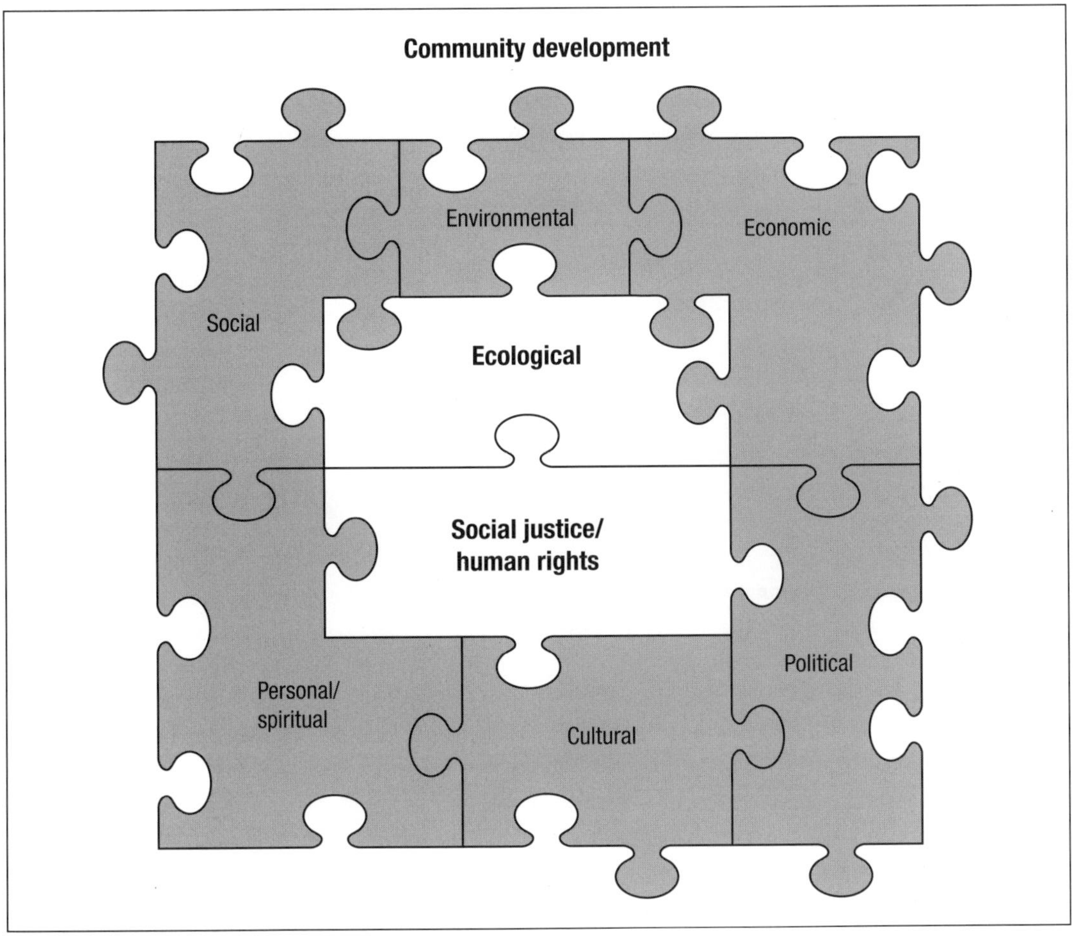

Figure 9.1 Integrated community development

Social development

Much of what is traditionally regarded as community development, in occupations such as social work, youth work, education and the health professions, can be understood as *social development*. Although there is considerable variety in the activities that constitute social development, they can be grouped into four types as follows: *service development, the neighbourhood house/community centre, social planning* and *social animation* (see Figure 9.2).

Service development

PROCESS ISSUES

Much traditional community development activity is essentially social service development, involving the identification of social needs and the provision of structures and services to meet them. This typically involves the following process: the identification of a concern; a more detailed or systematic study of the need or problem; a public meeting, forum or consultation, with all interested people encouraged to attend and participate to decide on some course of action; completion of the necessary formalities for the new body to be established; the development and ongoing operation of the new body, including encouraging people to become actively involved; and ongoing monitoring and evaluation of the new body and its services.

Each of these steps is itself a complex process, which raises many important issues and difficult problems. They are not unique to social development, but occur to some degree in the other forms of community development discussed in this chapter.

Social service development does not always follow the stages outlined above. In some instances the order of the first two steps is reversed and it is a broad-based consultation, study or survey of

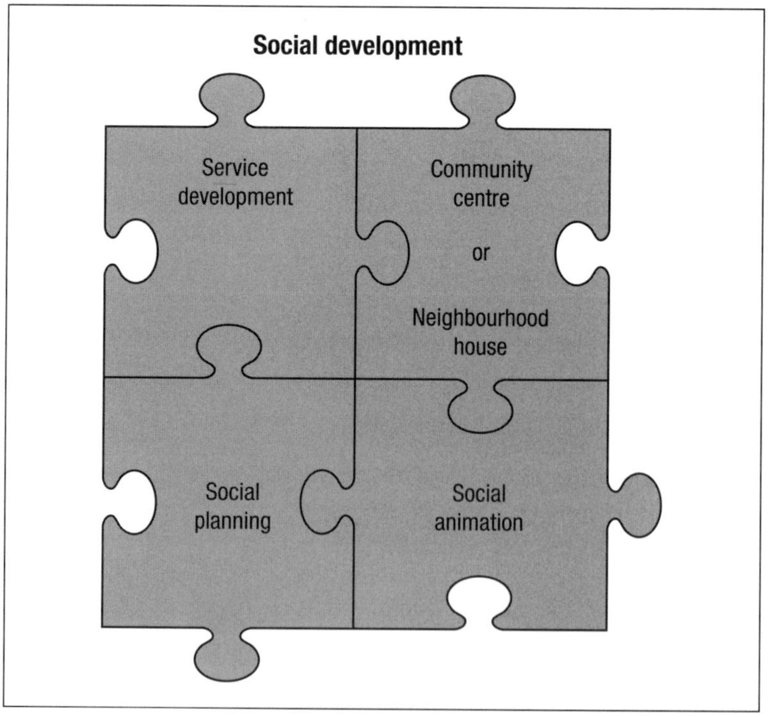

Figure 9.2 Social development

community needs, undertaken as a community planning process, which then highlights specific areas of concern. Sometimes a different form of consultation is used in the third step (public meeting, forum or consultation), where the more traditional public meeting would be inappropriate; for example, in a widely dispersed rural community a series of smaller meetings or electronic communication may be more realistic.

Sometimes the initiative is taken by a larger body, such as a church agency, and the development of the new program takes place within its structure, rather than independently. This can have important advantages, such as providing the program with an existing legal framework of incorporation, management expertise, service expertise, a funding base and access to various other resources (e.g. phone, fax, copier, computers, meeting rooms). The program may still have its own management committee, though the question of autonomy and independence may be an issue. However, it is worth noting that some of the most radical and innovative community-based social development programs have taken place under such auspices (Liffman 1978).

Sometimes a larger agency will establish a program and then encourage it to become independent once it has been properly established. At other times an initiative that began as an independent community action will be taken over by a larger agency because of its resources and infrastructure. Sometimes the initiative will come from government rather than the community as part of a government program to encourage decentralisation and community control; this can raise special problems as the government's agenda is not always the same as that of the community and governments are usually reluctant to give up all control and to support the kind of autonomy and citizen power discussed in Chapter 7. Indeed with the government tendering and 'purchase of service' approach to community funding, there is often less community control rather than more.

Another variant of the process is the development of a self-help group. This is where the primary instigators of the action are people directly affected by a particular problem, such as those suffering from a particular illness or those with relatives with a specific disability. Such groups tend to rely less on support from the rest of the community, though they will often seek support in the form of financial contributions.

Sometimes the aim of social development is not to establish a new community service, but to help the existing ones to operate more effectively through better coordination and planning. Hence the outcome of the process may be the establishment of new planning and coordination structures, ideally (though far from invariably) incorporating broad-based citizen participation and the representation of the views of the most disadvantaged.

STRUCTURAL ISSUES

The above discussion has focused on the provision of human services as this has been a traditional concern of social development. Many important community agencies were created through such processes—it is doubtful, for example, whether there would be many women's refuges in minority world countries if processes such as these had not been initiated at the community level. However, the view that community problems can be solved by the provision of social services, whether or not they are community-based, is problematic. While social services are, of course, often of crucial importance, an exclusive reliance on service provision can divert attention from some of the more fundamental structural issues, such as class, race and gender oppression. This can be seen in the 'typical' community processes described above—public meetings, committees, constitutions and so on. As discussed in Chapter 6, these have been characteristically the domain of the white middle-class male and it is small wonder that such people are often over-represented in such community-based structures. Hence this approach to social development can, in fact, reinforce structural inequalities of class, gender and race/ethnicity unless these issues are specifically addressed.

There is a further conservatism inherent in these processes. Services established in this way become part of the existing constellation of human services, organised along fairly traditional patterns and, through reliance on government funding, they take their place within the larger structures controlled by the welfare state. They do not necessarily represent an alternative in the post-welfare state and there are many examples of agencies that were started through such processes becoming extremely conservative and reactionary (it is worth noting that many of the most conservative 'old-style' non-government welfare agencies started life in this way). Thus this form of social development can simply reinforce existing welfare mechanisms, rather than becoming the genuinely community-based alternative to the welfare state advocated in Chapter 1.

This is not to deny the value of such service-based social development: many worthwhile results have been achieved through this process. Rather it is to emphasise that this approach to social development by itself is insufficient, and that an awareness of broader structural issues must be incorporated so that the process can be seen within a broader context.

The neighbourhood house/community centre

An alternative model is the neighbourhood house or community centre. A major forerunner of this approach to community development is the university settlement movement in the late 19th century (Woodroofe 1962), where settlement houses were established in low-income areas to support a variety of programs using the energy and skills of socially committed undergraduates. Other settlement houses were not attached specifically to universities, but were run by committed citizens interested in seeking an alternative to traditional forms of charitable relief. They were the forerunners of today's neighbourhood houses and community centres, as were the social programs run by local churches.

The community centre, then, is hardly a new concept and it has always been an important component of community development. The simple idea of providing a central meeting place, with some degree of resourcing (staff, volunteers, funds, equipment, etc.) is still an essential ingredient of much community development work and is often seen in the form of neighbourhood houses. Such a location can be used for a variety of activities—recreational, educational, political, cultural, health, advocacy, child care, education, skills development, information and referral, group discussions and human services at a local level (Welfare & Community Services Review 1984)—and can become the focal point for the other kinds of community development described in this chapter.

The initiative for developing a community centre or neighbourhood house can come from a number of quarters including local government, state government, non-government agencies, churches and local community groups. Experience has shown that it is critical for the local community to be fully involved in the planning. A community centre imposed from above by a well-intentioned government or non-government agency but without genuine community involvement will more than likely be located in the wrong place, have an inappropriate physical design and not meet the most important felt needs of the community, which will render the resulting 'community centre' virtually useless.

Similarly, there are different sources for support in the form of financial and people resources. More often than not, these involve government funding, whether directly or indirectly, and this poses problems in terms of the issue of autonomy (discussed in Chapter 5). For a community centre or neighbourhood house to work effectively, within the approach to community work outlined in earlier chapters, local people must have primary control over its operation and over the utilisation of the available resources. In practice this is often not possible in cases where it relies on government funding and this represents a major obstacle to a progressive approach to community centre work. These problems can often be minimised by seeking a variety of funding sources—for example, foundations, service clubs, business or churches. This, however, raises another problem common to many community projects. The ongoing search for funds and the satisfaction of the requirements of the various funding bodies can take so much time and energy that a community worker has little left for the actual program.

These difficulties aside, some form of neighbourhood house or community centre is an essential component of many of the other aspects of community development discussed in this chapter. Without such a focal point (whether or not it is formally designated as a 'community centre') it is hard to see how a good deal of other community development could take place.

Social planning

In the context of community development, the term *social planning* should not be taken as implying the imposition from above of a grand plan or the essentially technical activity implied in Rothman's (1974) model B in his much-quoted typology of community organisation practice. Rather, it implies the process of the people of a community defining their needs and aspirations and working out appropriate strategies, as well as how the existing services and resources can be coordinated and utilised to best effect. It is planning and coordination at a grassroots level and the role of the 'expert' is to facilitate this process to help people make their decisions on community priorities.

Such planning processes, of course, apply to other aspects of community development, such as economic development or cultural development. In the specific context of social development, the planning process is commonly carried out by a non-government agency, such as a local 'council of social service', a 'council of social development', a 'social planning council' or a local government body.

This local participatory planning is another vital aspect of community development and any community development strategy must incorporate some mechanism, whether formal or informal, for local people to have a genuine role in the making of such priority decisions. There are, of course, many potential problems associated with such processes, which were addressed in the discussion of participation in Chapter 6.

Social animation

Social development can also focus on the actual quality of social interaction within a community, rather than directly on the provision of human services. Thus a social development program might simply seek to facilitate people in the community talking to each other and interacting more in their everyday lives. Such community development is less goal-directed, at least in the initial stages, though specific service goals may subsequently develop out of the interaction. The community worker who lives in a community and tries to bring people closer together in a stronger experience of community interaction is adopting such a role. There are many examples of such work (e.g. O'Regan & O'Connor 1989), where what begins as simply an experience of community living can end up providing a focal point for a wide variety of human interactions with significant social, economic and political consequences for the quality of community life.

Here the role of the community worker is more one of catalyst, simply aiming to bring people together and to help them unlock their potential for an experience of community and for action. Community work concentrates on process rather than outcome, on the assumption that if the process is sound (and based on inclusive, non-violent and affirming principles), outcomes will be achieved based on the genuine needs and aspirations of the people concerned. Consciousness-raising, dialogical relationships and critically reflective practice (discussed in other chapters) are particularly important in such an approach to community work. Again, this mode of practice is relevant to other aspects of community development, as discussed below.

Economic development

The globalisation of the economy, under the influence of neoclassical economics and the power of transnational capital, has resulted in increasing numbers of people feeling that the mainstream economy is no longer meeting their needs or respecting their rights. This is seen in the high levels of unemployment in many communities, boosted by the 'hidden unemployed'—those who are not counted within the official statistics, who would like to have some kind of paid work or who have only casual part-time employment and would like more. It is also seen in the growing numbers of people in poverty, reflected not merely in official poverty-line statistics but also in the number dependent on emergency relief in one form or another (food vouchers, emergency cash, food banks, etc.). Whole communities can become economically disadvantaged as industry shuts down and relocates following the logic of the global market and 'free trade', leaving behind closed factories, lost jobs, devastated communities and personal despair. Conventional economics does not normally measure these personal and social 'costs'; but even if it does, industry is not required to take them into account. Even where industry has not relocated and there is still moderate local employment, much of the profit (or, in Marxist terms, surplus value) is immediately taken out of the local community and may be moved halfway around the world, maintaining low living standards for workers and their families. These mechanisms are justified by the rhetoric of neoliberalism—reducing deficits, increasing competitiveness, free trade, levelling the playing field, wealth creation and so on. The problem with this perspective is that the rights and needs of individuals, families and communities are effectively sacrificed in the interests of transnational capital (for a further analysis see Gorz 1989; Buarque 1993; Pusey 1991; Horne 1992; Max-Neef 1991; Daly & Cobb 1989; Rees et al. 1993).

From a community development perspective, the response to this economic crisis is to develop an alternative approach that seeks to relocate economic activity within the community, work towards the community's benefit, revitalise the local community and improve the quality of life. The current economic crisis has forced increasing numbers of people and communities to seek such alternatives in the realisation that the mainstream economy is no longer doing a very effective job of meeting their needs and respecting their rights—hence the heightened interest in community economic development (Shragge 1993).

Community economic development can take a variety of forms, but these can be grouped into two categories (see Figure 9.3). The first, the more conservative approach, seeks to develop

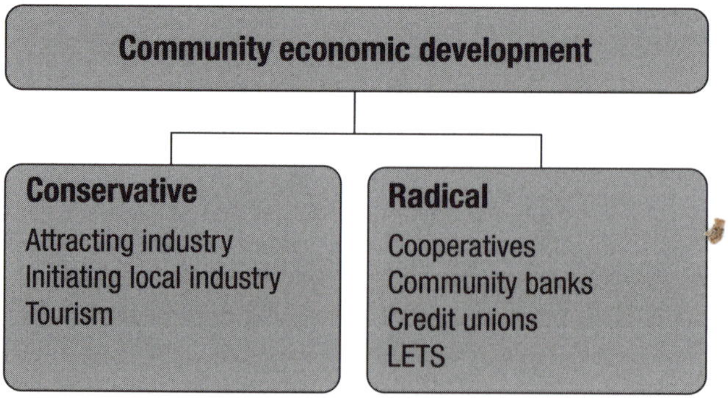

Figure 9.3 Community economic development

community economic activity largely within conventional parameters, while the second, the more radical approach, seeks to develop an alternative community-based economics.

The conservative approach to community economic development includes activities such as attracting industry to a local area, initiating local industry and tourism. It seeks to improve the economy of the community by helping it to operate more effectively within the existing economic order. The analysis of the earlier chapters, however, suggests that the existing economic order is part of the problem and is in the long term (or even fairly short term) unsustainable. The nature of the existing order is such that not all communities can hope to benefit from such a strategy; those that 'win' will do so at the expense of others because of the essentially competitive nature of the market.

A more radical approach to community economic development involves attempting to establish an alternative, locally based economy (Albert & Hahnel 1991). This is in line with the perspective of Chapter 5, embodying the principle of autonomy. It requires a community to be more dependent on its own resources and suggests that conventional economic wisdom often results in these resources being unrecognised and underutilised. It also ensures that the surplus value from local productivity remains in the community where it was created, rather than being exported.

COOPERATIVES

The establishment of cooperatives is one way in which this can be achieved; cooperatives, as discussed in Chapter 7, have proven effective in various locations. Cooperatives also have the potential to strengthen rather than to weaken community solidarity—the experience of many cooperatives bears this out (Craig 1993; Melnyk 1985).

A particularly interesting example of the strengths of cooperatives is in the Cape Breton region of Nova Scotia, where there has been a long history of cooperative structures initiated largely by the work of the extension department of St Francis Xavier University and its director, Father Moses Coady, in the 1920s and 1930s (Melnyk 1985; Macleod 1991). These efforts were aimed at counteracting economic hardship, such as the 1930s depression, but have resulted in a strong cooperative tradition and many cooperative structures that leave the people of the region in a better position to tackle their present economic problems (caused by the collapse of the fishing and steel industries). This is a good example of the potential long-term benefits of alternative community economic development; Father Coady's work had implications well beyond the immediate economic crisis facing communities in Cape Breton at the time.

There has been increasing worldwide interest in the worker cooperatives of Mondragon (Morrison 1991; Whyte & Whyte 1988) and it appears that, at least in some circumstances, co-operatives do represent a viable alternative to more conventional economic structures. Although there are certain fundamental principles of cooperatives (see Chapter 7), they can take many different forms, depending on local needs and the local culture. As with all community development, the imposition of a detailed plan of 'how to do it' is almost bound to fail, as each community needs to work out its own form of cooperative to suit its unique situation.

COMMUNITY BANKS AND CREDIT UNIONS

Large national or transnational banks are an important part of the global economic system and inevitably operate primarily in the interests of transnational capital (if they were to attempt otherwise, they would not survive at the national or global level). Thus they are not always well placed to meet the needs of a local community and its citizens. Indeed they provide an important mechanism for the export of profits from the local community and the control of the local economy by external forces. In recognition of this, some community initiatives have established local banking structures so that the community can have more control over its economy. This allows for local community control over, for example, what kind of businesses should receive loans, the rescheduling of mortgages for those unable to pay and interest rates on investments (Dauncey 1988; Meeker-Lowry 1988).

Credit unions are perhaps the commonest form of community banking. A credit union is simply a group of people who agree to invest their money together and to make loans to members. It operates like a local, small-scale bank. Some credit unions and building societies however, have grown so large that they have lost the characteristics of a small organisation, namely effective community or membership control and operation primarily in the interests of the membership. The lesson to be learned from this is that in establishing a community bank or credit union it is essential to ensure that its community base is maintained and it is unable to grow and join the national or international economies but remains a central feature of the local economy. If this can be safeguarded, such localised banking structures can be a very important component of alternative economic development.

LETS

The name *LETS* is applied to community-based schemes that create a community-based currency alternative (Macornick 2007). There is some confusion about what the letters stand for: 'local employment and trading scheme', 'local energy transfer scheme', 'local exchange and trading system' and so on. In some areas, particularly in Aotearoa, the name *green dollar* scheme is used instead.

In times of economic crisis, there is generally an increase in the 'informal' economy or the barter system, where people will exchange goods and services without money changing hands. There is always some level of such activity—much to the annoyance of conventional economists, who cannot count it in the gross domestic product, and politicians and treasury officials, who cannot tax it. While conventional economic wisdom frowns on the informal economy, from a community development perspective it can be understood in a different light. If the formal economy is failing increasing numbers of people, the use of the informal economy can be seen as a way for people to regain control over economic activity and to devise an economic system that does meet their needs.

The LETS approach seeks to formalise the local exchange economy by creating a community currency. Members of the scheme (who may be individuals or local businesses) have accounts that are kept at a central point and a directory of the services or products that members are offering is distributed regularly among the membership. A member wanting to purchase a service or product contacts the other member direct and arranges the transaction, after which the appropriate amount in 'green dollars' (or whatever local name is being used) is transferred from the account of the purchasing member to the account of the provider. For more details about the operation of LETS, see Dauncey (1988) and Dobson (1993).

There are many potential advantages to LETS. It enables people to engage in economic transactions even if they do not have a regular income. It values and rewards any contribution people can make to the community, not simply the skills that are valued in the traditional labour market. People can buy needed goods and services even if they have no money. The system has the potential to strengthen community solidarity and provide an economic focus for community interaction. The profits from economic activity stay in the local community.

There is no doubt that LETS is a very significant development and can provide the basis of an alternative community-based economy. But it can have mixed and complex impacts on dimensions of development beyond the economic dimension (van Kuik 2009; Walker 2009). It is certainly worth serious exploration by any community worker or community group interested in alternative economic development and the widespread establishment of LETS would represent an important challenge to the mainstream economy. The general enthusiasm about LETS in some quarters, however, has led to an assumption that LETS is the answer to everything, which it is not (North 2006). It can represent an important component of alternative community development, but expecting it to solve all of a community's problems is to fall into the trap of linear thinking, seeking a single answer and ignoring the other aspects of the complexity of community development. There are, in fact, some significant questions that need to be raised about LETS and about the other forms of alternative economic development outlined in this section. See the International Journal of Community Currency Research (freely accessible on the internet from several sites) for an excellent body of literature on these debates.

ISSUES AND PROBLEMS

A major question concerning cooperatives, community banks, credit unions and LETS must be their adequacy at coping with issues of structural inequality, such as class, gender and race/ethnicity. There is a danger of establishing alternative systems that challenge the existing economic order and provide alternatives, but do so primarily for articulate white males and therefore perpetuate oppressive structures at the community level. There is nothing inherent in the schemes themselves that means this will necessarily be the case, but, as pointed out in Chapter 3, unless such issues are explicitly addressed, social and economic structures will tend to accept and reinforce the existing forms of structural oppression. Some of the most enthusiastic supporters of LETS, for example, take little account of such factors and although gender issues have been addressed in many LETS there is still limited participation by people from cultural and ethnic minorities. It is also sometimes the case that many of the services traded in LETS would be seen as marginal by many people and reflect the interests of 'green trendies' rather than the population at large; when a listing of services available through LETS is dominated by reflexology, tarot readings, herb farms, aromatherapy and essential oils, one must question its relevance to the broader community and the possibility of LETS being exclusive rather than inclusive (whatever one may think of the value of the services traded). Of course many LETS are not like this, but the critical point is that for LETS to be acceptable within the community development perspective of this book, it must explicitly address such issues of inclusivity.

From a socialist perspective, many of these community-based economic schemes are open to question. If one accepts the Marxist position that the structures and relations of capitalism are the fundamental problem, little will be solved by replacing the large-scale structures of capitalism with smaller-scale versions of the same thing; they will simply perpetuate domination, oppression and exploitation on a community level rather than on a larger scale. They do not challenge the basic structures of capitalism and therefore become part of the hegemony maintaining the existing order. This criticism is not as significant for cooperatives: the cooperative can be a mechanism for changing the ownership and control of the means of production and has been an important component of socialist programs. LETS, however, might be considered a reaffirmation of the primacy of the market, which, from a socialist perspective, is to say the least a cause for concern.

From a Green perspective this need not be such a profound objection. If one accepts that it is the issue of scale that is the major problem, then the mechanism of the market is quite acceptable as long as it is maintained at a human scale. From this perspective the problem with big business is not that it is business but that it is big. Indeed, some form of localised market transaction is unavoidable and a socialist objection to the local market can be seen as unrealistic.

Rather than attempting to resolve this ideological issue here, it is simply worth noting that local economic schemes such as LETS are problematic in that they raise significant ideological issues. This is not to say they should not be pursued, but rather that they should not be regarded as a magic solution to all community problems and that they should be implemented only in the context of a wider analysis and other community development initiatives that address fundamental structural issues.

Political development

Much of the literature on community work or 'community organisation' has been concerned essentially with political development. This is closely related to the notion of empowerment, which was discussed at some length in Chapter 3, because political development is essentially about issues of power. In order to undertake a program of political development it is necessary to locate the program within an analysis of power, both at the macro level, in terms of structures and discourses of inequality/oppression, and at the more local level. Thus it is important to analyse power within the community itself, looking at how power is distributed and how it is maintained and exercised. This will, to some extent, vary from community to community, though it is likely to reflect the broader structural inequalities of class, gender and race/ethnicity, as well as local factors.

Altering the distribution of power within a community so that it can be more equitably shared is therefore one goal of political development. The other goal is to empower that community to operate more effectively within the wider arena. Just as people can lack power within their communities, communities can lack power within the broader society. Hence the analysis of power has to include an analysis of the power of the community itself, relative to other communities and to other institutions. It is the relative powerlessness of communities that lies at the heart of the need for community development and so political development is an essential component of a community development strategy.

Political development, therefore, seeks to enhance a community's capacity to operate in the political arena; it is aimed at increasing the power both of the community as a whole in its relation to the wider society and of individuals and groups within the community to participate in community processes, activities and decisions. There are two arenas of political development, which can be designated as internal and external. Within these two arenas there are three key processes of political development: consciousness-raising, organising and action (see Figure 9.4).

Internal political development

Internal political development is concerned with the processes of participation and decision making within the community. It seeks to maximise the effective participation by community members; this is achieved through two of the three key political development processes: *consciousness-raising* and *organising*.

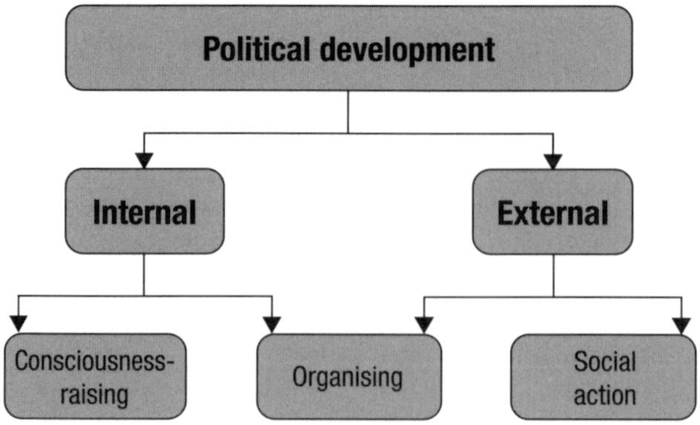

Figure 9.4 Political development

CONSCIOUSNESS-RAISING

Consciousness-raising was discussed at some length in Chapter 7 and so need not be considered in detail here. Consciousness-raising applies across all aspects of community development, but it is perhaps particularly significant in relation to internal political development (covered in this section). The ability to link the personal and the political and to help people to share their experiences and reflect on their situation in such a way that it opens up the possibilities for action, is of major importance in political development; indeed effective political development at community level cannot proceed without it.

ORGANISING

The other aspect of internal political development is the way in which the community organises itself in order to deal with its problems and, in the longer term, to develop alternative and autonomous structures of the type envisaged in Chapter 5. There is nothing about localisation and community control that *necessarily* implies that procedures will be democratic, socially just and rights-based and that women and men of different cultural, ethnic and class backgrounds will be included and able to participate equally in community decision making.

In order to achieve such participation it is often necessary to redefine the traditional decision-making processes, such as formal meeting procedures. Conventional procedures can be very alienating and excluding (as the example of the community member on a board in Chapter 6 illustrated), especially for people who are not accustomed to working in that way; this is especially a problem for Indigenous people in Australia, whose cultures may embody different forms of decision making based on consensus. In order to be more inclusive there are alternative forms of decision making that can be adopted, most notably consensus-oriented processes where discussion will continue until not just a majority but everybody is satisfied with the result. The discussion in Chapter 6 about supporting and encouraging participation articulated ways to develop alternative organising processes.

If a more community-based system is to replace traditional welfare-state structures, as was suggested in Chapter 1, local communities will have to assume extra responsibility for the planning, organisation and delivery of their own human services, such as health, education, financial assistance and care of the dependent. To do this, local management structures will need to be established and they will need to be integrated into an overall form of community governance. In some areas existing local government structures can provide a good basis for such a development, but even in such locations a community will need to come to terms with how it manages its own affairs. This approach requires the active participation of a large number of people if it is to work effectively and such participation would be seen as one of the rights and obligations of citizenship in a society based on community-level structures. Engaging citizens in the building of these structures and ensuring that broad-based participation is not only possible, but also encouraged, are major roles for a community worker, as was argued in Chapter 6.

External political development

External political development refers to empowerment of the community in its interactions with the wider social and political environment. This is more commonly referred to as 'social action' and has been seen as an important component of community work. However, from a developmental perspective, the empowering of a community to take such action is as important as the action itself.

While consciousness-raising, as discussed above, is an essential precondition of such empowerment, the main community development focus in external political development is on organising and action.

ORGANISING

By contrast with the internal organising discussed in the previous section, organising in the external context effectively means organising for social action. It involves the community in establishing structures that will not only enable it to operate in an inclusive, democratic manner ensuring maximum participation, but which will also assist in increasing its effective power in the wider arena.

These two aims can sometimes create tensions. An important principle of organising for social action is discipline: people must not be allowed to 'do their own thing', but must act in accordance with the agreed plan of action. This can conflict with the aim of maximum participation and self-determination that is important in internal political development. When a community delegation is meeting a political leader, for example, it is important that there be selected spokespersons (or often only one spokesperson), who should be the most articulate and forceful people available and the people most likely to influence the politician; issues of gender, race and so on will take second place to political objectives in the selection of the people to speak. Even if the politician is sensitive to such issues, and a gender and race balance is included among the spokespersons, this is done as a *tactical* decision and is not one based on principle. In an internal community meeting, one might want to encourage everyone to speak when they feel like it, but in a delegation or public meeting, where discipline is essential, this could be disastrous.

Because of such potential tensions, the development of a political strategy for use in the external arena is a critical process. Ideally, one would seek to use the more inclusive and consensus-based developmental structures that have been established within a community to determine external strategy and tactics. Thus the decision that only certain people will speak in a delegation, that only specific people will try to get themselves arrested by lying in front of a bulldozer or that only certain people will speak to the media, is one that is taken and owned by the whole community.

Such tensions reflect the difficulty of operating in a wider competitive and conflictual system while seeking to operate through principles of non-violence, consensus and cooperation (see Chapter 7). This is a major issue for a community worker and must be dealt with at the community level. Sometimes, indeed, it is better not to take the pragmatic political option but to remain true to the principles of non-violence, consensus and cooperation in the wider arena, as this itself can be a powerful statement. It may be that particular incidents, such as a delegation meeting, are not as effective as one would like, but the overall impact may be greater.

This approach was used with devastating effect by Gandhi (1964, 1982). A firm adherence to principles of non-violence would suggest that, in the long term, one's ends are better served by retaining such principles in all actions, rather than making a pragmatic compromise. In practice, however, most communities and community workers will find themselves making some compromises, and the critical question is when to compromise on tactics and when to hold firm to process principles. This will be answered differently by different workers in different situations, but it will never be an easy or straightforward decision. Asking the critical questions is the hallmark of the competent community worker.

Organising for external action is essentially a practical matter of getting things done and helping the community to get itself organised to implement effective action plans. Small, task-centred groups or cells are usually the most effective form of organisation (e.g. one for media relations, one for legal issues, one for publicity material, one for letter-writing and petitions, one for lobbying politicians, one for logistical support and one for recruiting membership; see Jay 1972). These groups would report to a coordinating group or collective, which may be the community as a whole or some smaller group directly responsible to the community in some way. There are manuals available with suggestions of how this could be achieved (e.g. Jay 1972; Coover et al. 1985; McLean & Stutter 1993;

McArdle 1993), but there is no single right way to do it and each community needs to make its own decisions based on its unique circumstances.

SOCIAL ACTION

The goal of this sort of community organising is the achievement of some form of change in the external environment, for example, stopping a freeway or high-rise development, gaining representation on a particular authority, achieving better public transport, reducing violence in television programs, preserving the natural environment or stopping the closure of a local industry. This commonly involves some form of social action and has long been seen as a critical component in community work.

The community work movement of the 1970s, relying heavily on the writings and films of Saul Alinsky (1969, 1971), tended to see social action as perhaps the only legitimate form of community work and community work became synonymous with organising action campaigns for so-called 'radical' social change. This limited perception led to the rejection of other forms of community work as not 'radical' and therefore conservative and not worth doing. While such campaigning is clearly important, community work suffered from this limited perception of its nature and scope. More recent approaches have sought to incorporate social action within a broader context of community development; it is simply one aspect of developmental work among many. It is also important to emphasise that other forms of community work can be radical and challenge the existing order while an approach of 'action for action's sake' can in fact be quite conservative. Alinsky, indeed, can be criticised for his inherent conservatism in that he simply helped certain disadvantaged groups to operate more effectively within the existing order rather than challenging that order itself (see Chapter 5).

Social action campaigns, however, remain an important part of community development and can be seen as an expression of broader social and political aspirations and of social movements (Baldry & Vinson 1991; Burgmann 1993). Such campaigns can cover a wide variety of issues, and incorporate a variety of strategies for change (Baldry & Vinson 1991). To be successful, the selection and development of campaigning strategies must arise from a careful analysis of the social, political and cultural context and must result from a developmental process within the community concerned rather than being imposed from outside. The NO WAR campaign against the war in Iraq and the so-called 'War on Terror' has been a prime example of mobilisation from within communities in response to broader political issues of imperialism and conflict. At times, NO WAR was part of enormous protest marches that occurred simultaneously throughout many cities of the world. The success of these particular events, in terms of numbers that have been mobilised, is reflective of the thoughtful planning and the astute reading of the political barometer at the times of organising. Although the United States and George W. Bush's 'coalition of the willing' persisted despite the protests, the protest marches in themselves were effective products of planning and community-based mobilisation. The failure of the Howard government to regain office in Australia in 2007 and the election of Barack Obama as President of the United States in 2008 were both outcomes of growing grassroots resistance, of which political protests were part.

There are a number of useful source books describing specific action campaigns (e.g. Baldry & Vinson 1991; Coover et al. 1985; Plant & Plant 1992; Hawke & Gallagher 1989). These can be used to provide some creative ideas, but simply copying somebody else's techniques is almost bound to fail; what worked for Alinsky in Chicago, for Stephen Hawke at Noonkanbah or for Bob Brown in Tasmania is unlikely to work by simple replication in a different place, time and culture. At a more general level, however, there are some basic principles that can be applied to social action that are common to other aspects of community work practice. These will be considered in Chapter 10.

A peace rally to protest against war in Iraq—mobilisation from within communities

Cultural development

The globalisation of culture has followed the same pattern as the globalisation of the economy. A universal culture is emerging, propagated through increasingly global media, which are largely controlled by and work in the interests of transnational capital. Television, music, architecture, food, drink, clothing, film, sport and other forms of recreation are becoming increasingly (and, for many, depressingly) similar wherever in the world one happens to be. One is never far from McDonald's, Coca-Cola, Western popular music, American television extravaganzas or a pizza shop. One city is very much like another, hotels have become the same the world over and television, advertising and computer technology seem to work relentlessly to bring about uniformity.

In the face of this globalisation of culture it is very difficult for communities to preserve their own unique local culture, yet this is a critical component of community development. The principle of diversity requires that diversity of culture be retained; it is culture which gives people that critical sense of identity and belonging, so cultural development is of paramount importance for community. Not only is culture becoming globalised, it is also becoming increasingly commodified. Cultural activity becomes something that is produced, packaged, bought and sold, rather than something that is the property of the whole community and in which people are free to participate. Conventional analysis sees culture as split across class divisions into so-called 'high culture' and 'popular culture' but both are influenced by this process. Music, drama, art and sport are becoming activities that are done by the few for the consumption of the many, rather than being widely participatory. Instead of making music, we listen to the elite performers on our stereos or portable media players. Instead of playing sport we watch it on television. Instead of acting, we watch a movie. Even if we go to live concerts, live theatre or live sport, our role is as passive and paying consumers; any attempt to participate in more than the prescribed 'acceptable' ways (such as through polite applause) is likely to lead to our forcible ejection from the event. More often, through electronic technology, the activity itself will be far removed from our own reality, in both time and place, and our participation is non-existent. These are activities that are reserved for the elite professionals; most of us are just not good enough and our occasional amateur efforts are looked on with at best tolerance and at worst scorn. We become embarrassed and are not inclined to continue to participate. The message is that such things are really the domain of the professional and our role is primarily the passive one of consumer of the packaged product.

This is a historically recent phenomenon, however, many rural communities in the majority world still preserve their own unique local culture. Until the 20th century, such cultural activities were largely local and highly participatory and regional differences were both significant and important. This cultural diversity helped to provide a sense of identity and community and the globalisation and commodification of culture is an important part of the loss of community that was so widely experienced in the late 20th century. Cultural development is thus an important component of a community development approach. Within the context of community development, cultural development has four components (see Figure 9.5): *preserving and valuing local culture, preserving and valuing Indigenous culture, multiculturalism* and *participatory culture*.

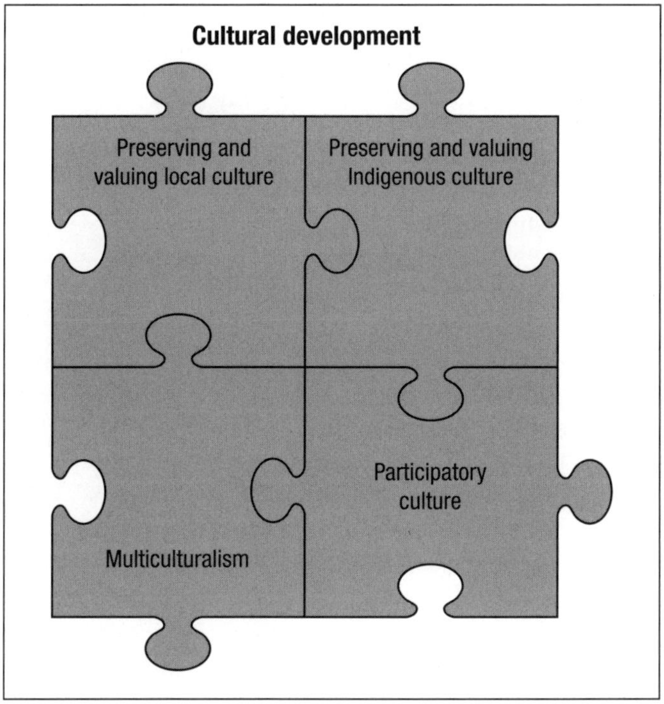

Figure 9.5 Cultural development

Preserving and valuing local culture

How we view culture is also critical. There are two aspects to this question. The first is how we construct 'culture' and the second is how we see its role in community development. Culture has been described as a phenomenon that is reasonably static and deeply rooted in groups. However, a more useful way of viewing culture is as a relational concept, where it is concerned with the many interrelationships between people and groups, between ideas and worldviews. As Rao and Walton (2004, p. 4) put it, 'culture is concerned with identity, aspiration, symbolic exchange coordination and structures and practices that serve relational ends, such as ethnicity, ritual, heritage, traditions, norms, meanings and beliefs'. It is a form of capital reserves. Its role in community, then, is to enhance community capacity and collective agency. This point is important to appreciate because, in the pursuit of human wellbeing, it takes the focus away from individual ability to a focus on collective capacity through relationships and the power to achieve. Culture, from this perspective, influences wellbeing through the expression of the arts. Some economic activities are shaped by the cultural milieu. Culture shapes the nature of participation and the sense of solidarity. Culture maintains continuity with the past and influences the future journeys of groups and societies (Sen 2004). In this sense, culture is a critical component of community development. This is not to deny that there are aspects of culture that are oppressive and exploitative, which contravene human rights. If culture is concerned with relationships, and relationships are embedded with power (including misused power) then culture can undermine the community development project too.

Culture, then, and local cultural traditions are an important part of a sense of community and help to provide a community with a sense of identity and solidarity. Community development, therefore, will often seek to identify the positive and important elements of the local culture and to strengthen, affirm and preserve them. These might include local history and heritage, locally based crafts, local foods or other products and, in some cases, local languages. Communities may have particular traditions, such as local festivals or fairs, a town band, a reputation for skill in football or links to a particular ethnic community.

External influences can effectively break down these local cultural traditions and to retain them requires a deliberate community strategy. As with other aspects of community development, there can be no simple recipe of how this can be achieved. The initiative must come from the community itself; the way in which this will be done will vary from community to community according to local conditions, culture, economics and so on. The community needs to identify what are the unique or significant components of its cultural heritage and determine which of these are worth preserving. Then a plan can be established about how this might be accomplished through, for example, activities at the local school or community centre, establishing a local industry based on

A local village festival is held annually and features contemporary cultural activities unique to that village in India

local culture, festivals, publications or making a video. The most effective plan will be one that involves many members of the community rather than just a small group or an elite and one that integrates the cultural traditions within the mainstream life of the community rather than being set apart from it.

Care must be taken that this form of cultural development does not create an artificial 'museum' approach to local culture, which sets the traditional culture aside from day-to-day reality and maintains it in a static rather than a dynamic form, as an oddity to be observed rather than as a way of life. The separate 'pioneer village' or annual folk-dancing festival, for example, can be so far removed from local community life that it in fact separates the community from its cultural heritage rather than the reverse. A local tourist industry can easily reinforce such an artificial separation. For cultural development to be effective within a wider community development context, it must not be separated in this way but must be seen as a real part of community life. If this is achieved, the local cultural tradition can become a focal point for social interaction, community involvement and broad-based participation and can become an important process in other aspects of community development, such as social development, economic development or political development.

Local cultural heritage can be emphasised in a variety of community contexts. As an example, a community health centre located in a community with a strong history of organised labour and working-class struggle through union solidarity might signify this with relevant wall posters,

In contrast to the village festival, this replication of Australian goldfields in the 1800s commodifies and artificially separates 'culture'

perhaps emphasising the important contribution of trade unions to occupational health and safety. It might be named in honour of a local union pioneer. It might have direct links with local unions, through active participation in union affairs, particularly those with a health focus. It might organise a good deal of its health promotion work using union structures. It might allow union-based groups to meet in the building and so on. In all these ways, the health centre would be helping to reaffirm the significance of this aspect of the local cultural tradition and strengthen its identification in the community.

Not all local cultural traditions are worth preserving. For example, one would not want to encourage a community with a tradition of racism, female genital mutiliation, domestic violence, alcoholism or female infanticide to perpetuate these with pride and to protect them on the grounds that they are important local traditions giving people a sense of identity. While cultural diversity is important, a cultural development strategy must also be informed by the social justice and human rights principles outlined in Chapter 3. This asserts the importance and universality of fundamental issues of human rights and the importance of class, gender and race/ethnicity, which in effect circumscribe the freedom of relatively autonomous and decentralised communities to develop as they wish. Cultural and religious festivals in rural Indian villages are central to their cultural life. However, they are also the reason for people to take loans, fall deeply into debt and further poverty and for moneylenders to increase their power and wealth. Such issues of social justice and human rights should be fundamental to all community development and must not be lost sight of in the interests of cultural relativism and diversity. They are essential in determining which aspects of a traditional community culture should be strengthened and preserved as part of the community development process.

Preserving and valuing Indigenous culture

Preserving and valuing the culture of Indigenous people is a critical issue for community development. While it might be argued that Indigenous culture is simply a particular case of local culture as discussed above, the different dynamics surrounding Indigenous culture mean that it has to be treated as a separate case. There are two principal reasons for this. One is the special connection that Indigenous people have to the land and to their traditional community structures, which developed in harmony with the land over a very long period. Community, and the integrity of traditional community, is essential to their cultural and spiritual survival; in this important sense the preservation of traditional culture is a more vital need for Indigenous Australians than for most others. The second reason is that a good deal of harm has been done, and in many cases is still being done, to Indigenous people in the name of 'community development' (Chambers 1993). It has at times been simply a euphemism for oppression, domination, colonialism, racism and the imposition of Western cultural values and traditions at the expense of those of Indigenous people. Because Indigenous people have a critical need for community development in one sense of the term, yet have been the victims of community development in another sense, there is a major contradiction that needs to be identified and thought through. While this contradiction exists for others as well, it is much stronger and more polarised in the case of Indigenous Australians, making community development with Indigenous people in Australia a special case deserving special treatment and careful consideration.

There are, in practice in Australia, two different contexts for community development with Indigenous people. One is the case of Indigenous communities where the community members are all or predominantly Indigenous people and the community itself is thus identified and the other is the case of Indigenous people belonging to a community along with people with other cultural backgrounds.

INDIGENOUS COMMUNITIES

Community development with Indigenous communities makes sense only if it is undertaken within Indigenous cultural traditions. To attempt otherwise is to participate in the further oppression of the Indigenous people and reinforce structures and discourses of domination. The primary aim of community development, therefore, is to legitimise and strengthen Indigenous culture through effective empowerment processes, which enables Indigenous people to have genuine control over their own community and their own destiny. Indigenous people themselves must set the agenda for development and have complete control over processes and structures.

For this reason there are limits to the effective and appropriate participation of non-Indigenous community workers. Such workers, while they may be genuinely sympathetic to the needs and aspirations of Indigenous people, nevertheless represent the dominant non-Indigenous culture and are themselves part of the structures of colonisation and oppression. They must always be aware that it is not 'their' community and that they will never fully understand or appreciate the culture and traditions of the people with whom they are working.

This is not to say that there is no role for non-Indigenous community workers. Such workers, if they approach traditional culture with genuine respect, goodwill and sensitivity, can make a significant contribution to the community development process in several ways. Indigenous people are some of the most oppressed, disadvantaged and powerless in Australian society, and it is simply not good enough for the dominant society and non-Indigenous community workers to ignore them, using as an excuse 'It is really their problem and we should not be telling them what to do'. The idea of Indigenous control also does not equate with non-Indigenous workers or organisations doing nothing. Support and partnerships and Indigenous control are not mutually exclusive concepts. As part of the structures of racist oppression, non-Indigenous community workers must be prepared to accept that it is indeed their problem and that they have a responsibility to support Indigenous people in their struggle to reverse these oppressive structures.

Non-Indigenous community workers can sometimes, by their very presence, act as a catalyst for community development as described in the earlier section on social development. In a more activist role they can play an important part in helping Indigenous people with their political struggle, by assisting them in developing their strategies for social action; often a community worker will have a more extensive understanding of the political processes of mainstream society, and this is vitally important knowledge for Indigenous people. A significant example is Hawke and Gallagher's account of the Noonkanbah conflict in Western Australia (1989); their role as effective political advisers to the community was very important in helping Indigenous people to fight for their land.

It is also important in such struggles for Indigenous people to know that they have the support of people and groups in the non-Indigenous community and community workers can have a vital role in demonstrating and organising such support. Church groups, such as the social justice units of the mainstream Christian denominations, have been particularly important in this respect.

While support for the struggle of Indigenous people is critically important, it must be emphasised that in the end it is the Indigenous people's struggle and non-Indigenous community workers and activists should never seek to own that struggle or to see it as theirs. Ultimately, non-Indigenous community workers are representatives of the oppressing culture and, with very few if any exceptions, cannot expect to become fully identified with Indigenous people in their struggle against that oppression. They can be very supportive and can provide a good deal of important assistance, but in the end it is the Indigenous people themselves who must provide the necessary leadership. Many of the skills of a community worker (see Chapter 11) are those that Indigenous people themselves will need if they are to achieve successful community development; hence community workers have an important role to play in skill-sharing as part of the empowerment process. This, however, must not be done in such a way as to devalue the skills that Indigenous people have developed; community workers have much to learn from the wisdom and skills of Indigenous people. Skill-sharing, therefore, must be a two-way process, with each learning from and valuing the other's experience, expertise and wisdom.

The ideal, of course, is that there be well-supported Indigenous community workers. In many instances this is already the case; it is just that non-Indigenous society does not readily recognise the existence of such people within traditional societies. But there is also a need for more Indigenous people to be involved in community development training courses—both as educators and as students—and for these courses to take more account of the needs and wisdom of Indigenous people.

Another important role for non-Indigenous community workers is working to counteract racism and racial oppression in the wider society. Structural racism is at the heart of the problems of Indigenous communities and community workers are in an important strategic position to help to challenge it. This is perhaps the way in which non-Indigenous community workers can be of most help to Indigenous communities.

Working with Indigenous communities can raise important issues of gender. Traditional Indigenous culture can seem to reinforce the oppression of women; while there is debate about the extent to which this is true in traditional Indigenous societies, there is no doubt that many women are oppressed and abused within many *contemporary* Indigenous communities, which have been influenced by the values of the dominant culture, especially where alcohol is readily available (Bolger 1991). This emphasises the importance of the social justice and human rights perspective outlined in Chapter 3 and is an important warning against a naïve romantic view that everything that happens in Indigenous communities is noble and virtuous.

Working with Indigenous communities requires a sensitivity to what is an essentially alien culture for the non-Indigenous worker. It is obviously important for the worker to be as well informed as possible about the culture, which can be accomplished through discussion with Indigenous people themselves, others who have worked in the community (though it is important to realise that not all such people will be well informed) and through reading relevant publications. Although the diversity among Indigenous communities makes generalisation hazardous, there are two critical elements that pervade all community work with Indigenous people: *land* and *spirituality*. The crucial relationship of Indigenous people to the land and Indigenous understandings of spirituality and the sacred are fundamentally different from those of Western non-Indigenous people and they pervade all aspects of Indigenous society and community. It is around such issues that many of the most important conflicts with non-Indigenous society arise, prime examples being land rights and the desecration of sacred sites through mining or 'development'. These also, however, provide a potential basis for a genuinely Indigenous alternative to the conventional forms of structures and services that have so conspicuously failed Indigenous people in the past.

A particularly important initiative is the establishment of programs using Indigenous spiritual values and traditions as a way of organising alternative approaches to social problems and human services, such as health, alcohol, housing and justice issues (Hazelhurst 1994). Programs in North America and Aotearoa as well as Australia are now being established along such lines, seeking to utilise the strengths of Indigenous cultures instead of denying their legitimacy or potential. These represent an important step in the general development of a community-based alternative, as such Indigenous societies are by their very nature community-based.

INDIGENOUS PEOPLE IN OTHER COMMUNITIES

Where there are substantial numbers of Indigenous people forming part of wider community groups, a different set of issues confronts the community worker in these cases. Here the goal of community development is not only the enhancement and protection of Indigenous culture, but also the legitimising and acceptance of that culture within the wider community. This requires working towards countering racism, acceptance by non-Indigenous people that the Indigenous group has something legitimate to contribute to the community and the integration of Indigenous culture in such a way that it is acknowledged by the wider community at the same time as not compromising its integrity for Indigenous people.

This is an extremely complex and delicate task that requires: cultural sensitivity; political sophistication; communication skills; the capacity to negotiate and advocate; a strong personal commitment to social justice; human rights promotion; time; patience and a thick skin. It is perhaps one of the most difficult challenges that can face a community worker. On one side, entrenched racist structures, attitudes, habits and practices, which have been reinforced for decades, need to be challenged and broken down. On the other side, the suspicion, mistrust and anger caused by decades of oppression, exploitation, discrimination, broken promises and well-intentioned but misguided 'charity' need to be acknowledged and overcome. Each group needs to learn to trust, value and respect the other, which means longstanding and well-entrenched patterns must be broken. This cannot be accomplished immediately—those who seek to achieve instant 'reconciliation' are bound to be disappointed.

This form of community development needs to work on a number of fronts at once. One key component is to work closely with the people who are at the interface between Indigenous and non-Indigenous people and who are crucial in defining relationships between the two groups: police, teachers, social workers, lawyers, magistrates, health workers, publicans, clergy and so on. Such people are crucial in any change strategy. A second component is to create public awareness by utilising every opportunity for consciousness-raising (see Chapter 7) among both Indigenous and non-Indigenous groups. Another is to work closely with community leaders (both formal and informal) in both groups. This includes local media, local government, employers, union leaders, influential citizens, power brokers and traditional Indigenous leaders. A further strategy is to look for every opportunity to bring people from the two groups together around as wide a variety of community activities as possible. Another is to make the most of every opportunity for education: the more people can learn about other people's culture and life experience, the easier it is to challenge racist stereotypes. Lastly it is important to support Indigenous people to build their own organisations within the larger community so that they are more readily able to negotiate, collectively, the interfaces between themselves and non-Indigenous people, institutions and organisations.

Such a multi-strategy approach (the details will vary according to local factors) can bring results, but it is a long and painful process. It involves the building of trust, encouraging people to change and take risks and negotiation and diplomacy of the highest order. The role is essentially one of an 'active catalyst'; the community itself must be the ultimate source of change, but good community work can help to bring about the conditions that will make it possible.

Multiculturalism

The common use of the term 'multiculturalism' generally denotes different *ethnic* groups living in one community but maintaining distinctive cultural identities. Thus the focus is on ethnicity and the cultural features of different ethnic groups. With increased global travel and personal mobility, massive migrations following the wars of the 20th century and continuing increases in the movement of refugees, multiculturalism has become the norm in most societies. The days of relatively homogeneous cultures appear to be gone and people and communities are having to come to terms with living in a multicultural society. For some this is a cause of enrichment, diversity and the embracing of new opportunities for cultural experience while for others it is cause for fear, threat, suspicion, racial and cultural tensions and exclusions. The issue of multicultural policy and politics is complex, and outside the scope of the present discussion, but a diversity of cultural backgrounds is a reality for many communities and it is therefore an important aspect of community cultural development.

As with Indigenous people, the challenge for community development is to help to preserve the integrity of a variety of cultures while seeking ways in which the different cultural traditions can integrate within a local community and enrich the cultural experience of all. This is a difficult task, and can be made more so by the enormous variety of cultural traditions, sensitivities, historical rivalries and conflicting values, and by the ambiguity within the wider community around issues of multiculturalism. A community worker seeking to develop a multicultural community must obviously be aware of and sensitive to these issues and will need very special skills in order to act as a catalyst for community development.

The clash of cultural values and the problems experienced by individuals and families as they seek to find a way through these conflicts provide an environment of instability and uncertainty. For community workers, however, instability and uncertainty should imply opportunity—in seeking to help people resolve these difficulties there are opportunities for creative development of alternative, community-based structures over which the people themselves can have control. For example, a good deal of creative community work can be undertaken from migrant resource centres or ethnic community organisations, through provision of the resources and support for people to establish their own programs, structures and services.

Many of the strategies outlined in the section on Indigenous people can be applied also to multicultural community work, though of course they need to be adapted to meet the specific requirements of local conditions. These include working with key community leaders, consciousness-raising, bringing people together and countering racism.

One important issue for community workers in multicultural settings relates to universal principles of social justice and human rights. In this area, particularly, one can come up against traditional community practices that offend against these principles (and some that are not so traditional, such as the use of physical violence to resolve conflict in communities that have come from war-ravaged areas, including those that have used child soldiers). An extreme—but very real—example is the issue of female genital mutilation; other examples include traditional gender relations, arranged marriages and parental attitudes to education. This is why a strong understanding of and commitment to the social justice and human rights issues discussed in Chapter 3 is a crucial component of the community development approach. Such commitment ensures that a community worker will not be tempted to avoid these issues on the grounds of cultural integrity and will not fall into the trap of 'culturalism' ('If it's cultural, it's good') (Booth 1999). Obviously such issues have to be addressed with sensitivity, but female genital mutilation and other human rights abuses cannot be tolerated from a social justice and human rights perspective and the challenge for the community worker is how to work *with* a community towards the abolition of such practices.

In doing so it is important, as discussed in Chapter 5, for community workers to remember that cultures are not static—cultural norms, values and practices change over time—and that cultures are not monolithic—many values and practices are contested within the culture and are not necessarily adhered to or supported by all members of the cultural group. Thus a practice such as female circumcision must be seen as something that is contested, not supported by everyone and under challenge from *within* the cultural community. Culture must be seen as dynamic. In the case of female circumcision, this can be seen as an example of the struggle for the liberation of women, which transcends cultural boundaries.

Other issues of class and gender are also important for community workers in multicultural settings. Often an ethnic 'community' will simply reflect the traditional highly stratified and oppressive divisions of the original society. Thus support for ethnic communities can inadvertently become support for oppressive structures and the exclusion of some members by privileging others as elites within ethnic communities, rather than support for the community as a whole. Gender-based oppression is often found within the structures of ethnic communities and migrant women are thus particularly disadvantaged. This means that a community worker, committed both to supporting cultural integrity and to social justice and human rights, is likely to be faced with difficult tensions and contradictions in working with ethnic communities. The social justice and human rights analysis of Chapter 3 is critically important in this regard and the task of resolving these contradictions and promoting community development that counteracts such oppressive structures and practices is complex and difficult.

Participatory culture

The final aspect of cultural development is related to participation in cultural activities, rather than the maintenance of cultural traditions.

Such cultural activity is an important focus for community identity, participation, social interaction and community development. One way to encourage healthy communities is to encourage broad participation in cultural activities so that art, music, theatre, dance and sport become things that people do rather than watch. This has been the focus of many programs of community cultural development; cultural participation is seen as an important way of building social capital, strengthening community and affirming identity. The possible activities will vary, depending on the location, the local culture and other factors.

The role of sport in community development raises a problematic issue. Most sport is by nature competitive and using sport as a form of community development can be seen as reinforcing structures of competition rather than cooperation. Some community workers, therefore, will choose not to encourage sporting activities, though this is an unpopular position in a sports-crazy community (as is often the case with country towns) and may become a problem for that worker in trying to gain credibility. Also such a position fails to recognise that in many instances the competitive aspect of social sport is of relatively minor importance and it is the social interaction that occurs during or around the sporting contest that is of greater significance. In one community racism against newly arrived refugees from the Horn of Africa was addressed by the community worker through facilitating teams to play soccer which, although competitive and gender-biased, was important as it was a common passion of both the young African males and their non-African counterparts. Thus, a categorical rejection of competitive sport may well be inappropriate for a community worker—it is perhaps through the encouragement of participation in organised sport, especially where the competitive element is not strong, that community solidarity can best be achieved.

In some sporting activities, however, the element of competition and aggression can be more blatant. It is hard to see the justification for the encouragement of boxing, for example, if one is interested in developing non-violent cooperative community structures. Motor sport is another that is hard to justify, especially from a Green or ecological perspective, given that it glorifies the use of the motor car and driving at high speed.

As with other community development activity, class, gender and race/ethnicity issues need to be identified and recognised in the encouragement of cultural participation. Some sporting or cultural activities will favour particular class groups (e.g. golf, sailing, symphony concerts), while others will tend to be gender-specific (e.g. football). It is important that participatory cultural activity should be inclusive rather than exclusive and the class, race and gender implications of any such community development need to be carefully monitored—otherwise oppression and structural disadvantage will simply be reinforced.

Cultural participation also has the potential to achieve more than the strengthening of social capital and community building. Participation in cultural activities is an important part of helping the people of a community to reclaim their own culture back from external definers, such as advertisers. Hence cultural participation is potentially political and can assist in community development at a more political level.

Cultural activities themselves have the potential for consciousness-raising, the exploration of oppression, the linking of the personal and the political and for coming to terms with social and community problems. Culture has the power to inspire, inform and unite a community. Revolutionary music, including songs of protest, has been very important as a focus and inspiration for earlier social movements. Augusto Boal (1979) has demonstrated the revolutionary potential of the theatre as a means of consciousness-raising and political development, allowing people to explore their context and the issues of power and oppression and to express their resistance. This has been used by others (van Erven 1992), who have shown that theatre can be a powerful technique for development and social change across a wide range of cultures. Indeed in some cultural settings (e.g. the Philippines), to attempt a program of consciousness-raising and community development *without* music, dance and theatre would be to condemn the program to immediate failure.

Environmental development

A consequence of the Green position described in Chapter 2, and the increased awareness of the importance of the environment, is that communities need to take responsibility for the protection and rehabilitation of the physical environment. The environment is a critical component of community and it needs to be incorporated in any integrated approach to community development. This applies to both the natural environment and the built environment.

Sometimes environmental issues will be important in bringing a community together and serving as a catalyst for community action. This has long been recognised in urban regions, where social action is most commonly discussed as a reaction to proposed freeways or property developments that have a direct impact on the local environment and are seen as posing a threat to the life of the local community. Specific pollution concerns, such as toxic waste disposal or lead emissions, can be another critical issue around which a community will readily mobilise. Such a threat can bring a community together and the initial action organisation can provide a basis for more long-term development. Environmental development, however, goes beyond simple environmental activism. It involves improvement of the community's environment in the broadest sense and requires the community to become aware of the importance of environmental issues and take responsibility for improving and protecting the local environment. At a less dramatic level than activist campaigning, a more general concern for the environment can be used as a way of bringing people together in a relatively non-threatening way. Establishing viable processes for recycling is an activity that can receive wide community support and is a practical way in which people can 'do their bit for the environment'. From a more considered Green perspective this is not nearly enough (see Chapter 2), but it provides a useful starting point for encouraging a broader ecological awareness and for bringing people together at a community level.

A community-based approach to urban and regional planning would require that there be adequate mechanisms for people to be involved in decisions about the physical attributes of cities, towns and regions. Decisions that are now seen as largely the domain of expert planners, or as being the province of developers, would be located more within the reach of ordinary people and would be seen as part of the local participatory decision-making process. Thus an important arena for community development activity is that of local planning and community workers will seek ways in which this can be undertaken within a more participatory model (as discussed in detail in Chapter 6). The urban renewal programs being introduced in many Australian cities are proving to be an important, while sometimes painful, experimental ground for community participation in urban planning.

Bioregionalism is a movement that has seen the local environment as a primary basis for community development (Sale 1991). This emphasises self-sufficiency and many of the principles of autonomy and localisation described in Chapter 5. It advocates a concentration on the local ecology, which can lead not only to sound environmental practices, but also to patterns of living, social interaction and economic activity that are localised, self-sufficient and sustainable. From this perspective, an initial concern for the local environment can be used as a starting point for more fundamental and broader-based community development. It is essentially applying the same principles of consciousness-raising as have been used in the women's movement, in Freire's 'conscientisation' (Freire 1972) and in work with low-income people (Liffman 1978) but starting instead with people's concern about the environment. This concern can be related to broader structural and political issues and can be related to other aspects of community life as the holistic perspective requires.

Environmental development can also be seen as moving beyond the local community. The Green analysis emphasises that we live in one finite world and that every citizen and every community has a responsibility to protect the global ecosystem. This provides not only a justification for moving beyond purely local concerns but also an imperative to do so. A concern to reduce the emission of greenhouse gases, for example, has little immediate local impact, but from a global perspective is critical to survival and is both a proper and a necessary concern of local communities. There is now a reasonable level of awareness about such global ecological imperatives and they can become a focus for organising local action. Thus organising to ensure that community activities have minimal impact on the wider environment (e.g. the ozone layer) as well as on the local environment is part of a community environmental development strategy.

Environmental concerns in the majority world are often related to more immediate human needs, such as survival, clean water, safe food and clean air (Shiva 1989, 1991). Here environmental development becomes even more important and any community development strategy has to incorporate environmental issues.

The techniques of environmental community development are similar to those discussed elsewhere in this chapter. They include consciousness-raising, education, organising the local community and setting goals and priorities. The results might include the creation of nature reserves, tree planting, soil conservation, building cycle paths, making the local economy more self-sufficient, introducing tighter pollution controls on local industry, altering local building regulations and establishing recycling (possibly as a new industry or on a cooperative basis). As with other aspects of community development, environmental development will succeed only if there is genuine and broad-based community involvement in identifying needs and determining appropriate courses of action. This is particularly important in relation to environmental development because of the technical nature of many environmental problems, which can result in an attitude of 'leave it to the experts' and runs counter to a community development perspective. Here the analysis of Chapter 2 is critically important: if environmental problems are the result of the social, economic and political order, they are essentially social, economic and political problems rather than technical problems. Hence they are matters for the whole community. Certainly the input of technical experts in environmental science is important, but effective solutions will be community-based, rather than the technical solutions demanded by the scientific technological paradigm.

Again, as with other forms of community development, class, gender and race/ethnicity issues are critical. It was shown in Chapter 4 that a Green perspective often does not take account of these factors and the result is an environmental activism which simply reinforces existing discourses of oppression and structural disadvantage. Thus the feminisation of the environment movement places undue blame and responsibility on women and there is the commonly heard complaint that the environment is a 'middle-class' issue because of the way it is treated in the media. Environmental development needs to overcome these problems and stereotypes; the fact that environmental issues are a matter of concern for the whole community is not of itself sufficient to ensure this and issues of class, gender and race/ethnicity must be specifically addressed in any development program. For this reason it is essential that environmental development and environmental activism be located within a broader context of integrated community development as outlined in this chapter.

Personal and spiritual development

Personal growth

It is important, in discussing community development, not to lose sight of the importance of personal growth and personal development. One of the main justifications for community development is that the community is a better context for personal development than the more impersonal bureaucratic structures of big government and big business. The loss of community is closely associated with the loss of personal identity as it is through one's sense of belonging in a community that one develops a sense of personal worth and the capacity to lead a more enriched and fulfilling life.

Some of the previously discussed aspects of community development are aimed at personal development. This is particularly so of social development where a major emphasis has been on the development and delivery of human services such as health, education, housing and care of the dependent. Such services, in the community context, are primarily aimed at improving people's quality of life and so they are an important component of a personal development agenda.

The idea of personal development and personal growth, however, is also associated with a variety of activities, including encounter groups, myriad kinds of therapy, *gestalt*, 'new age', cults, tarot readings, neuro-linguistic programming, mysticism and witchcraft. It has to be said that many of these, though certainly not all, are of doubtful value and represent a form of self-indulgence that fits in with the dominant individualist ideology and is contrary to community development. Indeed, a whole 'personal growth' industry has been set up. If such practices are divorced from a specific power analysis they can readily serve only to help people feel good about being disempowered.

The research evidence on the effectiveness of even the more mainstream and respectable therapeutic programs is less than fully convincing and a strong case can be made that the 'therapeutic state' has served to benefit the elite of the helping professions rather than the clientele it was supposed to serve (Polsky 1991).

The most unfortunate aspect of all this is that it has given personal growth a bad name. From a community development perspective, one of the most concerning things is that the personal growth industry has created an artificial environment for personal growth, rather than allowing and encouraging it to occur within a more natural and sustainable community context.

Personal growth can also be politically conservative. It is all too easy—from a personal growth perspective—to move to an essentially individual account of social problems (see Chapter 3), with its associated tendency to 'blame the victim'. It is also fully consistent with the individualism and competition of capitalism and the highly individualised society. Individualism is part of the problem—from a community development perspective it is most unlikely to be an effective part of the solution. It is important to note, however, that personal growth, therapy and counselling are not necessarily conservative; it is simply that, without a structural analysis of the sort outlined in Chapter 3, they have an inherent tendency towards such conservatism. It is essential, therefore, to base personal growth within an analysis of power, and to understand the 'empowerment' aims of personal growth within the context of power as discussed in Chapter 3. By incorporating such a structural social justice and human rights perspective one can develop an approach to personal growth that is more radical in nature. Such models have been developed within the radical streams of some of the helping professions (e.g. Fook 1993; Mullaly 1997) and within the feminist movement (Marchant & Wearing 1986). Such approaches specifically link a structural perspective to the therapeutic and see personal growth, counselling and therapy as potentially liberating and empowering by joining the personal and the political. This requires quite a different approach from more conventional counselling techniques—one which is in fact closer to Freire's dialogical praxis (1972).

This is not to deny that the need for personal growth and development is strong in modern society. However, other cultures and at other times people have had their needs for personal fulfilment met through means other than a professionalised industry, such as the family and the community. The therapy and personal growth industries are symptoms of individualism and the poverty of personal relationships in modern Western society. From a community development perspective, this points out the need for establishing alternative community-based structures to meet people's need for personal growth and development. A community-based approach to personal growth and development would seek to find ways in which people's individual needs could be met through community networks, structures and interactions, rather than through professionalised and packaged services. It therefore seeks to decommodify personal growth and relocate it within human social interaction. It is still largely the case that at times of personal trouble, stress and pain people will seek help and support first from their families and friends. However, the limited and fragmented social networks that are part of *Gesellschaft* society mean that people cannot always find such support. A community-based approach would aim to strengthen community interactions so that those supports were more readily available. Similarly, it can be suggested that in a flourishing, healthy community people are able to grow and develop personally through their interactions with others and that the artificial environment of the personal growth industry then becomes unnecessary.

The key to personal development, therefore, is the development of strong community interactive structures. This requires basic community development strategies of the kind discussed in Chapter 11. However, personal development can also be achieved through involvement in the various other community development processes discussed in this chapter and in Chapter 7. Personal growth and development can be an important consequence of other community activity; this is often likely to be much more effective than establishing a specific program of 'personal growth' within the community.

Spiritual development

Personal growth and development are important to provide people with more meaning in their lives—that is, a sense of purpose and worth. To many people, however, this need is better understood as a need for spiritual development. Modern society is essentially secular and has left little room for notions of the sacred or spiritual values. This can be seen to have denied one of the most important aspects of human existence. Hence there is a strong need for community development to incorporate notions of spiritual development.

In this context, the words *sacred* and *spiritual* are used in their broadest sense and do not equate solely to the understandings of mainstream religions, though such perspectives must be included. One can have a spiritual experience quite outside the confines of organised religion—experiencing the grandeur of a wilderness area, contemplating the ocean, reading poetry, being moved by an expressive piece of music or a painting, pondering the mysteries of the universe, finding fulfilment in sexual relationships, participating in making music, dancing or singing and in the experience of genuine human community.

For Indigenous people the sacred and spiritual transcend all of life and all human experiences; unless understood within a spiritual context, life has no meaning and no purpose. All people are spiritual and it is a feeling for the spiritual that unites people, animals, the land and all things into a whole and defines one's relationship to the natural environment. Thus the holistic perspective, an essential component of the approach to community development outlined in this book, is in Indigenous culture a natural consequence of a spiritual perspective. For Indigenous people one of the major criticisms of modern Western society is that it does not have this profound sense of the sacredness and spiritual nature of all things and has lost what gives meaning, sense and unity to life and to the world.

It is only in relatively recent times that Western society has lost its sense of the sacred and the spiritual. But the spiritual dimension is important to community development. A sense of the sacred and a respect for spiritual values are an essential part of re-establishing human community and providing meaning and purpose for people's lives. But the corollary is also true: genuine human community is in itself a spiritual experience and so the development of community is an important ingredient of spiritual development—the two belong together.

As with other forms of community development, the external imposition of a particular form of spirituality is bound to produce negative consequences; the colonialism of Christian missionaries is perhaps the most extreme example of this.

A more appropriate form of spiritual development is to begin by respecting and affirming the (often varied) religious and spiritual traditions of the community. On this basis, one seeks to provide an environment where a sense of the sacred and the spiritual can develop, where people can openly acknowledge the importance of spiritual values, where a variety of spiritual experiences is available to people and where various spiritual traditions—including those of the major religious faiths, Indigenous people and others—are all valued and respected. This requires the development of a sense of community (which itself can be a spiritual experience) and strong cultural development as discussed earlier in this chapter; art, music, literature, poetry and drama can all become ways in which people experience and express their spirituality and are, therefore, critical components of a community's spiritual development. Harmony with nature is also spiritual and so the spiritual dimension of development, in this respect, resonates loudly with the ecological perspective discussed in Chapter 2.

Balanced development

This chapter has outlined six aspects of community development: social, economic, political, cultural, environmental and personal/spiritual. Within each of them there is a further variety of community development activity and the picture that emerges is complex. Community development occurs on a number of fronts, and uses a variety of techniques. It is a complicated business and requires a wide range of skills and abilities, which will be discussed in Chapter 11. Community workers find themselves doing many different things (often all at once).

An effective approach to community development will take account of all of these six different aspects of community work, though in any particular situation some will inevitably be seen as higher or lower priorities or as opportunistic starting points in the community development process. A healthy community, however, must be well developed in all six; if any one is left out, the community will be poorer and its development uneven. It is therefore inappropriate to regard any one as a priori more important than the others, even though such views are often voiced. For example, much community economic development proceeds on the assumption that if only one can 'get the economy right' all else will follow. Others see personal development as the priority: if people are able to develop a sense of worth and personal fulfilment, then everything else can be easily accomplished. Another view emphasises political development, seeing political empowerment as the key element that will stimulate all the others. Similar claims are made for social, cultural and environmental development.

The holistic perspective emphasises that all are important and that they are interconnected. Each affects the others and development in any one of these areas tends to assist development in the others. Thus, although it is useful to identify these six aspects of community development, it must not be assumed that they are distinct. The purpose of the typology is not to make clear or rigid distinctions, but to emphasise the need for *balanced* development consistent with the ecological principle of equilibrium (Chapter 2) to ensure that a community development project takes all these aspects of development into account.

The discussion of the six aspects of community development also brought out the importance of the earlier discussion of the ecological and social justice/human rights perspectives. They enable and indeed encourage one to ask questions about such matters as sustainability, diversity, class, gender and race/ethnicity. Unless these questions are specifically addressed, there is a real danger that community development will simply reinforce existing patterns of structural oppression and ecological damage. This perspective effectively provides a screen for the planning and evaluation of community development—a set of criteria that must be met in any community work project. More than this, however, it points the way to some interesting and creative alternative ways of doing things: how to stimulate economic development that is truly sustainable, how to develop structures that do not favour white articulate men, how to engage in political campaigning in a genuinely inclusive and non-violent way, how to structure meetings and decision-making processes so that everyone can have input and so on.

Discussion of the six areas also indicated that a number of community work practice approaches are common to them. Consciousness-raising, bringing people together, the articulation of community aspirations and needs, management at community level, not imposing grand solutions from above and the role of community worker as catalyst were some of these common themes. Thus many of the actual principles of community work practice apply across the six areas and have more general utility in an integrated and balanced approach to community development. It must not be thought, therefore, that each area requires a separate range of skills, though inevitably there will be some skills that are more applicable in some areas than in others.

Such an integrated approach to community development suggests important elements in terms of both process and outcomes. Integrated community development is likely to have processes that entail development across a range of changes and outcomes which see parallel changes. The vision of a community-based alternative in which integrated community development is likely to result will include:

- Social relationships, including personal and other relationships within communities, and relationships with those outside communities where the balance of power in these relationships will shift from more oppressive to more liberating
- Economic relationships where there is increased local control and ownership of economic resources and processes and where sustainability is enhanced
- Cultural traditions where values within communities reflect more strongly a culture of human rights
- The environment, both human made and natural, where the community is more intimately identified with the ecology, rather than being seen apart from the rest of nature
- Employment and income generation which enables people to have access to all the resources they require to have their human rights to health, wellbeing, safety, freedom and dignity met
- Governance structures wherein participation in decision making has a broader base, is more inclusive and equitable and all members of a community are able to exercise social citizenship roles
- Social infrastructure which increases the capacity of the community to support its members.

From such considerations, a particular approach to community development practice can be seen to emerge. This will be discussed and outlined in subsequent chapters where the emphasis changes from the theoretical background of community development to actual community work practice.

Case studies

The following case studies will enable you to explore the relationships that exist between and within all six dimensions of community development discussed in this chapter. They will also alert you to situations where there might be gaps and an under-emphasis. Thinking about how these gaps could be addressed constitutes reflective practice. The following questions are guides for working your way through the case studies. Whenever a community embarks on a program of, for example, community economic development it is important to ask how the program relates to the other five aspects of community development. In each of the case studies, ask yourself these questions.

1 What aspect of development is the project mainly focusing on?
2 Will the project improve the community in relation to the other five dimensions of development?
3 How will the project relate to the particular dimension of community, both locally and on a larger scale?
4 Will it enhance or undermine any of the other dimensions?

5 Where are the gaps in the project among the six dimensions of community development?
6 As a result of answers to questions 1 to 5, it may be necessary to modify the program, or to establish other forms of community development activity to meet the other developmental needs of that particular community. What might some of these modifications be and what are the barriers to enacting the changes?
7 What opportunities exist to change practices?

CASE STUDY: Addressing safety in a local reserve

A local woman, a volunteer in a church-based coffee shop was overheard talking with another woman about her reluctance to take her grandchildren into the local reserve because used syringes were being found there. Community workers, overhearing the conversation, asked her if she had some time the next day and if she thought she and the workers knocking on the doors of homes around the reserve to see if others shared the same fear, would be a good idea. She did. Although her initial concern was for her own grandchildren, she readily identified as a member of the community and understood the importance of identifying community energy and mobilising local people to collectively address the issue.

The next day they canvassed many homes and found there was a common concern about a range of safety issues, especially at night. The volunteer invited people to a meeting in the coffee shop and 50 people turned up. A small organising group was formed and they began a campaign to lobby the local government body for lights to be installed in the reserve. There were delegations to the local government authority. The local free newspaper was used effectively and extensively to publicise the issue and the campaign. The campaign was successful and lighting was erected through the reserve. This success was also splashed across the newspaper.

Six weeks later, two young mothers arrived at the coffee shop looking for the volunteer. They each lived on opposite sides of a busy arterial road. There was a children's playground on each side of the road, but the local government authority was planning to close one. This would mean parents would have to take their children further, and across a busy road, to access the remaining playground. They had read in the newspaper about the volunteer and her success in her role as 'reserve expert' and had come to seek her support for them to mount their campaign.

It was noteworthy that another local woman, not the community workers, was considered to have the knowledge, skills and resources to mobilise local people and to influence local government decisions.

CASE STUDY: Social action to keep a city's green lung

In Kuala Lumpur, Malaysia, a community valued their local forest as a 'green lung' in a large city and as precious forest amid much deforestation in the country and around the globe. So when plans were announced by the Federal Territories Minister to free 39 hectares for 'development' the community responded. Twenty NGOs, resident associations and community-based groups formed an environmental alliance to lobby government

continued

through petitions and representations and to garner mass support among the people of the area and among community groups nationwide. The alliance also set up a website to distribute information, provide updates on the campaigns and conduct a public opinion poll to demonstrate to decision makers the will of the people.

The Malaysian Nature Society executive director said that the joining together of so many groups across the nation demonstrated that this green-lung issue was not an isolated one; it was part of a wider concern for the environment which was shared by many Malaysians and community groups. Taking a stand on these 39 hectares was important not only to save this forest—people and groups were also aware that, unless a stand was taken here, the government would continue to develop other forests unchecked by protest or resistance. After three years of campaigning, the government had promised to gazette the forest as a green lung, but no legislative changes had been made. The campaign continues and though the outcome is uncertain, the failure of the government to proceed with the development, the widespread support for the environmental alliance and the multiple strategies used by members of the alliance continue to give the people in communities across Malaysia hope.

CASE STUDY: Promoting Indigenous culture

The Indigenous communities in the Coorong, an area south-east of Adelaide, South Australia, have developed a number of projects designed to strengthen their communities. One such project is the Coorong Wilderness Lodge established and run by members of the Ngarrindjeri people. The project consists of restaurant facilities (including meals using Indigenous foods), caravan and camping facilities, bunk-house accommodation, video presentations, kayaking, ocean walks, bird watching, bush tucker and cultural dancing. The local community started the project on the assumption that tourism was an industry with great potential and that the project would create jobs for local Indigenous youth in a remote area with a paucity of employment opportunities. The project also offered the potential for skill training, cultural awareness, ecological sustainable living and ensuring that the local culture remained living, dynamic and growing and was seen by others as such.

The first stage of the project, after farmland had been purchased and returned to Indigenous hands, was to address the land degradation. The local community entered into partnerships with others to obtain the resources to regenerate the land. These partners included Greening Australia, Local Action Planning committees and the University of South Australia. Seedlings were direct-planted and, with the help of the university, the area was grid-referenced to enable a systematic plan of regeneration using local vegetation. The partnerships were described by the manager of the Lodge as the 'coming together of theory, the land and traditional culture' where technical knowledge, available local seeds and community knowledge of traditional uses of plants shaped the regeneration process. Now, after successful regeneration of much of the area, the project has well-established greenhouses to continue the process.

The next focus was on the business aspect of the project. Over some years, infrastructure has been built. A modern restaurant takes advantage of the beauty of the natural environment. In addition, accommodation has been built, roads constructed and water supplies guaranteed. The project is able to rely on rainwater for ten months of every year and wind power and solar power provide 50 per cent of electricity needs and also feed electricity back into the electricity grid. The area has also been restocked over time with native fauna.

Training of local people has been put in place in such areas as kayaking, hospitality, marketing and promotion and tour guiding. The training has been undertaken in the community, which has meant that organisations such as TAFE (Technical and Further Education) colleges have delivered their courses onsite at the project.

The project is now a viable tourist venture of a scale that uses but does not exploit the natural and cultural assets of the area. The impact on the local Indigenous community is positive and the project challenges many of the racist stereotypes that exist in Australia. The project has had many hurdles to overcome, including bureaucratic requirements, which have often been experienced barriers to Indigenous communities being able to establish successful business ventures elsewhere. However, the project has successfully responded to many external demands by ensuring its work is of very high quality—both its business practices and its tourism products.

The restaurant at Coorong Wilderness Lodge

CASE STUDY: Hoi Sinh—addressing drug use

The Hoi Sinh project was initiated by sections of the Vietnamese community in an Australian city. It was a community response to growing concern by Vietnamese parents, who came to Australia as refugees, about illicit drug use among the younger generation. 'Hoi Sinh' means 'rebirth' or 'regeneration'. The project had three objectives: 'To raise awareness about drug and alcohol issues with a purpose of proactive primary prevention in the community; to increase harm minimisation amongst young people; to develop, implement evaluate and document an assessment and referral process and network for young Vietnamese people with drug and alcohol issues' (South Australian Community Health Research Unit 1999).

Funding from various sources enabled a research officer to be employed in the project. Subsequently an advisory committee was formed to guide the project. After some time an action report was completed and a drug and alcohol worker, employed by the government drug agency, was placed at the Vietnamese Community Association one day per week. In the first two years, the major activities of the project were securing funding for a street worker, producing educational information, running a community-based conference and supporting a Vietnamese peer education program among young people in the Vietnamese community.

The project committee consisted of the Vietnamese Community Association and representatives from a local health service, a government drug agency, a peer-run community-based service for drug users, the Police Department, a human-relations training NGO and a crime-prevention program. The committee's aims were:

- raising awareness about drug and alcohol issues with the purpose of proactive and primary prevention in the community
- increasing harm minimisation among young people
- developing, implementing, evaluating and documenting an assessment and referral process for young Vietnamese people with drug and alcohol issues
- actively promoting Vietnamese community involvement and engagement in relation to alcohol and other drug issues
- networking in relation to youth alcohol and other drug issues that are impacting on the Vietnamese community
- developing an action strategy for monitoring and resolving issues relating to youth alcohol and other issues
- lobbying for appropriate and responsive approaches to alcohol and other drug issues.

>> discussion questions

1 What is meant by the claim that a one-dimensional approach to community development is likely to fail because it is not holistic?
2 Describe some of the activities that constitute social development. For each of these, there are different meanings. What particular meanings of the activities would constitute social development within an ecological and social justice/human rights approach?
3 What are the key differences between the more conservative approach to economic development and the more radical approach? What aspects of social development would you consider need to be included in economic development activities to make them a more holistic economic venture?
4 How would you describe political development and what place or roles would it have in (a) social development activities and (b) economic activities?
5 How would you explain the relationship between culture, identity and community?
6 What are some of the important roles for non-Indigenous community workers in working with Indigenous communities? What is the special significance of these roles, taking into consideration the special circumstances of Indigenous communities historically, politically and economically?
7 What do you understand to be the significance of land and spirituality for Indigenous communities?
8 What may be involved in working to counter racism, which is one of the greatest challenges facing workers in Indigenous communities?
9 What is meant by the statement: 'The key to personal development is the development of strong community interactive structures'? How does this differ from the usual personal growth services offered in Western cultures?
10 In what ways is the spiritual dimension important in community development?

>> reflective questions

1 If you are a non-Indigenous person, how will you approach the issue of racism when working with Indigenous communities and interfacing with non-Indigenous people and systems, given that you are positioned in the latter? What values and assumptions do you hold that may enhance or hinder your work? Where do these values and assumptions stem from?
2 If you are in a privileged position in terms of your life opportunities, how might this affect your work and your relationships with people in Indigenous communities?
3 How have you achieved personal growth in your own life? Has community been a part of this or has it been a more private process?
4 What does spirituality mean for you and in your own life? What impact might this have on your appreciation of spirituality for others with whom you will work?
5 Think of any community development activity you may have been involved in or may be in the future, or one that you have heard of or read as a case study in this book. Drawing on the discussions in this chapter, how would you incorporate into the activity each of the three components discussed? Reflect on your thoughts and identify in what ways the incorporation of these three components would enrich the activity and make it more aligned to an ecological and social justice/human rights approach.

CHAPTER 10

The application of principles to practice

Introduction

This chapter outlines a number of principles of community development, which emerge from the discussion in the previous chapters and are intended as a basic set of principles that should underlie a developmental approach to all community work practice. They represent a summary of the book thus far; the reader will find little new material here that was not present in previous chapters. Some community workers have found such a summary a handy checklist for practice, while others have found it useful in developing a framework for evaluating community development projects.

The principles outlined here are not a series of 'how to do it' prescriptions. One of the themes of previous chapters, particularly Chapter 5, is the need to allow structures and processes to develop organically from the community itself. This, together with the ecological principle of diversity, requires that things be done differently in different communities, depending on a host of local social, economic, political and cultural factors. Therefore, any 'how to' list, such as 'how to start a LETS', 'how to organise a community campaign', 'how to measure community need', 'how to save your local environment' or 'how to run a community meeting' is unlikely to be fully applicable; it will have been formulated out of experience in a different context and the fact that it may have worked there does not imply that it will work somewhere else. At the heart of many such prescriptions is a colonialist assumption of superiority and a desire to impose one's own grand scheme on others; this is diametrically opposed to the fundamental ethos of community work.

The development of actual practice will vary from community to community and from community worker to community worker. Each situation calls for a process of seeing how the important principles of community development can be applied within the specific local context. Further issues of practice, including the problems of the 'how to do it' approach, will be discussed in the following chapters, whereas this chapter will be devoted to identifying those principles of community development that transcend local conditions and therefore guide one's practice at a more general level.

The principles are grouped according to the discussion in Chapters 2, 3, 5, 6, 7 and 8; for a fuller discussion the reader is referred to these chapters. However, it must be emphasised that these principles are not independent and that they relate to each other in a variety of ways. Taken together they represent a coherent approach to community development that is consistent with the previous analysis.

Be mindful of the language used in this chapter and how it reinforces a sense of 'holism'—in other words, the interrelationships and connections amongst the principles.

Ecological principles

The first five principles are derived from the discussion in Chapter 2 about ecological principles as a basis for community development. Unless communities and structures are based on principles of ecological sustainability, they will be inevitably short term and will not address the major ecological issues facing the contemporary world. However, these ecological principles also inform community development in a more process-oriented way and have significant implications for effective community work.

1. Holism

The principle of holism applies to all aspects of community development. It applies at the level of analysis as well as at the level of practice. In terms of analysis, it can be summarised by the idea that everything relates to everything else and hence it is necessary to take a broad systemic perspective in understanding any particular issue, problem or process. For example, if a community is concerned with a perceived rise in violent crime, this needs to be understood not only in terms of who is committing the crimes of violence, how to catch the criminals and how to prevent the crimes from occurring. It must also look at the other issues that relate to violent crime, which might include growing social and economic inequalities, media coverage, town planning, racism, employment opportunities, policies around drug use and legalisation, the powerful message of the consumer society, legitimisation of violence in entertainment and so on. These in turn lead to a consideration of other issues, such as globalisation, corporate power and levels of social expenditure. All community issues need to be understood in their broad context if a community development strategy is to be successful.

A holistic understanding also affects practice. In the above example, holism suggests that the community needs to concern itself with a range of issues if it is to be effective in dealing with community issues; this validates a broad 'organic' approach to community development. Holism in practice also emphasises the importance of the 'ripple effect'—the idea that we can never do only one thing but that every act has an effect like ripples in a pond, reaching out to the furthest ends of the system. Every act we commit changes the world, often in ways we will never know. Every conversation we have with another person changes both of us in perhaps small but nevertheless significant ways; each of us, from that moment on, will be a slightly different person as a result and this will affect our future words and actions, which in turn will affect the words and actions of others who themselves will be changed as a result.

2. Sustainability

The principle of sustainability is an essential component of the ecological approach (see Chapter 2). It is essential that any community development activity occurs within a framework of sustainability, otherwise it will simply reinforce the existing unsustainable order and will not be viable in the long term. If community development is to be part of the establishment of a new social, economic and political order, its structures and processes must be sustainable.

Sustainability requires that the use of non-renewable resources be minimised and, if possible, eliminated. This has implications for local communities in terms of land use, lifestyle, conservation, transport and so on. Community development should aim to minimise dependence on non-renewable resources and to substitute these with renewable resources. Projects and strategies that might be encouraged include the promotion of bicycles as an alternative to motor vehicles, choosing economic development projects that do not plunder natural resources and not using old-growth forest timbers as building materials.

Sustainability also requires that outputs to the environment, such as pollution, be minimised and that materials be conserved and recycled where possible. This too can become a focus for community development, both in terms of minimising pollution, such as fertiliser run-off, and in the more positive sense, such as establishing community-based recycling, which is an important contemporary initiative in many communities (with or without official support). Recycling projects can also have the added benefit of being ideal mechanisms for establishing stronger community-level contact and for encouraging broad-based participation.

Another important feature of sustainability is limiting growth. Growth has become the norm in many mainstream structures, yet growth is, by its very nature, unsustainable. Establishing structures, organisations, businesses and industries that do not have to grow to survive is a major challenge for community development. It is important to help communities to accept a philosophy of 'small is beautiful' and to enable them to work out what this means in practice. This in turn brings in notions of 'steady-state', balance, equilibrium and harmony, which are critical aspects of the ecological perspective.

Community development has the responsibility of piloting local sustainability in practice if an alternative and ecologically sane social, economic and political order is to be established. By demonstrating that such an approach is viable at the community level, community development can be, and indeed must be, at the forefront of social change. Thus sustainability is not merely a principle that limits certain forms of community development, but in a more positive sense can also become a critical part of the community development agenda.

3. Diversity

The ecological principle of diversity has been discussed, implicitly or explicitly, in several of the previous chapters. Valuing diversity addresses the ecological dangers of monocultures, the modernist tendency to impose a single order onto everything, the colonialist erosion of other identities, cultural globalisation and the exclusionary discourses of racism, sexism, ageism and so on. This makes it an essential component of any community development practice. There is always a danger, in any activity such as community development, of seeking to impose one way of doing things, one world view, one 'right' structure, in an attempt to encourage unity or conformity. This is a significant aspect of colonialism (see Chapter 7) and of structural oppression (see Chapter 3). Valuing diversity is an important way of framing opposition to such modernist and oppressive tendencies.

For community workers, diversity is important at two levels, namely *diversity between communities* and *diversity within communities*. Diversity *between* communities suggests that one community does not have to be like others; indeed a community, instead of trying to follow a process or 'model' from elsewhere, can celebrate the differences that make it unique. One of the strengths of community development is that it values diversity between communities and accepts that different communities will have different ways of doing things, rather than imposing a 'right' way to do things. A community is free to experiment, innovate, do and express things in its own way. For community workers diversity between communities reinforces the idea that there is no one 'right' way to do community development, that each community is different and that what is 'right' for one community is not likely to work in another one. Diversity between communities means that a community worker must always be prepared to work 'from below' in the way described in Chapter 5.

Diversity *within* communities emphasises the importance of inclusive structures and processes in the community so that the community is able to affirm and celebrate not only its own differences from other communities, but also the differences within the community itself. Diversity is necessary for a healthy community—it contributes a richness and dynamism to the community experience. Encouraging diversity within the community and helping to find ways to validate that diversity is therefore an important aspect of community development work. This will be a particular challenge in communities with a history and tradition of exclusion, such as racism or homophobia, and this is where a community worker needs a strong social justice/human rights perspective to ensure that such exclusion is actively confronted.

4. Organic development

An easy way to think of the concept of organic development as opposed to mechanistic development is to think of the difference between a machine and a plant (Macleod 1991). A machine works independently of its environment: it can be moved to another location and will work in the same way, it can be taken away to be repaired, it requires a small number of specific inputs and its principles can be readily understood. While it is working, it basically retains the same structure and form (it may wear out, but it does not grow or change in any fundamental way). A plant is far more complex and the principles of the totality of its operation cannot be easily understood. It is highly dependent on the environment and interacts with it in many different ways; if moved to a different environment it is likely to wither and die. It grows, changes with the seasons and reproduces. It needs to be nurtured and requires much more than maintenance'. Such tending and nurturing must take into account a wide variety of environmental factors—climate, aspect, soil, water, shelter and so on.

A community is essentially organic (plant-like) rather than mechanistic (machine-like). Therefore, community development is not governed by simple technical laws of cause and effect but is a complex and dynamic process; tending and nurturing this development is more an art than a science. The community has its own inherent capacity to develop its true potential and community development is about providing the right conditions and nurturing to enable this development to occur.

Organic development means that one respects and values the community's particular strengths and resources and allows and encourages the community to develop in its own unique way through an understanding of the complex relationship between the community and its environment. Such an approach requires a holistic rather than a linear perspective (see Chapter 2). Development will take place in a variety of ways at the same time, as discussed in Chapter 9, and this diversity and the complex interaction between the various components of community development is critical to the process.

5. Balanced development

The idea of balance, or equilibrium, was another of the important aspects of an ecological perspective outlined in Chapter 2. This can be translated to the idea of balanced or integrated community development using the six dimensions identified in Chapter 9. Social, economic, political, cultural, environmental and personal/spiritual development all represent essential aspects of any community's life (Suzuki & McConnell 1997). A program of community development, therefore, must take all six into account. This does not necessarily mean that all six will be part of every community development strategy; as noted in Chapter 9, it is likely that a community will be stronger in some of these six areas than in others and that as a result certain areas will require more concentration. The important point, however, is that all six must be considered, so that a decision to concentrate on, say, social and economic development rather than the other four is made consciously, and preferably by the community itself, rather than simply being assumed as a result of the interests of a community worker or the mandate of a government agency. Such a decision must be taken in the full understanding of the critical importance of all six areas, not assuming that any one is 'fundamental' and basic to change in the others.

It is possible that development in one area can have positive spin-offs in other areas, and can be planned and implemented in such a way that its developmental goals link to other aspects of community development. Community economic development, if pursued using a local cooperative model, can easily lead to cooperatives becoming the basis of other community activity (e.g. cultural development or the delivery of human services).

The important thing for a community worker, therefore, is always to keep all six aspects of community development in mind, ensure that they are all addressed by the community and seek ways in which development in any one of the six might link to and stimulate development in the other five.

Social justice and human rights principles

The next set of principles can be grouped around the ideas of social justice and human rights. As argued in Chapter 4, an ecological approach to community development, though necessary, is not sufficient as a basis for practice. It is also necessary to incorporate the ideas of social justice and human rights—that community development is working not only towards a more ecologically sustainable world, but also towards a fairer world. The principles summarised here were discussed in more detail in Chapter 3.

6. Addressing structural disadvantage

The fundamental nature of class, gender and race/ethnicity oppression has been a theme throughout this book. Community development—if it is to be consistent with the social justice and human rights perspective of Chapter 3—must always take account of this oppression. At the very least, community development projects must ensure that they do not reinforce these forms of structural oppression; community development should preferably seek to confront and counter them in whatever ways are appropriate within the specific context.

This requires a community worker to be aware of the complex, subtle and pervasive ways in which class, gender and race/ethnicity oppression operate through the media, the education system, organisational structures, the welfare system, language, the economy, the market and advertising. It also requires community workers to be critically aware of their own backgrounds, their own (often unconscious) racist, sexist and class-based attitudes and their own participation in the structures of oppression.

Other forms of oppression are important too—in particular age, disability and sexuality. These need to be taken into account by community workers to ensure that community development projects serve to counter rather than reinforce these forms of oppression.

Community development structures and processes can easily reinforce the dominant structures of oppression, for example, by unthinkingly following meeting procedures that favour articulate white middle-class males, ignoring the need for child-care provision, scheduling meetings at times when it is difficult for some people to attend or by not providing translation or interpreter facilities. The discussion in Chapter 9 identified a number of areas where an unthinking or uncritical approach to community development reinforces rather than challenges structural disadvantage.

More positively, community development should *address* issues of class, gender, race/ethnicity, age, disability and sexuality. While there is oppression or disadvantage in any of these dimensions, a community will not reach its full potential and the goals of social justice will not be achieved. Community development should incorporate strategies specifically designed to overcome such disadvantage, such as strategies for affirmative action, positive discrimination, equal opportunity, consciousness-raising and education. The extent to which these issues can be explicitly addressed will depend on many contextual factors and a community worker may need to exercise a degree of caution. It may be necessary for the explicit acknowledgement and addressing of structural disadvantage to wait until the community itself is ready to embrace it; after all, it is the community's project, not the worker's, and the community must set its own agenda.

A critical issue for community workers can arise when a community process leads to a decision that will reinforce dominant oppressive structures. An extreme example is where a community, after a lengthy consultation process, asks a community worker to 'help keep the blacks out of town'. More subtle and less dramatic examples also arise, such as a women's group deciding to set up a pyramid franchising operation or local industry seeking protection against 'militant unionism'. Another important aspect of addressing structural disadvantage is the critical link between the personal and the political, the individual and the structural or private troubles and public issues. It is only when this link is made that individual needs, problems, aspirations, sufferings and achievements can be translated into effective community-level action.

All personal experience can be linked to the political; this has been one of the most important contributions of feminism. In C. Wright Mills' terms (1970), every private trouble can be related to a public issue; this needs to be understood if effective change strategies are to be undertaken. The dominant paradigm has tended to break the link between the personal and the political, resulting in the individualising of social problems (see Chapter 3), which has reinforced the dominance of conservative and 'therapeutic' solutions that ignore structural issues.

As well as there being a political side to every personal issue, the reverse is also true: there is a personal side to every political issue. Unemployment, the economy, free trade, health insurance, industrial development and so on all affect people in a personal and individual way. The human impact of political issues is also often ignored or minimised in mainstream political discourse, except for highly sensationalised treatment by the commercial media.

Community development has the potential to make these links as it is able to provide a forum in which the political aspects of the personal, and the personal aspects of the political, can be identified and explored. Indeed unless these links are made, the potential of community development to transform society is severely limited.

These links are not addressed explicitly in many community development contexts. However, it is clearly possible to make and emphasise the link between the personal and the political in many aspects of one's day-to-day work, helping people and groups always to think about each in terms of the other. A person who is out of work can be helped to see their personal problem as one that they share with many others and which is related to national and international politics, the global economy and so on. Simply bringing people together—a basic function of community work—can help people to share their problems and concerns and to begin to explore ways whereby together, rather than individually, they might do something about them. Politicisation does not have to be controversial, dangerous or extreme; it can simply be a case of helping people to talk about their problems and their lives and helping them make connections. And for a community worker this represents the first step towards addressing structural disadvantage.

7. Addressing discourses of disadvantage

The above section dealt with disadvantage from a structural perspective. Another perspective, as identified in Chapter 3, is the poststructural where, rather than structures of power, it is discourses of power that are of particular concern. If power relations are defined and redefined in continually changing discourses of power, and if these discourses then become the way in which power is exercised and perpetuated (Foucault 1972), then it is important for community development to address discourses of power as well as structures of power. The position of this book is that both structures and discourses of power are important in shaping power relations and in affecting people's lives; it is not a case of one or the other, but rather a more inclusive paradigm that encompasses both.

Discourses of power and oppression therefore need to be addressed in community development. The worker needs to be able to identify and deconstruct discourses of power and understand how those discourses effectively privilege and empower some people while marginalising and disempowering others. This deconstruction is a critical component of consciousness-raising and is discussed below. But it is not simply a case of being able to identify and deconstruct, as this can simply result in feelings of powerlessness. It is also important for community development to seek actively to engage with the dominant discourse and to become part of the *reconstruction* of discourse, so that people in the community can contribute to the discursive construction of power. This means that community members can be empowered to help identify approaches to power and power relations and to articulate relationships of power from their own perspective rather than from somebody else's point of view. Further, they can be helped to articulate their view within the wider societal discourse (e.g. through use of the media) and thereby contribute to the redefinition of power relationships. A simple example might be for a group of people with disabilities to mount a concerted effort to write letters to newspapers, stage media events for television and print journalists, phone radio talkback shows, speak to university classes and influence prominent media commentators, politicians and opinion leaders in order to promote a more positive view of the experience of people with disabilities and the contribution they can make to society, rather than defining them as dependent and in need of 'charity'.

Influencing discourses of power can be undertaken in different ways, depending on the context, but from a poststructural perspective it is the capacity to articulate an alternative vision, and to have it validated within the dominant discourse, that is at the heart of community empowerment.

8. Empowerment

Empowerment should be an aim of all community development. The word 'empowerment' has been much overused in recent years (Parker et al. 1999), but in the sense in which it was discussed in Chapter 3 empowerment means ensuring people have the resources, opportunities, vocabulary, knowledge and skills to increase their capacity to determine their own future and to participate in and affect the life of their community.

A complete strategy of empowerment requires that the barriers to people exercising power be understood, addressed and overcome. These include the structures of oppression (class, gender and race/ethnicity), language, education, personal mobility and the domination by elites of the structures and discourses of power. Understood in these terms, then, empowerment is a form of radical change, which would overturn existing structures and discourses of domination.

It is too much to expect that any community development project will be able to achieve this single-handedly. Indeed any project that explicitly attempted to do so would be almost bound to fail. Community development, however, can have more modest empowerment aims. Any increase in empowerment for more disadvantaged sections of the community will help to bring about a more socially just and human rights-based society and the empowerment of members of a local community will strengthen that community and will enable more effective community-based structures to be put in place. Similarly, any strategy that reinforces the structures and discourses that oppose empowerment is likely to weaken rather than strengthen community activity.

The extent to which any community development program will explicitly address empowerment will vary. In many instances empowerment will be a by-product of another developmental process, rather than being a stated aim. For example, a community recycling program, an adult literacy class or the establishment and operation of a women's refuge can be done in such a way that the people involved, and the community as a whole, are empowered by the process. To achieve this, people must be encouraged to take control of the project themselves and through it to learn that they can indeed have more control over their community and their lives. They are then not seen simply as 'volunteer helpers' but as a vital part of the process; the project becomes 'their' project.

The other principles in this chapter will at times limit empowerment; if people are 'empowered' so that they can live an extravagant and ecologically unsustainable lifestyle or so that they can more effectively exploit others then that 'empowerment' project cannot be justified. There are limits to empowerment outcomes (as there are limits to all community outcomes) imposed by the ecological and social justice/human rights perspectives of Chapters 2 and 3.

9. Human rights

An understanding of and a commitment to fundamental human rights, as discussed in Chapter 3, is an essential and central principle of community development. The Universal Declaration of Human Rights provides a powerful definition of basic human rights. Other agreements, such as the UN covenants on Civil and Political Rights and on Economic, Social and Cultural Rights, spell out these commitments in more detail. It is well worth the community worker becoming familiar with these documents as well as others that may be particularly important in specific community circumstances (e.g. the UN Convention and Protocol relating to the Status of Refugees; such documents are available on the website of the UN High Commissioner for Human Rights: www.ohchr.org).

Human rights are important for community work in both the negative sense (the *protection* of human rights) and the positive sense (the *promotion* of human rights). In the negative sense, it is important that any community development project conform to the principles of basic human rights. The human rights as defined in the UN documents are meant to apply to the decisions and practices of nation, but they apply just as readily to communities. Community structures and programs should be established in such a way that they do not contravene these principles. For example, the right to meaningful work, the right to freedom of association and the right to freedom of expression need to be safeguarded. Human rights conventions can also provide an answer to a common issue for community workers: when a community seeks to do something that contravenes basic human rights principles (such as the right to join a union or the right to be free from racial discrimination), the use of human rights declarations and conventions can give a community worker strong grounds for opposing such a development.

In the more positive sense, the achievement of the ideals of the Universal Declaration of Human Rights can be used as a goal for community development. The right to an adequate standard of living, the right to education, the right to participate in the cultural life of the community, the right to participate in decision making that affects the community, the right to self-determination, and the right of the family to protection and assistance are some of the rights defined in the Universal Declaration and the UN covenants, which could well become the focus for community development activity in countries of both the minority world and the majority world. Many of the ideals of the Universal Declaration are only imperfectly realised in any national context and the promotion, not just the protection, of these fundamental rights can be an important community development goal.

Furthermore, the criteria for claims for human rights and the notion of building a culture of human rights are both powerful tools for community workers' processes and objectives. Building a culture of human rights, because it entails enabling the voices of the marginalised and oppressed to be heard and to challenge dominant discourses, is a critical tool for empowerment practice. A human rights approach to practice is a powerful means for individuals to practise citizenship and to engage in social citizenship processes in this consumerist era. Participation, as discussed in Chapter 6, becomes both a means and an end in the venture of reclaiming citizenship. Within a global context, as outlined in Chapter 8, local people can become global moral citizens.

10. Need definition

The concept of need, and need definition, was discussed in Chapter 3. It is important at this point, however, to emphasise the critical importance of need definition in community development. There are two key community work principles relating to need which have to be identified here.

The first is that community development should seek to bring about agreement between the various need-definers identified in Chapter 3, namely the population as a whole, service users, service providers and researchers. Where there are different perceptions between these need-definers, there is less likelihood that people's needs will be effectively met and the various actors will be working at cross-purposes. Community work should, therefore, seek to bring about an effective dialogue between these need-definers, each of which has a legitimate and important role to play to develop a consensus about the community's needs. In reality, many of these need-definers seldom communicate effectively with each other around issues of need. For example, how often do demographic researchers doing 'need analysis' and service users actually talk to each other—and if they did, would either understand what the other was talking about?

The second principle is that, despite the importance of various other need-definers, it is the need definition of the people themselves (i.e. community members) that should take precedence, as long as ecological and social justice/human rights principles are not thereby compromised. The important focus of a critical social practice (Fay 1987) is to engage people in a dialogue that will lead them to be better able to articulate their 'true' needs (Marcuse 1964) and not have those needs defined for them by others. This is essential if community work practice is to be liberating and empowering rather than the reverse. Community development, indeed, can be defined as helping communities to articulate their needs and then to act so they can be met. For this to happen, in light of the ecological and social justice/human rights perspectives discussed in earlier chapters, the people themselves must own and control the process of need 'assessment' and definition.

Valuing the local

The principles implied by the idea of change from below, or 'bottom-up' development, are central to the idea of community development. Yet, as discussed in Chapter 5, they often conflict with the taken-for-granted ideas of top-down rationality, planning and change. These principles centre on the idea of valuing the local, and not privileging knowledge, skills, processes and resources that are 'imposed' on a community from 'above'.

11. Valuing local knowledge

The principle of valuing local knowledge simply states that local knowledge and expertise are likely to be of most value in informing community development and that they must be identified and validated rather than subordinated to the knowledge and expertise of the outside expert. Of course there are times when external knowledge will be needed, but this must be, where possible, a last resort only after the community itself (not just the community worker) is satisfied that the necessary knowledge is not available within the community. If knowledge is understood as either universal or local (i.e. contextualised), it is clear that in community development most of the knowledge that will be useful is local knowledge. Some universal principles, such as those discussed in this chapter, may apply in a general way, but they must be shaped and mediated by local knowledge so that they can become relevant in the specific community context and do not devalue and disempower.

A community development process should seek to identify local knowledge to assess the extent of local expertise, whether formally recognised or not, realising that external expertise can help a community only in a general way rather than in terms of specific programs. Such an approach can help to persuade members of a community that they may actually have the knowledge necessary to work on their particular issues—this can be a first step towards action for change.

12. Valuing local culture

Cultural globalisation is robbing communities around the world of their cultural identity. The principle of valuing local culture requires that this be addressed and that local cultural traditions and processes be validated and supported as part of a community development process. This principle cannot, of course, be applied in disregard of other principles, such as human rights, sustainability or the need to confront structures and discourses of disadvantage. Uncritical reinforcement of local culture can sometimes entrench exclusive, unsustainable and marginalising practices. However, it must always be remembered that cultures are dynamic rather than static and that cultural traditions are often contested within local contexts. This enables principles of human rights, inclusiveness, sustainability and so on to be addressed by the community within the context of its ongoing development, but this does not mean that local culture is devalued in the process. It is particularly important to encourage a local *participatory* culture.

13. Valuing local resources

The idea of self-reliance, discussed in Chapter 5, implies that the community should seek to utilise its own resources wherever possible rather than relying on external support. This applies to all forms of resources—financial, technical, natural and human—and can be achieved in a variety of ways. Seeking local financial support for community projects is not always possible, but it is normally preferable to relying on external sources of funding as these inevitably impose their own conditions, which may not correspond with the community's interest. Simply making an inventory of the interests and expertise available within the community and then making this widely accessible can be a useful developmental activity; the very act of compiling the inventory can itself stimulate community interest and involvement and help to get people talking together.

The dominant 'welfare state' way of thinking means that people will often ignore such local resources and seek support from elsewhere—normally from governments. This can weaken local community structures and is of doubtful long-term value. It is important to ask the question: *If it can't be done with local resources, is it worth doing at all?* Self-reliant communities are going to be in a much better position to cope with a future of uncertainty and crisis. Therefore community development should aim to strengthen community self-reliance wherever possible and community development projects should aim always to increase self-reliance and to seek ways in which self-reliance can be initiated and reinforced, rather than adopting strategies that reduce self-reliance and increase dependency, such as state-sponsored and state-funded community development. In general, the more a community can do without government funding, the better.

An approach to community development that seeks to minimise government funding might be criticised as 'playing into the hands of the right' by providing governments with a ready excuse to cut social spending on the grounds that programs are better run by autonomous, self-reliant communities. However, it must also be pointed out that if a community is independent of government it is in a much stronger position to criticise government, propose progressive or radical alternatives and be free of government control, whereas a group that receives government funding inevitably has this independence compromised. Governments, whether of the right or the left, have much more to fear from the actions of independent, autonomous and self-reliant communities than from groups that can effectively be controlled through government financial support. Hence a move towards reducing a community's dependence on government can hardly be seen as a right-wing conspiracy. The community development vision, after all, seeks to provide an eventual alternative to government and it is therefore necessary to break free of the constraints of operating within the government system.

Other sources of funding, such as churches and foundations, are often less restrictive than government as such funding bodies are often more able to accept the legitimacy of a community-based alternative. It does not, after all, threaten their very existence in the way that it may do for governments. However, the same principles of self-reliance and independence eventually apply.

Another way in which the resources of a local community can be realised and valued is through community ownership. Very few material resources are owned at community level. Most commodities, land, buildings and so on are owned either by individuals or small businesses on the one hand or by larger units such as corporations or governments on the other. Community ownership tends to be confined to such things as the community hall, local parks and gardens and the plant and equipment of local government. A widening of community ownership is an important aspect of building community; it can help support a community's sense of identity, it can give people more reason to become actively involved at community level and it can be a more efficient use of resources.

Many of the things owned on an individual or household basis lie unused for most of the time. Examples include garden tools, woodworking tools, washing machines, lawn mowers, books, recreational equipment, games, bicycles and computers. This is grossly inefficient from an economic point of view and ecologically wasteful. Community or group ownership of such items makes far more sense, though it contradicts the ethic of individual ownership and private consumption, which is the main obstacle to such an alternative. It is essential, however, if we are to move towards a society where there is a lower level of material consumption (which, from an ecological point of view, is inevitable) without a corresponding reduction in the quality of life.

14. Valuing local skills

One of the greatest temptations for a community worker is to think that they are the person with the 'skills' to do community development. Such a perspective not only privileges the community worker over those with whom they are working, but also devalues the important skills that community members have; after all, they are the ones who know the community and the local context and the skills that have been developed locally are likely to be the ones that will work best in that environment. A community development approach must therefore seek to value and maximise these skills rather than devaluing and marginalising them.

This does not mean that the skills the community worker brings are unimportant or irrelevant. Obviously there are skills in community development that a worker is able to bring to a community—otherwise why have a community worker at all? However, these skills have to be located within the local context and need to be applied appropriately to the specific location; it is not a case of skills being like a toolkit, where the same tools can be used everywhere, but rather that skills will be modified and applied differently in different contexts.

More importantly, community workers must always realise that community members themselves possess important skills and that ultimately these are what will drive the community development process. Often it is important to reinforce this in working with community members, many of whom will not see the things they can do as 'skills' and therefore as being important to the process. Much of a community worker's time is spent in reinforcing, supporting and valuing the work of community members and helping them to apply their particular skills in the interests of the community as a whole.

An important aspect of community work skills is the idea of *skill-sharing*. This means that the community worker and community members do not seek only to apply their particular skills, but also to skill each other. A community worker may come to a community with particular skills, but must always look for ways in which relevant skills can be learned by community members. Thus when the worker leaves the community, their skills remain behind and, as a result, people are more empowered.

However, it must not be thought that skill transfer is only one-way, with the worker 'skilling' the community members. Community workers are also able to learn skills as part of the process; community members will undoubtedly have many skills that the worker does not have and a good community worker is learning all the time. A community work approach that does not privilege the worker's skills over those of the community thus results in a two-way exchange of skills—hence the idea of *skill-sharing*, a process whereby both worker and community members can develop new skills that can be applied in community development.

15. Valuing local processes

The imposition of specific answers, structures or processes from outside the community seldom works. This, indeed, is one of the main rationales for the community development approach; it is because things do not work very well when they are imposed from outside that community-based structures and processes are seen as providing a more appropriate alternative. This implies that the community development approach itself cannot be imposed, but must be genuinely offered to the community and then developed within the community in a way that fits the specific context and is sensitive to local community culture, traditions and environment.

The ecological principle of diversity emphasises that there is no one right way of doing things and no single answer that applies to every community. What works in one environment will not work in another. Therefore a fundamental principle of community development must be to be deeply mistrustful of any process imposed from outside, however well intentioned. For a government to attempt to develop a 'policy' on community development that sets out a model of how it should be achieved is futile and contradictory. Governments can certainly assist the processes of community development through the provision of resources, communication, support and networking, but they cannot determine how community development should occur. Similarly, any textbook or manual that specifies 'how to do' community development or 'how to do' a particular community task (e.g. set up a LETS, run a community meeting or assess needs) is likely to be at best ineffective and at worst dangerous; such texts inevitably devalue local process and should be treated with extreme caution.

This does not mean that a community development process cannot benefit from experience from elsewhere. Clearly something that has been shown to work well somewhere else is worthy of serious attention. If such ideas are examined to see how they might be adapted to the local community and whether they might help improve local processes then they can be extremely valuable. Outside experts or consultants may have something valuable to contribute if they are prepared to do so in a way that respects the unique features of the local community and does not seek to impose externally derived answers. Communities can learn from each others' experiences; what they cannot do is simply apply a formula that has worked somewhere else without critically evaluating it in terms of its local context.

All community development processes are context-specific and they cannot be understood in terms of universal rules. The different context means that each community development experience will be unique and the community must develop in its own particular way. It can learn from the experiences of others, but should never slavishly copy them.

The community development perspective requires horizontal communication (learning from each other, not from imposed expertise), accountability to the community and the encouragement of diversity—this applies as much to process as it does to knowledge, skills, culture and resources.

16. Participation

Participatory democracy and the participation of all in community activities is an important ideal in community development. This does not ensure that all people will participate—the ideal is never reached. Nor does it imply that those who participate will do so in the same way. Different people have different skills, interests and capacities. Good community work will provide the broadest possible range of opportunities for participation and will legitimise equally all people who are actively involved.

It is imperative that community workers understand the complexities of participation, the contested ways in which it can be used and the different objectives that it may serve. An analysis of participation as empowerment is essential. An appreciation of the array of knowledge and skills necessary to maximise participation and the use of these skills is central to bottom-up processes. An understanding of the barriers and the factors conducive to participation will enable more effective and fuller participation in community-based services and programs.

Class, gender and race/ethnicity need to be taken into account in participation. As discussed on several previous occasions, many of the most traditionally valued community activities, such as committee membership, are characteristically white, male and middle-class activities; in fact, that is why they are traditionally valued above other forms of contribution. If the structural disadvantage of class, race and gender is to be overcome, three processes need to occur. One is to allow and encourage other people to learn the skills of participation in traditionally 'white male' activities. The second is to change the nature of those traditionally exclusive activities to enable more people to participate effectively. The third is to value equally other forms of participation, seeing each as critically important and dependent on the others.

The issue of participation was discussed in detail in Chapter 6. For present purposes, it is sufficient to emphasise that encouragement, recognition and active nurturing of broad participation are vital to a community development program.

Process principles

A number of principles relating to the process of community development have been discussed in previous chapters, principally in Chapter 7, and they are summarised here. Community development is essentially about a process rather than an outcome, about a journey rather than the arrival and hence many of the most important practice principles focus on the idea of process.

17. Process, outcome and vision

The tension between process and outcome has been a major issue in community work. A pragmatic approach tends to emphasise outcome: what is seen as most important is the result that is actually achieved—how it is achieved is relatively unimportant. The alternative to pragmatism (such as that of Alinsky 1971) is the Gandhian approach (Gandhi 1964, 1982), which sees process and outcome as integrated. Hence one cannot achieve a non-violent society by using essentially violent processes; the process itself is important in determining the outcome. Violent or unprincipled means will corrupt the end and the process must reflect the outcome, as the outcome will most certainly reflect the process. Ethical and moral issues of process, far from being unimportant (as in the Alinsky approach) become central. The approach to community development outlined in this book clearly reflects the Gandhian rather than the Alinsky view.

Concentrating on process, however, can lead one to lose sight of the ultimate vision and can result in an obsession with process and an ignoring of the structural context; this characterises a good deal of 'new age' practice, where feeling good and communicating honestly with other people are seen as sufficient to change the world. This is both potentially conservative and largely ineffective in bringing about progressive change. It is essential that the process always be located in its wider context using the structural analysis of earlier chapters.

Rather than outcomes, it is therefore important to talk about vision; this is less specific than the idea of an outcome, but still emphasises the importance of having some idea of where we are headed and what it is all for. The idea of *vision* in community development has been a recurring theme in earlier chapters and it is important that this be incorporated in any consideration of process, as it is the vision that provides the purpose for the process.

There is always a tension in community work between the achievement of immediate goals and the ultimate vision of a better society. Focusing specifically on either one can mean that the other becomes forgotten, the result being either undirected pragmatism or unproductive dreaming. The two are sometimes seen as being in conflict and community workers often criticise each other for being either too pragmatic or too idealistic. For community development, as understood in this book, both elements are important and it is essential to maintain the balance between the immediate and the long term (this is consistent with the ecological principle of balance discussed in Chapter 2). The ultimate vision is of critical importance and community work must always be undertaken within the context of such a vision. However, the immediate goal is also critical: it is the way that vision is translated into something that has immediate relevance for people and it locates community development firmly within the life experience and consciousness of the people concerned. People have immediate needs that must be addressed and they will, for the most part, not accept simply being told to 'wait for the revolution'.

The challenge, then, is to link the immediate goal and the ultimate vision and to show how each is not only relevant to the other but is indispensable for the achievement of the other in a sustainable way. This relates closely to the connection between the personal and the political, as it is through the link between the immediate goal and the ultimate vision that the personal can be connected to the political and that consciousness-raising (see Chapter 7) and the relating of individual understanding to action can be achieved. In a sense, each acts as a constant check on the other; immediate actions cannot be justified unless they are compatible with the ultimate vision and the ultimate vision cannot be justified unless it relates to people's immediate day-to-day concerns. Thus it is not a case of the outcome *or* the vision, but rather of encapsulating the outcome *and* the vision.

18. The integrity of process

Not only is the process in community development more important than the outcome, in a very real sense it *is* the outcome: the aim, after all, is to establish viable community *processes*. Hence the process must conform with the expectations of any vision or outcome in terms of such issues as sustainability, social justice and human rights. If community development can use processes which themselves express these ideals, then it is more likely to be able to achieve its longer-term vision.

This means that some of the more conventional 'political' approaches to process are unacceptable. To attempt to achieve change towards the kind of society envisaged in earlier chapters by stacking meetings, pushing through decisions, 'playing the numbers game', using confrontationist tactics, working behind people's backs or generally being devious and manipulative will only reinforce the patterns of interaction one is trying to change and will neither empower people nor be effective in the longer term. Such tactics may sometimes be better at achieving a short-term specific result as the alternatives generally take a lot longer, but they have no place in community development understood from the broader perspective of sustainability, social justice and human rights.

The processes of community work always need the closest scrutiny to ensure that the integrity of the process is maintained. They need to be subject to the constraints of the ecological and social justice principles outlined in earlier chapters and need to be critically evaluated in their own right for what they really are, which means breaking through the illusions of acceptability sometimes created by technical or professional language where 'lying' is called 'being strategic', 'railroading' and 'manipulating' called 'group skills' and so on.

19. Consciousness-raising

The principle of consciousness-raising can underlie all community development. It does not have to be a deliberate process, labelled as such (e.g. a 'consciousness-raising group'), though this may sometimes be appropriate. Rather, a community worker can look out for any opportunity to undertake consciousness-raising informally in the course of day-to-day conversation with people in the community.

Consciousness-raising seeks to help people to explore together their personal experiences of life and the links between their experiences and the structures or discourses of power and oppression, with a view to creating space for effective action for change. As described in Chapter 7, there are four aspects or stages of consciousness-raising: the linking of the personal and the political, the development of a dialogical relationship, the sharing of experiences of oppression and the opening up of possibilities for action. These are not, of course, discrete categories, nor do they necessarily occur sequentially; in the rather messy and uncertain reality of community work few things happen neatly and processes such as these will merge with each other. The important principle is that consciousness-raising is an essential part of empowerment and it is therefore an essential part of community development. A community worker should always be seeking opportunities to engage in consciousness-raising practice and to incorporate consciousness-raising into every aspect of their work. For example, talking with someone who is unemployed provides a real opportunity to examine together the structural reasons for unemployment, the unequal distribution of work, the exploitation of the workforce and so on. This need not be done in a threatening, arrogant or 'intellectual' way, but can simply be introduced into regular conversation through discussing how many people are out of work, speculating about why there has been an apparent rise in unemployment, talking about what it must be like for young people whose only option is casual work at a fast-food outlet and so on. At other times it is simply allowing a safe space for people to talk, to share their ideas, hopes, fears, triumphs and disappointments; the sharing of experiences is important for any consciousness-raising process and for building community solidarity.

20. Cooperation and consensus

The ecological perspective and the non-violent approach both emphasise the need for cooperative structures rather than competitive structures. Many of the structures, processes and institutions of modern society are built on the assumption of the virtue of competition; these include the education system, the economy, business, employment, the media, the arts, recreation and health care. Thus ecological and non-violent community development challenges a core assumption of many basic institutions.

Community development, then, should seek to challenge the dominance of the competitive ethic, and to demonstrate that it is largely based on false assumptions (Kohn 1986). Therefore it should aim at establishing alternative structures and processes premised on cooperation rather than conflict. Consensus decision making is one of these, but also included is the establishment of cooperatives in their various forms (Craig 1993; Melnyk 1985; Macleod 1991; Morrison 1991; see also Chapter 7).

At a more basic level, community development can seek to bring about more cooperation in community activities by bringing people together and by finding ways to reward the cooperative behaviour of individuals or groups (such as by reducing municipal rates for housing cooperatives). Community recreation activities can emphasise the cooperative rather than the competitive. Cooperation extends beyond a community's boundaries and implies cooperation with other communities around common aspirations or problems and issues of concern. Often it is assumed that communities will be in competition with each other (e.g. for economic development funding), whereas cooperation between communities can, in the long term, prove far more beneficial. The cooperative imperative can even be extended to an international level, which would lead one to question the wisdom of a system of world 'trade' based on competition. Should a wealthy nation really be seeking a 'competitive edge' in its dealings with other countries in the world? What does that really mean? Who will be the losers if that country does turn out to be the winner? What are the long-term implications of such competitiveness in terms of regional conflict, world peace and international understanding? These questions might seem remote from community development, but it is important to understand the implications of competition and the need to begin to establish a viable alternative. The cooperative ethic is more likely to flourish at the international level if there is a solid foundation for it in the everyday lives of 'ordinary' people—in other words, at the community level.

Hand-in-hand with cooperation goes consensus. Indeed consensus might be thought of as a particular form of cooperation—cooperation in decision making—while a conflict approach can be seen as a competitive model of decision making. The principle of seeking to overcome competitive structures and replacing them with cooperative ones is therefore paralleled by seeking to replace conflict models of decision making and practice with consensus models. As discussed in

Chapter 7, consensus does not mean that everyone has to agree, but rather that everyone has agreed on a process and is satisfied that the outcome of that process represents the best decision that could be reached in the interests of the group, and where everyone has a stake in both the process and the outcome. In this sense, it really represents an extension of the principle of cooperation to the field of decision making.

21. The pace of development

A natural consequence of organic development is that it is the community itself that must determine the pace at which development occurs. Attempting to 'push' a community development process too quickly can result in the process being fatally compromised, the community losing any sense of ownership of that process and a loss of commitment by the people involved. Successful community development will move at the community's own pace; successful community workers will be able to judge that pace and act accordingly, not push the community to move faster than its own dynamics will allow.

Community development is by its nature a long-term process; one cannot bring about autonomous, active and participatory communities of the type envisaged in earlier chapters within a short space of time. Immediate results tend to be transitory and the basic developmental process, while it can be stimulated and encouraged, cannot be speeded up. This is often frustrating for community workers and can be even more so for managers, politicians and bureaucrats who want to see results (and preferably 'measurable' ones). This is another reason why the bureaucratic mode is an inappropriate one for community development.

Community development is a learning process for the community concerned and it can be very tempting for a community worker to try to speed up the process by telling people what to do or, more subtly, by making polite but persuasive suggestions before the need has been articulated by the people themselves. Community processes take time—sometimes an apparently interminable length of time—but there is usually no alternative but to stay with the process and allow it to 'take as long as it takes'.

22. Peace and non-violence

In order to bring about a society based on principles of non-violence, non-violent processes need to be used; from the point of view of the preceding sections, non-violent ends cannot be met using violent means.

In this context, non-violence implies more than simply the absence of physical violence between people. The notion of *structural violence* implies that social structures and institutions can themselves be seen as violent. A coercive society or a society that oppresses people, even though it may not use overt violence, is seen as violent in these terms. Hence gross inequality in the distribution of wealth and opportunity, sexism, racism and other forms of structural disadvantage represent a form of violence. Similarly, the legal system, the education system and the social security system, because of the elements of coercion involved and because of the way they perpetuate social control, reflect a violent society. The family can be a violent environment even if physical violence itself is never used.

A non-violent approach will, of course, oppose and seek to counter the more obvious and immediate manifestations of violence: militarism, the arms trade and physical violence in all its forms, such as domestic violence, street violence, corporal punishment, the death penalty and police brutality. It will seek to provide non-violent alternatives (e.g. mediation), remove the causes of such violence (e.g. by providing more support to families) and it will seek to do so through non-violent means. Thus it is unacceptable to counter juvenile crime by imposing harsh penalties on young offenders as this is simply to respond to violence by using the methods of violence. Such an approach only reinforces violence and reaffirms the notion that violent solutions to problems are acceptable and effective.

At a more fundamental level, the non-violent perspective will also recognise structural violence and other forms of coercion, and will seek to counter them. This inevitably links non-violence to ideas of liberation, freedom from class, race and gender oppression, and reform of coercive structures such as the education and social security systems.

From a community development perspective, it is important for community development both to seek to change the structures of violence and to seek to do so through non-violent means. This means that the Alinsky tactics of crystallising and essentially provoking conflict are not normally acceptable in community development. It means that processes must seek to affirm rather than to attack, to include rather than to exclude (see below), to work beside rather than to work against, and to mediate rather than to confront. This often requires changing the 'rules' by which people operate and refusing to play by the established unwritten rules of politics or community processes. It means that meetings, discussions and other forms of interactions will have different formats, as discussed in previous chapters.

23. Inclusiveness

Inclusiveness is one of the important principles of the non-violent perspective. Gandhi did not seek to isolate and 'defeat' his 'opponents' (these are the words of violence rather than non-violence). Rather, while disagreeing with their ideas, values and politics, he sought to respect and value them as people, and hence to include them rather than to exclude them from his movement. He sought to allow them to change 'sides' and join him while retaining dignity and self-respect. The more conventional approach is to enter into conflict, which only serves to entrench people in opposing positions. This can be resolved either by one side 'winning' and the other 'losing' (which involves loss of dignity, reinforcement of domination and essentially violent structures) or by compromise, where each 'side' will indeed feel 'compromised' and nobody will be fully satisfied.

Applying the principle of inclusiveness to community development requires valuing diversity through processes that always seek to include rather than to exclude, where all people will be intrinsically valued even if they hold opposing views and where people are allowed space to change their position on an issue without 'losing face'. Confrontation is sometimes inevitable and indeed desirable, but there are non-violent principles of confrontation, as clearly demonstrated by Gandhi. They can be summarised as follows.

Never seek to provoke and always respond to the provocation of others by non-violent means. Always seek to establish dialogue and increase mutual understanding. Seek to understand the other's point of view and to respect the right of that person to hold that position even if you disagree. Be prepared always to examine your own position and do not claim a monopoly on truth and wisdom; you can always learn from another, especially from someone who thinks differently. Always see the other as a potential friend and ally and seek ways in which they can become a real friend and ally with dignity and self-respect (Bishop 2002). Always respect and value the other person as a fellow human being and seek to work with, rather than against, them. The essence of non-violence is to oppose structures and ideas but not people (Gandhi 1964, 1982).

These principles are very difficult to maintain, especially if one has been socialised in a society that values competition and where confrontation, conflict and violence are well entrenched;

they are difficult to apply while doing community work in such a context. Nevertheless they are critically important for successful community development and they represent an important ideal of practice.

24. Community building

The principle of community building simply states that the process of community development should always seek to bring people together, to strengthen the bonds between community members and to emphasise the idea of *interdependence* rather than *independence*. In a society where independence and individualism are highly valued it can be difficult to introduce the alternative view of *interdependence*, namely the idea that, rather than being rugged individualists who are fiercely independent, human beings are actually dependent on each other in many different ways, some of which are mediated by the market and others of which are not. From this point of view, the idea of independence is a myth and we should rather be celebrating our interdependence and seeking to strengthen the links between people, namely community building. Simply emphasising this interdependence and seeking ways in which it can be validated and encouraged can be a critically important aspect of community development.

All facets of community development can incorporate community building. This can include simply taking every opportunity for fullest participation, to introduce people to each other, creating space for people to talk, trying to make activities group-oriented rather than individualistic and specific team-building exercises. The encouragement of reciprocity and mutual obligations within the community—people doing favours for each other—can help create social capital and strengthen community ties in a way that makes further community development possible.

Global and local principles

The relationship of the global and the local is now a significant part of all community development practice and needs to be part of the consciousness of every community worker. An understanding of globalisation and its impact and an awareness of how international issues affect practice is critical to community development; if community workers are to remain relevant in the 21st century, they need to practise from an internationalist perspective.

25. Linking the global and the local

In a globalising world, the practice of community development cannot ignore global issues, however local its focus may appear to be. Global forces affect all communities and are a contributing factor to the problems and issues that a community faces. Hence, in understanding a community, a worker has to be able to understand the global as well as the local, and how they interact.

But it is not just a case of understanding—the linking of the global and the local has to move beyond analysis to action. The community needs to be able to link the local and the global in ways that will lead to change. *Practising* locally and globally is the big challenge for community workers. This can be achieved by using the approach of globalisation from below, seeking to reconstruct an agenda of globalisation that is in the interests of ordinary people and communities and which links them in global yet grassroots action for change. There are various approaches that can be implemented for such global/local practice, which were discussed in Chapter 8; like most things in community development there is no simple 'how to do it' procedure, but different issues, in different contexts, will lead to different approaches to practice.

The important point for the community worker is always to be aware of the links between the local and the global and, with the community, to explore ways that the community can link to global movements for change.

26. Anti-colonialist practice

Colonialism can affect community workers in any setting; it is not confined to international development work, though it is in that context that colonialism can be most apparent. Community workers can readily colonise those with whom they are working, taking over the agenda, devaluing the culture and experience of the community and stripping the people of their identity. Colonialism can be an extremely seductive ideology; there is only a short step from believing that as a community worker 'I have something to offer' and from valuing one's own cultural background and experience to a colonising practice that simply perpetuates colonialist domination.

As discussed in Chapter 8, there are seven ways in which a community worker can guard against colonialist practice: (i) through critical self-awareness, political awareness and reflection; (ii) by the worker locating themself within the dominant or colonising culture and exploring the implications of that; (iii) by allowing space for an alternative discourse and action to emerge and for the natural resistance of the colonised to be expressed and worked through; (iv) by stepping back, to listen and learn, before rushing into action; (v) by working in solidarity with the people and sharing a common agenda; (vi) by working *with* the community; and (vii) by applying the test of reciprocity and asking how the worker would feel if the situation were reversed and they were subjected to the 'development' that is proposed for the community.

The temptations of colonialism are strong and it is easy to persuade oneself that one is acting 'in the best interests' of the people with whom one is working. Indeed, because much colonialist practice is undertaken from the best of intentions, it can be hard to identify and challenge. But it is necessary to do so if a community development program is to be genuinely empowering and if structures and discourses of oppression are to be overcome. Here, postcolonial thinking is an important perspective for the community worker.

Conclusion

The principles outlined in this chapter represent a summary of the book thus far. They have been brought together here as a convenient checklist of community development principles that can be applied in practice. But this chapter is more than a summary and checklist because it gathers together in one place all the principles and so enables a fuller appreciation and clearer grasp of the holism of the approach to community development taken in this book. Each principle is in itself more complex and problematic than can be covered in this chapter and the reader is referred to the discussion in other chapters for a fuller explanation.

These principles of community development need to be adapted, considered and reconstructed according to the context. They cannot be too specific or directive, but simply represent guides for practice that workers will inevitably interpret in different ways.

>> discussion questions

1 Explore and describe how can you use the principles of practice summarised in this chapter to apply to community work practice and as a framework for evaluating community development projects.
2 Examine the ways in which the principles in this chapter can constitute a coherent approach to community development.

>> reflective question

After thinking carefully about the principles of community development summarised in this chapter, explore how they may contribute to your own identity as a community worker. How do they resonate with you, your values and your life experience? How does each one resonate? How do they together resonate with you personally? What does this say about who you are as a community worker? What changes would you like to make in terms of your values, expectations and where you locate yourself as a professional in relation to communities? If there are some mismatches between the principles and your sense of self, in what ways would you see yourself as different in terms of the community development approach constructed throughout this book?

CHAPTER 11

Roles and skills

Introduction

This chapter moves from the principles to the actual practice of community development. Talking about *practice* can reify or mystify community work, if it is assumed that practice is something done by a professional, a specialist or at least a paid worker. Certainly these people can (and do) practise community work, but in the context of this chapter the idea of practice (or praxis, as will be discussed below) is not limited in this way. Community work can be undertaken by anyone and this discussion of practice is meant to be inclusive rather than exclusive. It is concerned with both the roles that a community worker can occupy and the skills that are necessary to fill those roles effectively. Before considering these specific roles and skills, however, it is important to make some general points about both roles and skills.

The problem with 'cookbooks'

There are no short-cuts to developing and learning the skills of community work practice. A number of books, manuals or resource kits aim to 'teach' the community worker 'how to do it' by using a cookbook approach—giving a set of clear, sequential instructions about the way to do community work, including how to assess needs, how to run a community meeting, how to write a funding submission, how to mount an education campaign and so on (e.g. Flood & Lawrence 1987; McArdle 1993; Ward 1993; Coover et al. 1985; Rothman et al. 2001; Tropman et al. 2001). At first sight these cookbook approaches might seem to be the ideal way to learn about skills, but experienced community workers tend to look on these approaches in a rather different light. These books and manuals have their uses, certainly, and can be a good source of new ideas and perspectives, but you cannot 'learn' community work skills from such a text. There are four principal reasons why such a cookbook approach to learning skills is inadequate.

The first is that such manuals, because of the way they structure the process of community work, tend to assume that it is an ordered, linear process, typically moving from 'getting started' through stages such as needs assessment, building an organisation, obtaining funding, mounting a campaign, and monitoring and evaluation. Each of these stages is itself also seen as a linear process; for example, there are steps that are defined for doing needs assessment. In reality, community development is seldom like that. It is much more chaotic and tends not to proceed in a logical order. A community worker is constantly moving backwards and forwards between tasks and stages and things tend not to have an ordered and predictable beginning, middle and end. Indeed, in applying the holistic and 'bottom-up' principles described in earlier chapters, one might conclude that there would be something seriously wrong if they did. The carefully ordered manuals tend to represent a process that reflects an idealised view of community work rather than the much more messy and uncertain reality of practice. They reflect the world as the writers of textbooks would like to see it, rather than as it really is. The world of real human experience is, after all, an unpredictable and chaotic place despite the attempts of positivist social scientists and economic rationalists to convince us otherwise.

The second problem with the 'cookbook' approach is that every community is different. What works in one community may not work in another because of differences in culture, history, tradition, geography, resources, climate, income and so on. Community workers have to work towards solutions, structures and processes that are grounded in the local culture and which make sense to the local people. What might have worked in inner-city communities, for example, is unlikely to work in isolated and remote areas, in outer suburbs or in a rural community and any attempt to slavishly apply a cookbook community work solution is almost certain to fail.

The third reason for mistrusting cookbooks is that not only is every community different but every community worker is different. A community worker has to develop their skills in such a way that they are consistent with their own style, personality and methods of communicating. One can, of course, learn from other workers, but one should never try simply to emulate another worker's style without critical reflection and an evaluation of how it fits one's own way of doing things. Finally, the cookbook approach tends to treat skills in isolation, as if they can be learned in and of themselves. Skills, however, are intimately tied up with values and knowledge and to discuss them in isolation from values and knowledge is to make an artificial separation that is characteristic of a mechanistic paradigm rather than the holistic approach outlined in earlier chapters. This is not to say that books and manuals of the 'how to do it' variety have no value; on the contrary, many community workers have found them extremely useful. There is always value in looking at how others have worked and in their accounts of what has been effective for them in their particular situations. One can obtain many good ideas from such reading and it can stimulate a community worker to think about and try alternatives. Looked at in this light, practice manuals are valuable and this is how they tend to be used by experienced community workers. The danger is in assuming that they represent the 'right' way to 'do it' because in reality there is no such thing.

For these reasons, the reader who has come to this chapter hoping to be told 'how to do it' will be disappointed. The discussion of roles and skills will raise some critical issues and will identify a number of problems and dilemmas about community work practice. It will even identify some of the ways a community worker goes about acquiring and improving skills and what some of those skills might be. But it will not provide an easy or simple textbook guide to 'learning' the skills of community work.

Competencies

There is a good deal of current interest in the notion of competencies in the human services (and indeed in all occupational groupings). Jobs are increasingly being described in terms of the specific competencies required of a worker and training courses are designed with defined competencies as the end-product. This approach is problematic for community work. The term *competencies* is largely synonymous with the term *skills* and a narrow prescriptive approach to defining competencies is clearly inappropriate given the fluid and context-specific nature of community work skills as discussed above. Just as a broad and grounded understanding of *skills* is necessary in talking about community work, so is a broad and grounded approach to *competencies* necessary if community work is to be defined within the 'discourse of competencies'. Unfortunately competencies are not usually understood in this way; they tend to be defined in terms of specific tasks that a worker should be able to perform. To reduce community work to such a series of specific tasks is to remove much of what is important about community work practice—flexibility, commitment, passion, art, the holistic perspective and a theoretical base. It is to turn community work into an essentially technical exercise and also to deny the legitimacy of people who may wish to practise community work but do not possess those specific measurable competencies. This tends to remove community work from the domain of many people and reinforces the notion of community work as an 'expert' activity, which is counter to the principles on which this book is based.

For community workers, therefore, the current discourse of competencies raises an important question: whether to oppose the whole competency movement on the grounds of its irrelevancy to community work or to seek to alter the definitions of competencies to incorporate a broader perspective. There is no easy answer. The danger of the former is that it could leave community workers outside any form of job classification, while the latter could lead to community work being co-opted into a paradigm with which it is fundamentally incompatible. Such dilemmas are inevitable in an activity that is conceptualised from within an alternative paradigm, but which has to some extent to be accommodated within old paradigm structures and frameworks, of which competency is a prime example. Whichever approach is taken, it is important that community workers seek to challenge the assumptions behind the competency-based approach and look for other ways of defining the practice of community work.

Practice, theory, reflection and praxis

To discuss *practice* in isolation is to divorce it from its context and to minimise its links to theory. The distinction between theory and practice has been a core component of the mechanistic, Western, Cartesian, modernist world view (Capra 1982; Rifkin 1985), but the alternative paradigm seeks to emphasise their integration rather than their difference (Fay 1975).

The relationship can perhaps best be understood by referring to one of Marx's more famous dictums: that it is through trying to change society that we come to understand it. Thus from *action* we derive *understanding*, which is the reverse of the more conventional approach, which assumes that from *understanding* we derive *action*. The two positions can be characterised as 'to understand the system you need first to try to change it' and 'to change the system you need first to understand it'; the former represents the Marxist (materialist) view, the latter the more conventional (idealist) view.

Within the holistic approach of a critical paradigm of social science, as advocated in earlier chapters, neither perspective by itself is sufficient and understanding and action (or theory and practice) belong together. Successful practice, therefore, involves learning and doing at the same time and in order to separate this from more conventional and limited understandings of practice some writers in the Marxist tradition have used the word *praxis* as an alternative. The essence of praxis is that one is involved in a constant cycle or spiral of doing, critical reflection and learning so that each informs the others and the three effectively become one. This is represented in Figure 11.1. It is from such a continuous process that both theory and practice are built at the same time. Praxis is more than simply action: it is understanding, learning and theory building as well, all

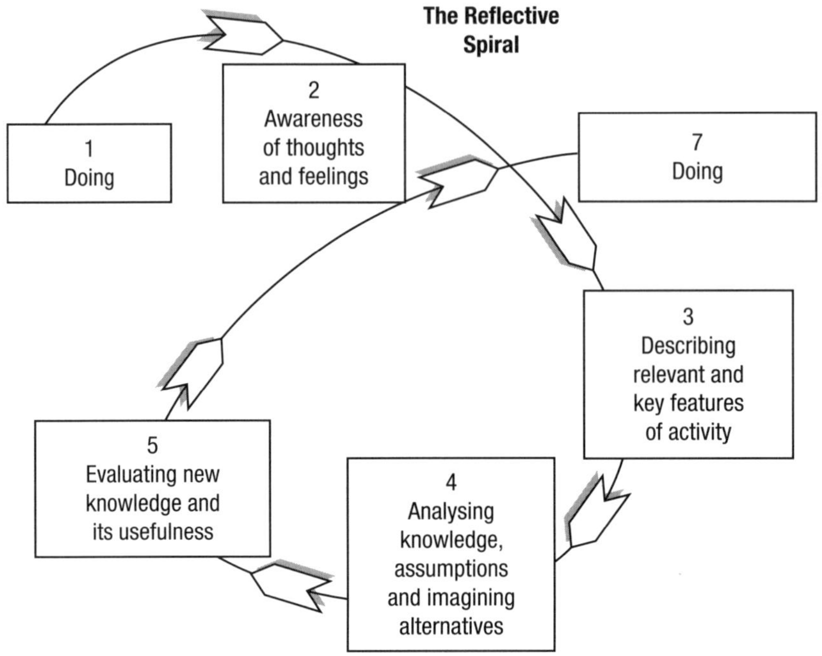

Figure 11.1 The Reflective Spiral

emerging out of reflection. This is knowledge building, the generation and regeneration of knowledge for practice.

Community work practice, from this perspective, is much more than 'just doing it'. It requires the community worker to be constantly reflecting on the nature of their practice, to be using the experience of practice to gain a deeper understanding of the community, society and social change and to be evaluating theory in terms of practice and practice in terms of theory. Critical reflection, analysis and action go hand in hand.

One of the problems facing community workers is to ensure that this critical reflection actually occurs. One can easily become so 'busy' that there is no time and space for critical reflection, and this will only serve to limit the effectiveness of one's community work and one's capacity to grow and develop in the role. Some community workers try to set aside a regular time for such reflection, but this is often not easy: the nature of community work is that it is irregular so trying to set aside a 'regular time' for anything is not generally very successful. Keeping a diary can be a very good form of writing to help the process of critical reflection—not a mere record of 'what I did today', but also why I did it, what questions it raises, what I learned from it, what was frustrating or rewarding about it, how it relates to the broader picture and so on. Sometimes critical reflection is better achieved by talking things through with others; some community workers have found it valuable to meet with others to share experiences and discuss common problems. Some community workers prefer a more formal process of 'supervision', while others prefer informal networking. Talking things over with someone who has nothing at all to do with community work can be both refreshing and enlightening.

Reading is another important aspect of critical reflection. This does not include only books or articles about community development, but a much broader range of writing (including fiction) relating to community life, social and political issues, change and development. The community worker is of necessity a generalist rather than a specialist and the broader one's knowledge base, the more likely one is to be able to make critical connections and to help develop innovative ideas. Broad general reading is an important component of improving one's knowledge and skills—and hence of critical reflection related to practice.

It would be wrong to assume that the process of critical reflection stops with the community worker. In community development one should seek to involve the whole community in critical reflection on its processes, where it is going and what people are learning. How one does this will obviously vary from community to community, but a good community worker will always be seeking to extend the process of critical reflection on practice to involve as many community members as possible. The processes of community development, and the theory and practice of community work, belong ultimately to the community itself rather than to the worker and control of the process requires that critical reflection be part of the whole community's agenda.

The language of roles

From the holistic perspective advocated in earlier chapters there are problems with a discussion of specific roles in community work. It is easy to fall into the trap of breaking community work down into 'constituent parts', a characteristic of the Newtonian paradigm. A typology of roles can lead a community worker to thinking about the job as if they are doing just one thing at a time. One thinks of oneself, for example, as being an 'enabler', an 'organiser' or an 'educator' and as moving from one specific role to another. The reality of community work, however, is that in a single activity a community worker is often performing several of these roles at one time. A rigid separation of roles may look neat in a textbook or a classroom, but it seldom reflects the more fluid context of practice and it can lead a community worker into creating artificial distinctions.

A sole concentration on roles can also lead a worker to thinking about practice in terms of the job at hand ('How can I best fill this role?') and not in terms of the overall purpose or vision of community work. Any form of analysis that distracts the worker from the 'big picture' is likely to be counterproductive, lead to fragmented practice and encourage community work 'for its own sake' rather than locating it in the broader context of the earlier chapters.

Thus the delineation of community work roles can be seen to provide a vocabulary that may allow for fragmented practice within an 'old paradigm' and which can discourage a more holistic approach. Nevertheless it is still necessary to find some way of making sense of the variety of activities community workers do and the skills they need to do them. That is the aim of this chapter, rather than attempting a rigid and prescriptive definition of specific identifiable practice roles. Community work tends to be about doing a lot of things at once and in any single activity or project a community worker is likely to be filling several roles and will move between one and another all the time, using a variety of skills in the process. The following discussion, therefore, must be read as an outline of the different things a community worker does and the skills required to do them, rather than as a rigid separation of activities that are conceptually distinct or mutually exclusive.

For the purposes of this discussion community work roles have been grouped into five clusters, namely *facilitative* roles, *educational* roles, *representational* roles, *technical* roles and *critical questioning* roles. Within each, a number of more specific practice roles are outlined and the skills needed to fill those roles are identified (see Figure 11.2.).

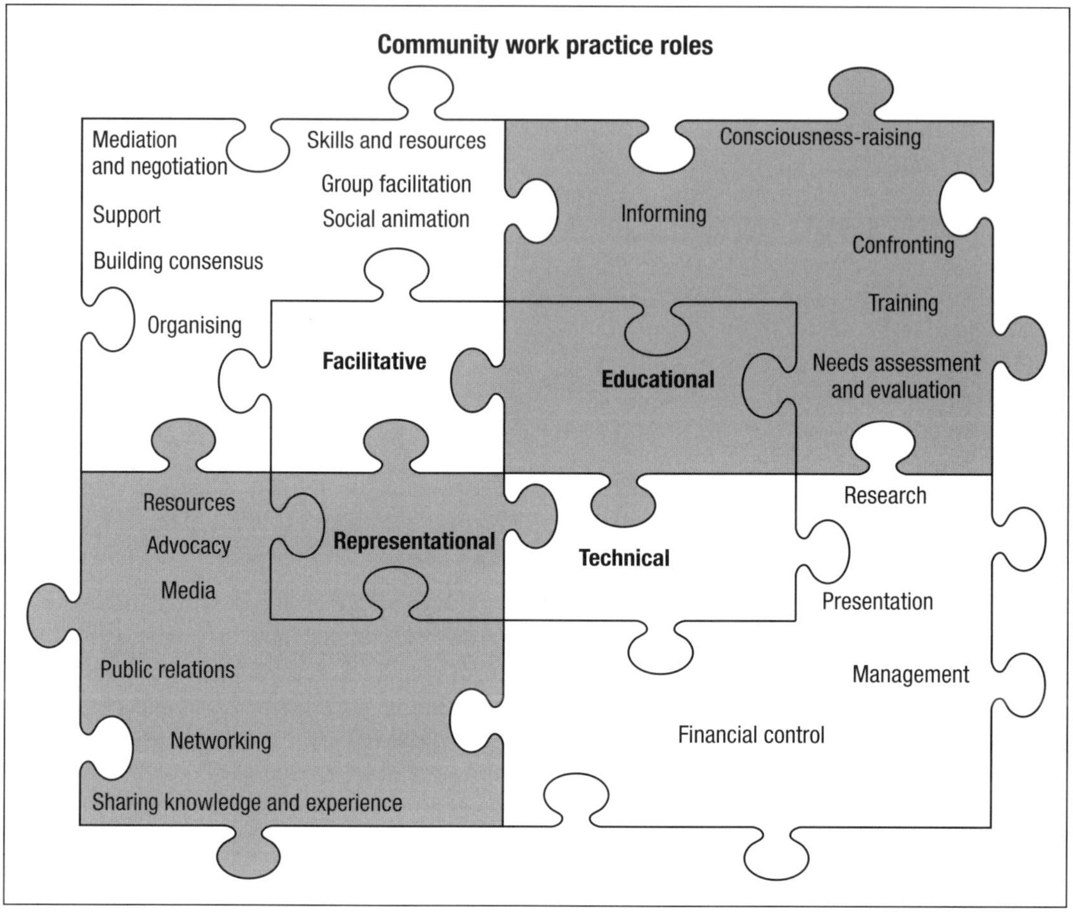

Figure 11.2 Community work practice roles

Facilitative roles and skills

The practice roles grouped as *facilitative* roles are those that are concerned with stimulating and supporting community development. The community worker can use a variety of techniques to facilitate the process, effectively becoming a catalyst for action and helping the process along. Within this category, a number of more specific roles can be defined. These are *social animation, mediation and negotiation, support, building consensus, group facilitation, utilisation of skills and resources* and *organising*.

Social animation

The term *social animation* describes an important component of community work practice, namely the ability to inspire, enthuse, activate, stimulate, energise and motivate others to action. The role of the community worker is not that of the person who does everything themself but instead enables others to become actively involved in community processes.

Six aspects of successful social animation can be identified, which can become the focus for a more explicit description of this community work role. The first, and arguably the most important, is *enthusiasm*. The worker who has genuine enthusiasm for the task at hand will communicate that enthusiasm to others. While genuine enthusiasm tends to be infectious, false enthusiasm is easily seen through, so it is a waste of time for a worker to try to be artificially enthusiastic about a project. But if a worker is embarking on a project about which they are genuinely enthusiastic, it can only benefit the project if the worker is able to display that enthusiasm openly. Unfortunately some workers who try to adopt a 'professional' role sometimes see enthusiasm as unprofessional and seek to project an image of detached objectivity. While it can be argued that this is a misrepresentation of professionalism, there can be little doubt that this sort of pseudo-professional detachment is not very helpful for a community worker.

The next characteristic of a good animator is *commitment*. The worker who is strongly committed, either to the idea of community development as a whole or to the achievement of a particular developmental objective, will inevitably convey that commitment to others and will also be able to speak with passion and conviction about the cause at issue. This relates directly to the community worker's values and is one reason why a community worker who is not strongly committed to community development, but is simply 'doing it as a job' is unlikely to be very successful. The approach to community development outlined in this book has identified the source of that commitment firmly in the two aims of social justice/human rights and ecological sustainability. Commitment to such ultimate causes generally lies at the heart of successful community work practice.

Integrity is the next important attribute of the successful animator. Like enthusiasm and commitment, integrity (or the lack of it) is easily communicated to others in the community. If a community worker is seen as genuine, consistent and non-manipulative in dealings with others it will be much easier to play a successful role as animator within a trusting relationship. The community worker who attempts to manipulate or play off one person or group against another, will rapidly lose credibility. Thus the principle of the integrity of process, which was identified in Chapter 7, is not only important as a matter of principle but also has a very practical importance as it is only by following such a principle that one's integrity will remain intact.

Communication is a critical component of social animation, as one cannot be a good animator unless one can communicate clearly and appropriately. This applies not only to a worker's ability to communicate facts, ideas or opinions but also to one's ability to communicate the enthusiasm, commitment and integrity that have been discussed above. Such communication is often unconscious and flows from a community worker's entire way of operating. Community workers will inevitably spend a good deal of time talking to other people and good interpersonal communication skills are, therefore, vital and pervade all community development. While much successful social animation may be unconscious, it results from the community worker's *understanding and analysis* as part of the reflexive practice approach described above. This itself is a conscious process and, to that extent at least, animation is not just a matter of 'being there'—almost as a kind of mystical presence that magically makes things happen—but is also a deliberate and planned activity. Such practice analysis leads a community worker to be aware of the different ways in which they can engage constructively with others and stimulate community-based action.

Many of the skill prerequisites for social animation are difficult to acquire if one does not already possess them as they are, to a large extent, grounded in the worker; some people naturally have the ability to motivate and activate the people around them, and others do not. One cannot just go to a course on how to be a successful animator as it is a very complex activity and cannot be described in terms of simple discrete skills.

Qualities such as enthusiasm, commitment and integrity cannot be termed *skills*: they are attributes or characteristics of a worker rather than things they can actually do. Some aspects of social animation, however, are more skill-related—namely those to do with communication. There are ways in which a community worker might seek to develop skills in this area, though these will vary according to the characteristics and situation of the individual worker. These include seeking feedback from colleagues, community members and others, critical reflection and analysis, self-awareness, observing other workers and learning from experience. Some communication skills may be picked up through formal education, but for the most part this is an area (like much of community work) where community workers must take responsibility for their own skill development, and cannot expect anyone else to do it for them.

Mediation and negotiation

Community workers will often have to deal with conflicting interests and values within the community. These conflicts are often strongly felt, partly because of issues of personal power, but also because many of the issues facing communities are ones about which people feel strongly. Passionate views can be a positive sign for community development as they indicate that people do feel strongly about their community and what happens to it, but that can be of small comfort to a community worker attempting to deal with strong conflict and build consensus.

In order to deal with these conflicts, a community worker will sometimes have to play the role of *mediator*. This requires an ability to listen to and understand both sides, reflect the views of each side to those on the other, help people to respect the legitimacy of views other than their own and help people to seek areas of common ground and eventually reach some sort of consensus. It is not always possible for a community worker to play such a role, especially if they are strongly identified with one side or have been known to express strong views on the issue involved. Often, however, the community worker will be in a position to take the neutral non-partisan position required for mediation. Strict neutrality is impossible in community issues so the term *neutral* in this context carries a relative implication and has more to do with the perceived integrity of the community worker.

Where a community worker is clearly identified with one side of a conflict, and *mediation* is impossible, it may still be possible for the worker to play a useful *negotiation* role. It is not appropriate for a worker to attempt to maintain perceived neutrality and impartiality on all issues, especially where fundamental questions of social justice and human rights are involved. From the social justice and human rights perspective of Chapter 3, for example, it would be quite impossible for a worker to be anything other than totally and openly opposed to blatantly racist regulations or practices. Here the role of negotiator requires the worker to be able to represent only one side of a particular conflict, in such a way that its claims are most powerfully articulated, but also remembering the principles of non-violence, the importance of criticising ideas rather than people and the need to allow one's opponents to 'change sides' without losing face.

Mediation and negotiation skills involve the ability to intervene in an issue without necessarily taking sides, acknowledge the legitimacy of different points of view and to enable others to do the same, separate issues from personalities so that people can disagree without it becoming a matter of personal attack, help people to reframe their concerns and points of view so that dialogue can be encouraged and sense where a consensus might lie in order to help the parties concerned to work towards it in such a way as not to lose face.

Such mediation and negotiation skills again involve many skills that a community worker will have acquired simply as part of being human, but the worker needs to use them in a special way. As with communication skills, group skills and others, the community worker needs to maintain a strong awareness of structural issues in the form discussed in the social justice and human rights approach of Chapter 3.

Support

One of the most important roles for a community worker is to provide support for people involved in community structures, processes and activities. This involves affirming people, recognising and acknowledging their value and the value of their contribution, giving encouragement, being available for people when they need to talk something through or ask questions and so on. Support can also take a more practical form, such as ensuring that arrangements are made for tea and coffee after a meeting. While some support can be formal and structured, for example, praising someone's work on a committee or speaking in support of someone at a public meeting, most support is given informally and in unstructured ways. This involves the community worker in being available and accessible to people and being prepared to spend time with people informally—say, over a cup of tea or a drink in a tavern, in the supermarket or at a football match. The community worker who is too busy to stop for a chat is too busy to do their job effectively.

It is easy for a community worker to forget the importance of simple support or the nurturing and affirmation of others and get carried away by the more glamorous aspects of the job. But community development can be a difficult and discouraging experience for all those involved and if a project is to succeed it is necessary to provide ongoing support to build and maintain self-confidence. Self-confidence is the foundation on which consciousness-raising and empowerment rest.

There are no special community work 'skills' involved in the support role. It is simply a matter of being genuine, being there for people when needed, being able to affirm them, and being sufficiently reliable and dependable that people will know that they can rely on you when necessary.

Building consensus

The consensus approach to community development runs counter to the conflict approach, which is taken for granted in many social, economic and political interactions. Challenging the values of conflict and the structures of competition, so that they can be replaced by the values of consensus and the structures of cooperation, is a major task for the community worker.

Building consensus is an extension of the mediation role discussed above. It involves emphasising common goals, identifying common ground and helping people move towards a consensus position that is acceptable to all. It is important to emphasise that a consensus does not mean that everybody has to agree on everything—where there is a diversity of opinion that would clearly be impossible. Rather, a consensus represents an agreed-on course of action, which everyone has decided would be the best course *taking into account and respecting the diversity of views in the group*. This may not be the preferred option for some, perhaps most, of the people involved. It requires group members to make a commitment to each other, and to finding the course of action that represents the best option for the whole group and each individual in it, and to which each individual can be committed.

Building consensus can take a long time and for this reason it is often tempting to move into conflict mode and accept the will of the majority rather than continue to talk through the issue until a consensus is reached to which all group members can commit themselves. This temptation needs to be resisted if the principles of non-violence, cooperation and consensus are to be maintained. Consensus is different from 'the majority rules' and, although it can take longer to achieve, the result will be greatly preferable in terms of building group solidarity and commitment.

While the consensus approach may seem a strange concept to people used to the conflict model epitomised by such things as formal meeting procedure, speaking 'for' and 'against', crystallising conflict and voting and winning, it is important to point out that the consensus approach is more widely used than one might think. Most informal discussions in fact work more or less on this principle, where people try to find a way of agreeing on a course of action. Many formally constituted meetings (especially small groups, executive committees, task forces, staff meetings, etc.) will spend most of their time in informal and loosely structured discussion where people are effectively seeking consensus and they move into formal mode and actual voting only when it seems that consensus cannot be reached. In fact, most important decisions in organisations are taken in informal consensus-oriented groups, to be later presented to a meeting for formal ratification. Formal conflict-based meetings do not seem to be very good mechanisms for making decisions and people generally prefer to follow a consensus model if possible. Indeed, Indigenous people have characteristically worked from a consensus decision-making model and have found the conventional Western conflict approach patently absurd and inappropriate to making good decisions. When all this is taken into account it can be seen that perhaps consensus decision making is the norm rather than the exception; perhaps it is only the structures and requirements of Western culture and industrial capitalism that have marginalised it and led to a more artificial and inadequate conflict approach, which people will naturally avoid if possible.

The task for a community worker, therefore, is to help legitimise the consensus model and help make it work. This requires helping people to understand that the informal consensus-based perspective they will use for many of their most important decisions is not inferior in some way to the formal conflict model but is in most cases superior to it. It also involves helping to set up different structures and planning meetings in different ways (see Chapter 9) so that the consensus model is supported and becomes part of the formal processes of the meeting.

In order to build consensus, the community worker needs to have skills in listening, empathising, reframing and communication. It is often necessary to reframe what someone is saying in such a way that allows for dialogue and inclusion rather than confrontation and exclusion. It is also important to be able to 'sense' a consensus emerging, help the group identify and name it, and encourage discussion to clarify its meaning and implications.

Group facilitation

Much of a community worker's time is spent in groups and the effectiveness of a community worker will depend very much on how well they are able to operate in a small group. The groups in which a community worker will be involved include action groups, management committees, planning groups, consciousness-raising groups, training groups, task groups, recreation groups, self-help groups and local decision-making bodies. While in most groups the main or sole activity will be talking among the members, this is not always the case. Groups may be involved in cooking, building, painting, renovating, child care, gardening, bushwalking or other forms of physical activity, yet in all these groups the need for good facilitation is critical.

In many instances a community worker will play a facilitative role with such a group, whether formally as chairperson or convenor or informally as a group member who is able to help the group achieve its goal in an effective way. Either way, group facilitation is a critical community work task as many of the goals of community development can be achieved only through effective and well-functioning groups, which are able to reach decisions and which allow and encourage meaningful participation by group members.

It is in a group setting that the consensus building described above can best be achieved. Hence the approach to community development outlined in previous chapters requires a particular consensus-oriented approach to working in small groups. Some degree of conflict is almost inevitable in a community group, especially when it is dealing with an issue about which people feel strongly, as is usually the case with community development. It is important that a community worker is able to manage the conflict and mistrust that may accompany different agendas and views and help the group to move beyond conflict towards consensus, rather than creating winners and losers within the group.

Most discussions of group work make a distinction between task-oriented and process-oriented roles. The former are focused on helping the group to achieve its outcomes (e.g. to make decisions, to construct a playground, to employ a child-care worker), while the latter (process-oriented roles) are concerned with how the group gets there, how people participate and how they feel about it. This relates to the discussion in Chapter 7 about process and outcome where it was pointed out that in community development the emphasis is on process, but that because of the artificiality of the means/ends distinction a clear dichotomy between process and outcome cannot be sustained: the process is, in effect, the outcome.

The distinction between task and process in community groups, therefore, is often more apparent than real. It may in some instances represent a useful way of thinking about group work and helping to ensure that one does not become too restricted in one's understanding of what happens in groups, but it is an oversimplification to see the two as distinct. It is important to concentrate on how they are related and how process and outcome are involved in all aspects of group facilitation.

Group facilitation is complex and sophisticated, reflecting the complexity of dynamics within a group. It can involve the community worker in a number of different types of activity. These include formal or informal 'chairing' or convening where other group members will look to the community worker to lead or coordinate the discussion or activity. It can involve talking to group members beforehand, encouraging them to participate and helping them to think through how they are going to approach the meeting. It can involve actively seeking the views of people in the group, reflecting and interpreting what others have said, seeking to summarise, coming up with suitable forms of wording, representing the views of people who are not present and using a variety of group techniques such as brainstorming.

Community workers, therefore, need to be able to operate effectively in groups, which requires a broad range of skills. These include the capacity to encourage others to take a leadership and facilitating role and manage mistrust, among other things. Group work skills can be developed through ongoing critically reflective praxis, as discussed above, and the worker's primary responsibility is to ensure that there is an environment in which this can occur. This means finding ways to become more sensitive to one's own role in group situations, receive feedback from others including co-facilitators, to read, observe, watch how others operate, and learn from one's own experiences, mistakes and successes.

Utilisation of skills and resources

Another important facilitative role a community worker can play is to identify and utilise the skills and resources that exist within a community or a group. As well as a role, this can be considered as an approach to community development because it implies valuing strengths within. One of the consequences of the centralised, market-based labour market with which we are so familiar is that unless someone's skills are recognised through a 'job' or through some sort of formal accreditation, they tend to be marginalised or ignored. Similarly, the segmentation of various forms of human activity means that there can be many resources and facilities that are untapped or under-utilised because they are commonly understood as having only one specific purpose (the most obvious example, perhaps, being school buildings and grounds, which remain largely unused outside school hours or in vacation periods). Thus it is usually the case that in any community there is more potential in terms of people's skills and expertise and in terms of community resources and facilities than most people have realised.

An important role for a community worker is to identify and locate these resources and help people see how they might be utilised. One of the first tasks of a worker stimulating community economic development is often to take a skills inventory of the local population: listing the skills and experience that represent an untapped economic resource in the community. A similar inventory of unused or under-used resources (school buildings, disused workshops, etc.) can then be matched with the skills inventory and as a result of these two processes some potential local economic projects emerge as likely possibilities.

It is important for the community worker to have a good understanding of just what is available in the community (whether it be finance, expertise, raw materials, manufactured products, community facilities or volunteer labour) so that it can be drawn on where necessary. Too often the temptation is to seek resources externally, through grants or consultations, when the intelligent use of local resources would not only be easier but also would help restore the confidence of a local community, stimulate local activity and facilitate the kind of autonomy and self-reliance described in Chapter 5. Often, in fact, community work will involve simply linking people to other people or to resources and facilities, or having the imagination to identify the usefulness of a group or facility that has been there all the time, but which nobody has thought of using for the purpose at hand.

Organising

Another important facilitative role of the community worker is that of organiser. This can simply be described as being the person who makes sure things happen. It involves being able to think through what needs to be done and, by working alongside others in the community, to ensure that it all happens and the skills are shared. This may include making sure that a hall is booked for the meeting, the press release has been distributed, notification of the meeting has been sent out, tea and coffee have been organised for after the meeting, the washing up will be done, the request for a permit for a street protest was submitted on time, the mayor and the local member have been invited, there is a proper amplification system for an open-air meeting, child care has been organised, the minutes of the last meeting do not get lost and letters of invitation have been sent. If these things are not done, community processes will be stifled; if they are properly organised, things will 'run smoothly' and there will be more opportunity to realise the goals of community development.

Sometimes this is a case of doing it oneself, but if one is genuinely committed to the community development process it is better to help others to take these responsibilities by providing appropriate support, encouragement, tactful reminders and so on. In doing so a community worker must not be seen to be 'above' such 'mundane' tasks; the worker who gets everybody else to do all the work and never does any themself will quickly lose the respect of the community. It is essential to be prepared to get one's hands dirty and do the unpopular jobs along with others; this is, among other things, a way of demonstrating one's commitment to the community.

Being well organised, aware of what has to be done and making sure (if possible, unobtrusively) that it all happens becomes second nature to a community worker. The unstructured and flexible nature of community work means that a worker has to be efficient and organised in terms of, for example, time management, keeping track of documents, being aware of deadlines and keeping appointments. It may be a less glamorous role than some of the others discussed in this chapter, but it is one of the most important. It is through this sort of day-to-day organisation that one can often do effective empowerment and consciousness-raising work with community members; it can be the easiest way to affirm the skills and values of many people who have become used to seeing themselves as having little to offer, but who perhaps can make a good cup of tea or make a sound system work properly.

Educational roles and skills

The second category of practice roles and skills can be classified as *educational*. Whereas facilitative roles involve the worker in stimulating and supporting community processes, educational roles require the worker to take a more active role in agenda-setting. The worker is not simply helping a process along but is actually having a positive and directive input, as a result of their knowledge, skills and experience. Community development is an ongoing process of learning: workers are constantly learning new skills, new ways of thinking, new ways of looking at the world and new ways of interacting with others.

Education is one of the most important aspects of a community worker's role and so skills in education are critically important. In some instances this seems to imply relatively straightforward training, for example teaching people how to keep minutes of meetings, how to keep basic accounts and how to use a computer to establish a database. It is, however, not this simple. Even basic tasks like these have particular significance and tend to reflect the culture of the powerful rather than the powerless. In order for the empowerment principles of Chapters 3–7 to be effected it is important that a community worker does not decide what basic skills need to be taught, but rather allows people in the community to set their own learning agenda. To many people, taking minutes of a meeting, using a computer or keeping financial records might seem like a boring waste of time and so to teach such people these skills will have little lasting value. But if a community group has arrived at the point of realising that it needs some way of keeping track of the money, that it has to keep track of its previous decisions or that there must be an easier way of maintaining a membership list, then some form of training activity becomes relevant to their own defined needs. It also then becomes possible to develop, for example, a form of record keeping that best meets the needs of the group, rather than simply adopting 'accepted practice' according to some outside expert.

Such an approach to training requires that the worker is always sensitive to the articulated needs of the community and responds to the community's agenda rather than set their own. It requires a relationship based on dialogue and equality, rather than the inequality of institutionalised expertise. Very importantly, it also means that all learning has a purpose and is located in a wider context. Teaching and learning is a two-way process and the community worker learns just as much from the process as they contribute to it. Thus the approach, even to teaching basic skills, is more closely related to Freire's critical pedagogy than to conventional didactic 'training'. In this regard, it is worth emphasising that Freire based his whole consciousness-raising approach on one of the most basic skills of all, namely literacy (Freire 1972).

The challenge for a community worker is to 'teach' in such a way as to open up possibilities while responding to the community's agenda rather than reinforce structures of control and domination and fit the agenda of a government, funding body or professional association. This can be a significant challenge and emphasises the importance of the broader structural analysis discussed in earlier chapters.

Many of the basic skills associated with education, as with group and interpersonal interactions, are not particularly mysterious and are part of the life experience of most people. They include being able to present an idea clearly using language people will understand, being able to listen and respond to other people's questions and to their felt need to know more, being able to build on the ideas of others, being able to enter into a dialogue with another person from which both will learn and grow, and being able to help other people to set their own agendas and learning goals.

The educational roles of a community worker are *consciousness-raising, informing, confronting, training* and *needs assessment and evaluation*.

Consciousness-raising

The process of consciousness-raising has been described in earlier chapters; it is not necessary to revisit it in detail here. However, it is important to emphasise that consciousness-raising is a critically important role for a community worker and it pervades all aspects of practice.

One of the characteristics of consciousness-raising is that it should aim to provide an awareness of structures and strategies of social change within which people can participate and take effective action. In some cases these structures may already be in place, while in other cases it may be necessary to help people to see how they can establish such structures themselves. Sometimes it may simply involve helping people to realise ways in which they can change their own lives so that they do not contribute to or reinforce oppressive structures. Sometimes it may involve linking people with already existing action groups, movements or campaigns. But it always involves helping people to move beyond a state of seeming apathy and passive acceptance (or silent resistance) to one of activism. Many people are passive not because they want to be but because they have not been introduced to structures and strategies through which they can become activists relatively easily. Activism has too often been seen as an activity for the minority and too little attention has been given to making it readily accessible to ordinary people. Emphasis on the citizen's *obligation* to participate, as well as the *right* to participate (which was discussed in detail in Chapter 6), is a central feature of the community development perspective of earlier chapters. Hence helping people to become active participants is critically important to a community worker.

As discussed in earlier chapters, there is some opportunity for consciousness-raising in most forms of community development activity. It is one of the most pervasive roles of a good community worker as almost any situation has consciousness-raising potential. Indeed, as Freire (1972) has so clearly pointed out, consciousness-raising is at its most powerful and effective when it is located in the context of the ordinary realities of day-to-day life (with Freire's work, in the need to read and write) rather than being seen as something special or removed.

A good community worker will always be looking for the opportunity to engage in consciousness-raising and dialogue and to relate people's experiences to a wider social, economic, cultural and political context. This affects the way everyday problems and issues are discussed and the way in which actions are initiated. A busy or dangerous road, for example, can become a stimulus for a discussion of public transport, urban planning decisions, the interests represented in local government, the rights of older people to safety and mobility, the road lobby, the transport of toxic chemicals and so on. This can be done informally and casually; one doesn't have to make a major issue of it—one can simply allow it to emerge in general conversation. Much of this consciousness-raising is best undertaken at the informal level.

There are many skills involved in consciousness-raising. A community worker needs to be able to link the personal and the political and to help others to make that connection. They also need to be able to listen, communicate and enter into a dialogical relationship. The interpersonal and group skills described above are essential for any consciousness-raising practice, as is the ability to motivate and to work alongside others in a spirit of solidarity.

Informing

Simply providing people with relevant information can be a useful role for a community worker. This can cover a very wide range. An important area is demographic information and social indicators such as age structure, suicide rates, rates of juvenile offending, income distribution and ethnic origin; these can be used to construct a community profile. This information is very important for a community in planning how best to meet its needs and how to involve as many people as possible in community development processes. It can help to highlight what is special or different about that particular community and where it differs from a national average.

A community worker will also be in a good position to provide information about programs in other communities; one must be wary of simply transferring a successful program from one place to another because of local social, cultural and political variations, but it is still important for people to have some idea about how things have worked elsewhere so that they can learn from other communities' successes and mistakes.

Information about external resources, such as funding guidelines, expertise, manuals, audio-visual presentations and training packages, is another area where simply informing people of what is available can be an important community work service. The principle of self-reliance requires a worker to be careful not to ignore local resources, but with this caveat it is still important for communities to be able to utilise external resources appropriately.

Often it is appropriate for a community worker to inform a community of matters of economic or political reality with which they need to deal. Sometimes community members will be well aware of these themselves, but in a community where people have limited access to external sources, where people have chosen an isolationist lifestyle or where a community has been deliberately 'kept in the dark' by powerful interests, it is important for a community worker to be able to inform people of things that may directly or indirectly affect them. A community worker may be the first to know, for example, that a significant regional employer is considering closing a manufacturing plant or that a major freeway is proposed that will cut the community in two.

Finally, a community worker will often be in a position to inform people about what is happening within their own community. Often the community worker will be able to move between different subgroups (e.g. ethnic groups or different socioeconomic groups)—in many so-called communities these groups are profoundly ignorant of each other's experiences or even existence. Simply informing people of what is going on in their own community can fill an important gap in local communication.

Confronting

Sometimes it is necessary for a community worker to confront a community or community group. Confrontation is very directly and clearly communicating how one sees a situation, its context and its consequences.

Sometimes a community worker will become aware that if a community group continues in a direction in which it has started it is headed for serious problems. While at times this may be a useful and necessary learning experience for the group, in some circumstances the problem will be of such a magnitude that the group or community could not afford *not* to deal with it and it is necessary for a worker to confront the group with the consequences of its actions. For example, a community group that is managing a community-based child-care centre may receive complaints about suspected child sexual abuse by one of its staff and choose to ignore these complaints because that person is a good friend and loyal community member. This is clearly a potentially disastrous course for the group to take and it is in the interests of both the children involved and the community development process that the group be confronted with the possible consequences of their action as a matter of extreme urgency.

At other times, confrontation may be necessary because of the legal implications of individual or group action. For example, an incorporated community group that does not bother to get its books properly audited or a group that fails to take out workers' compensation insurance for its employees could be headed for legal difficulties as well as potential embarrassment and financial loss. Again, confrontation may be necessary in order for the group to accept its legal responsibilities.

Sometimes it is necessary to be confrontationist over moral issues or issues of principle rather than legal issues. If a community group is pursuing programs that are effectively racist or sexist, bring about thoughtless environmental destruction or represent a health hazard, again it may be necessary for a worker to confront a group with the consequences of its actions.

The final form of confrontation that is sometimes used by community workers relates to the internal dynamics of a community or group. For example, an individual might be extremely disruptive and obstructionist, preventing effective consensus or action and frustrating (and driving away) other group members. Such a situation has to be dealt with if the group is to survive; this will usually involve having to confront that person about the consequences of their behaviour. If a community group is strong, this will be effectively done by other group members, but sometimes a community worker will have to assume this role.

In all these cases of confrontation it is the ultimate effectiveness, integrity and viability of community structures and processes that make the confrontation necessary.

Training

Training is the most specific educative role, in that it involves simply teaching people how to do something. In many cases the community worker will not be the trainer but they will help the group to find someone who can provide the necessary training, preferably from within the community but otherwise from some external source. However, there will be times when it is most appropriate for a community worker to provide training, either because of that worker's particular expertise or because of simple convenience.

Training is most effective when it is provided in response to a request from the community itself. The community worker who decides that a group needs some form of training and then provides it is likely to be disappointed; training is much more productive when the people themselves have identified a need for it. In training, as in all other aspects of community development, a worker has to resist the colonialist temptation (which can often be both subtle and powerful) to define other people's needs for them.

Training may be specifically in processes of community development or community management, for example, minute-taking, simple bookkeeping, meeting procedures and consensus decision making. Sometimes it will be more specifically oriented to a task a community group wants to undertake, such as care for the aged, how to construct a playground or how to cook for large numbers. At other times, training may be focused on the specific needs of people or groups within the community, for example, literacy training, assertiveness training, nutrition, budgeting or fluency in the dominant language. In other settings, training may be more recreational or cultural, in an attempt to enrich lifestyles rather than meet basic needs, for example, orienteering, rock climbing, public speaking, health and fitness, music, drama and a host of other physical, social and cultural activities. Finally, training may be more specifically oriented to economic development—to give people skills that they can use to obtain a job and work productively in the labour force or skills they can use to start a local community economic project.

It is obviously impossible for any community worker individually to provide all this training; in most instances the worker will be playing the role of finding the relevant resources and expertise. But in some cases the worker may wish to provide the training directly and will assume a primarily educative role with the community group.

Needs assessment and evaluation

Many texts on community work or social planning will discuss both needs assessment and evaluation as if they are technical activities in which a worker needs to be highly skilled and which are essentially jobs for the experts. There is a tendency, as a result, for them to be seen as areas where the experts must be consulted and they tend to be tasks for which consultants are often employed.

Such a view of needs assessment and evaluation tends to ignore their most important aspect—that they are essentially value judgements.

From the community development perspective outlined in earlier chapters it is essential that people be able to define their own needs; this, after all, is the basis of empowerment. Defining needs assessment as a technical undertaking for the expert is a way of disempowering ordinary people and handing over to that expert the power to define people's needs for them. It is also denying the essentially value-laden nature of needs assessment. (Even the word *assessment* carries strong objectivist implications.)

From this view of need definition, the role of a community worker is to facilitate the process of people defining their own needs in such a way that they can act to have those perceived needs met. To do this a community worker might well wish to collect and analyse relevant social and economic data to present to the community in order to help people make need judgements (note that the worker does not make the need judgement themself). The worker will also want to facilitate the process of need definition by bringing people together, helping groups to reach consensus and so on. These are all roles that have been described earlier in this chapter as part of community work. Hence needs assessment is not really a separate specialist role for a community worker. It is, rather, a task for the community and the community worker will facilitate the process just as they will facilitate any other community process.

The same argument applies to evaluation. The very word implies a judgement of the value of something and so the evaluation of a community project is a judgement of its value. This may be further defined in terms of worth, effectiveness or efficiency, but in each case it still involves somebody making a value judgement and, as with need, a judgement of evaluation will reflect the particular person's values, ideology and world view. Again, as with need, the technical approach of much of the literature has tended to mask this central aspect of value judgement and has made evaluation seem as if it is a complex task that can be done objectively—hence the urge to call in an expert consultant to 'do' evaluation. As with need, from a community development perspective it is essential that it is the community that makes the evaluative judgement—asking an outside 'expert' or even a community worker to do it will effectively disempower the community.

The role of a community worker with evaluation, as with need definition, is to facilitate the process of the community making its own evaluative judgements. This will involve data collection and analysis and process facilitation. The community worker has no business doing the actual evaluation (i.e. the making of the evaluative judgement) itself.

Representational roles and skills

The term *representational roles* is used to denote the roles of a community worker in interacting with external bodies on behalf of, or for the benefit of, the community. While much of a community worker's activity will be focused within the community it is also necessary for a worker to relate to the wider system. These representational roles are *obtaining resources, advocacy, using the media, public relations and public presentation, networking*, and *sharing knowledge and experience*.

Many of these roles are highly problematic for a community worker committed to genuine self-reliance and empowerment. Although they are roles often filled by conventional community workers, they are often at odds with the principles of community development discussed in earlier chapters. It is in this set of roles—perhaps more than in any other—that community work as practised from within the perspective of this book differs from much of what has been traditionally seen as community work in many Western countries.

Obtaining resources

Community workers often help a community or community group to obtain the information, resources, skills and expertise it needs in order to be able to establish its own structures and meet its own objectives. While a community worker cannot be expected to provide everything themself. it is reasonable to expect that a community worker will know what is likely to be available from different sources and how to help the community to obtain what it needs.

Community workers play an important role as information brokers: knowing how to gain access to information, helping community groups to do so and then helping them to use that information effectively. Thus an important area of skill for community workers is in using and processing information: knowing how to use a library, what can be obtained from the Australian Bureau of Statistics, how to use computer databases and so on. A community worker cannot be expected to know everything, but can be expected to know where to go to find out about almost anything a community group may need.

The same applies to expertise. A community worker will not be an expert in all areas, but should know where to go to find expertise in such diverse fields as accounting, literacy training, health and fitness, diet, recreation, planning regulations, legal drafting, small business management and photography. Part of this skill is in knowing what one can do oneself and for which things one needs to seek help—in other words, having a realistic view of the limits of one's own expertise. Knowing when to seek outside expertise and then where to go for it is an important skill not always acquired by community workers.

Obtaining resources—most commonly financial resources—is often the most time- and energy-consuming aspect of community work. A community worker usually needs to become an expert in 'getting funding', which requires knowledge of various government and non-government grant bodies, the ability to write a successful funding application and the ability to play the politics of funding (i.e. lobbying key individuals or obtaining support from powerful backers). These skills can be learned through experience, by observing others and from various publications that are available from different grant bodies.

External funding is more readily justifiable if it is clearly time-limited and is used to *initiate* or *establish* a program rather than to support it in the long term. Community workers who seek external funding need to consider whether it will be possible to establish alternative community-based resources over a longer period to move away from community dependence. Sometimes, of course, this will not be possible and the community will have to rely on long-term external funding to provide the services and facilities it needs.

Advocacy

A community worker will often adopt an advocacy role on behalf of the community or on behalf of a group or an individual within that community. Here the community worker is representing the interests of that person, group or community and putting their case for a better deal. This might involve appearing at hearings or tribunals, lobbying politicians or other key powerbrokers or making representation to local or central government.

An advocacy role raises serious questions about empowerment. The very act of advocacy assumes that the advocate is better able to represent the case than the person or people directly affected. It is based on the model of the legal system where a client engages a lawyer to present a case and represent the client's interests. As such, it is potentially disempowering rather than empowering. It reinforces a view that people are unable to speak up for themselves and establishes a power relationship between the community worker and the community. It is worth noting the way in which the advocacy model has been associated with one of the most conservative and powerful professions; community workers should think twice before accepting the legal profession as their preferred role model.

The advocacy role is a powerful one and it is easy for a community worker to be seduced into a power position, especially when it is associated with apparently radical rhetoric, as is often the case with the discourse of advocacy. This is not to say that community workers should never adopt an advocacy role—sometimes it is essential, especially when working with a particularly disempowered community that has immediate and urgent needs. The important point is that a worker must not assume that by adopting an advocacy role they are necessarily working for empowerment. Rather advocacy must be accompanied by some form of power analysis and must always be seen as a short-term measure. The goal of a community worker must be to enable people to represent their own interests rather than to feel that they always need someone else to do it for them.

Using the media

Community workers in many instances need to make effective use of the media. This can be in order to highlight particular issues and to help to place them on the public agenda. It can also be a part of an action campaign undertaken by a community group or it can be in order to publicise community processes, meetings and events. Sometimes it is necessary to be able to use the media in a crisis situation where, for example, there has been a public scandal relating to the community, where there have been accusations of corruption or where the community is engaged in some form of controversial action.

This can involve a community worker in issuing press releases, doing interviews for radio, television or the print media or participating in a debate or forum. It can also involve things such as making sure there are good 'photo opportunities', staging events or demonstrations bearing in mind their appeal to the media and building rapport with key journalists.

As with the other roles discussed in this section, it is important for the worker to involve community members as much as possible, from an empowerment perspective, rather than simply taking on the role of media representative. Ideally responsibility for relating to the media would be shared by various people in the community, but realistically it is often important in the short term for an experienced community worker to accept this responsibility within a longer-term process of skill sharing. Empowerment of community members themselves to deal with the media must then be the long-term goal.

Public relations and public presentation

It is important for a community worker to be conscious of the image projected by a community project and to promote an appropriate image in the wider context. At a more basic level, it is necessary for a worker to seek publicity for community projects so that people will know about them and become involved and also so that the projects will receive appropriate support from elsewhere.

This can involve a community worker in a variety of roles, such as speaking at meetings of service clubs, women's groups, local councils and ratepayers' associations. It also means putting notices in community newspapers, preparing posters or leaflets and getting them distributed and other similar work. Good public relations requires creativity and imagination, looking for every opportunity and 'gimmick' to obtain public exposure.

Part of this role is the ability to make public presentations. A community worker will at times have to make public presentations, either within the community (e.g. to a community meeting) or externally. This will be much more effective if the community worker can present facts fluently, clearly and in an interesting fashion.

Again it is important for a community worker not to see media roles and skills as their sole responsibility, but to work consciously to involve and thereby empower other community members.

Networking

Networking means establishing purposive relationships with a variety of people and being able to use them to effect change. It is one of the most important change strategies used by community workers, and a community worker will not only network within the community, though this is obviously very important, but will also establish a working network that extends well beyond those boundaries.

A community worker will typically establish networks with community members, other community workers, workers in related fields (e.g. social workers, psychologists, clergy, health workers), key people in government, politicians, academics, researchers, community leaders and representatives of various interest or lobby groups. A community worker maintains contact with them, discussing issues of common concern and using those contacts to mobilise resources and support. The people with whom the worker networks will, of course, be using their contacts with the community worker in a similar way.

Networking is essential and it is part of the practice of every community worker, but it too has its potential problems. Networking can lead to the development of an unofficial elite, which can effectively control social and political processes. Thus the community worker may in fact be setting up a new kind of control resulting in the community (or certain processes) being effectively run by a small group consisting of the community worker and their network. Because these are people with whom the community worker is likely to feel comfortable, networking can easily seduce a community worker into establishing a social change elite while being convinced that they are undertaking empowering community development. Like other roles discussed in this section, this is potentially disempowering and all the more dangerous because it is easy for a worker to feel comfortable in this role and not realise its negative impact.

There are two important principles to ensure that this does not happen. One is for the worker to keep the network open and to network with a variety of different people who do not necessarily network with each other. This prevents the formation of a 'closed' elite. The other principle is to involve grassroots community members in one's network and to encourage and help community members to establish their own networks as a form of empowerment.

Sharing knowledge and experience

It is important for community workers to share with each other, and with other people the fruits of their experience. Community workers, if they engage in reflective practice and critical reflection, are always learning from the job; they will never be in a position of 'knowing it all'. But they also learn from each other and from experience in other community projects. An important community work role is the sharing of knowledge and experience with others. This can be done at either a formal or an informal level.

In many ways, however, it is the informal sharing of knowledge and experience that is most useful. Even at formal conferences many participants will comment that it is the informal interaction (during meals and coffee breaks) rather than the formal program that is of most benefit. Many community workers seek opportunities for informal interaction with other community workers through, for example, regular lunches or social gatherings. It is in this way that practice wisdom and experience can be effectively shared.

Again the community worker needs to be aware of the danger of creating an elite and of not involving the local community. As with networking, it is important to seek to include community members in this knowledge dissemination and to encourage community members to find ways to share their experiences with people from other communities.

Technical roles and skills

Some aspects of community development involve the application of technical skills to aid the community development process. As discussed above, community development is for the most part best understood not as a technical activity (if one thinks of 'technical' as the application of specific skills using a 'cookbook' approach). However, there are some aspects of community development where a community worker will use technical knowledge in this way. These are: *research, verbal and written presentation, management* and *financial control*. In some cases a community worker will not have the necessary skills to perform these roles and will need to seek other expertise, but these are commonly occurring activities for community workers and most workers will develop a degree of competence or expertise in them either as a result of training or from experience (or, most commonly, both).

There are two other community work roles that are usually regarded as being essentially technical exercises—*needs assessment and evaluation*—and the reader may be surprised at their exclusion from the above list. These will be discussed in a separate section as it will be argued that to treat them as technical is in effect disempowering, and that in each case the technical role of the community worker should be limited to the technical skills described in this section.

With the roles listed below it should not be assumed that because of their technical nature they are limited to the skilled or trained community worker. Two of the most important aspects of community work are skill-sharing, which will be discussed at the end of this chapter, and community ownership of processes. For this reason a community worker will seek to involve other people in these technical processes as much as possible.

Research

Community workers are inevitably involved in research processes using a variety of social science research methodologies to collect relevant data and analyse and present them. This includes designing and conducting social surveys, analysing the data from such surveys, using and analysing census data, collecting and analysing data about demand and utilisation of various services (e.g. how many people use public transport, how long are waiting lists for aged persons' accommodation). This is an area where technical knowledge of such things as sampling, questionnaire construction and statistical analysis is necessary if the job is to be done properly.

The aspiring community worker who feels inadequate when the words *research* and *statistics* are mentioned should not be unduly frightened by this community work role. In general the methodology and statistical analysis required for community development purposes is not at a highly sophisticated level. What is important is for the community worker to be able to design and implement relatively straightforward projects, such as community surveys, in ways that remain methodologically sound, and to be able to analyse the results appropriately and present them to the community in such a way that they can be used. The aim is to provide a community with useful information rather than to undertake learned research for a PhD. A more detailed discussion of the various tasks a community worker might undertake in this area is beyond the scope of this book, but there are many good texts available, such as Wadsworth's *Do It Yourself Social Research* (1997).

There is an important warning to be issued about community surveys. While they can be very useful, they can also be overused. When faced with a community problem or issue often the first response of a community worker, especially one with a social science degree, is to 'do a survey' without thinking through the reasons or asking what that survey would actually achieve. Partly this is because of the concentration on surveys in many social science courses, as a result of which they can be easily seen as the primary tool for problem solving. It is also a classic case of using an essentially technical process to solve what is often not a technical problem; doing anything else might be difficult, messy and challenging, whereas doing a survey is a clear, technical and apparently 'value-neutral' process. In many cases the survey is carried out, the results are presented, but there is no ready answer to the inevitable question of 'So what?'. The community development process is not enhanced—indeed, it may have been retarded because energy put into the survey could more profitably have been directed elsewhere. Also, as communities have only limited tolerance to surveys, it will be more difficult to do surveys there in the future. It is, therefore, irresponsible to undertake a survey unless it is clearly necessary and there is no viable alternative.

Before embarking on a survey, then, it is essential for the community worker and the community itself to be clear on why the survey is being done, what it will achieve and to decide whether the same outcome could not be better achieved through another process, such as calling a public meeting, asking key community members or simply analysing data that are already available.

ALTERNATIVE RESEARCH APPROACHES

The research process described above is a fairly conventional—many would say limiting—understanding of the research process. There is also a rich field for community workers in ideas of research that include action research and collaborative research. *Action* research is where the research is actually undertaken by a program of action—trying both to understand the world and change the world at the same time. This, of course, is fully consistent with the idea of praxis in community work, as described earlier, as it refuses to see understanding and action as separate. *Collaborative* research is not done by a single researcher looking at a community, but is a cooperative exercise involving all people concerned in designing the project, gathering data and implementation. It is therefore a shared project, which does not privilege the researcher over the researched and does not see the flow of knowledge as one-way (from researched to researcher), but rather sees it as a collaborative dialogical process of education. It, too, is fully consistent with community development principles.

Combining action and collaborative research produces an approach to research that has been termed *participatory action research* (Fals-Borda & Rahman 1991; Rahman 1993; Kirby & McKenna 1989). This is essentially community development, as it incorporates the principles and practices described in this and earlier chapters and in this sense community development can be framed as a research process. Community workers can thus make use of the literature within the participatory action research paradigm, including feminist research, naturalistic research and so on. In this sense, research is not just a process that *informs* community development (as is the case with more traditional research paradigms), but research *is* community development and the same principles apply to both.

Verbal and written presentation

A community worker will inevitably do quite a lot of writing. This involves writing reports, funding submissions, minutes of meetings, discussion papers and letters. The capacity to write well, and to present oneself clearly, is thus a major asset and greatly increases one's effectiveness in community development. While many community workers will have good writing skills as a result of previous life experience, those who do not are well advised to improve their writing skills through available courses. There are also more specialist writing skills that a community worker may need to acquire. A good example is the media release, which requires a particular form of writing that does not come easily to someone whose writing skills have been developed in an academic environment. With such specialist writing skills, the community worker needs a high level of self-awareness, to make a realistic assessment of what they can do and what skills need to be further developed. This will vary from one community worker to another.

Community workers also need to be able to express themselves well verbally to make oral presentations to community groups, use audiovisual techniques and information technology appropriately and so on. Community workers will collect a lot of useful information and need to be able to communicate it in the appropriate forum in such a way that it leads to effective action.

Written and verbal communication by community workers has to be clearly presented to its audience in a form that will be readily understood. Thus long or obscure words, inaccessible jargon and long complex sentences should be avoided. Use of lists, tables, illustrations, graphs and cartoons can significantly enhance a written presentation, and can help to present material in an accessible form. Sometimes humour can add significantly to a presentation, though at other times it will detract from it.

As with many aspects of community work there are no hard and fast rules of how to do it; so a lot depends on the audience and the social and cultural context. A technique that works well in one community or group will be a disaster in another. A community worker needs to have a good understanding of the audience and the context and to be able to present the message accordingly.

As well as being grounded in the social and cultural context, a community worker's verbal or written presentation should include the possibility of action. Material can be presented in such a way that it leaves the listener powerless, effectively saying 'So what?'. Alternatively material can be presented in such a way that it opens up the possibility for action and helps people to articulate a plan of what to do next.

The linking of a presentation to the possibility of action demonstrates the connection between presentation (whether written or verbal) and consciousness-raising and empowerment. Communication, in this sense, can never be a neutral conveying of information. It either reinforces or undermines existing power structures and therefore either facilitates or retards the process of empowerment.

Management

When a community takes responsibility for managing its own projects, management roles become important. Some of the activities that are identified as 'management' in the conventional management literature do not apply in the community setting because of the size and scale of the operation;

many management principles are based on an assumption of large organisations, whether government or non-government. At community level, for example, concepts like 'middle management' do not normally apply—organisations being sufficiently small that there is no 'middle' level necessary. Other conventional management concepts are inappropriate for community development because they are based on different assumptions and values; for example, the notion of accountability in conventional management tends to be accountability upward rather than accountability downward or outward and accountability for outputs.

Possibly more than any other activity, 'management' has become reified as something so precious that it needs a highly trained professional 'expert'—hence the current popularity of MBA degrees. For a community worker the management and organisational skills required for the job should not be thought of in this way. The management of a community-based organisation requires special skills and attitudes, such that an MBA would in all likelihood be a liability rather than an asset. The community worker's job is, by definition, not to be a 'manager' in the sense of controlling other people as the essence of community work is to enable the community to manage its own affairs rather than to entrust that task to a professional. However, the reality of practice is that a community worker will need to have a certain level of management competence, if only to help a community-based organisation to set itself up on a sound footing.

Management therefore remains an important role and some management skills are necessary in the organisation of community-based services. Community workers may well find themselves in a management position having to deal with issues like the performance appraisal of staff, building an effective team, helping an organisation to define its goals and objectives, deciding on an appropriate allocation of responsibilities within the organisation, making sure there is good communication between different people, dealing with conflicts and tensions and ensuring that appropriate authorisation is obtained before certain decisions are taken (especially those involving money). These processes may be undertaken very differently in a community-based organisation if compared with a larger conventional organisation, but the management role remains important.

The principle of 'community management' requires that it be the community that effectively manages the organisation and this means that highly participatory models of management will be more appropriate. However, the community worker will inevitably be involved not simply in establishing community management structures but in some aspects of the management process itself.

Many of the skills of community management are subsumed under the other skills discussed in this chapter, such as interpersonal skills and group skills. But it is also important for a worker to have skills in such things as decision making, staff management, financial management and record-keeping, if only so that these skills can be shared with community members who will, it is hoped, take over such responsibilities in due course.

Financial control

The final technical role is that of financial control. Even with a highly devolved structure of local community autonomy, there is still an important need for adequate financial record-keeping, accountability for expenditure and budgetary control. A community worker has an important role to play in assisting the community to make sure that appropriate mechanisms are in place for this to happen and may play some role in the actual operation of control systems. This is often an area where a community worker will have little background or experience and it may be appropriate to seek the assistance of someone with accounting expertise. Ideally that expertise can be obtained from within the community, though that will not always be the case.

As with management, financial control may be achieved in a very different way from more conventional accounting practices, which are better suited to traditional organisations. But despite the differences, with a community-based organisation there is still a need for financial accountability and for mechanisms to ensure that financial resources go where they are intended to and are not lost or misappropriated.

This can be a very real issue for an employed community worker, who in some instances may be legally liable if funds are misspent or misappropriated. In addition, a financial scandal can be disastrous for a community group struggling to be innovative and creative in its work; a scandal can engender public mistrust in the project and the people involved, lead to calls for its closure and set the cause of community development back many years. For these reasons, despite the fact that financial control may seem to be conservative, controlling, disempowering and 'old paradigm', it is essential that community workers deal with the issue adequately and ensure that appropriate (and one hopes also community-based) control mechanisms are in place.

Developing skills

Community work skills cannot be learned from a practice manual nor can they be learned in a classroom. This is not to say that practice manuals and classroom teaching are irrelevant—indeed, they can be very important in exposing people to new ideas and in beginning the process of skills development.

Rather than *learning* community work skills, it is more appropriate to talk about *developing* those skills. This implies not that skills are universally common attributes to be acquired (like the skill of riding a bicycle) but that community work skills will be different for each individual worker and that each worker will both define and acquire them in a unique way. The responsibility is on the worker themself to develop the skills, rather than on a teacher, trainer or supervisor to impart the skills to the worker. Community work skills are developed as part of one's practice because community work is in essence more of an art than a science. It does not proceed along predictable paths—the community worker is constantly faced with new situations and with the need to adapt and change in different and creative ways. In making such adaptations there is always a lot of 'flying by the seat of the pants' and quick (often intuitive) decisions as well as coping with uncertainty rather than predictability. In such a form of practice, one's experience, practice wisdom, creativity, initiative, intuition, imagination and *informed* 'gut reaction' are often more important than specifically defined and learned skills. These qualities, in the final analysis, can be acquired only through experience and through an accumulation of critically reflective practice. It is through such experience and reflection that a community worker will develop (and constantly refine) skills and each worker will do this in a different way, consistent with their own personality, style and ideology. Education and training can open up various possibilities and can suggest potentially productive directions as well as potential pitfalls, but it is up to the individual to develop their own unique skills.

There are five important components of the process of skills development, each of which is critical in helping a community worker to establish their own particular variant of community work skills. They are: *analysis, awareness, experience, learning from others* and *intuition*. Together these amount to an openness to learning and an engagement with reflective practice.

Analysis

Good practice is integrated with good analysis. If one is able to analyse what is happening in, for example, the complex process of a community meeting, one is much more likely to be able to intervene appropriately and constructively in that process. In order to be able to analyse, the community worker needs relevant theoretical frameworks from a variety of disciplines, which can help them make sense of what is going on, whether at the micro-level of a small meeting or the macro-level of national and transnational politics. Some relevant frameworks have been developed in earlier chapters of this book, but there are others that a community worker will be able to find and adapt to a particular practice context.

The significance of analysis as a component of skills development is that it emphasises the importance of theory and the need for the intellectual development of the community worker. It also emphasises that skills development in community work goes beyond a simple *training* model to a more comprehensive *education* approach. The *trained* community worker will probably have limited usefulness, but the *educated* community worker can be a powerful force for social change.

Awareness

The second component of skills development is awareness: both self-awareness and an awareness of what is happening in the community.

A high level of self-awareness is essential for community workers. It is important for a worker to understand how others perceive them, and how they characteristically interacts with others. It is also essential for a worker to be aware of their own prejudices, blind spots and idiosyncrasies. The worker must seek opportunities to develop sensitivity and self-understanding. This can be achieved through thoughtful reflection, asking friends or colleagues to provide honest feedback, watching oneself on videotape or participating in some form of group interaction.

Awareness of what is happening externally is just as important as self-awareness. This requires one to be sensitive to others, ready to listen to what they have to say (rather than always pursuing one's own agenda) and able to understand local community politics, culture and traditions. The community worker must be a good listener as well as an activist and organiser—it is far more effective and appropriate to listen to what people have to tell you and reflect it back to them in new ways than simply telling people what to do.

Experience

In community work there is no substitute for experience. Community work is more an art than a science and this requires a community worker to make decisions based on wisdom, understanding and intuition rather than based on abstract universal rules of how to do it. In the final analysis, one can acquire that practice wisdom only through experience and any aspiring community worker is well advised to gain as much experience in community-based organisations as possible.

Anyone contemplating becoming a community worker, therefore, is well advised to become active in one or several community organisations as a way of gaining experience and developing skills. Such organisations include political parties, conservation groups, development and human rights NGOs, welfare groups, women's groups, trade unions, action campaigns, church groups and lobby groups. There is a wide choice, depending on one's particular interests and commitments. It is important in joining such organisations, however, not to become just an ordinary member, but to become an active member, prepared to serve on committees, task forces or action groups. Most organisations are always looking for committed activists and will welcome you with open arms. This provides a potential community worker with a wealth of relevant experience, the opportunity to learn from mistakes and to develop skills in small groups, meetings, lobbying, 'playing politics' and so on.

There are two important factors to be remembered here. First, it is possible to develop skills through experience only if one is able to develop analysis and awareness as described above. Many activists in community organisations remain ineffective because they do not have the perspective to learn from their experiences and develop their skills. The capacity to do that comes from analysis and awareness—experience by itself is insufficient. The second factor is the conservatism and 'old paradigm' nature of many community organisations. The vision of the earlier chapters of this book is not always well articulated in such groups. A traditional political party, for instance, is not a good example of a cooperative, non-violent organisation. A community worker seeking experience must be careful not to become co-opted (or corrupted) by conservative organisations. By all means use them as a way of gaining essential experience, but it is important to keep sight of the alternative vision and to maintain one's critical perspective in terms of the principles outlined in earlier chapters.

Learning from others

There is no substitute for experience and an essential part of that experience is observing how others work and discussing this with them. Watching a skilled 'operator' in a committee meeting, for example, can be a very good way to develop one's skills. It is always worth observing closely the work of an experienced and 'skilled' community worker and talking to them about what they are doing and why. Often that community worker will be unable to explain it very clearly, which is an indication of how an experienced worker effectively internalises knowledge, wisdom and skills.

In learning from others, however, it is important to remember that each community worker is different and that what works for one will not work for another. Attempting to copy slavishly the style and methods of another worker is likely to lead to disaster, as many aspiring Alinskys have found; one can work in the style of Alinsky (1969, 1971) only if one has the personality of Alinsky and (perhaps fortunately) there are very few who do.

Intuition

Making decisions on the basis of intuition, rather than by using more 'rational' conscious procedures, has often been criticised as 'unscientific' and as resulting in a bad decision that has not been properly thought out. But in real life most of our everyday decisions are made on the basis of intuition, or what feels to be right at the time, and more often than not those decisions are good ones. Trusting one's immediate judgement or 'gut feeling' often turns out to be a wise course of action and one often regrets having had 'second thoughts' and not pursuing one's 'hunches'. The reason for this, of course, is that intuition is not random. Making an intuitive decision is simply relying on various principles, feelings, values and experiences that are so thoroughly internalised that one becomes unconscious of their contribution to decision making. This does not make them any less valuable—there is a degree of rationality about them that leads to intuitive decisions often being better than those made on the basis of more formalised considerations based on conscious deliberation.

Intuition should not be undervalued; it has an important role in skills development (England 1986). It is a primary source in determining what to do and how to do it. In valuing intuitive understandings and insights, however, it is important to try to understand the source of this intuition—in this way intuition relates closely to self-awareness. If, for example, one's values, knowledge and life experience are heavily influenced by racism, then one's intuitive judgements are also likely to have racist elements. It is not enough simply to trust to intuition—one must seek to understand the source of those intuitive judgements and subject them to critical reflection as discussed above. One should not deny the importance of intuition, but one should seek to understand it and how it affects one's decisions.

Demystifying skills

There is nothing special, unique or remarkable about the actual skills of a community worker. They are not like the skills involved in, say, flying an aircraft, performing a surgical operation or programming a computer, in that they do not involve a specialised activity outside the experience of most of the population. Rather, community work skills involve such basic activities as talking to others (often very informally), listening to what people have to say, being an effective part of a group, organising and making decisions. These are things that are part of everyday life, which people have learned to do since they were very young. Thus, at one level everyone can be regarded as having the basic skills necessary for community work and community workers do not have to learn new activities in order to become effective. The important thing is how they are able to use those basic human skills they have already acquired. To become a community worker you do not have to be taught to do anything new or different, you just have to understand and use in a particular way the skills you have already developed from life experience.

Unfortunately, as with other occupations or roles in human services, community work skills have often been mystified by jargon or by complicated diagrams and models so that they sound more 'precious' and special than they really are. This is one of the consequences of professionalisation (discussed in Chapter 12) that serves to disempower rather than to empower many who might see themselves as potential community workers. It also tends to limit the extent and effectiveness of skill-sharing, which will be discussed below.

An important task for community workers therefore is to seek every opportunity to demystify the idea of community work skills. This can be done by refusing to use jargon and by seeking every possible opportunity to express ideas in ordinary language. Thus, one could talk about 'deciding what to do' instead of 'planning an intervention strategy', 'helping people to agree' instead of 'facilitating consensus', 'using' instead of 'utilising', and 'planning' instead of 'strategic planning'. Technical terms can be useful—when they have a precise meaning that cannot readily be expressed in other words or when they provide a common language for practitioners meeting to discuss their work (as long as everybody present knows the code). But jargon is often a form of pretentious language that serves only to reinforce the power of those who understand what it means and to disempower those who do not. As such it is directly in conflict with the aims of community development and has no place in the practice of a community worker.

Using straightforward language serves to make the skills and ideas of community development more accessible to more people and makes them seem less special, precious and expert. It also reflects reality. If one examines the way community workers spend most of their time, one finds it is spent on many very 'ordinary' activities: getting to know other people, setting up meetings, innumerable phone calls, talking to people—whether individually or in small groups—and seemingly endless cups of tea, lunches, informal chats and so on. To use technical, professionalised jargon for such activity makes community work sound much more precious than it really is and can serve primarily to flatter the egos of those community workers who see themselves as 'professionals'.

This is not to say that community work is necessarily easy, or that anyone can do it. Community work is difficult, demanding and challenging and is not for everyone. But what makes it so is not the technical difficulty of the actual task, but rather the essentially problematic and contradictory context of community development in modern societies, the competing and excessive demands placed on a worker, and the political, moral, ethical and value issues that are involved. It is these, rather than the technical aspects of doing the job, which tend to result in worker burnout, feelings of inadequacy, disillusionment, tension, conflict and disagreement for community workers. Most people possess the basic skills to do community work, though of course there is always room for improvement and refinement. It is how those skills are used that can cause problems.

Skill-sharing

One of the problems about identifying the skills of a community worker is that the very act of defining skills can locate the community worker as separate and apart from the rest of the community. If the worker is seen as having special skills the implication is that other community members do not and this leads to a special status for the community worker as the 'expert'. It is then only a small step to a model of community work based on professional expertise, which can become a power game for the community worker and can effectively disempower the very community the worker is supposed to be empowering. An empowerment perspective requires a particular approach to skills—one that is contrary to the way in which skills are understood in the conventional professional model.

A professional approach will emphasise the exclusivity of skills, seeing them as attributes of someone who has been professionally trained. If skills can be clearly defined, there are likely to be mechanisms (whether formal or informal) to ensure that the 'unqualified' are not allowed to 'practise' and that the skills concerned are perceived as exclusively the province of a professional elite. This is seen most strongly in the medical and legal professions and to varying degrees in other professions such as accountancy, engineering, psychology, nursing and the therapies.

The empowerment perspective, however, emphasises skill-sharing as the more important approach. Instead of restricting the learning and application of particular skills to a professional elite, skills are shared with as wide a group as possible. The skills of community development need to be defined and constructed in such a way that they can be understood by everybody and can be learned not just by a community worker, but by other community members. The role of the community worker is to ensure that she/he does not have exclusive possession of a set of skills, but rather uses all the skills within the community, and helps others to acquire whatever skills the community worker may have. Many community workers have defined their purpose as to make themselves redundant by this process of skill-sharing, and this can be seen as the ultimate end of the empowerment process.

For this reason the skills of a community worker must be seen in the same light as the skills of other people in the community: to be shared with others in a mutual learning exercise and used for the purpose of community development. This also means that a community worker will seek in practice the opportunity to learn additional skills from other community members—skill-sharing cannot be a one-way process, as this would only reinforce the community worker in a position of perceived power. If a community worker is able to value the skills of community members, and is genuinely able to learn from them, skill-sharing can become a foundation for the kind of dialogical practice discussed in earlier chapters.

Critical questioning roles and skills

Doing community work is not an easy or straightforward task; many conflicts, dilemmas and problems will confront a community worker and the nature of the work is such that there are usually no easy answers. However, there are questions a community worker will need to address in order to resolve them including *conflict, information and communication* and *laws and regulations.*

A health centre mural, designed and painted by community members to reflect the centre's aspirations for community-based services

Some of the major conflicts, dilemmas and problems are related to *values and ethics* and to *moral and ethical dilemmas* including *conflicts with the community, conflicts with employers or funding bodies, issues of information and communication* and *laws and regulations*.

Values and ethics

Community work, by its very nature, cannot be a value-free, technical activity. The very act of community work implies certain values, such as that of community itself, and the values of democracy, participation, self-determination and so on. More specifically, the model of community development derived in earlier chapters implies a number of value positions arising from the ecological and social justice/human rights perspectives. The first seven chapters of this book established such a value base for community work. There are also a number of values that are either implicit or explicit in the practice principles of Chapter 10 and it is equally clear that there are other value positions that are antithetical to this approach to community work, such as racism, sexism, violence and competition.

Personal values

Any community worker will approach the task with a set of personal values in addition to those which 'come with the job'. Some of these may well be seen by others to be opposed to community work values, which can be a cause of major conflict for a community worker. For example, while it might be argued that one's views on abortion need not conflict with the values of community work, there are many who would disagree with such a stance. A community worker who took a strong 'pro-life' position would be likely to earn the condemnation of many fellow workers who would see this as reinforcing gender oppression. Another worker who strongly advocated the opposite view would be unlikely to win the respect of, for example, a traditional Roman Catholic community and might be accused of not endorsing a basic human right, thus questioning their commitment to other human rights. In either case, the worker's capacity to work as an effective community worker would be seriously compromised.

There are no easy solutions to such value conflicts, but there are ways in which they can be more effectively managed. It is important for a community worker to be very aware of their own values, which is part of being a critically reflective practitioner. It is also important to understand how these values might conflict with the values of people in the community and with the values of one's fellow workers. This can result in a more considered approach to the way one communicates one's values. Sometimes it is better to keep quiet about particular issues, especially if one believes that others are not able to listen and accept what one has to say. At other times it may be important to communicate one's personal values clearly and openly. Here it would be necessary to think carefully and reflectively about how this might best be done rather than jumping straight onto a soapbox.

The imposition of values

Another important value issue is that relating to the imposition of one's values on a community, especially when one is working with a disempowered group on a consciousness-raising model. As discussed in Chapters 7 and 10, the way to deal with this is to make sure that the relationship is a genuinely dialogical one rather than an uneven relationship of domination. But that is an effective answer at only one level. At another level, community work *is* about imposing particular values on a community, namely the values of community development. Community development requires certain value positions, such as the value of participatory democracy, non-violent change, social justice, human rights and ecological sustainability. In this sense, community work is a process of advocating and imposing certain values and a community worker need not be apologetic about it or pretend that this is not so.

For this reason, it is important for a worker to make a clear distinction between those values that are inherent in community development and those that are not. It is entirely legitimate to seek to impose the former while it is clearly unacceptable to impose the latter. The community worker must be able to think through these value dilemmas clearly and have a good analysis of what values are critical to the community development process and what values are essentially personal and must not be imposed on others. This is not always an easy distinction to make—it might be argued that it is a false dichotomy and amounts to a separation of the personal and the political in terms of the community worker's personal life. However, if one is concerned to promote 'community development' while at the same time not disempowering others by imposing one's values on them, one must make such a distinction as a guideline for practice.

Moral and ethical dilemmas

Value conflicts in practice are often defined in terms of ethical dilemmas. Although there is no formal code of ethics for community workers (unless they are acting as members of a profession such as social work, law or psychology), a number of ethical principles are implied by the discussion in earlier chapters. An ethical dilemma requires a worker to make a moral judgement about what is the 'right' way to behave in a certain situation; it is more than just a value conflict because an ethical dilemma carries with it the notion of obedience to a moral law or a conflict between moral laws. The moral/ethical dilemmas that commonly confront community workers can be grouped into four categories.

1. CONFLICTS WITH THE COMMUNITY

Dilemmas can arise when the expressed values of a community, which may have been determined through a participatory democratic process, directly conflict with a worker's values or with ecological or social justice/human rights principles discussed in Chapters 2 and 3. Three examples serve to illustrate the complexity of these dilemmas. The first is a community that incorporates strong racist values and which, through a process of democratic participation, decides to exclude Indigenous people from the community in some way and seeks the community worker's assistance. The second example, where there is a conflict with an ecological principle, is a coal-mining community struggling to maintain the coal industry as a major employer and wishing a community worker to support its campaign for an environmentally unacceptable coal-fired power station. The third example, where the worker's personal values are offended, is the case of a community worker with a strong commitment to animal rights and animal liberation working in a rural community that is seeking to save its economic base through live sheep exports and the maintenance of an abattoir.

In each case the worker must make a decision about the importance of the value that is being threatened by the community and whether it amounts to a sufficient justification for the worker to take a principled stand and reject the community position by refusing to cooperate in implementing the community's decision. This would be a serious step as it amounts to a betrayal of the fundamental community development value that the community knows best. It represents the worker taking a position of moral superiority and can disempower rather than empower. It is also likely to make the community worker less effective—the worker will be less accepted and trusted by the community and may even run the risk of losing their job. It is therefore a decision that cannot be taken lightly.

In some circumstances a worker is fully entitled to take such a principled stand. The first example, of the racist community seeking to exclude Indigenous people, is an occasion on which one would expect a community worker to take a clear stand against racism and refuse to accept the community's position. The other two examples, however, pose more of a problem for the community worker: to what extent is the worker justified in imposing alternative values on the community by taking a stand on principle? The worker must come to a decision based on an analysis of the importance of the value under threat, the extent of 'damage' that will result if the community has its way, the potential damage to the worker's ability to work with that community, the consequences of compromising the worker's integrity, likely levels of support the worker may receive and the worker's personal strength. In reality, a community worker has to be prepared to make *some* compromises as part of day-to-day work. Local communities can be very conservative and reactionary, and there might be little to be gained and much to be lost by taking a principled public stand on every issue, large or small. A community worker, for example, may choose to tolerate mildly sexist language in order to maintain good working relationships with local councillors. But a worker will not wish to compromise on every issue—some matters are clearly too important to ignore. It might be argued that many community workers are too ready to compromise their principles and that both their integrity and their effectiveness suffer as a result. From a Gandhian perspective, indeed, it is essential to maintain integrity by not compromising principles. So a community worker is faced with a series of moral/ethical dilemmas to which there are no easy or clear-cut solutions; different workers will 'draw the line' at different points. The danger lies with a community worker who fails to recognise these dilemmas and who is unaware of the consequences of such moral choices.

2. CONFLICTS WITH EMPLOYERS OR FUNDING BODIES

Another area of potential conflict is when a community worker, as a result of a genuine participatory process, finds the community taking a position that conflicts with the interests of either the worker's employer or the body that has funded the community project. Often community development programs are established with the tacit assumption that they will not 'rock the boat', but will serve as a mechanism for maintaining stability and reinforcing the existing order. Thus there can be serious constraints on community development; these may be either explicit or implicit. Such constraints are particularly likely when governments are either running or funding community development programs, but they can also apply to non-government employers and funders.

In such a situation, the worker may face considerable pressure to 'make the community change its mind', and as a result the worker's job and the program itself may be at risk. Again the worker is required to make a moral decision, often in the face of considerable pressure to compromise on an issue of principle. The central issue is whether the community worker (and the community development project) is *primarily* accountable to the employing or funding body or to the community itself. From a community development perspective, the answer must clearly be the latter, although the worker obviously has an important level of accountability to the employer or funder. But such decisions in practice are never easy and the realities of the situation may make it inappropriate for a worker to take an 'all or nothing' stand. Sometimes the extent of compromise required is small and the worker may feel able to negotiate an acceptable change without sacrificing the integrity of the program. At other times the issue may be such that the worker feels there is no alternative to making a firm stand.

A good community worker will often be able to avoid such conflicts by anticipating them and by working to ensure that they do not reach crisis point. Ideally the community group will be made aware of the potential conflict so that the community itself can take responsibility for the decision and can plan its program bearing in mind likely risks to both the worker and the program itself. It then becomes the community's issue, rather than the worker's, and it may be possible for the worker to distance themself to some extent in the perception of the employer or funder. Also the worker could have clarified the situation with the employer or funder and sought to negotiate an acceptable position.

Often when a community worker is 'caught in the middle' in this way it is as a result of the worker taking responsibility for what is really someone else's problem. A community worker needs to ensure that they are not made the scapegoat for problems that really belong elsewhere—in this case with the community or with the employer/funder. Part of the empowerment of a community must be to enable the community to take responsibility for its own actions and the community worker who allows themself to become the scapegoat for such conflicts is contributing to the community's disempowerment.

Conflicts such as this do not arise in the ideal situation, where a community is actually self-reliant in the way described in Chapter 5 and where the community worker is employed by, and accountable to, the community itself. The need to avoid such conflicts is another argument for the self-reliance model of community development. However, the reality of practice is that a good deal of community work does involve external employers and funders and this is an important area of potential conflict for most community workers.

3. ISSUES OF INFORMATION AND COMMUNICATION

A number of moral and ethical dilemmas can arise around issues related to information and communication. For example, a community worker may learn that a trade union or protest group is planning an illegal action and so will have to make a decision about whether to inform the police or other authorities. A community worker may come across evidence of corrupt practices by local officials and need to determine whether to expose this corruption. There are occasions when a community worker has to balance the expectations of confidentiality (often implicit rather than explicit) with the general good in deciding whether to 'go public' on an issue or not.

Because the community worker works with information of varying kinds, the politics and ethics of communication are very important and dilemmas of this type are likely to arise. While the issue is sometimes clear-cut—as might be the case, for example, with serious corruption—at other times the decision will be rather more difficult and carefully established relationships of trust and confidence may be threatened for little real benefit. Confidentiality is an important value when dealing with personal issues, but when one moves to the political dimension 'confidentiality' can turn into secrecy and conspiracy. If community work is indeed about linking the personal and the political, there will inevitably be conflicts in this area. As a general rule with the notion of non-violence and openness, it is better for a worker to be open and honest and not to engage in conspiracies of silence or secrecy; the worker would then need to establish a strong justification before breaking this rule. Even if some immediate relationships might suffer, it is generally better in the long term to maintain one's integrity and not compromise on issues of principle. To do otherwise is to use corrupt means to achieve one's ends, which, from a Gandhian perspective, will inevitably corrupt both the end and the worker in the process.

As with other ethical issues, the reflective community worker will often be able to avoid such conflicts by being aware of the politics and ethics of information and by setting guidelines in interactions with others. This can be achieved by being clear with other people about one's position and responsibilities and by explaining what will happen to any information the worker receives. Above all, establishing a reputation for honesty and integrity will do much to prevent a worker from being caught in such a dilemma.

4. LAWS AND REGULATIONS

Community workers can be faced with the question of the extent to which they are bound to obey laws, rules and regulations. While a community worker is under an obligation to obey the law, and to work within the lawful regulations of governments, local authorities and funding bodies, there are two occasions when a community worker may feel justified in taking a different position.

The first is where it can be argued that the law or regulation is unjust or oppressive, and where disobeying the law is a conscious act of civil disobedience (Herngren 1993). This is most likely to occur as part of a development process where social action is undertaken in order to bring about change. Sometimes as part of that action there will be a deliberate decision (for example, to trespass on 'private' property) as has been the case with many environmental or peace protests. Sometimes this will also involve deliberate acts of 'vandalism' such as the painting of slogans on the side of a visiting warship. On other occasions it may be appropriate to hold an 'illegal' demonstration or street march. Sometimes public servants have felt morally compelled to break government regulations by releasing information they believe the public has a right to know and this can apply to a community worker as well.

In making such a decision, those involved are taking a conscious risk of arrest and conviction and for this reason alone the decision must not be taken lightly. There are three questions that must be carefully considered before deciding to break the law as part of community development.

1 Is there a strong moral justification for breaking the law in this particular circumstance?
2 What are likely to be the personal consequences for those involved in the action?
3 What will be the public consequences in terms of whether the cause will be advanced, public perceptions, favourable or adverse publicity and so on?

A community group and a community worker must be satisfied on each of these criteria before embarking on such a venture.

The other occasion when breaking laws or regulations can be justified is of quite a different nature. Many laws and regulations are commonly broken out of necessity or simple common sense; indeed Lipsky (1980) has argued that it is only as a result of rule breaking and rule bending that many bureaucracies are able to survive and provide an adequate public service. Community workers and community groups will inevitably be involved in such 'benign' rule breaking as a matter of course. Examples might include: not managing to get a formal notice of an annual general meeting in the newspaper within the time specified by the constitution, accepting nominations for a committee after the deadline simply because not enough people had nominated by the closing date, not being able to get an audited financial statement to the local council by the due date and letting an employee take an extra day of sick leave beyond their entitlement. It should be noted that each of these examples could be significant under certain circumstances—for example, if there are contested elections at the annual general meeting, if there is a suspicion of financial mismanagement or if the employee has a poor work record. But in the normal course of events they are not of great significance and amount to the kind of 'normal' rule bending that is unlikely to cause excitement.

A community worker, therefore, needs to be able to exercise a degree of discretion and common sense in deciding whether rule bending or rule breaking can be tolerated. Pedantically sticking to the letter of the law on all occasions can be extremely disempowering for a community group and it is reasonable to expect that there will be some degree of flexibility. However, a community worker must be aware of the problems that can be created by any instance of rule breaking and the dangers that are always present—particularly if one is working in a program that is controversial and has attracted some powerful opposition. Under such circumstances any breach of the regulations, however technical, may be seized on by one's opponents; in such a case it is simply good tactics to be scrupulous in observing all rules and regulations to the letter.

Summary

Moral and ethical dilemmas such as those described above are never easy to resolve and there are no moral principles that can be readily applied in all circumstances. In each case the worker needs to make a moral judgement, which will be based on both moral principles and practical exigencies. There are, however, some general points that can be made.

1 It is important to have clearly thought through one's moral justification for any action and to have a set of guiding principles such as those outlined in earlier chapters. The worker who does not have such a background is likely to make inappropriate decisions.
2 The decision must be based on a realistic assessment of the situation at hand, including the likely consequences for the people involved, the worker and the community program.
3 Many potential ethical conflicts can be avoided if the community worker is aware of the dangers and is able to set clear rules and expectations for themself and for others.

4 Where possible, the community should own and deal with the moral/ethical dilemma rather than making the community worker the scapegoat.
5 Principles of openness, honesty, integrity and non-violence must underpin all ethical decisions and these must be violated only if the worker is convinced that there are strong moral and practical reasons for doing so.

The use and abuse of power

There is a fundamental paradox for a community worker in relation to the worker's power. The community worker, as a result of their training, education and experience, possesses knowledge and skills that can be very influential in community processes and hence has a good deal of power—or at least potential power—to influence the community. On the other hand, the community development perspective requires that power not be wielded by specific individuals such as community workers, but be located within the community itself; the good community worker must be able to let go of power or it is possible that the worker will become part of the problem rather than part of the solution. The more skilled, experienced and effective a community worker is, the more they will be able to work against the very processes and structures that community work aims to establish. In other words, the more effective the worker becomes, the more the community could be disempowered in the process and the more the worker could be setting back the process of community development. This paradox raises the whole issue of power and emphasises how important it is for a community worker to be aware of the nature of power in the community and the potentially exploitative nature of community work knowledge and skills, especially when constructed within a paradigm of professionalism.

Professions, as Illich has argued (Illich et al. 1977), tend to mystify, alienate and disempower the users of services. The professional model sees knowledge and skills as the exclusive property of the professional and works against them being accessible to others, either formally through registration and certification or informally through mystification and jargon. The professional is seen as the expert and this serves to undervalue the expertise of the service user, which will be more securely based in the local culture but not legitimised with the trappings of formal qualifications, professional journals, certification, conferences and so on. Thus the relationship between professional and service user is one of unequal status and power. The professional becomes the expert in need definition (Illich et al. 1977; Ife 1980), which effectively denies the service user the right to define their own needs in their own way.

This approach to professionalism is contradictory to community development.

In the sense of a professional commitment to a shared value and ethical position, there are more grounds for supporting a professional model of community work. Thus one might wish community workers, although not being members of a body called a profession, nevertheless to act 'professionally'. In this sense, being professional implies the importance of values and ethical integrity as a basis for practice; this is surely an admirable quality in any community worker. This has led some writers (Andrews 1992; Wilding 1982) to argue for a redefinition of professionalism to incorporate its perceived benefits while rejecting its undesirable baggage.

But there are problems even with this approach to professionalism as a basis for community work practice. Many professionals relate to their perceived common value/ethical base as a fact of life and a parameter of practice, rather than as being an ideal or a vision to which they are passionately committed and in which they deeply believe. Indeed many professionals are more concerned with being competent than with being passionate, especially given the current dominance of the discourse of professional competency, and the worker who shows 'too much' passion and commitment is often seen as naïve, unstable or not sufficiently 'balanced'. Such a balanced, detached, clinical approach is largely ineffective in community work. One needs to be passionate and committed, with a sense of vision that is rather more internalised and fundamental than a professional's commitment to a code of ethics. For a community worker, the value base takes on a much stronger and more personal meaning than it does for most professionals. Coupled with this is the dilemma, discussed in previous chapters and earlier in this chapter, of how to engage in a process of development and consciousness-raising without imposing one's own values on the community. This is also a question of the way a community worker will use or misuse power.

There are three ways in which a worker can seek to overcome this contradiction. The first is through self-awareness. A good community worker will have a high degree of self-insight, will be aware of the dangers of the misuse of power and will be constantly reflecting on the power relations involved in community work practice; this is essential to effective community work. Such self-awareness, though important, is not sufficient as the worker must also be able to take effective action to prevent such problems occurring but it is an essential prerequisite for the other two safeguards.

The second safeguard is to ensure that decisions, processes and programs are not the result of the worker's individual initiative, but are controlled and owned by the community. Thus community work is not a case of a worker 'doing things to' a community, but rather is a case of the worker and other community members doing things together. This is done within a context of open and honest communication so that the worker is not tempted to conceal specific motives or objectives and is open with the community about just what they are doing and why. If decisions are taken as a result of a genuinely dialogical relationship between the community worker and community members, and open communication is always maintained, the chances of a community worker becoming a manipulator and a power broker are greatly reduced.

The third way in which this paradox of power can be resolved is if the community worker is actually seen to be a member of the community itself so that the worker's fortunes are inextricably tied to the fortunes of the community. It is only when a worker is seen as coming from 'outside', in an external interventionist capacity, that the danger of manipulation and power play becomes a problem. If the worker is seen as a community member, they will be subject to the same controls and structures as other community members and will have (and be perceived to have) common interests with the rest of the community.

Long-term commitment

The length of commitment of a community worker, especially of an external worker or a worker who has come to work in a new location, needs to be considered from the perspective of community development as promoted in this book. For an Indigenous worker or a worker who has been a member of that community for many years this is not an issue as their commitment to the community can be assumed to be long term. However, a community worker who is appointed to work with a particular community may not see this as a lifetime commitment and it is important to consider just what degree of time commitment is reasonable and realistic if that worker is to be effective in a community development role.

Community development is not something that can be achieved quickly. It is simply not possible to undertake community work of the type described in this book for a brief period. It can take many months for community development processes to be set in place and several years before they begin to show significant results. It is true that in some circumstances results can be achieved quickly—for example, the setting up of an action group, a campaign to save a valued natural feature of the environment, a better bus service or the building of a community centre. But this is only scratching the surface of the more fundamental process of community work, incorporating the six dimensions of social, economic, political, cultural, environmental and personal/spiritual development. If a community worker really wants to make a significant contribution to a community a commitment of years rather than months is necessary. It is impossible to place an exact figure on the minimum time commitment required as so much will depend on local factors, but any worker who is not prepared to commit at least three years either has utterly unrealistic expectations or does not have a clear understanding of the nature of community development. Even three years will in many cases be too brief a period to achieve anything of lasting significance, though it would be enough at least to get some processes started and perhaps to have stimulated local community leadership to take over the project.

Unfortunately many of the people or organisations that sponsor or administer community development programs do not take this long-term view. There are many projects or consultancies that run for only a few months, usually with an external worker, and these are naïvely expected to make a major difference to the life of a community. Such projects are often futile and result in reports that are seldom used and community structures that do not last. As a result they can give community development a bad name. Communities would be well advised to have nothing to do with such short-term projects unless there are clear and achievable short-term objectives, or unless they can be clearly identified as being just one component of an ongoing and long-term community development process. Such projects or consultancies are often not particularly empowering—they rely on the outside expert and can undermine community autonomy and self-reliance. In addition, they are most likely part of somebody else's agenda rather than meeting a need that has been identified by the community itself.

Contemporary society is in many ways obsessed with the short term. We require instant solutions and immediate results; if something cannot be achieved within a fairly short time span, it is generally not regarded as worth doing. This attitude was identified in Chapter 2 as being associated with ecological unsustainability and the wish to find quick technological solutions to problems that are in reality endemic to the social, economic and political order. Such problems cannot be resolved by quick-fix technology: they require more fundamental and inevitably long-term structural change.

The same is true of community work. It is necessary to move away from the obsession with quick results and realise the need for longer-term processes aimed at more significant change. There is little place for the 'quick and dirty' approach within this model of community work and community development.

Sometimes a worker will have no option but to limit a community work project to a relatively brief period. In such a case it is important for the worker to set clear expectations and limits, for both worker and community, in the light of a realistic assessment of what is achievable. This can itself be difficult as the very setting of such limits is counter to the holistic, developmental approach described in earlier chapters. More importantly, however, the worker can seek to *initiate* community development processes in such a way that they will be able to continue—and to grow—after the worker has left. In many cases this sort of initiation of community development is all that a worker will be able to do.

The worker who *is* able to make a longer-term commitment can be faced with a different problem. In many ways the role of a community worker is eventually to work themself out of a job and to enable the community in due course to take over all its own developmental processes. This means that, while a community worker's commitment is ideally long term, it usually should not be indefinite (the exception being where the community worker is a permanent member of that community). The worker who makes a long-term commitment faces the danger of having such a personal stake in the continuation of the community work role that they are unable to let go, or even recognise when the time to let go has arrived. This again emphasises the critical importance of self-awareness for a community worker.

Securing support

Community work can be a difficult job, but it need never be lonely. Those who see it as a lonely job are probably not taking a realistic view of community work and are almost certainly not seeing the opportunities around them to seek and find support from others. The idea of the lone community worker, struggling in isolation, is anathema to the very basis of community development, which is above all a collective and social activity. The problem for the community worker is often not loneliness and isolation but the reverse—the inability to get away for some time alone for personal reflection and fulfilment.

Despite this, community workers certainly need a good deal of support from others because community work is a challenging and difficult task; it is personally demanding and frustrating, and at times depressing and causes disillusionment. Any community worker will need to develop sources of personal and expert support in order to make sense of the job and for the simple needs of personal survival. This support can come from six different sources: *employers, co-workers, workers in other communities, community members, activist networks* and *personal networks*.

Employers

If a community worker is employed by a government authority or some other external agency, that employer has a responsibility to provide the worker with adequate support, encouragement and assistance. This is of two kinds: logistical support and supervisory support.

Logistical support involves those things that a worker needs in order to do the job, such as a vehicle, office facilities, telephone, fax, computer, stationery and, where appropriate, secretarial or clerical support. While this may seem obvious, it is surprising how often such basic supports represent a problem for community workers who have to spend a good deal of energy fighting to secure these to a reasonable level. It is naturally a particular problem for a worker employed by a small community agency or group that itself has very limited resources; here the worker cannot blame the employer. However, the lack of basic supports can be a blessing in disguise. The worker is forced to seek more imaginative ways of securing such logistical support, often from within the resources of the community itself, and this can be an important step towards the ideal of community autonomy and self-reliance. There may be, for example, someone in the community with typing or secretarial experience who has not had a job for many years and who is happy to help out as a way of relearning the skills needed to seek employment again. Or there may be retired people with particular skills who are more than happy to provide them on a voluntary basis, if only so that they can feel they are still able to make a useful contribution.

Supervisory support is another right that a community worker should be able to expect from an employer. This involves the community worker being able to discuss the job with another, probably more experienced, worker who can help to put the work into perspective and offer useful suggestions. While this may sound fine in theory, it is relatively seldom the case in practice for two important reasons. One is that people in supervisory positions are often not the most appropriate people to offer such supervision (often they are bureaucrats and managers rather than community workers and do not have a good understanding of the actual needs of practice). Indeed the best and most committed community workers—and therefore the ones who should be offering the supervision—are more likely to be out doing community work rather than occupying a supervisory position in a government bureaucracy. The second reason the traditional supervisory model is often inadequate is the varied nature of community work. It varies from worker to worker and from community to community, so it is often inappropriate for one worker to be trying to 'supervise' the work of another. The very idea of external supervision implies that the work of a community worker can be examined and evaluated in isolation from its community context, which is contradictory to the principles of the community-based perspective. Supervision can thus become like the form of 'cookbook' learning described earlier in this chapter. This is not to say that good and appropriate supervision can never be found. It certainly can, especially in non-government organisations, and the community worker who is able to have access to it is indeed fortunate. The problem is that it is relatively uncommon and is much more the exception than the rule.

Co-workers

A community worker will seldom be the only person in the community who has a community work role. There is likely to be a number of people who have closely related roles, even if they do not regard themselves as having the label 'community worker'. They include community health workers, recreation officers, community arts workers, clergy, Indigenous leaders, aged-care workers and some human service professionals such as social workers, teachers, lawyers and medical practitioners who take a community development perspective in their work.

This group represents a good source of support and encouragement for a community worker. It is important to form good working relations with such people and to seek to work together as much as possible. Often such workers will meet on a regular basis for a 'contact lunch' or similar function, the main aim of which is to facilitate communication and to provide a mutual support network. In many ways this group acts as a primary reference group for a community worker, is the group most likely to give a worker constructive feedback and new ideas and is a critical source of emotional and moral support. Such workers often share similar values and are more or less committed to community work principles and ideals, so it is a group that will understand what a community worker is trying to do and is therefore likely to be supportive.

Unfortunately the politics of the local community, or 'welfare politics' in the broader sense, can interfere with the development of such a cohesive group—particularly if the workers concerned see themselves as competing with each other for resources, territory, clients or power. Such competition can divide communities and work against effective community empowerment. It is important for a community worker to work as much as possible to break down such competition and to seek genuine consensus and cooperation. This is easier said than done, but it may prove impossible for a community worker to follow a community development agenda unless at least a majority of such local community workers are working together.

Workers in other communities

Another important source of support is fellow community workers who are working with other communities. One is more likely to be able to obtain support from those with whom one is personally comfortable and from those who share a common practice perspective and a common world view. This gives a worker a wider choice than simply the group of workers in one's own community. It can also be important to find out what is happening in other communities—not necessarily to copy slavishly other people's ideas, but to learn about alternative approaches and seek fresh ideas that might be able to be adapted in one's local situation.

A community worker generally has to seek out such contacts, but for the worker who is prepared to make the effort there are plenty of opportunities, even for those working in isolated communities. At a formal level there are conferences, seminars and training courses. Although these may have a formal program, usually their most useful purpose is to bring workers together and provide an opportunity for them to talk to each other. There are also regular or irregular meetings of community workers involved in particular fields—for example, local government, youth services or aged care. There have also been attempts to form larger organisations of community workers to provide another structure that allows workers to meet.

As well as these formal structures, many community workers are able to maintain contact through more informal meetings such as regular lunches, parties and other social occasions. These can serve the dual purpose of being informative and pleasurable.

It is not necessary, of course, for community workers to find this kind of support only in face-to-face contact. Newsletters can be used as a way of keeping workers in touch with each other and community workers can also make use of various forms of electronic communication, such as teleconferencing, the Internet, online forums and discussion groups and email. While it may be true that modern technology can be disempowering, as discussed in Chapter 2, electronic communication also provides a useful mechanism for community workers to keep in touch with each other—in fact it is particularly important for workers in rural or isolated communities who have limited opportunities to attend conferences or meetings. Such forms of electronic communication can widen the potential network of a community worker greatly, as they can involve communications with community workers all over the world in a wonderfully rich and varied exchange of ideas and perspectives.

Community members

From a community development perspective, the most critical form of support for a community worker will come from the community itself. Indeed, if a worker is not receiving support from the community and sees the community as somehow 'them' rather than 'us', it is likely that the worker is not doing a very effective job. The ideal of the community-based alternative would see the community as being able to provide all necessary supports for its members; this would include the community worker as well.

It is a common experience for a community worker to see community members as the most important, exciting and dynamic people with whom they come into contact and as the people most able to offer support and encouragement. Certainly if this is not the case a community worker should be working to establish a climate in which such support from the community is both possible and usual. Ultimately it is community members to whom a community worker is responsible, with whom the worker will have to work in community development and who have a responsibility to look after and support their community worker. Thus the relationship between worker and community members is a critical one in community work practice and it is also a potential source of immense pleasure, joy and enrichment, as well as support, for the community worker.

If the worker is really to make the most of this potential it is necessary to have a high level of personal commitment to the community and to the community development process, as discussed earlier in this chapter. Although the costs will at times appear high, the rewards can be beyond measure. It is a common experience of community workers, and of all social activists, that the personal investment in a community or a cause is repaid many times over in the rich rewards of personal involvement. As Peter Singer (1993) has argued, such commitment can provide a justification for moral and ethical behaviour in a secular society where for many people life has lost much of its meaning.

Activist networks

Another important source of support for many community workers is their involvement, in a personal capacity, in various organisations or social movements. Community workers by nature tend to be activists and to be committed to various causes aimed at making the world a better place. This means they are often members of activist organisations, including political parties, conservation or Green groups (such as Greenpeace), overseas aid organisations (such as Oxfam), human rights organisations (such as Amnesty International), the peace movement, the women's movement, groups working for Indigenous rights or religious social justice groups.

Active membership in such organisations provides an important form of support for community workers. It provides an opportunity for workers to meet others who share similar values and reinforce their personal commitment to principles such as social justice, human rights and peace, which are critical in community work. It therefore allows the worker to stay grounded in a basic personal commitment, as well as being personally rewarding.

At another level, involvement in such organisations is directly relevant to one's work as a community worker. Many activist organisations rely at least in part on community development principles, such as democratic participation, consciousness-raising, empowerment and action at a small-group level. And all of them are committed to bringing about change that is generally quite consistent with community development principles. Active involvement in such activist organisations thus provides an excellent source of new ideas for a community worker and represents important practical experience. It is also excellent training in how to operate effectively in meetings (both formal and informal) and how to influence organisational change.

Community workers can make a significant contribution to activist organisations. Many such organisations are seeking precisely the skills and expertise a community worker possesses and a good community worker is able to help activist groups in many ways. It is hardly surprising that many staff employed by activist organisations come from a community work background and that many community workers are elected or appointed to positions of responsibility in those organisations.

Personal networks

The final form of support for a community worker comes from that worker's personal networks, such as family, friends, partner and housemates. Because the work can be difficult, stressful and demanding it is essential that a community worker have a good personal support network of people who are sympathetic to what the worker is trying to do and who value and support that worker on a personal level. Many community workers say that their job would be impossible without a high degree of personal support and nurturing from those to whom they are closest.

This raises the issue of the worker looking after themself. There is no point in a worker becoming so committed and involved that they end up with burnout; this serves the interests of neither the worker nor the community. A community worker must, therefore, be able to manage their own life in such a way as to maintain mental health and reduce stress levels to a minimum. How this can be done will depend on the individual worker—there can be no set prescription, simply a reminder to make sure that it is on the worker's personal agenda.

>> discussion questions

1 Work through the case studies presented in earlier chapters. What roles and skills are important in each of these case studies?
2 What are the dangers in taking a 'cookbook' approach to community development roles and skills?
3 What is meant by 'praxis' and what is the importance of the action/understanding relationship for the community worker?
4 In what ways do each of the roles and skills described in this chapter (those within the facilitative, educational, representational and technical clusters) fit into the overall integrated approach to community development—an ecological and human rights/social justice approach?
5 What is involved in *developing* community development skills, in contrast to the idea of *learning* skills?
6 What are the general points to be considered when making moral judgements to resolve moral and ethical dilemmas?
7 What are the issues of power and its potential abuse that must be considered in community work?

>> reflective questions

1 Identify occasions on which you have given yourself some time and space to think about an action you have undertaken. How have you done this reflection? What things have you explored and what questions have you asked yourself? How might these experiences build up your own process and ways of engaging in critical reflection?
2 How would you go about involving the community in your reflective practice and critical reflection on practice?
3 Think about your reactions to your position in relation to skill development: your attitude towards being analytical and your ability to be analytical, your level of self-awareness and awareness of context, your degree of openness to learning from experience and from others and your willingness to trust your intuition. What has helped form these reactions? Which reactions will assist you as a community worker and which may hinder you? What changes may you need to consider to minimise the barriers to your skill development as a community worker?
4 Clarify your own values in relation to community development by reviewing your answers to the reflective questions throughout this book.
5 There will be moral and ethical dilemmas in community development. How have you resolved value or ethical dilemmas in your own life? What have been the criteria you have used in such resolutions?
6 How will you ensure that your awareness is such that you avoid using power exploitatively and do not impose your personal values on a community?
7 Complete the mapping of who you are as a community worker. What does this look like? Describe it to another person and share your personal and professional growth with them.

CHAPTER 12

Practice issues: struggles and journeys in community work

Introduction

Doing community work is not an easy or straightforward task—it can be a journey of struggles and puzzles; of many conflicts, dilemmas and problems, which will confront a community worker and the nature of the work is such that there are usually no easy answers. This chapter identifies some of these practice issues and discusses some of the questions the reflective community worker will need to address in order not to be immobilised by the complexities. The way in which this is approached is through storytelling. Selected stories from my practice are used throughout this chapter to narrate the journeys and struggles. Reflections on these stories illustrate how tensions and conflicts need to be negotiated. The stories and reflections reinforce the message given throughout this book that community work cannot be practised from a recipe-like handbook (a cookbook approach) or a prescriptive framework. Before embarking on the storytelling, I will spend some time explaining strengths-based practice as a critical resource for me in ensuring I maintain an integrated approach to my community work.

In 1981 Rein and White made an important statement about knowledge in social work that is as true for community work as it is for any other discipline:

> The knowledge that social work seeks cannot be made in universities by individuals who presumptively seek timeless, contextless truths about human nature, societies, institutions and policy. The knowledge must be developed in the living situations that are confronted by the contemporary episodes in the field . . . (p. 37)

Knowledge is not static and what appears in books are not grand truths. They are resources that community workers use as they themselves continually generate and regenerate, over and over, knowledge in every living situation of their practice. Therefore, what is to follow in this final chapter is not a prescription for your practice in community development. Rather, I would like to share my journeys and struggles with you and it is my hope that this sharing will reassure you about the importance of process and the normality of uncertainty—not the need for prescription.

Practice frameworks

Every community worker will conceptualise practice in a different way and will build a different practice framework that will develop and continue to change with each living experience. Such a framework is simply the way in which a community worker makes sense for themself what community work is all about. During the course of this book a particular framework has been developed, which makes sense to me and which it is hoped you will find useful. However, there is a danger in a community worker simply adopting this or any other framework uncritically and making it their own. To seek to impose a single framework on all community workers is to fall into the positivist and modernist trap of assuming there is only one 'right' or 'best' way to do community work. This would be contrary to the principle of diversity and the need to establish 'bottom-up' constructions of wisdom, which are central themes of this book. It is important to develop one's own framework—if the ideas here have helped present or future community workers to do that, the book will have served its purpose. The reflective questions at the end of each chapter are designed to enable you to construct *your* identity as a community worker and *your* framework for practice.

It is appropriate at this stage to represent the framework of this book in summary form; this is done in Figure 12.1. The various sections of this diagram can be expanded and this has been done in the diagrams in previous chapters, of which Figure 12.1 represents a synthesis. Using a jigsaw pattern with different sections, and jigsaw pieces within them, emphasises the interconnectedness of the various ideas represented and the importance of a holistic perspective. Each section and each jigsaw piece should be seen as interconnecting—there is no particular significance to be attached to the positioning of one section and one piece in relation to any other. Rather, each segment must be seen as relating to all others, not just those next to it.

'Strengths' as a vehicle for maintaining the visions of integrated community development

The term 'strengths' appears throughout this book. Here I dwell on its special significance. I have found that working from a strengths perspective, rather than from a problem or deficit base, is a most important support in my community work. For me drawing on this approach was a radical departure from my professional training, where I learned that my knowledge was to help others solve their problems. For me there was an intuitive and inherent disconnection between deficit-based practice and community development. The principles of strengths-based work have served to keep me focused on an integrated approach to community development and as a catalyst for alerting me to the complexities of the community work I have engaged in and the need for reflection. A common criticism of strengths-based practice is that it tends to deny problems and therefore discourages people from expressing their pain, frustrations, anger and so on. This criticism is based on a misguided and superficial understanding of strengths.

Since the 1980s, St Luke's in Melbourne has done an immense amount of reflection and work in developing alternative, strengths-based approaches to practice. During this journey, the organisation has questioned its conventional values and has developed some core principles for strengths-based practice

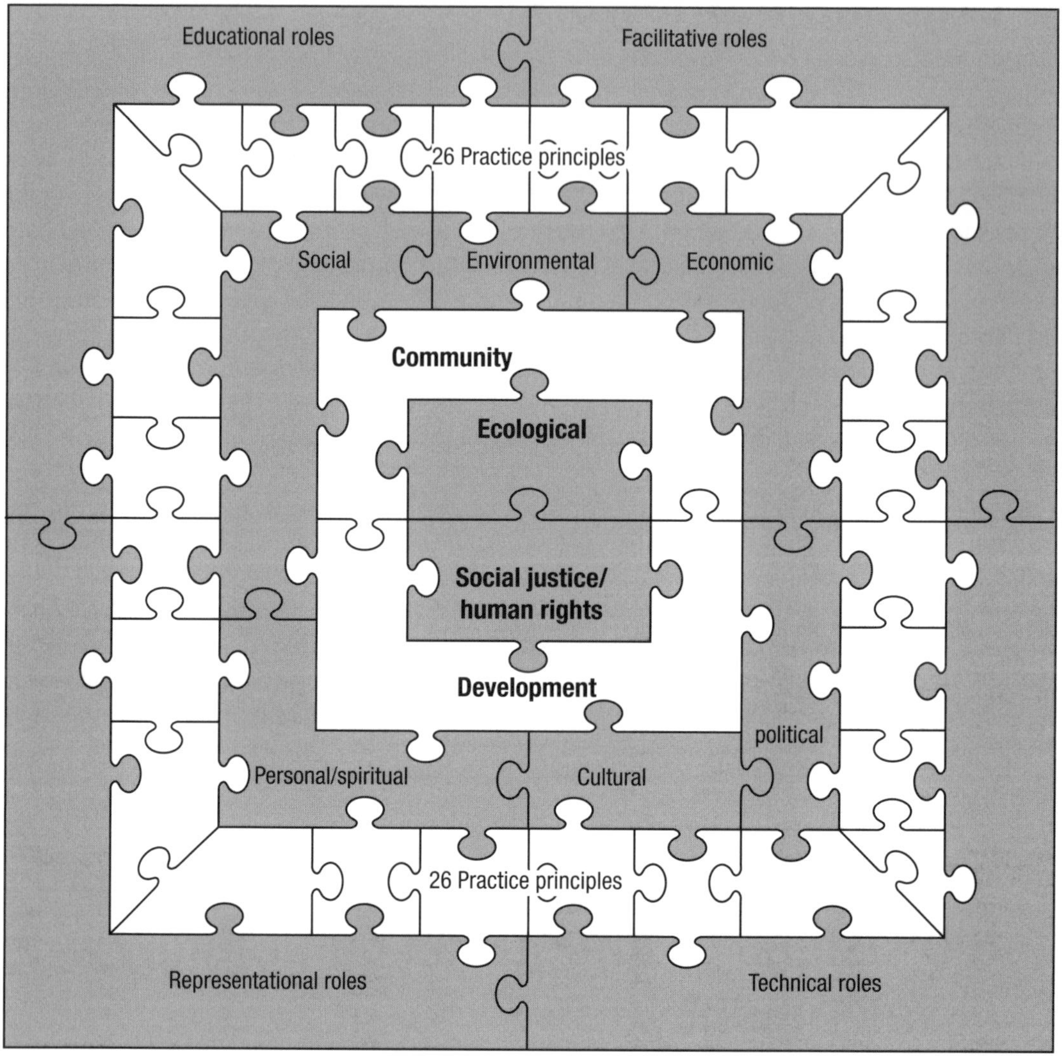

Figure 12.1 A framework for community work

(Beilharz 2002; McCashen 2005). It is worth summarising some of the main principles of strengths-based practice to ensure that the depth and comprehensiveness of the approach is clearly understood.

The strengths perspective is firstly a philosophy, a way of thinking and a way of working that guides practice. It frames how we see communities, the people in them and our relationships with them. It requires that our attitude towards those with whom we work in community development is a positive attitude, which is very congruent with the framework of community development presented in this book and the principles outlined in it. A strengths perspective demands an attitude that acknowledges the inherent human dignity of every person, their capacities and rights, and that respects the diversity and commonalities among people and groups. At the same time it gives agency to people in the change process; it does this not in a patronising way, but by creating the conditions around them which enable them to collectively participate in change and development through mobilising the resources within the community. It gives 'solidarity and agency' (Bhattacharyya 2004: p. 5). The notion of mobilising resources and abilities to create visions and change is crucial. It is a radical alternative to what is much more common, which is focusing on deficits and using professional knowledge and skills to 'fill the gaps' that deficits represent. It is important to know the strengths in a community because people always take some of their past on the change journey, which is a journey of unknowns. If people take part of their past, their strengths will be of far more use than deficits and will represent much more powerful resources to address community issues, needs and aspirations. Because the strengths perspective creates conducive conditions for people to participate in change, it of necessity addresses power imbalances, social disadvantage, exclusion, oppression and marginalisation. The purpose of addressing these issues is closely related to social justice and human rights. It is clear that a strengths perspective can build a belief in people's ability to create change and can build hope, which is realistically based on capacity. People can therefore envision an alternative future for their community, which is possible because it is firmly based in available local skills, knowledge, assets and resources.

Deficit-based practice, on the other hand, is not consistent with the framework for integrated community development developed in this book. A focus on deficits tends to problematise communities, leading to dependency relationships between worker and community and to an expectation that the outside experts will come with solutions. Community leadership is undermined. Efforts are fragmented as they are mobilised to produce many different solutions to the many different problems. Resources often go to service providers, not community (Kretzmann and McKnight 1993). This is a sure recipe for colonialist, imposed, top-down community work. A deficit approach rarely represents a positive development process.

The three narratives and reflections that follow are snapshots of my practice. They are not intended to prescribe how to practise community development (or, regarding the aspects in which we failed, how not to practice). Rather, they are intended to deepen an appreciation of the struggles and complexities of community development processes and outcomes when theoretical frameworks and reality intersect in practice.

Freud's restaurant

I would not have predicted that I would ever engage in community development within the walls of a psychiatric hospital. When I commenced work in the social work department of a psychiatric hospital a colleague asked me if I would take over the men's group he had been running. While this group was part of the day hospital program, its members, numbering about twelve, were from the hospital's long-stay wards. They were mostly diagnosed with chronic schizophrenia and had been in the hospital for a number of years. I was told they were 'chronic schizophrenics'.

It was clear that over time the members had developed a strong identification with their group and they considered their meeting time as a very special part of their week. As they articulated this and the value they placed on their relationships with each other the group became a safe place to encourage each other, share personal experiences in their lives and to reassure each other of their value as friends. They shared many issues, including failures in relationships and frustrations in their struggles to reach their aspirations in their lives. I was aware that I was part of a system that readily labelled and dehumanised people with mental illness. I was also aware of the power of the group members, through their interactions in the group, and ensured that I was constantly mindful of their dignity, humanity, pain and strength and their immense ability and commitment to support and nurture each other.

Often the men would express a view of being controlled by their illnesses. They saw themselves as disadvantaged, stigmatised and discriminated against in many areas, including accommodation and employment. They expressed anger and frustration at experiences of being evicted, ridiculed and rejected for jobs. At the same time, there was also a sense of resignation—that this was indeed their lot. They felt powerless and helpless to change the conditions in which they found themselves. Some saw that the only hope lay in a cure for their illness, but the prospect of this was distant. I would respond with understanding but always challenge the men to find alternatives in their day-to-day experiences of frustration. Their ability to engage in relationships was evident in their group participation. When they were angry at other patients 'bludging' their cigarettes, I would explore alternative responses, no matter how limited their choices may have been. The important thing was that they were faced with choices, once conditions around them enabled them to have these choices. I attempted to maintain a theme in the group that challenged their identity as helpless and powerless. On one occasion a group member's teenage son had been lost, and then found dead, in one of the deserts in Central Australia. The son had been working on a large farm and had become lost. The reassurance and support given by other members over the course of the group session was inspirational and I reflected with them on the very significant human qualities they were able to bring to bear on a very sad and distressing experience.

After one year, I reviewed the group by asking members to write down what they thought they had gained from the group and what they would like in the future. One of the things in the list of what they would like was to have books about interpersonal relationships in the patient library. The review presented yet another opportunity to reinforce the abilities of the men and their part in the development of their group. However, it was the request for books that dramatically changed the direction of the group. We visited a specialist bookshop and the men browsed and listed the books they wished to have. I then submitted this list to the hospital's volunteer coordinator. One group member followed this up with the coordinator and was told that it was not possible to have those books in the patients' library because the information in them may upset the doctor–patient relationship. In other words, that knowledge was for professionals, not psychiatric patients! When this was reported back to the group the response was anger. I explored the anger with the men and amidst animated and heated discussion we began to discuss the issue as a violation of their right to have access to information and knowledge. They tried to get the volunteer coordinator to attend a meeting. After several apologies, the coordinator did not materialise, but a cheque arrived for the amount needed to buy the books. We went to a local coffee lounge to celebrate their victory. They had won the right to information. 'What shall we fight for next?' was the question raised. The first response was 'the right to work'. From here the discussion led to their resolve that they would not fight for the right to work, but they would work! A number of the men had worked in hospitality as waiters, a chef and a restaurant manager. They decided they would open a restaurant and it would be called 'Freud's'. Eventually the group was successful in opening their restaurant which ran as a small business for three years. The process of development was both a struggle and an inspiration.

The group formed an organising committee. They carefully planned all that they needed to do to establish their restaurant. Their search for funding was a long struggle, but they were persistent and their actions included meeting with the Minister of Health. They activated many of their old professional networks and I assisted them to establish new contacts. They negotiated with the hospital for space in a heritage building on the campus. They met with resistance along the way, but they remained powerful. For example, once the Minister of Health declared his support after their meeting with him, the hospital much more readily gave the resources needed. They were also met with rules. Once they got permission to paint the interior of their space, the hospital painters declared that only union members could do painting in the hospital. The group agreed but insisted that they would carry the cost of the painting. This debt was eventually paid back with great dignity. They approached cotton mills for tablecloth material, paint retailers for paint, old contacts for used kitchen equipment. In this way they accumulated all the equipment they needed for their venture. Alongside their planning, they had long discussions about the other people in their wards. They wanted the project to include anyone who wished to participate. They knew the abilities of many of the people were limited, but they saw opportunities for others to gain some self-esteem, be more active and learn some skills. The group divided into subgroups—one to continue the restaurant planning and the other to work with other people in the wards, to talk with them, encourage them and to identify roles they could play. They decided all profits would be shared among the workers and they incorporated under state government legislation as the Eastwood Workers Cooperative.

Over the time the restaurant operated, it was open for lunch every day and for dinner for special functions. There were several large evening functions catered for, but the main activity was lunch. Their patrons included other patients, hospital staff (both clinical and administrative) and patrons from the general community. The group saw themselves as having two main ongoing functions: operating the restaurant and training and supporting other people from their wards.

Over time the hospital raised a number of issues that had severe impacts on the restaurant. One major issue was insurance. The hospital finally made a decision that people from outside the hospital were not covered by insurance and so the scope of the restaurant to remain viable shrank. Other such issues impinged on the project and together these compounded to finally force the project to finish. In the last four months, the group worked without personal income because they had decided that they would finish the project with no debts and their last priority was to repay the loans and other debts. After the project, relationships remained strong and some participants commenced other educational ventures, including one man who enrolled in a university course and successfully completed it.

Reflections on Freud's

When I first commenced work at the psychiatric hospital, community development was not part of my role description and I did not envision working with people in the hospital to develop a stronger, more supportive community. However, opportunism has always been a feature of my practice—opportunism within clear principles and values. This 'tight–loose' framework allows me to seek unexpected opportunities for community development towards human wellbeing. I saw this opportunity early in my time at the hospital. I was clear from the outset that my practice would challenge those aspects of the system that maintained dependency and which labelled people and related to them according to those labels. I was not interested in diagnoses. I wanted to support the members of a group to reach their aspirations. I knew this would create and build tensions within the system.

My initial response to the men's idea of opening a restaurant was fear and a sense of being out of control. The tensions emanating from my professional training began to surface. What did I know about business and the hospitality industry? What would be the response of the hospital authorities to a demand from a group of patients to open a small business? Power and control issues rose to the surface in my practice. Embarking on something I knew nothing about would mean a loss of my power. But I had to interrogate my own needs and prescriptions from my professionalisation and how I was becoming blind to the skills and knowledge of the group members. They were the experts; I did not have to be the expert in hospitality. These people were capable and they had the right to have their capacities recognised and be the resources with which they could participate in reaching their aspirations. My responsibility, from a human rights perspective, was to acknowledge and value their expertise. My roles were support, building consensus in the decision making that would ensue and group facilitation in the forthcoming planning meetings, which the soon-to-be-formed organising committee would convene. The apparent power of the mental health system seduced me into a sense of powerlessness. This did not have to be. My skills were in mobilising the resources of the group as a collective, assisting them to obtain external resources and using media, advocacy and engaging with systems to ensure they supported, rather than thwarted, the men's aspirations. I reminded myself that at the core of this campaign was a struggle by a group that was oppressed, disadvantaged and stigmatised to fight for social justice and their right to reach their aspirations. From this perspective, their vision for an alternative future became compelling. It represented community development because, if successful, the restaurant would be a structure within the hospital community that could support people and create radical alternatives for their personal identities and their sense of contribution and belonging. As my immediate supervisor was a senior psychiatrist, I found trusted social work colleagues to discuss my situation, my tensions, my puzzles, my values and practice frameworks and what these implied for the paths ahead.

Still, it was difficult for me to imagine that the restaurant would eventuate. My mind entertained the interface of this small oppressed group and the complex systems it would have to negotiate: the hospital, the health system, legislative requirements and obtaining expensive equipment, among others. I saw the group members as relatively powerless. The experience challenged these views of power as static. The group formed strategic alliances, such as with the Minister of Health and with commercial companies. Their efforts to raise funds, which included everything from the grant they received from the Minister of Health to selling raffle tickets, were successful. They taught me again that solidarity and collective action were powerful. However, over time, the project was building contradictions within the psychiatric system that the system found intolerable. How could it be that the professionals, who for so many years cared for these long-stay patients, became the clients of these very people when they came to lunch? Longstanding relationships of dependency and power, upon which so much relied, were being disrupted. Eventually the system's power was overpowering. I initially saw the project as a failure because the restaurant eventually closed. The group enlightened me. The process and the struggles; the joys and the successes; the group cohesion and strong and sustained mutual support and respect; the changes in people's identities, skills and confidence and the new horizons some individuals had set for themselves were what the group alerted me to. The restaurant itself was important, but the processes and other outcomes were of greater importance to the group. They saw achievements that nobody could take from them. They taught me about process and outcomes and the importance of integrity of process.

In the early stages, when the group first entertained their dream of a restaurant, I wondered about participation and inclusion. Here was a small group among many other people in the long-stay wards who had similarly suffered oppression. What of those others? The group demonstrated their strengths and sense of responsibility to their fellow community members when they made their commitment to include as many others as wanted to be part of the project. My role then became one of facilitating this and supporting the group to develop ways of encouraging others to participate and to create safety for them to belong to the venture. Valuing the local culture of respect among the people was an important lesson for me.

On reflection, the notion of developing community through such a project in a psychiatric hospital still seems unimaginable. The conditions surrounding people in the psychiatric system are oppressive, powerful and extremely entrenched. Professional knowledge dominates. The power of psychiatric diagnostic labelling is enormous and pervasive. Personal identity is often reconstructed by individuals and is built upon a diagnostic category. People become 'schizophrenics'. Their full human capacity is judged by their label and they are so often considered to be globally incapable. However, the processes of solidarity, collective action and mutual affirmation of each others' strengths that this group engaged in and the fluidity of power that was evident over the three years taught me much about how people can have the agency to create their visions if the conditions around them are addressed along the way. Allowing space for people to collectively contribute to development enables communities to develop and achieve those things that are important for them, even within the most oppressive of conditions.

Tamil Tendril Tailoring Unit

This is a narrative about, and includes reflections on, community work in a poor, rural South Indian community (Tesoriero 2006a, 2006b, 2008a, 2008b). For many years a non-government agency (NGO) in South India has been working in a local rural area. I had worked in partnership with this NGO for twelve years, working on community projects that the NGO initiated. Over the years its efforts have not been evenly spread across its catchment area. There were some parts that remained relatively underdeveloped and under-serviced. One such part was the Vasaikanapatti Panchayat.

The Vasaikanapatti Panchayat comprises a main village, eight hamlets, field huts and two colonies. The colonies are inhabited by harijans, or outcastes, who are known also as dalits.

Living in separate colonies, dalit communities generally have fewer basic amenities (such as toilets), live in greater poverty, are relegated to doing the most menial tasks and, being largely landless, are economically dependent on caste people for income. Income security and food security are generally less than for caste people. Many dalits rely on 'coolie' work, which refers to casual, daily work in fields and other areas. This work is both seasonal and unreliable. Payment can be in grain rather than in cash. There is a history of discrimination against dalits.

The caste system in India is a complex system and there are thousands of castes and sub-castes throughout the subcontinent. The Indian government has determined a limited number of categories into which castes are placed for the purpose of access and equity policies and practices, such as reserved places in education, public employment and so on. These categories are (from highest to lowest in the hierarchy): forward castes; backward castes; most backward castes; scheduled castes (dalits); scheduled tribes. Vasaikanapatti Panchayat consists of most backward castes and scheduled castes. Ninety per cent of people are of the Vanniyar caste, which is a most backward caste.

Within the partnership with the NGO in 2006 we mobilised resources to work with the people of the Vasaikanapatti Panchayat. The team of community workers comprised social work students from Australian universities, myself and the community worker from our partner NGO. Before embarking on community work, we sought advice from a large and well-established NGO in Bangalore, which had been instrumental in establishing some of the first women's self-help groups (SHGs) in India. Over ten years it had established and supported several thousand local groups, assisting women to gain power collectively and to develop income-generation projects. The approach used was a strengths-based approach called Appreciative Inquiry (Ashford and Patkar 2001). After consultation with the organisation and listening to their stories of success, we decided that Appreciative Inquiry fitted well with our community development framework, its principles and concepts. It was amenable to a human rights approach. It also appeared to be appropriate to the local Indian context.

Appreciative Inquiry is a change strategy that is fully participatory and which focuses on the conditions and environments in which people live. It works from the strengths and resources that exist within people and their communities. Appreciative Inquiry is depicted as a four-stage process, which moves in cycles. The four stages are *Discovery*, *Dreaming*, *Design* and *Delivery*.

In the *Discovery* stage, people in groups and communities are encouraged to identify their strengths and the factors that have enabled past achievements. The *Dreaming* state enables people to envision the future they would like, to identify the ways in which their community would be most supportive of its members and the roles they and their local groups or organisations could play in creating such positive changes. In the *Design* stage people devise particular strategies and action plans to achieve their goals. The *Delivery* stage involves the implementation of the action plans.

The Dreaming stage builds on the community strengths to envision a better community. The visions are likely to be holistic in their scope, taking in social relationships, economic relationships, cultural traditions, the natural and human-made environment, governance structures in the community, income generation and money-earning visions and social infrastructure.

The central feature of the Design stage is dialogue through which community members devise ways of realising their dreams; of building and strengthening capacity, participation, social relations, governance structures and leadership in the community. Devising strategies includes identifying roles and responsibilities. It also includes building new relationships with external organisations and mobilising necessary resources.

The Design stage yields an action plan, which includes planning for short- and long-term objectives and for structural changes that may transform the conditions in which people live.

In the Delivery stage the action plans are implemented. Resources are mobilised, new relationships with external organisations are formed, new skills are developed in members and there is much collective action towards the collective vision.

In Vasaikanapatti, we embarked on Discovery with an established local women's self-help group in one of the villages. We were advised to begin with an already established community group. At the first meeting, after discussing whether they wanted us to join with them in development and their agreement to this, we asked them to teach us about their community by collectively drawing a village map on the ground. This was done with great enthusiasm and much animated discussion.

We discussed together the village map and linked this with storytelling about their village, asking what they liked about it. This exercise started the process of discovering their strengths and the factors that enabled their achievements, a process which continued through several sessions.

They told us 'how they liked their village, it was a nice place to live, with fresh air, fresh water every day; they had fresh vegetables, fresh fruits; how it was healthy to live here, no pollution; they had good coconut and papaya trees; there was a very good atmosphere in the village, everyone knew each other, they were all somehow related, very calm, no disturbance, no fighting, there was a good community spirit'.

They explained to us their SHG and its processes, how it functioned, and its rules, norms and achievements, such as their success in getting a water tap installed in the village.

At the next meeting we highlighted the strengths we found from their stories and shared these with the participants to ensure they resonated with them. The strengths we discovered and shared with the participants included: awareness of positive aspects of their environment and the village; feelings of happiness within their environment, the village; awareness of sense of living 'healthy' through fresh food; good community spirit and harmony; awareness of women's situation in India; awareness of members' rights as women in India, in the world; awareness of changes in Indian society; awareness of pressure from society's taboos; awareness of the importance and impact of education; desire to learn; desire to be leaders of their own changes; being determined.

The group members concurred with these strengths and themes. During this session, we related all these strengths back to the stories and to the themes that emerged from them. The strengths were written in English and Tamil languages on two large white cardboard sheets. After having asked the group about their thoughts and if they agreed about these strengths, one woman said, 'We were not aware of these until you told us, but now we can see how we can come up in life'. The other women nodded and smiled in agreement.

In the next session, to introduce the Dreaming phase, we asked them to close their eyes and visualise their village and how they would like it to be in five years' time. After this they were each given white flip-chart paper. They were asked to draw what they had visualised on the paper. Children also participated in the exercise.

During the subsequent session, to further progress their dreaming, we did the exercise of prioritising their dreams. Each of their 18 dreams were hand-drawn on a card and placed on the ground. Each participant was handed three stones, ranging in size from large to small. They each used the three stones to vote for their three top priority dreams, the largest stone for the top priority dream, the smallest stone for their third priority dream. They did this by placing each of the three stones on three chosen cards. We noted each person's vote and afterwards worked on tabulating the results to take back to the next session.

During that next session, when asked to identify, from 'the most important' chart, which two dreams they would like to work on they spontaneously voted by raising their hands. The dream of a collective tailoring unit received the most votes.

Actions to be undertaken in the Design stage of the tailoring unit were identified and discussed among the group: getting the land, building the tailoring unit, organising further training, contributing money on a weekly basis, opening a bank account, getting sewing machines and convincing some doubting or anxious fathers and husbands to let their daughters and wives participate. These action plans addressed and involved a complex array of systems, skills and structures, such as defining member roles, developing relationships, creating partnerships, expanding capacity building, increasing social and financial resources, implementing documentation and creating a financial base and other management systems, as well as challenging gender-based power relations.

The outcome was the commencement of a tailoring unit, comprising 50 women from eight of the ten communities in the Vasaikanapatti Panchayat. The unit, named Tamil Tendril (meaning Tamil Breeze), included ten women from the dalit colonies among its members and the tailoring teacher was also from one of the dalit colonies. The women negotiated for and secured eight sewing machines from the local partner NGO and they secured a temporary rental building (the rooftop and two rooftop rooms of a caste family home) in which the group held tailoring and embroidery classes. The group was assisted with the legalities to enable it to form a society with office bearers and a bank account. The women commenced skill training in areas such as collaborative decision making, conflict resolution, roles and responsibilities of group members, making linkages with outside organisations and finance and accounts.

With regard to a range of external relationships, contacts were established with possible retail outlets in Australia with a view to the unit becoming an export production unit. Support was requested from and subsequently offered by a nearby community-based export tailoring unit and a local weavers' cooperative agreed to supply cloth to Tamil Tendril. After discussions with the panchayat council, agreement in principle was obtained for assistance in being allocated land and for state government and NGO assistance in providing building materials for a permanent office and a tailoring unit building in the panchayat.

The women of Tamil Tendril Tailoring Unit

Individual participants learned skills, which ranged from technical skills to those which increased their social power, such as skills of negotiation and harnessing resources. However, these achievements at the community and individual level were only part of the picture of change.

At the time when discussions started in the village about establishing the group as a more formal tailoring unit the project team members were approached by a non-SHG member who was upset because information about meetings and other matters was being withheld from her and other women. At the same time, the SHG leader and one other woman approached us by making a special visit to us to tell us that other women in the project, the dalit (and SHG non-member) women, were 'bad', that they should not be given any positions of responsibility and that we should not interact socially with them.

We were aware that all previous programs run in the community had been divided into those for the dalit people and those for other castes. On the other hand, we were adamant and very clear that our community work would provide opportunities for all members of the community to be involved in ways that encouraged dialogue, not separation.

We made several attempts to combat the influence of these exclusionary practices and deeply ingrained forces in a caste-based community. We unmistakably reiterated our community development principles to the women. We clearly told the women that the development of the Vasaikanapatti community was to include everyone and that this meant that women who had previously chosen not to be in their SHG and dalit people would be part of the tailoring unit if they so chose. This was met with a repeated message that these were 'bad' people. As Westerners we were somewhat perplexed by this as we had observed the caste and dalit women interacting amicably on many occasions, their children playing together and, at times, the women entering each others' homes.

In one of the early meetings one young woman from one of the dalit colonies told the group that she had completed courses in embroidery and at the next meeting, with the support of team members, she brought with her samples of her work. This woman continued to attend the meetings, completed an application form to join Tamil Tendril and encouraged other young women from her colony to join. This resulted in ten out of the 50 participating women coming from the two dalit colonies. With our support and advocacy this young woman with embroidery skills demonstrated good leadership skills in the classes, she quietly and confidently assisted other members and other women consulted her, along with the teacher, during the tailoring and embroidery classes.

We had much difficulty in securing a tailoring teacher, but eventually one was found by the NGO worker. The woman was local to the panchayat and, to our astonishment, from one of the dalit colonies! We met her, invited her to the next meeting and she met with the women. We discerned looks of reservation and reluctance on the faces of some of the women. The teacher brought out her certificates and samples of her work. She handed them to the project team members, who nodded in approval and the certificates were circulated by the women around all of the group members. By the end of the meeting there were warm exchanges and the teacher spoke in a confident voice to the women. It was agreed that she would teach six days a week for six months.

Subsequently, on several occasions, the NGO community worker told us that there were problems. First we were told the teacher was not competent. Then we were told her husband would not allow her to teach. On each occasion, these reasons appeared to dissolve as we asked probing questions, met with her and her husband and so on. Eventually classes began and the teacher settled into her role.

While we seemed to be able to maintain involvement of the dalit women and to successfully resolve each particular incident as it arose, the underlying issue of power and exclusion being exerted by the SHG leader and a few other women persisted. We reflected on this and it seemed as though we could only win battles but that the war would continue and caste and other divisions would remain intact. We thus decided to seek a more structural solution to the issue of exclusion within the communities. We were not under the illusion that we could replace the current exclusionary caste structures, but we wanted to build a viable alternative, even if it sat beside the old structures for some considerable time to come.

Our work felt like a real struggle to us. Our struggle was concerned with maintaining a strengths perspective in the face of a seeming onslaught of exclusionary practices within the community. It sometimes became difficult to appreciate the community in a positive way. We were becoming deficit-focused so we deliberately turned our attention and our discussions to the alternative question 'What are the strengths in this community?'. Our vision immediately broadened beyond a few SHG members to the whole Vasaikanapatti community. There were other people in Vasaikanapatti who were involved in other civic activities, including other women's self-help groups and the panchayat council. We firmly believed that collective power worked for the good of a community as well as in other ways. We were increasingly convinced that our short-term tactics for each discrete incident were not an adequate solution; that a more durable solution must lie in our facilitative and consultant roles, through partnership with all the local people in building a much broader community-based structure, owned by them, which could address issues competently and capably. We had somehow fallen into the colonialist trap of providing the solutions and so, by default, of assuming a deficient community. We needed to realign our perspective towards a reinvigorated belief in the indigenous ability of the community and walking alongside it to build structures based on its strengths.

We went back to talk with the groups we were working with. We contextualised the tailoring unit as one project, but only the first of many more projects that our community work would initiate. That the tailoring unit originated in one village did not mean that it belonged to that village. Anyone from the broader community could participate. But we would be involved only for three years and the project would need to continue after that, totally in the hands of the community. We proposed that we establish a community-wide Community Committee. Our rationale for this was that it would be representative of all communities across Vasaikanapatti, including the two dalit colonies. If the Community Committee was assisted to develop the skills to manage and govern the project in ways consistent with the values and principles of our community development framework, then this would be an effective alternative mechanism within the communities and one that may be able to deal with exclusion issues into the future. We considered our assistance as providing training in such areas as collaborative decision making, conflict resolution and so on. This committee would consist of panchayat council representatives and two nominees, one woman and one man, from each village, hamlet and colony. We would visit each community, explain the Community Committee, its role and the roles of its members. We would then ask each community to select its two nominees.

The longstanding relationships between NGO workers and community leaders (all male and from caste communities) were central to our work being accepted in the communities. However these relationships also circumscribed the boundaries between acceptable and unacceptable interventions and acceptable and unacceptable change. The NGO partnered with us because development was its core work, but also there was potential kudos from achieving outcomes in an underdeveloped part of its patch. However, its approach to community development within a rural Indian context was highly patronising, in alliance with the traditional power holders. This approach was also one which, over the years, had cemented its status and power and the status of its workers, who were almost exclusively professional, university-educated males from higher castes. In other words, despite engaging in community 'development', the NGO was itself an embedded part of the social structure and its activities reinforced and perpetuated traditional social relations and power imbalances. So when the NGO became aware of the increasing power of people in the community—particularly dalit women—and their demonstrated ability to work collectively, self-reliantly and to achieve goals, and heard more and more of their demands, the NGO perceived its traditional position of power as being threatened and began to withdraw its support. The NGO's support of the project was essential because of its credibility. It held long-standing power in the community and provided resources to it. Above all else, local people were afraid to risk the NGO's disapproval and suffer the likely loss of support and resources. Accordingly, the NGO workers, keen to maintain their positions and alliances within the organisation, responded to subtle but powerful messages from their director and withdrew support. Workers who had been critical allies in change began actively but subtly to undermine the project work and the achievements that had been made at the community level with Tamil Tendril and the community committee. While the workers' actions were clearly a withdrawal of support, their personal feelings, as they expressed them in different ways, were very ambivalent.

In the end longstanding dependency relationships in Vasaikanapatti proved to be the stronger forces. The perceived costs of gaining power at the local level were considered by local people as ultimately too great. So the sustainability of the Tamil Tendril as a self-reliant, income-generation project benefitting women from both caste and dalit communities was eroded. The intended expansion of community-building activities beyond Tamil Tendril to other groups in the community, such as youth, was now not possible. The resources that were held by the NGO or which it could harness externally to support the local people's aspirations were denied to Tamil Tendril. Hopes and expectations were not realised.

Reflections on Tamil Tendril

The divisions in the Vasaikanapatti community have important implications for strength-based practice. For us the divisions and fractures initially represented threats to the project. We appreciated the exclusion issues arising within the community as indicative of deeply embedded divisions. We therefore concentrated on ameliorating the situations as they presented. On each occasion we devised tactics to counteract the divisive processes. In so doing, we inadvertently and insidiously fell into a deficit framework. We discarded our belief in the community's strengths and internal resources and sought to redress weaknesses as we saw them. Our tactics did not work beyond immediate 'band-aiding'.

When we stood back, reflected and took a community-wide view and reminded ourselves of strength-based practice, we began to reframe the divisions as diversity. In a community that had separatist programs in the past, we had dalit and caste people joining together and, indeed, a dalit woman as teacher. Where many self-help groups had traditionally excluded non-members, we had the privilege of non-SHG members, including dalit women, participating. Not only were they participating, but they were developing leadership roles. They were taking initiative, taking on responsibilities and influencing the directions of Tamil Tendril. The tensions were emerging out of radical change.

Reframing *divisions* as *diversity* unearthed for us many more rich resources in the community and for our work. We had young and old; we had literate and illiterate; we had an individual who was both a health worker and a member of a caste. Valuing diversity, we realised, brought new and more perspectives to the processes. People from diverse backgrounds working together, even with understandable tensions, represented a new dimension of dialogue, of listening and being together, rather than retreating into their corners of Vasaikanapatti and each holding tightly to their own 'truth'. We then moved to 'institutionalise' or formalise this resource by establishing the community committee where the diversity was represented on a body that would become the decision-making body for community development in Vasaikanapatti.

The strengths perspective was crucial in our work with exclusion because it enabled us to reframe deficiencies (divisions) as community strengths and resources (diversity; and with diversity coming together, dialogue; and with dialogue, richer processes and outcomes). The perspective proved to be more powerful an influence on our practice than the caste and membership issues confronting us. Conversely, when we realigned ourselves with a strengths-based approach, it proved crucial in developing structures that would embrace the diversity, which is in stark contrast to our attempts to 'remedy divisiveness'. The strengths perspective became a vehicle by which we remained alert to our community development framework and its principles.

The caste system's influence appeared early in our community development work and consistently through the process. This challenged us to examine the place of our values in relation to local values, customs and practices concerning caste and exclusion. The terrain was akin to a murky swamp. Were our values pertaining to social justice, human rights, participation and inclusion universally applicable or were we engaging in colonialist practices? How were we to value the Indian caste system which, while it certainly excluded, was also endowed with an immense capacity to give a sense of belonging to its members? The caste system is valued negatively as well as positively across India and in some parts of India, especially in urban areas, its place in Indian society is very quickly eroding. Difference and dynamism, universal and local, all contributed to an extremely complex terrain for our community development.

We used Bennett's (1993) concept of intercultural sensitivity as a guide to practice across cultures. Specifically, he describes the most developed form of intercultural sensitivity, 'integration', as:

> . . . the attempt to integrate disparate aspects of one's identity into a new whole while remaining culturally marginal. The goal of this new definition of identity is not to reaffiliate with one culture, nor is it simply to reestablish comfort with a multiplicity of worldviews. (1993, p. 60)

Here Bennett is describing a position that sits on the margins of a culture but engages in processes that build identity and culture and so 'allow for ethical choice and action in the profoundly relativistic world implied by an ethnorelative identity' (1993, p. 60). Integration, in this context, depicts a relationship that allows for an ethical position and this, in turn, implies values upon which ethical choices and actions are based. We drew on our community development principles and, where contradictions arose between particular principles, developed a hierarchy. Where human rights, social justice, inclusion and participation jarred with valuing the local, we gave the latter a lower place in the value hierarchy. The resultant value stance then provided us with the scaffolding for ethical choice and action—a process that redefined identity, the relationship to culture and culture itself. In other words, this process was part of a larger transformative process where culture itself, as a dynamic concept, is influenced.

In our community development work caste women attempted to exclude dalit women from membership of Tamil Tendril. They attempted to bar them from office-bearer positions. They tried to refuse to utilise essential skills possessed by some of the dalit women and needed by the group—skills such as embroidery and leadership .

The most significant change that occurred was that the local people had experienced, at least for a short time and to some extent, success as well as their agency in achieving their goals in solidarity, which cut across traditional differences and caste practices. Empowerment and asserting rights was realised, but not in a sustainable way. Appreciative Inquiry strategies had worked, but the broader development processes, which should have supported those successes, were not adequately or effectively attended to by us.

The turn of events in the project highlighted the need to break those traditional dependency relations that make the cost and the risks of embracing radical alternatives too great for local people. This requires a more holistic approach than we had taken because dependency is not only social and political, but also economic. Dalits, as noted previously, mostly depend on caste landowners for day work as their only source of income, which is meagre and often in-kind.

In terms of human rights work, our processes fell short of conforming to a human rights framework. Working within human rights framework entails a dual focus—working with rights claimants and working to change the duty bearers (those who have a responsibility to ensure rights are upheld, whether they are NGOs, decision makers, politicians or other leaders). We failed to effectively include the second focus in our work. Our processes failed to adequately build local capacity and networks (Uvin et al. 2000) in the political sense and to generate transformed relations that could change the traditional power relations. By neglecting to aim explicitly for sustainable community outcomes, the project neglected to adequately address structural power relations where duty bearers held power but failed in their duty to uphold basic human rights.

There were many lessons learnt and the Vasaikanapatti community were powerful teachers. The power of community development and the partnership model of working with communities was strongly reinforced. Having a genuine belief in and a commitment to identifying, working with and sharing discoveries of strengths in a community is central to development work. A belief in and commitment to a strengths-based approach is equally potent in a community that is poor, relatively underdeveloped and with relatively poorer health status than other communities. The ease with which barriers to development work can seduce one into a deficit framework is frightening. The strength of a team and the power of reflection in practice as a foil to reverting to what professionals love—deficits—was also reinforced.

We developed a more useful and more sophisticated understanding of the meaning of 'the environment as a helping resource'. We came to understand that this is not a given or simple fact—it can only come from strategically engaging in what is partly a developmental and partly a political process. The helping aspect of the environment is only one aspect of a contradictory phenomenon. In other words, there are alienating forces as well as supportive forces in the environment. Alienating forces involve the use of power in ways that are socially unjust and which violate human rights. The community worker must understand that power is a dynamic force, that they can also muster power and thus build supportive structures in the community. These structures can, in turn, counter the alienating forces and so enable community work to more fully conform to a social justice/human rights and ecological framework. It is clear from this view of the environment that a belief in strengths does not mean a naïve view of community. Rather, it must include a thoughtful and balanced analysis of all dynamics and interests within and external to a community and it must also then include a clear set of strategies to build supportive features and a set of strategies that challenge those with vested interests who use power abusively and exploitatively.

Kalyyur Nagar

Kalyyur Nagar is one of several villages south of Chennai in South India, which were affected by the 2004 Tsunami and which are inhabited by tribal communities, in particular, members of the Irula tribe. The Irula tribe was dislocated from forest regions and in the dislocation process lost their traditional means of sustainable livelihood and became dependent on landowners, quarry owners and others who controlled means of production in the plains. These communities are one of the scheduled communities, which means they are very disadvantaged and are subject to affirmative action under Indian legislation. Kalyyur Nagar is one of the sites we moved to after Vasaikanapatti and the establishment of the Tamil Tendril Tailoring Unit.

We are still in the early days of working in this area but the beginning of the story is inspirational. When we first arrived in the village, early in 2009, we were told that the village had very recently been freed from bonded labour in a local quarry and that a local NGO, led by a Catholic priest, had freed the village from bonded labour. Those living in many other nearby tribal villages remain as bonded labourers in local quarries. Bonded labour is slave labour where families, over several generations, have been bonded because of a debt incurred many years ago, which was never able to be repaid because of exorbitant interest rates. The practice is illegal but persists across India. Many NGOs work tirelessly to free people from bonded labour.

Several days after we arrived one of the villagers, a young married man, was enticed back to the quarry by the quarry owner. The next morning his body was found. He had been murdered. Neither the police nor the local politician were interested in pursuing the case at that time, but the villagers mobilised and made numerous deputations and protests to try to force action.

We met most evenings with the villagers in their village under a failing street-light. Here they told us numerous stories of their struggles and the strength of and resources in the community became very apparent. When we reflected back to the community the strengths we saw in their stories, they were clearly shocked that outsiders would consider affirming their community. But at the same time they were clearly resolute in the importance of their struggles.

When we asked them about their dreams for their village, they identified many and prioritised three: (1) to renovate their small village temple; (2) to build a tuition centre so that the young women of the village could have greater access to education and (3) to build a small office so that they could organise to fight for the freedom of other bonded-labour villages.

Reflections on Kalyyur Nagar

I felt very ambivalent about engaging in Appreciative Inquiry with a community that had such a history of dislocation and oppression and which was currently so traumatised by the murder of one of its young men and the system's discounting of his life and his death.

The villagers' prioritised dreams reinforced all the principles of community development that, for me, tend to dissipate at times when I am faced with almost unbelievably terrible circumstances. The shock of this community's history and its present trauma blinded me to a holistic view of the community. My own ethnocentric and individualistic interpretations and perceptions of what I heard and observed precluded me from understanding the complexity of a community and all that is entailed in that—local beliefs, knowledge, skills, resources, resolve and an ability to act collectively and to engage in solidarity in struggle. As a team (the local Indian community worker, the Australian social work students and myself), we valued reflection as a core part of our community work practice. Reflection and dialogue, which drew on our community development framework and its principles as well as on the principles of the strengths perspective that operationalised our framework, enabled me to change my view from one of a crushed group of people to a view of a strong and resilient community whose members were clear about their rights, outraged at the violation of their human rights and determined to struggle to reclaim their rights. Without the support of a clear community development framework and its principles, and without the support of the community and my colleagues to reflect on my practice I was in danger of having a very myopic picture and of drifting into a sense of powerlessness and hopelessness.

The lessons we learned in Vasaikanapatti enabled us to more readily recognise the place our principles must retain in our work. We more readily recognised our responsibility to address the injustices created by those with power and support a community to challenge those injustices and the perpetrators of them.

At the time of writing, the people of Kalyyur Nagar had saved the money to renovate their temple and were repainting it. They were well on their way, with the support of a local NGO, to establishing their tuition centre. They were also on the path of planning for their organisation to be established and housed in a small office.

Passion, vision and hope

Community work is not simply a technical exercise that can be done by anybody and where effectiveness is measured in the essentially clinical and sanitised language of 'competence'. Certainly technical knowledge, skill and expertise are important, but they are not enough. They are not enough because the conditions in which they find themselves are often so complex and unpredictable. Good community work must also include embarking on unknown journeys, embracing the puzzles and tensions and asking questions along the way. Therefore good community workers also must have passion, a sense of commitment, a real enthusiasm for their work and something that drives them on. Good community workers will not see their work as simply a job, but also as something that is intrinsically important, worth doing and part of making the world a better place. These qualities enhance good community workers' knowledge and skills and carry them through the troughs of uncertainty and doubt.

This approach to one's work (particularly if it is paid work) is not popular or widespread at the present time. It is more common to see one's work as a job, which one may or may not enjoy (though it is preferable if one does), the primary motivation for which is personal gain in terms of monetary reward and possibly also status and recognition. While undoubtedly for many paid community workers the salary is an important part of the job, community work should be about much more than that, and involves the worker seeing their role as part of a larger movement for social change. Community workers are thus somewhat deviant in their attitude to work, though it is important to remember that they are not the only deviants—others, such as clergy, workers in activist organisations and at least some politicians also see their work in this way. However, if the kind of transformation that is envisaged in Chapters 2–5 were to take place, the nature of 'work' would have to be very different and the attitude of community workers would be more 'normal'.

This difference helps to explain why many of the trappings that normally go with the workplace do not apply readily to community workers. These include rigid definitions of specific competencies, the importance placed on promotion, the lure of high salaries, formal supervision, accountability upward, time sheets, books of regulations and a clear distinction between work and non-work. Where these are imposed on a community worker they are almost always found to be wildly inappropriate and the values of community development would specifically challenge such ideas. This is, at least in part, because of the importance of passion and commitment in community work; this gives community work a dimension that is totally foreign to traditional workplace structures and norms.

Yet this dimension is vital to community work. Community members will quickly pick up a lack of enthusiastic commitment and passion on the part of a worker and, in turn, are unlikely to become passionately committed themselves. By contrast, the community worker who is able to convey a sense of passion and enthusiasm and is able to infect others with it has taken a giant step towards effective community development.

Where, then, does a community worker find this sense of passion and commitment? What makes a worker enthusiastic about community development? How can a worker maintain that level of commitment in the long term? It is for precisely this reason that community workers need to find and use as much support as possible. The question of where passion, commitment and enthusiasm come from is appropriately the subject of this final section.

Essentially the answer has already been provided in the discussion in earlier chapters on empowerment and consciousness-raising. There it was emphasised that what was required was an understanding of how things come to be the way they are, that there really are genuine alternatives for a better future and that there are possible forms of action through which that change could be effected. The same is true of community workers themselves and it can best be summarised as a combination of vision and hope. Put simply, the community worker needs both a *vision* of a better society and a *hope* that change is indeed possible. Both are essential—vision without hope leads to despair and disillusionment, while hope without vision leads to reactive and pragmatic action with no purpose or goal. But the community worker who has both vision and hope will also have that passion and drive needed for bringing about genuine community development.

This vision and hope can come from a number of sources. One is from analysis and critical reflection. Indeed the purpose of this book has been to try to provide a theoretical framework for the development of a vision of an alternative and a hope that change is possible. But this is not the only source—few people become social activists purely as a result of intellectual study, though it can be an important part of the process.

Developing a sense of vision and purpose is a personal matter for each community worker. For some, religious commitment is an important component of inspiration; others will not find religion an important source, but for all community workers the experience of a sense of outrage at injustice, intolerance and exploitation can be a crucial factor in motivating a worker to action and in lighting a 'fire in the belly'. Being confronted with such injustice through documentaries, reading, encounters with others or personal experience is a major factor in motivation. There is also great potential in art, music, literature, poetry, radio, film and drama. All these media have been used to expose injustice, present alternative visions and fire people to take action. They can be important sources of inspiration for community workers.

A sense of history is also important. An understanding of historical processes helps one realise that the present social, economic and political system, with its injustice, inequality and loss of community, is a relatively recent phenomenon and that major change is not only possible but is normal and inevitable. The obstacles to change seem insurmountable only if one takes an a historical view, whereas a historical perspective helps to open up other possibilities and helps one realise that we are living in a period of massive change and that it is in precisely such periods that new options become real possibilities. It is an exciting period in which to be alive and community workers have a real opportunity to help shape a new society.

A further source of vision and hope is in the many stories of successful change and intense struggle that are to be found in many parts of the world. From the highly publicised work of people such as Mahatma Gandhi, Martin Luther King, Nelson Mandela and Barack Obama to the less well-known work of people involved in different local community development projects, there are many stories to inspire and motivate a community worker (Seabrook 1993a). To this must be added the many examples of grassroots citizen action where people have taken matters into their own hands and set up alternative community-based systems to meet needs that are no longer being met by a global economy and a political process that has become removed from the reality of ordinary people (Ekins 1992). These include LETS, cooperatives, Transition Towns and a myriad of self-help groups, action groups and simple informal neighbourhood social organisations. That this is happening in spite of the current social and global political and economic forces, which militate against human community, is testimony to the power of the ideal of community development. These many stories show not only that change is possible, but also that it is actually happening, which is the most inspiring and empowering message that a community worker could hear.

References

Albert, M. & Hahnel, R. 1991, *Looking Forward: Participatory Economics for the Twenty First Century*, South End Press, Boston.

Alinsky, S. 1969, *Reveille for Radicals*, Random House, New York.

Alinsky, S. 1971, *Rules for Radicals: A Practical Primer for Realistic Radicals*, Random House, New York.

Andrews, D. 1992, 'Beyond the Professionalisation of Community Work', *Social Alternatives*, vol. 11, no. 3, pp. 35–8.

Argyle, M. 1991, *Cooperation: The Basis of Sociability*, Routledge, London.

Arnstein, S. 1969, 'A Ladder of Citizen Participation', *Journal of the American Planning Association*, vol. 35, no. 3.

Ashford, G. & Patkar, S. 2001, *The Positive Path: Using Appreciative Inquiry in Rural Indian Communities*, MYRADA, Bangalore.

Ashok, B. 2008, 'What Do Rivers Mean to Us as a Society?', *The Hindu*, 21 September, p. 16.

Avonius, L. & Kingsbury, D. (eds), 2008, *Human rights in Asia: a reassessment of the Asian values debate*, Palgrave Macmillan, New York.

Aziz, N. 1999, 'The Human Rights Debate in an Era of Globalization', in P. Van Ness (ed.), *Debating Human Rights: Critical Essays from the United States and Asia*, Routledge, London.

Baird, V. 2008, 'Yasuní – Is This The Way Beyond Petroleum?', *New Internationalist*, no. 413, July, pp. 4–10.

Baldry, E. & Vinson, T. (eds) 1991, *Actions Speak: Strategies and Lessons from Australian Social and Community Action*, Longman Cheshire, Melbourne.

Bannerjee, M. 2005, 'Social Work, Rawlsian Social Justice, and Social Development', *Social Development Issues*, vol. 27, no. 1, pp. 6–24.

Barber, B. 1995, *Jihad vs McWorld: How Globalism and Tribalism Are Reshaping the World*, Ballantine Books, New York.

Batten, R., Weeks, W. & Wilson, J. (eds) 1991, *Issues Facing Australian Families*, Longman Cheshire, Melbourne.

Bauer, J. & Bell, D. (eds) 1999, *The East Asian Challenge for Human Rights*, Cambridge University Press, Cambridge.

Bauman, Z. 1998, *Globalization: The Human Consequences*, Polity Press, Cambridge.

Beck, U. 2000, *What is Globalization?*, Polity Press, Cambridge.

Beier, J. 2002, 'Beyond Hegemonic State(ments) of Nature: Indigenous Knowledge and Non-state Possibilities in International Relations', in Geeta Chowdhry & Sheila Nair (eds), *Power, Postcolonialism and International Relations: Reading Race, Gender and Class*, Routledge, London.

Beilharz, L. 2002, *Building Community: The Shared Action Experience*, St Luke's Innovative Resources, Bendigo.

Beilharz, P., Considine, M. & Watts, R. 1992, *Arguing About the Welfare State: The Australian Experience*, Allen & Unwin, Sydney.

Bell, C. & Newby, H. 1971, *Community Studies*, Allen & Unwin, London.

Benello, C.G. 1992, *From the Ground Up: Essays on Grassroots and Workplace Democracy*, Black Rose Books, Montreal.

Benhabib, S. 1996, 'The Democratic Moment and the Problem of Difference', in S. Benhabib (ed), *Democracy and Difference: Contesting the Boundaries of the Political*, Princeton University Press, Princeton NJ.

Benhabib, S. 1996, 'Toward a Deliberative Model of Democratic Legitimacy', in S. Benhabib, (ed), *Democracy and Difference: Contesting the Boundaries of the Political*, Princeton University Press, Princeton NJ.

Bennett, M. 1993, 'Towards Ethnorelativism: a Developmental Model of Intercultural Sensitivity', in R.M. Paige (ed), *Education for the Intercultural Experience*, Intercultural Press Inc., Yarmouth, ME.

Bhabha, H. 1994, *The Location of Culture*, Routledge, London.

Bhattacharyya, J. 2004, 'Theorizing Community Development', in *Journal of the Community Development Society*, vol. 34, no. 2, pp. 5–34.

Bickman, W., Rifkin, S.B. & Shrestra, M. 1989, 'Towards the Measurement of Community Participation', *World Health Forum*, vol. 10, pp. 467–72.

Bishop, A. 2002, *Becoming an Ally: Breaking the Cycle of Oppression*, Allen and Unwin, Crows Nest, New South Wales.

Boal, A. 1979, *Theater of the Oppressed*, Pluto Press, London.

Bolger, A. 1991, *Aboriginal Women and Violence*, Australian National University, North Australia Research Unit, Darwin.

Bolman, W. 1974, 'Policy Aspects of Citizen Participation', in L. Bellak (ed.), *A Concise Handbook of Community Psychiatry and Mental Health*, Grune & Stratton, New York.

Bookchin, M. & Foreman, D. 1991, *Defending the Earth*, Black Rose Books, Montreal.

Bookchin, M. 1990, *Remaking Society—Pathways to a Green Future*, South End Press, Boston.

Bookchin, M. 1991, *The Ecology of Freedom: The Emergence and Dissolution of Hierarchy*, Black Rose Books, Montreal.

Bookchin, M. 1995, *Re-enchanting Humanity: A Defence of the Human Spirit Against Anti-Humanism, Misanthropy, Mysticism and Primitivism*, Cassell, London.

Bookchin, M. 2004, *Post-scarcity Anarchism*, AK Press, Edinburgh.

Bookchin, M. 2005, *The Ecology of Freedom: the Emergence and Dissolution of Hierarchy*, AK Press, UK.

Booth, K. 1999, 'Three Tyrannies', in T. Dunne & N. Wheeler (eds), *Human Rights in Global Politics*, Cambridge University Press, Cambridge.

Botes, L. & van Rensburg, D. 2000, 'Community Participation in Development: Nine Plagues and Twelve Commandments', *Community Development Journal*, vol. 35, no. 1, pp. 41–58.

Bowers, C. 2000, *Let Them Eat Data: How Computers Affect Education, Cultural Diversity and the Propects of Ecological Sustainability*, University of Georgia Press, Athens, GA.

Bracht, N. & Tsouros, A. 1990, 'Principles and Strategies of Effective Community Participation', *Health Promotion International*, vol. 5, no. 3, pp. 199–208.
Bradshaw, J. 1972, 'The Concept of Social Need', *New Society*, vol. 30, pp. 640–3.
Bradshaw, T. 2008, 'The Post-Place Community: Contributions to the Debate About the Definition of Community', *Community Development*, vol. 39, no. 1, pp. 5–16.
Bramble, T. 1992, 'Conflict, Coercion and Co-option: The Role of Full-time Officials in the South Australian Branch of the Vehicle Builders' Employees' Federation, 1967–80', *Labour History*, vol. 63, November, pp. 135–54.
Brecher, J. & Costello, T. 1994, *Global Village or Global Pillage: Economic Reconstruction from the Bottom Up*, South End Press, Boston.
Brieland, D. 1971, 'Community Advisory Boards and Maximum Feasible Participation', *Australian Journal of Public Health*, vol. 61, no. 2.
Brown, L. 1994, *State of the World, 1994: A Worldwatch Institute Report on Progress Towards a Sustainable Society*, W.W. Norton, New York.
Brownlea, A. 1987, 'Participation: Myths, Realities and Prognosis', *Social Science and Medicine*, vol. 25, no. 6, pp. 605–14.
Bryant, B. (ed.) 1995, *Environmental Justice: Issues, Policies and Solutions*, Island Press, Washington, DC.
Bryson, L. & Mowbray, M. 1981, '"Community": The Spray-on Solution', *Australian Journal of Social Issues*, vol. 16, no. 4, pp. 255–67.
Bryson, L. 1992, *Welfare and the State*, Macmillan, London.
Buarque, C. 1993, *The End of Economics: Ethics and the Disorder of Progress*, Zed Books, London.
Burbach, R., Nunez, O. & Kagarlitsky, B. 1997, *Globalization and Its Discontents: The Rise of Postmodern Socialisms*, Pluto Press, London.
Burgmann, V. 1993, *Power and Protest: Movements for Change in Australian Society*, Allen & Unwin, Sydney.
Burkett, I. 2001, 'Traversing the Swampy Terrain of Postmodern Communities: Towards Theoretical Revisionings of Community Development', *European Journal of Social Work*, vol. 4, no. 3, pp. 263–74.
Campfens, H. (ed.) 1997, *Community Development around the World: Practice, Theory, Research, Training*, University of Toronto Press, Toronto.
Capra, F. 1982, *The Turning Point—Science, Society and the Rising Culture*, Wildwood House, London.
Carter, A. 1999, *A Radical Green Political Theory*, Routledge, London.
Castells, M. 1996, *The Information Age: Economy, Society and Culture. Vol. 1: The Rise of the Network Society*, Blackwell, Malden, MA.
Castells, M. 1997, *The Information Age: Economy, Society and Culture. Vol. 2: The Power of Identity*, Blackwell, Malden, MA.
Castells, M. 1998, *The Information Age: Economy, Society and Culture. Vol. 3: The End of Millennium*, Blackwell, Malden, MA.
Castles, F. 1985, *The Working Class and Welfare*, Allen & Unwin, Wellington, New Zealand.
Cawson, A. 1982, *Corporatism and Welfare: Social Policy and State Intervention in Britain*, Heinemann, London.
Chambers, R. 1993, *Challenging the Professions: Frontiers for Rural Development*, Intermediate Technology Publications, London.
Cleaver, F. 2004, 'The Social Embeddedness of Agency and Decision-making', in S. Hickey & G. Mohan (eds), *Participation: From Tyranny to Transformation?*, Zed Books, London.
Clegg, S. 1989, *Frameworks of Power*, Sage, London.
Community and Family Commission (WA) 1992, *Speaking Out, Taking Part: A Report to the Government from the Community and Family Commission on Behalf of the People of Western Australia*, Office of the Family, Perth.

Connors, P. 2008, 'Community Development and Ecology: Links and Possibilities', in Clarke, M. et al., *Community Development and Ecology: Engaging Ecological Sustainability through Community Development*, Conference Proceedings, Deakin University, Geelong, Victoria.

Conservation Council of Victoria 1993, *Work and the Environment: Background Papers*, Work & the Environment National Workshop, Melbourne.

Cooke, B. & Kothari, U. 2001, 'The Case for Participation as Tyranny', in B. Cooke & U. Kothari (eds), *Participation: The New Tyranny*, Zed Books, London.

Coote, A. & Campbell, B. 1982, *Sweet Freedom: The Struggle for Women's Liberation*, Blackwell, Oxford.

Coover, V., Deacon, E., Esser, C. & Moore, C. 1985, *Resource Manual for a Living Revolution*, New Society Publishers, Philadelphia, PA.

Corrigan, P. & Leonard, P. 1978, *Social Work Practice Under Capitalism: A Marxist Approach*, Macmillan, London.

Cox, E. & Caldwell, P. 2000, 'Making Policy Social', in I. Winter (ed.), *Social Capital and Public Policy in Australia*, Australian Institute of Family Studies, Melbourne.

Cox, E. 1995, *A Truly Civil Society*, ABC Books, Sydney.

Cox, K.R. (ed.) 1997, *Spaces of Globalization: Reasserting the Power of the Local*, The Guildford Press, New York.

Craig, J. 1993, *The Nature of Co-operation*, Black Rose Books, Montreal.

Craig, W. 1987, *A Community Work Perspective*, Massey University, Palmerston North, New Zealand.

Crotty, M. 1998, *The Foundations of Social Research: Meaning and Perspective in the Research Process*, Allen and Unwin, St Leonards, New South Wales.

Dahl, R. 1961, *Who Governs?*, Yale University Press, New Haven, CT.

Daly, H. & Cobb, J. 1989, *For the Common Good—Redirecting the Economy Toward Community, the Environment and a Sustainable Future*, Beacon Press, Boston.

Dauncey, G. 1988, *After the Crash—The Emergence of the Rainbow Economy*, Green Print, Basingstoke.

Dawson, S. & Dargie, C. 1999, 'New Public Management: An Assessment and Evaluation with Special Reference to UK Health', *Public Management*, 1(4), pp. 459–81.

de Beauvoir, S. 1988, *The Second Sex*, H. Parshley (trans. & ed.), Picador, London.

de Schweinitz, K. 1943, *England's Road to Social Security*, Barnes & Co., New York.

Deacon, B. 1997, *Global Social Policy: International Organizations and the Future of Welfare*, Sage, London.

Denzin, N. & Lincoln, Y. (eds) 2000, *Handbook of Qualitative Research*, 2nd edn, Sage, London.

Deudney, D. & Matthew, R. (eds) 1999, *Contested Grounds: Security Conflict in the New Environment Politics*, State University of New York Press, Albany, NY.

Dinham, A. 2006, 'Raising Expectations or Dashing Hopes? Well-being and Participation in Disadvantaged Areas', *Community Development Journal*, vol. 42, no. 2, pp. 181–93.

Dobson, A. (ed.) 1999, *Fairness and Futurity: Essays on Environmental Sustainability and Social Justice*, Oxford University Press, Oxford.

Dobson, A. 1995, *Green Political Thought*, 2nd edn, Routledge, London.

Dobson, R. 1993, *Bringing the Economy Home from the Market*, Black Rose Books, Montreal.

Donnison, D. 1991, *A Radical Agenda: After the New Right and the Old Left*, Rivers Oram, London.

Doorman, F. 1998, *Global Development: Problems, Solutions, Strategy: A Proposal for Socially Just, Ecologically Sustainable Growth,* International Books, Utrecht.

Doyal, L. & Gough, I. 1991, *A Theory of Human Need*, Macmillan, London.

Earth Charter Commission 2000, Earth Charter, final version, at <www.onecountry.org>, accessed 1 September 2009.

Eaton, H. 2005, *Introducing Ecofeminist Theologies*, T&T Clark, New York.
Ebers, M. 1997, 'Explaining Inter-organizational Networks', in M. Ebers (ed.), *The Formation of Inter-Organizational Networks*, Oxford University Press, Oxford, pp. 3–40.
Eckersley, R. 1992, *Environmentalism and Political Theory*, SUNY Press, New York.
Economic Commission for Latin America 1973, 'Popular Participation in Development', *Community Development Journal*, vol. 8, no. 3.
Ehrlich, P. & Ehrlich, A. 1990, *The Population Explosion*, Simon & Schuster, New York.
Ekins, P. & Max-Neef, M. (eds) 1992, *Real-Life Economics: Understanding Wealth Creation*, Routledge, London.
Ekins, P. (ed.) 1986, *The Living Economy—A New Economics in the Making*, Routledge & Kegan Paul, London.
Ekins, P. 1992, *A New World Order—Grassroots Movements for Global Change*, Routledge, London.
Ekins, P. 2000, *Economic Growth and Environmental Sustainability: the Prospects for Green Growth*, Routledge, London.
England, H. 1986, *Social Work as Art: Making Sense for Good Practice*, Allen & Unwin, London.
Escobar, A. 1996, 'Constructing Nature: Elements for a Poststructural Political Ecology', in R. Peet and M. Watts (eds), *Liberation Ecologies: Environment, Development, Social Movements*, Routledge, London.
Esping-Andersen, G. 1990, *The Three Worlds of Welfare Capitalism*, Polity Press, Cambridge.
Evatt Research Centre 1989, *State of Siege: Renewal or Privatisation for Australian State Public Services?*, Pluto Press, Sydney.
Evers, A., Nowotny, H. & Wintersberger, H. 1987, *The Changing Face of Welfare*, Gower, Aldershot Hampshire.
Ewalt, P., Freeman, E. & Poole, D. 1998, *Community Building: Renewal, Well-Being and Shared Responsibility*, NASW Press, Washington, DC.
Ezzy, D. 2004, 'Old Traditions and New Ages: Religions and environments', in R. White (ed), *Controversies in Environmental Sociology*, Cambridge University Press, Cambridge.
Falk, R. 1993, 'The Making of Global Citizenship', in J. Brecher et al. (eds), *Global Visions: Beyond the New World Order*, South End Press, Boston.
Fals-Borda, O. & Rahman, M.A. (eds) 1991, *Action and Knowledge: Breaking the Monopoly with Participatory Action-Research*, The Apex Press, New York.
Fanon, F. 1961, *The Wretched of the Earth*, Penguin, Harmondsworth.
Fanon, F. 1967, *Black Skin: White Masks,* (trans. C. Markman), Grove Press, New York.
Fanon, F. 1994, 'On National Culture', in P. Williams & L. Chrisman (eds), *Colonial Discourse and Post-Colonial Theory: A Reader*, Harvester Wheatsheaf, Hemel Hempstead, Hertfordshire.
Fay, B. 1975, *Social Theory and Political Practice*, Allen & Unwin, London.
Fay, B. 1987, *Critical Social Science: Liberation and Its Limits*, Polity Press, Cambridge.
Feher, F., Heller, A. & Markus, G. 1983, *Dictatorship Over Needs*, Blackwell, Oxford.
Fellin, P. 2001, *The Community and the Social Worker*, 3rd edn, F.E. Peacock Publishers, Itasca, IL.
Ferro, M. 1997, *Colonization: A Global History*, Routledge, London.
Findlay, P. 1994, 'Conscientization and Social Movements in Canada: The Relevance of Paulo Freire's Ideas in Contemporary Politics', in P. McLaren & C. Lankshear (eds), *Politics of Liberation: Paths from Freire,* Routledge, London, pp. 108–22.
Flood, M. & Lawrence, A. (ed.) 1987, *The Community Action Book*, 2nd edn, Council of Social Service of New South Wales, Sydney.
Fook, J. 1993, *Radical Casework: A Theory of Practice*, Allen & Unwin, Sydney.

Foucault, M. 1972, *The Archaeology of Knowledge*, Tavistock, London.
Foucault, M. 1973, *Madness and Civilisation: A History of Insanity in an Age of Reason*, Vintage Books, New York.
Foucault, M. 1979, *Discipline and Punish: The Birth of the Prison*, Penguin, Harmondsworth.
Foucault, M. 1980, *Power/Knowledge: Selected Interviews and Other Writings 1972–1977*, C. Gordon (ed.), Pantheon, New York.
Fox, W. 1990, *Towards a Transpersonal Ecology: Developing New Foundations for Environmentalism*, Shambhala, Boston.
Freire, P. 1972, *Pedagogy of the Oppressed*, Penguin, Harmondsworth.
Friedman, M. & Friedman, R. 1980, *Free to Choose*, Penguin, Harmondsworth.
Friedmann, J. 1992, *Empowerment: The Politics of Alternative Development*, Blackwell, Oxford.
Fukuyama, F. 1992, *The End of History and the Last Man*, Hamilton, London.
Galiher, C., Needlemen, J. & Rolf, A. 1971, 'Consumer Participation', *Health Services and Mental Health Administration Reports* (USA), vol. 86, pp. 96–106.
Gandhi, M. 1964, *Gandhi on Non-Violence: Selected Texts from Mohandas K. Gandhi's 'Non-Violence in Peace and War'*, Thomas Merton (ed.), New Directions Publishing, New York.
Gandhi, M. 1982, *An Autobiography, or the Story of My Experiments with Truth*, Penguin, Harmondsworth.
Gaudiano, E. & de Alba, A. 1994, 'Freire: Present and Future Possibilities', in P. McLaren & C. Lankshear (eds), *Politics of Liberation: Paths from Freire,* Routledge, London, pp. 123–41.
George, S. 1992, *The Debt Boomerang: How Third World Debt Harms Us All*, Westview Press, Boulder, CO.
George, V. & Wilding, P. 1984, *The Impact of Social Policy*, Routledge, London.
Germain, C. & Gitterman, A. 1980, *The Life Model of Social Work Practice*, Columbia University Press, New York.
Germain, C. 1991, *Human Behaviour in the Social Environment: An Ecological View*, Columbia University Press, New York.
Giddens, A. 1994, *Beyond Left and Right: The Future of Radical Politics*, Polity Press, Cambridge.
Goodin, R. 1992, *Green Political Theory*, Polity Press, Cambridge.
Goodin, R., Headey, B., Muffels, R. & Dirven, H. 1999, *The Real Worlds of Welfare Capitalism*, Cambridge University Press, Cambridge.
Gordon, A. & Suzuki, D. 1990, *It's a Matter of Survival*, Allen & Unwin, Toronto.
Gorz, A. 1980, *Ecology as Politics*, Black Rose Books, Montreal.
Gorz, A. 1983, *Paths to Paradise—On the Liberation from Work*, Pluto, London.
Gorz, A. 1989, *Critique of Economic Reason*, Verso, London.
Gough, I. 1979, *The Political Economy of the Welfare State*, Macmillan, London.
Guamán, F. 2008, 'Speak to us First!', *New Internationalist*, no. 413, July, pp. 12–13.
Haque, M. 2000, 'Environmental Discourse and Sustainable Development', *Ethics and the Environment*, vol. 5, no. 1, pp. 3–21.
Harcourt, W. (ed.) 1994, *Feminist Perspectives on Sustainable Development,* Zed Books, London.
Harrison, J. 1984, *The Common People: A History from the Norman Conquest to the Present*, Fontana, London.
Harrison, P. 1983, *The Third World Tomorrow: A Report from the Battlefront in the War Against Poverty*, Chapter 2, pp. 23–42, Chapter 15, pp. 342–50, Penguin, Harmondsworth.
Haug, E. 2000, *Writings in the Margins: Critical Reflections on the Emerging Discourse of International Social Work*, Masters Thesis, Department of Social Work, University of Calgary, Alberta.

Hawke, S. & Gallagher, M. 1989, *Noonkanbah*, Fremantle Arts Centre Press, Fremantle.

Hawthorne, S. 2002, *Wild Politics: Feminism, Globalisation, Bio/diversity*, Spinifex, North Melbourne.

Hazelhurst, K. 1994, *A Healing Place: Indigenous Visions for Personal Empowerment and Community Recovery*, Central Queensland University Press, Rockhampton.

Healey, J. 2000, *Global Warming*, Spinnery Press, Balmain, New South Wales.

Held, D. 1980, *Introduction to Critical Theory: Horkheimer to Habermas*, Hutchinson, London.

Held, D. 1987, *Models of Democracy*, Stanford University Press, Stanford, CA.

Held, D., McGrew, A., Goldblatt, D. & Perroton, J. 1999, *Global Transformations: Politics, Economics and Culture*, Polity Press, Cambridge.

Helgason, K. 1998, 'New voices, new partners in the search for better governance', *Co-operation South,* no. 1, pp. 21–35.

Henderson, H. 1988, *The Politics of the Solar Age: Alternatives to Economics*, Knowledge Systems Inc., Indianapolis.

Henderson, H. 1991, *Paradigms in Progress—Life Beyond Economics*, Knowledge Systems Inc., Indianapolis.

Henderson, H. 1995, *Paradigms in Progress*, Berrett-Koehler, San Francisco.

Henderson, H. 1996, *Building a Win–win World: Beyond Global Economic Warfare*, Berrett-Koehler, San Francisco.

Herngren, P. 1993, *Path of Resistance: The Practice of Civil Disobedience*, New Society Publishers, Philadelphia.

Hickey, S. & Mohan, G. 2004, 'Towards Participation as Transformation: Critical Themes and Challenges', in S. Hickey & G. Mohan (eds), *Participation: From Tyranny to Transformation?*, Zed Books, London.

Hines, C. 2000, *Localization: A Global Manifesto*, Earthscan, London.

Hobsbawm, E. & Rudé, G. 1969, *Captain Swing*, Lawrence & Wishart, London.

Holland, J. & Blackburn, J. (eds) 1998,*Whose Voice? Participatory Research and Policy Change*, Intermediate Technology Publications, London.

Holmes, S. & Sunstein, C. 1999, *The Cost of Rights: Why Liberty Depends on Taxes*, Norton, New York.

Hoogvelt, A. 1997, *Globalization and the Postcolonial World: The New Political Economy of Development*, Palgrave, Basingstoke.

Horne, D. (ed.) 1992, *The Trouble with Economic Rationalism*, Scribe, Melbourne.

Hudson, B. 1987, 'Collaboration in Social Welfare: A Framework for Analysis', *Policy and Politics*, vol. 15, pp. 175–82.

Hurrell, A. & Woods, N. 1999, *Inequality, Globalisation and World Politics*, Oxford University Press, Oxford.

Ife, J. 1980, 'The Determination of Social Need: A Model of Need Statements in Social Administration', *Australian Journal of Social Issues*, vol. 15, no. 2, pp. 92–107.

Ife, J. 1991, 'Social Policy and the Green Movement', *Australian Quarterly*, vol. 63, no. 3, pp. 336–46.

Ife, J. 1993, 'Community Based Services: Opportunity or Con Trick?', in P. Saunders & S. Graham (eds), *Beyond Economic Rationalism: Alternative Futures for Social Policy*, Social Policy Research Centre Reports and Proceedings, no. 105, University of New South Wales, Sydney.

Ife, J. 1999, 'Postmodernism, Critical Theory and Social Work', in R. Pease & J. Fook (eds), *Transforming Social Work Practice: Postmodern Critical Perspectives*, Allen & Unwin, Sydney.

Ife, J. 2001, *Human Rights and Social Work: Towards Rights-Based Practice*, Cambridge University Press, Cambridge.

Ife, J. 2004, 'Linking Community Development and Human Rights', Community Development, Human Rights and the Grassroots Conference, Deakin University, Melbourne, April.

Ignatieff, M. 1984, *The Needs of Strangers*, Chatto & Windus, London.

Illich, I. 1973, *Tools for Conviviality*, Calder & Boyars, London.

Illich, I. 1976, *Limits to Medicine: Medical Nemesis, the Expropriation of Health*, Penguin, Harmondsworth.

Illich, I., Zola, I., McKnight, J., Caplan, J. & Shaiken, S. 1977, *Disabling Professions*, Marion Boyars, London.

Ishay, M.R. (ed.) 1997, *The Human Rights Reader*, Routledge, New York.

Jacobs, M. 1991, *The Green Economy—Environment, Sustainable Development and the Politics of the Future*, Pluto Press, London.

Jahan, R. 1995, *The Elusive Agenda: Mainstreaming Women in Development*, Zed Books, New Jersey,

Jamrozik, A. & Sweeny, T. 1996, *Children and Society: The Family, the State and Social Parenthood,* Macmillan, Melbourne.

Jamrozik, A. 1991, *Class, Inequality and the State*, Macmillan, Melbourne.

Jamrozik, A. 2005, *Social Policy in the Post-Welfare State*, Pearson Education Australia, Frenchs Forest, New South Wales.

Jarman, M. 2007, *Climate Change*, Pluto, London.

Jay, A. 1972, *A Householder's Guide to Community Defence Against Bureaucratic Aggression*, Jonathan Cape, London.

Jennett, C. & Stewart, R. (eds) 1989, *Politics of the Future—The Role of Social Movements*, Macmillan, Melbourne.

Jones, M.A. 1996, *The Australian Welfare State: Evaluating Social Policy*, 4th edn, Allen & Unwin, Sydney.

Kamerman, S. 1974, 'Participation, Leadership and Expertise: Imbalance or In Balance', *Social Service Review*, vol. 48, pp. 403–11.

Kannan, P. 2002, *Understanding Women's Participation in Community Development: A Fieldwork Experience*, PRIA and Department of Social Work, Stella Maris College, Chennai.

Kaplan, T. 1997, *Crazy for Democracy: Women in Grassroots Movements*, Routledge, New York

Karliner, J. 2000, 'Grassroots Globalisation: Reclaiming the Blue Planet', in F. Lechner & J. Boli (eds), *The Globalisation Reader*, Blackwell, Malden, MA.

Kaufman, M. & Alfonso, H. (eds) 1997, *Community Power and Grassroots Democracy: The Transformation of Social Life*, Zed Books, London.

Kelly, A. & Sewell, S. 1988, *With Head, Heart and Hand: Dimensions of Community Building*, Booralong Publications, Brisbane.

Kelly, L. 1992, *Community Development: From Technology to Transformation*, unpublished PhD thesis, University of Melbourne.

Kemp, P. & Wall, D. 1990, A *Green Manifesto for the 1990s*, Penguin, London.

Kennedy, R. (ed.) 1989, *Australian Welfare: Historical Sociology*, Macmillan, Melbourne.

Kenny, S. 1992, 'A New Professionalism', *Community Quarterly*, no. 22, pp. 6–8.

Kenny, S. 2007, *Developing Communities for the Future: Community Development in Australia*, 3rd edn, Thomson, South Melbourne.

Kingsbury, D. 2008, 'Universalism and Exceptionalism in "Asia"', in L. Avonius and D. Kingsbury (eds), *Human Rights in Asia*, Palgrave Macmillan, New York, pp. 19–39.

Kirby, S. & McKenna, K. 1989, *Experience, Research, Social Change: Methods from the Margins*, Garamond Press, Toronto.

Kleymeyer, C.D. (ed.) 1994, *Cultural Expression and Grassroots Development: Cases from Latin America and the Caribbean*, Lynne Riener, Boulder, CO.

Knudtson, P. & Suzuki, D. 1992, *Wisdom of the Elders*, Allen & Unwin, Sydney.

Kohn, A. 1986, *No Contest—The Case Against Competition*, Houghton Mifflin, Boston.

Kretzmann, J. & McKnight, J. 1993, *Building Communities from the Inside Out: A Path Toward Finding and Mobilizing a Community's Assets*, ACTA Publications, Chicago.

Kristol, I. 1978, *Two Cheers for Capitalism*, Basic Books, New York.

Kropotkin, P. 1972, *Mutual Aid: A Factor of Evolution*, Garland, New York.

Kuhn, T. 1970, *The Structure of Scientific Revolutions*, 2nd edn, University of Chicago Press, Chicago.

Kuyek, J. 1990, *Fighting for Hope: Organizing to Realize Our Dreams*, Black Rose Books, Montreal.

Kweit, R. & Kweit, M. 1981, *Implementing Citizen Participation in a Bureaucratic Society*, Praeger, New York.

Laris, P., Verity, F., Baum, F. & Project Team 2000, *Improving Health Services through Consumer Participation: A Toolkit for Organisations*, Report of a consultancy for the Commonwealth Department of Health and Aged Care, Adelaide.

Larsen, M. 2000, 'Imperialism, Colonialism, Postcolonialism', in H. Schwarz & S. Ray (eds), *A Companion to Postcolonial Studies*, Blackwell, Malden, MA.

Latham, M. 1997, 'The Search for Social Capital', in *Social Capital: The Individual, Civil Society and the State*, Centre for Independent Studies, Sydney.

Latouche, S. 1991, *In the Wake of the Affluent Society: An Exploration of Post-Development*, Zed Books, London.

Lawson, H. 2000, 'Globalization, Knowledgescapes and the Social Work Imagination', paper presented at Joint Conference of International Federation of Social Workers and International Association of Schools of Social Work, Montreal.

Le Grand, J. 1982, *The Strategy of Equality*, Allen & Unwin, London.

Leys, C. 1996, *The Rise and Fall of Development Theory*, EAEP, Nairobi, Indiana University Press IN & James Currey, London.

Liffman, M. 1978, *Power for the Poor: The Family Centre Project, an Experiment in Self-Help*, Allen & Unwin, Sydney.

Lincoln, S. & Guba, E. 1985, *Naturalistic Inquiry*, Sage, Beverly Hills, CA.

Lipietz, A. 1992, *Towards a New Economic Order: Postfordism, Ecology and Democracy*, Malcolm Slater (trans.), Polity Press, Cambridge.

Lipsky, M. 1980, *Street-Level Bureaucracy: Dilemmas of the Individual in Public Services*, Russell Sage Foundation, New York.

Lister, I. 1994, 'Conscientization and Political Literacy: A British Encounter with Paulo Freire', in P. McLaren & C. Lankshear (eds), *Politics of Liberation: Paths from Freire,* Routledge, London, pp. 62–73.

Lloyd, M. & Thacker, A. (eds) 1997, *The Impact of Michel Foucault on the Social Sciences and Humanities*, St Martin's Press, New York.

Lovelock, J. 1979, *Gaia: A New Look at Life on Earth*, Oxford University Press, Oxford.

Lowe, I. 2005, *Living in the Hothouse: How Global Warming Affects Australia*, Scribe Publications, Melbourne.

Lowe, I. & Paavola, J. 2005, 'Environmental values in a globalising world', in I. Lowe & J. Paavola (eds), *Environmental Values in a Globalising World: Nature, Justice and Governance*, Routledge, Abingdon, Oxfordshire, pp. 3–12.

Luke, T. 1999, *Capitalism, Democracy and Ecology: Departing from Marx*, University of Illinois Press, Urbana, IL.

Lutz, M. 1992 'Humanistic Economics: History and Basic Principles', in P. Ekins & M. Max-Neef (eds), *Real-Life Economics: Understanding Wealth Creation*, Routledge, London.

Lyotard, J. 1984, *The Postmodern Condition: A Report on Knowledge*, Manchester University Press, Manchester.

Macleod, G. 1991, *The Community Business Series: Cheticamp*, Tompkins Institute for Human Values and Technology, University College of Cape Breton, Nova Scotia.

Macornick, J. 2007, 'Local Currency Loans and Grants: Comparative Case Studies of Ithaca Hours and Calgary Dollars', *International Journal of Community Currency Research*, vol. 11, pp. 1–22.

MacPherson, C. 1977, *The Life and Times of Liberal Democracy,* Oxford University Press, New York.

Macy, J. 1991, *World as Lover, World as Self*, Parallel Press, Berkeley.

Mander, J. 1991, *In the Absence of the Sacred: The Failure of Technology and the Survival of the Indian Nations*, Sierra Club Books, San Francisco.

Marchant, H. & Wearing, B. 1986, *Gender Reclaimed—Women and Social Work,* Hale & Iremonger, Sydney.

Marcuse, H. 1964, *One Dimensional Man: Studies in the Ideology of Advanced Industrial Society*, Routledge & Kegan Paul, London.

Marshall, P. 1992a, *Demanding the Impossible: A History of Anarchism*, HarperCollins, London.

Marshall, P. 1992b, *Nature's Web: An Exploration of Ecological Thinking*, Simon & Schuster, London.

Marshall, T.H. 1965, *Social Policy*, Hutchinson, London.

Martin, S. & Schumann, H. 1997, *The Global Trap: Globalization and the Assault on Democracy and Prosperity,* P. Camiller (trans.), Pluto Press, Sydney.

Maslow, A. 1970, *Motivation and Personality*, 2nd edn, Harper & Row, New York.

Mason, M. 1999, *Environmental Democracy*, St Martin's Press, New York.

Matthews, R. (ed.) 1988, *Informal Justice?*, Sage, London.

Max-Neef, M. 1991, *Human Scale Development: Conception, Application and Further Reflections*, Apex Press, New York.

McArdle, J. 1993, *Resource Manual for Facilitators in Community Development*, Employ Publishing Group, Windsor, Victoria.

McCashen, W. 2005, *The Strengths Based Approach: a Strengths-Based Resource for Sharing Power and Creating Change,* St Luke's Innovative Resources, Bendigo, Victoria.

McCowan, L. 1996, *A Social Work Approach to Post Genocide Trauma Recovery for the Rwandese Community*, Master of Social Work thesis, University of Newcastle, Newcastle, New South Wales.

McDonald, J., Murphy, A. & Payne, W. 2001, 'Ballarat Health Consortium: A Case Study of Influential Factors in the Development and Maintenance of a Health Partnership', *Australian Journal of Primary Health*, vol. 7, no. 2, pp. 75–82.

McKibbin, B. 1990, *The End of Nature*, Penguin, London.

McKibbin, B. 2007, *Deep Economy: The Wealth of Communities and the Durable Future*, Time Books/Henry Holt and Co., New York.

McLaren, P. & Leonard, P. (eds) 1993, *Paulo Freire: A Critical Encounter*, Routledge, London.

McLean, R. & Stutter, H. 1993, *Advocacy Training in Community Services: a Training Package for Consumers and Service Providers*, TasCOSS/Tasmania TAFE.

Meadows, D., Meadows, D. & Randers, J. 1992, *Beyond the Limits—Global Collapse or a Sustainable Future*, Earthscan, London.

Meadows, D., Meadows, D., Randers, J. & Behrens, W. 1972, *The Limits to Growth—A Report for the Club of Rome's Project on the Predicament of Mankind*, Signet, New York.

Meeker-Lowry, S. 1988, *Economics as if the Earth Really Mattered*, New Society Publications, Philadelphia, PA.

Mellor, M. 1992, *Breaking the Boundaries: Towards a Feminist Green Socialism*, Virago, London.

Melnyk, G. 1985, *The Search for Community: From Utopia to a Co-operative Society*, Black Rose Books, Montreal.

Mendlovitz, S. & Walker, R.J.B. (eds) 1987, *Towards a Just World Peace—Perspectives from Social Movements*, Butterworth, London.

Merchant, C. 1980, *The Death of Nature: Women, Ecology and the Scientific Revolution*, HarperCollins, San Francisco.

Merchant, C. 1992, *Radical Ecology: The Search for a Livable World*, Routledge, New York.

Meyer, B. & Geschiere, P. (eds) 1999, *Globalization and Identity: Dialectics of Flow and Closure*, Blackwell, Oxford.

Midgley, J. 1986, (ed.), *Community Participation, Social Development and the State*, Methuen, London.

Mills, C.W. 1956, *The Power Elite*, Oxford University Press, New York.

Mills, C.W. 1970, *The Sociological Imagination*, Penguin, Harmondsworth.

Mishra, R. 1981, *Society and Social Policy*, 2nd edn, Macmillan, London.

Mishra, R. 1984, *The Welfare State in Crisis*, Wheatsheaf, Brighton, East Sussex.

Mishra, R. 1999, *Globalization and the Welfare State*, Edward Elgar, Cheltenham, Gloucestershire.

Mittelman, J. 2000, *The Globalization Syndrome: Transformation and Resistance*, Princeton University Press, Princeton, NJ.

Mongia, P. 1996, 'Introduction', in Padmini Mongia (ed.), *Contemporary Postcolonial Theory: A Reader*, Arnold, London.

Moran, E. 2006, *People and Nature: an Introduction to Human Ecological Relations*, Blackwell, Malden, MA.

Morrison, R. 1991, *We Build the Road as We Travel*, New Society Publications, Philadelphia, PA.

Mowbray, M. 1985, 'The Medicinal Properties of Localism: a Historical Perspective', in R. Thorpe & J. Petrucheria (eds), *Community Work or Social Change? An Australian Perspective*, Routledge & Kegan Paul, Melbourne.

Mullaly, R. 1997, *Structural Social Work: Ideology, Theory and Practice*, Oxford University Press, Toronto.

Mullaly, R. 2002, *Challenging Oppression: a Critical Social Work Approach*, Oxford University Press, Toronto.

Murphy, J. & Cauchi, J. 2004, 'What's Wrong with Community Building II: It's Much Worse Than We Thought', Community Development, Human Rights and the Grassroots Conference, Deakin University, Melbourne, April.

Naess, A. 1989, *Ecology, Community and Lifestyle*, Cambridge University Press, UK.

Nair, S. 2002, 'Human Rights and Postcoloniality: Representing Burma', in G. Chowdhry & S. Nair (eds), *Power, Postcolonialism and International Relations: Reading Race, Gender and Class*, Routledge, London.

Narby, J. 2006, *Intelligence in Nature: an Inquiry into Knowledge*, Penguin, New York.

National Social Welfare Commission 1973, Australian Assistance Plan: Discussion Paper No. 1, National Social Welfare Commission, Canberra.

National Social Welfare Commission 1974, Australian Assistance Plan: Discussion Paper No. 2, National Social Welfare Commission, Canberra.

National Social Welfare Commission 1976, Report on the Australian Assistance Plan, National Social Welfare Commission, Canberra.

Neumann, R. 2005, *Making Political Ecology*, Hodder Arnold, London.

Norberg-Hodge, H. 1991, *Ancient Futures: Learning from Ladakh*, Rider, London.
Norgaard, R. 1994, *Development Betrayed: The End of Progress and a Coevolutionary Revisioning of the Future*, Routledge, London.
North, P. 2006, *Alternative Currency Movements as a Challenge to Globalisation? A case study of Manchester's local currency networks*, Ashgate, Aldershot, Hampshire.
North Sydney Municipality 1990, *Public Participation and Direct Democracy in North Sydney Municipality*, North Sydney Municipal Council, North Sydney.
Nozick, M. 1992, *No Place Like Home: Building Sustainable Communities*, Canadian Council on Social Development, Ottawa.
Nurick, J. (ed.) 1987, *Mandate to Govern: A Handbook for the Next Australian Government*, Australian Institute for Public Policy, Perth.
O'Connor, J. 1973, *The Fiscal Crisis of the State*, St Martin's Press, New York.
O'Neill, K. 1997, 'Local Responses to Globalisation', in J. Wiseman (ed.), *Alternatives to Globalisation: An Asia-Pacific Perspective*, Community Aid Abroad, Melbourne.
O'Neill, M., Lemieux, V., Groleau, G., Frotin, F-P. & Lamarche, P. 1997, 'Coalition Theory as a Framework for Understanding and Implementing Health-Related Interventions', *Health Promotion International*, vol. 12, no. 1, pp. 79–87.
O'Neill, P. & Trickett, E. 1982, *Community Consultation*, Jossey-Bass, San Francisco.
O'Regan, P. & O'Connor, T. 1989, *Community: Give It a Go!* Allen & Unwin, Wellington, New Zealand.
O'Riordan, D. 1999, *Public Health Partnerships: An Integrated Approach to Addressing Health Inequities*, Centre for Health Promotion and Cancer Prevention Research & Centre for Primary Health Care, University of Queensland St. Lucia, Brisbane.
Oakley, A. et al. 1991, *Projects with People: The Practice of Participation in Rural Development*, International Labour Organization, Geneva.
Offe, C. 1984, *Contradictions of the Welfare State*, Hutchinson, London.
Ornstein, R. & Ehrlich, P. 1989, *New World, New Mind*, Touchstone, New York.
Pakulski, J. 1991, *Social Movements: The Politics of Protest*, Longman Cheshire, Melbourne.
Pakulski, J. 2004, *Globalising Inequalities: New Patterns of Social Privilege and Disadvantage*, Allen Unwin, Crows Nest, New South Wales.
Parker, S., Pease, B. & Fook, J. 1999, 'Empowerment: The Modernist Social Work Concept *par excellence*', in B. Pease & J. Fook (eds), *Transforming Social Work Practice: Postmodern Critical Perspectives*, Allen & Unwin, Sydney.
Pascall, G. 1986, *Social Policy: A Feminist Analysis*, Tavistock, London.
Pateman, C. 1970, *Participation and Democratic Theory*, Cambridge University Press, Cambridge.
Payne, M. 2001, 'Knowledge Bases and Knowledge Biases in Social Work', *Journal of Social Work*, vol. 1, no. 2, pp. 133–146.
Pearce, D., Markandya, A. & Barbier, E. 1989, *Blueprint for a Green Economy*, Earthscan, London.
Pease, R. 1991, 'Dialectical Models Versus Ecological Models in Social Work', in *Ecology and Deprivation: Implications for Social Work*, Proceedings of 11th Asia–Pacific Regional Seminar on Social Work, Asia & Pacific Association for Social Work Education, Hong Kong, pp. 107–12.
People Together Project & Victorian Local Government Association 2000, *The Power of Community*, Melbourne.
People's Health Movement 2000, *People's Charter for Health*, PHM, Dhaka, Bangladesh.
Pepper, D. 1991, *Communes and the Green Vision: Counterculture, Lifestyle and the New Age*, Green Print, London.

Pepper, D. 1993, *Eco-Socialism: From Deep Ecology to Social Justice*, Routledge, London.

Pierson, C. 1991, *Beyond the Welfare State?*, Polity Press, Cambridge.

Piette, D. 1990, 'Community Participation in Formal Decision Making Mechanisms', *Health Promotion International*, vol. 5, no. 3, pp. 187–97.

Plant, J. & Plant, C. (eds) 1992, *Putting Power in its Place: Create Community Control!*, New Society Publications, Philadelphia, PA.

Plant, R. 1974, *Community and ideology*, Routledge & Kegan Paul, London.

Plumwood, V. 1993, *Feminism and the Mastery of Nature*, Routledge, London.

Polsky, A. 1991, *The Rise of the Therapeutic State*, Princeton University Press, Princeton, NJ.

Porritt, J. 1984, *Seeing Green: The Politics of Ecology Explained*, Blackwell, Oxford.

Postman, N. 1993, *Technopoly: The Surrender of Culture to Technology*, Random House, New York.

Pusey, M. 1991, *Economic Rationalism in Canberra*, Cambridge University Press, Cambridge.

Putnam, R. 1993, *Making Democracy Work: Civic Traditions in Modern Italy*, Princeton University Press, Princeton, NJ.

Rahman, A. 1993, *People's Self-Development: Perspectives on Participatory Action, Research*, Zed Books, London.

Rao V. & Walton, M. 2004, 'Culture and Public Action: Relationality, Equality of Agency, and Development' in V. Rao & M.Walton (eds), *Culture and Public Action*, Stanford University Press, Stanford, California, pp. 3–36.

Rawls, J. 1972, *A Theory of Justice*, Oxford University Press, Oxford.

Rawls, J. 1999, *A Theory of Justice*, revised edn, Belknap Press, Cambridge, MA.

Rayner, M. 1998, *Rooting Democracy: Growing the Society We Want*, Allen & Unwin, Sydney.

Reason, P. (ed.) 1988, *Human Inquiry in Action: Developments in New Paradigm Research*, Sage, London.

Rees, S. 1991, *Achieving Power: Practice & Policy in Social Welfare*, Allen & Unwin, Sydney.

Rees, S., Rodley, G. & Stilwell, F. (eds) 1993, *Beyond the Market: Alternatives to Economic Rationalism*, Pluto Press, Sydney.

Rein, M. & White, S. 1981, 'Knowledge for Practice', *Social Service Review*, vol. 55, no. 1, pp. 1–41.

Reynolds, H. 1981, *The Other Side of the Frontier: Aboriginal Resistance to the European Invasion of Australia*, Penguin, Harmondsworth.

Reynolds, H. 1989, 'The End of a Long Love Affair', *Australian Society*, April, pp. 18–19.

Reynolds, H. 1998, *This Whispering in Our Hearts*, Allen & Unwin, Sydney.

Rifkin, J. 1985, *Entropy: A New World View*, Paladin, London.

Robertson, R. 1995, 'Glocalization: Time–Space and Homogeneity–Heterogeneity', in M. Featherstone, S. Lash & R. Robertson (eds), *Global Modernities*, Sage, London, pp. 25–44.

Rodger, J. 2000, *From a Welfare State to a Welfare Society: The Changing Context of Social Policy in a Postmodern Era*, Macmillan, London.

Rose, H. 1990, 'Activists, Gender and the Community Health Movement', *Health Promotion International*, vol. 5, no. 3, pp. 209–18.

Rosenau, P.M. 1992, *Post-Modernism and the Social Sciences: Insights, Inroads and Intrusions*, Princeton University Press, Princeton, NJ.

Rostow, W.W. 1971, *The Stages of Economic Growth: A Non-Communist Manifesto*, Cambridge University Press, Cambridge.

Rothman, J. 1974, 'Three Models of Community Organization Practice', in F. Cox, J. Erlich, J. Rothman & J. Tropman (eds), *Strategies of Community Organization: A Book of Readings*, 2nd edn, F.E. Peacock, Itasca, IL.

Rothman, J., Erlich, J. & Tropman, J. (eds) 2001, *Strategies of Community Intervention*, 6th edn, F.E. Peacock Publishers, Itasca, IL.
Rouse, R. 1994, 'Power/Knowledge', in G. Gutting (ed.), *The Cambridge Companion to Foucault*, Cambridge University Press, Cambridge.
Roussos, S. & Faucett, S. 2000, 'A Review of Collaborative Partnerships as a Strategy for Improving Community Health', *Annual Review of Public Health*, vol. 21, pp. 369–402.
Rowland, C. (ed.) 1999, *The Cambridge Companion to Liberation Theology*, Cambridge University Press, Cambridge.
Ryle, M. 1988, *Ecology and Socialism*, Radius Century Hutchinson, London.
Sachs, W. (ed.) 1992, *The Development Dictionary: A Guide to Knowledge as Power*, Zed Books, London.
Said, E. 1993, *Culture and Imperialism*, Chatto & Windus, London.
Said, E. 1995, *Orientalism*, Penguin, London.
Sale, K. 1991, *Dwellers in the Land: The Bioregional Vision*, New Society Publishers, Philadelphia, PA.
Salleh, A. 1997, *Ecofeminism as Politics: Nature, Marx and the Postmodern*, Allen & Unwin, Sydney.
Sarker, S. 1999, *Eco-socialism or Eco-capitalism: A Critical Analysis of Humanity's Fundamental Choices*, Zed Books, London.
Saul, J. 1992, *Voltaire's Bastards: The Dictatorship of Reason in the West*, Vintage Books, New York.
Saunders, P. 1994, *Welfare and Inequality: National and International Perspectives on the Australian Welfare State*, Cambridge University Press, Cambridge.
Save the Children, 2007, *Getting it Right for Children: a Practitioners' Guide to Child Rights Programming*, Save the Children UK, London.
Savoie, D. 1995, 'What is Wrong with the New Public Management?', *Canadian Public Administration*, vol. 38, no. 1, pp. 112–21.
Saward, M. 1998, *The Terms of Democracy*, Polity Press, Cambridge.
Schumacher, E.F. 1973, *Small Is Beautiful—A Study of Economics as if People Mattered*, Blond & Briggs, London.
Seabrook, J. 1993a, *Pioneers of Change: Experiments in Creating a Humane Society*, New Society Publishers, Philadelphia, PA.
Seabrook, J. 1993b, *Victims of Development: Resistance and Alternatives*, Verso, London.
Seidman, S. (ed.) 1994, *The Postmodern Turn: New Perspectives on Social Theory*, Cambridge University Press, Cambridge.
Selznick, P. 1966, *TVA and the Grass Roots: A Study in the Sociology of Formal Organisations*, Harper & Row, New York.
Sen, A. 2004, 'How Does Culture Matter?', in V. Rao and M.Walton (eds), *Culture and Public Action*, Stanford University Press, Stanford, California, CA, pp. 37–58.
Serageldin, I. 1995, *Nurturing Development: Aid and Cooperation in Today's Changing World*, The World Bank, Washington, DC.
Shannon, P. 1991, *Social Policy*, Oxford University Press, Auckland, New Zealand.
Shaw, M. and Martin, I. 2000, 'Community work, citizenship and democracy: re-making the connections', *Community Development Journal*, vol. 35, no. 4, pp. 401–413.
Shaw, T. 2008, 'An Ecological Contribution to Social Welfare Theory', *Social Development Issues*, vol. 30, no. 3, pp. 13–26.
Shiva, V. 1989, *Staying Alive: Women, Ecology and Development*, Zed Books, London.
Shiva, V. 1991, *The Violence of the Green Revolution: Third World Agriculture, Ecology and Politics*, Zed Books, London.

Shragge, E. 1990, 'Community Based Practice: Political Alternatives or New State Forms', in L. Davies & E. Shragge (eds), *Bureaucracy and Community: Essays on the Politics of Social Work Practice*, Black Rose Books, Montreal, pp. 137–73.

Shragge, E. (ed.) 1993, *Community Economic Development: In Search of Empowerment and Alternatives,* Black Rose Books, Montreal.

Simmons, I.G. 1997, *Humanity and Environment: A Cultural Ecology*, Addison Wesley Longman, Harlow, Essex.

Singer, P. 1993, *How Are We to Live: Ethics in an Age of Self-Interest,* Text Publishing Company, Melbourne.

South Australian Community Health Research Unit 1999, *Hoi Sinh Evaluation Report*, Adelaide.

Spergel, I. 1969, *Community Problem Solving: The Delinquency Example,* University of Chicago Press, Chicago, IL.

Spivak, G. 1987, *In Other Worlds: Essays in Cultural Politics*, Methuen, New York.

Spivak, G. 1994, 'Can the Subaltern Speak?', in P. Williams & L. Chrisman (eds), *Colonial Discourse and Post-Colonial Theory: A Reader*, Harvester Wheatsheaf, Hemel Hempstead, Hertfordshire.

Stiefel, M. & Wolfe, M. 1994, *A Voice for the Excluded: Popular Participation in Development, Utopia or Necessity?*, Zed Books, London.

Stilwell, F. 1993, *Economic Inequality: Who Gets What in Australia?*, Pluto Press, Sydney.

Strange, J. 1972, 'The Impact of Citizen Participation on Public Administration', *Public Administration Review*, vol. 32, pp. 457–70.

Strauss, A. & Corbin, J. 1990, *Basics of Qualitative Research: Grounded Theory Procedures and Techniques*, Sage, Newbury Park, CA.

Stretton H. & Orchard L. 1994, *Public Goods, Public Enterprise, Public Choice*, St. Martins Press, Basingstoke, Hampshire.

Stretton, H. & Orchard, L. 1987, *Political Essays*, Georgian House, Melbourne.

Sullivan, W. & Kymlicka, W. (eds) 2007, *The Globalization of Ethics*, Cambridge University Press, New York.

Sulman, M. (ed.) 1998, *Ecology Politics and Violent Conflict*, Zed Books, London.

Suzuki, D. & McConnell, A. 1997, *The Sacred Balance: Rediscovering Our Place in Nature*, Allen & Unwin, Sydney.

Tacey, D. 2000, *Re-Enchantment: The New Australian Spirituality*, HarperCollins, Sydney.

Tapper, A. 1990, *The Family and the Welfare State*, Allen & Unwin, Sydney.

Taylor, B.R. (ed.) 1995, *Ecological Resistance Movements: The Global Emergence of Radical and Popular Environmentalism*, State University Press of New York, New York.

Taylor-Gooby, P. & Dale, J. 1981, *Social Theory & Social Welfare*, Edward Arnold, London.

Taylor-Gooby, P. 1985, *Public Opinion, Ideology and State Welfare*, Routledge & Kegan Paul, London.

Taylor-Gooby, P. 1993, *Postmodernism and Social Policy: A Great Leap Backwards?*, Social Policy Research Centre Discussion Paper no. 45, University of New South Wales, Sydney.

Terchek, R. 1998, *Gandhi: Struggling for Autonomy*, Vistaar Publication, New Delhi.

Tesoriero, F. 2006a, 'Strengthening Communities through Women's Self Help Groups in South India', *Community Development Journal*, vol. 41, no. 3, pp. 321–33.

Tesoriero, F. 2006b, 'Personal Growth towards Intercultural Competence through an International Field Education Program', *Australian Social Work*, vol. 59, no. 2, pp. 126–40.

Tesoriero, F. 2008a, 'Learning from Failure: Generating Knowledge and Strategies to Advance Human Rights at the Community and International Levels', *Community Development and Ecology: Engaging Ecological Sustainability through Community Development*, Centre for Citizenship and Human Rights, 26–28 March 2008, Melbourne.

Tesoriero, F. 2008b, 'Change and Resistance to Change: Community Development in a Rural Caste Community in South India', in D. Bottrell & G. Meagher (eds), *Communities and Change*, Sydney University Press, Sydney.

Thoreau, H.D. 1854, *Walden* (1983 edn), Viking Penguin, New York.

Titmuss, R. 1958, *Essays on the Welfare State*, Allen & Unwin, London.

Titmuss, R. 1968, *Commitment to Welfare*, Allen & Unwin, London.

Titmuss, R. 1970, *The Gift Relationship: From Human Blood to Social Policy*, Penguin, Harmondsworth.

Titmuss, R. 1974, *Social Policy: An Introduction*, Allen & Unwin, London.

Toman, M. & Sohngen, B. (eds) 2004, *Climate Change*, Ashgate, Aldershot.

Tong, R. 1989, *Feminist Thought: A Comprehensive Introduction*, Routledge, London.

Tönnies, F. 1955, *Community and Association* (trans. C. P. Loomis), Routledge, London.

Torgerson, D. 1999, *The Promise of Green Politics: Environmentalism and the Public Sphere*, Duke University Press, London.

Towle, C. 1965, *Common Human Needs*, National Association of Social Workers, New York.

Trainer, E. 1985, *Abandon Affluence*, Zed Books, London.

Trainer, E. 1989, *Developed to Death: Rethinking Third World Development*, Green Print, London.

Tropman, J., Erlich, J. & Rothman, J. (eds) 2001, *Tactics & Techniques of Community Intervention*, 6th edn, F.E. Peacock Publishers, Itasca, IL.

Uhr, J. 1998, *Deliberative Democracy in Australia: The Changing Place of Parliament*, Cambridge University Press, Cambridge.

UN-HABITAT 2005, *UN-HABITAT: The Agency for Cities and Shelter*, Nairobi.

United Nations Development Program (UNDP) 1996, Guiding principles for development, monitoring and evaluation of people-centred, SHD-oriented programme support strategies, JJL/96/12/19, New Delhi.

Uphoff, N. & Cohen, J. 1979, *Feasibility and Application of Rural Development Participation: A State of the Art Paper*, Cornell University, Beacon Press, Boston.

Uvin, P., Jain, P. & Brown, D. 2000, 'Think large and act small: toward a new paradigm for NGO scaling up', *World Development*, vol. 28, no. 8, pp. 1409–19.

VanDeVeer, D. & Pierce C. 1998, *The Environmental Ethics and Policy Book*, 2nd edn, Wadsworth, Belmont, CA.

Van der Ryn, S. & Cowan, S. 2007, *Ecological Design*, Island Press, Washington, DC.

van Erven, E. 1992, *The Playful Revolution: Theatre and Liberation in Asia*, Indiana University Press, Bloomington, IN.

van Kuik, M. 2009, 'Time for each Other: Working Towards a complementary Currency Model to Serve the anti-Poverty Policies of the Municipality of Landgraaf, the Netherlands', *International Journal of Community Currency Research*, vol. 13, pp. 3–18.

Vinson, T. 2007, *Dropping off the Edge: The Distribution of Disadvantage in Australia*, Jesuit Social Services, Richmond, Victoria.

Voth, D. & Jackson, V. 1981, *Evaluating Citizen Participation: Rural and Urban Community Development*, Center for Responsive Governance, Washington, DC.

Wadsworth, Y. 1997, *Do It Yourself Social Research*, Allen & Unwin, Melbourne.

Walker D. 2009, 'The Impact of Community Currency Systems on Gender Relations in Rural Northeast Thailand: A hybrid Social Audit – Gender Analysis Approach', *International Journal of Community Currency Research*, vol. 13, pp. 36–60.

Wall, D. 1990, *Getting There—Steps to a Green Society*, Green Print, London.

Wallace, H. 1996, *Developing Alternatives: Community Development Strategies and Environmental Issues in the Pacific*, Victoria University of Technology, Melbourne.

Ward, C. 1977, 'Topless Federations', in G. Woodcock (ed.), *The Anarchist Reader*, Fontana/Collins, Glasgow, pp. 319–26.

Ward, C. 1988, *Anarchy in Action*, Freedom Press, London.

Ward, J. 1992, 'The Participating Professional', *Community Quarterly*, no. 22, pp. 22–6.

Ward, J. 1993, *Australian Community Development: Ideas, Skills and Values for the 90s*, Community Quarterly, Windsor, Victoria.

Warren, K. 2000, *Eco-feminist Philosophy: A Western Perspective on What It Is and Why It Matters*, Rowman & Littlefield, Lanham, MD.

Watson, D. 1980, *Caring for Strangers: An Introduction to Practical Philosophy for Students of Social Administration*, Routledge & Kegan Paul, London.

Weber, M. 1970, 'Bureaucracy', in H. Gerth & C.W. Mills (eds), *From Max Weber: Essays in Sociology*, Routledge, London.

Welfare & Community Services Review (WA) 1984, *The Wellbeing of the People: Final Report of the Welfare and Community Services Review in Western Australia*, vol. 1, Perth.

Whyte, W. & Whyte, K. 1988, *Making Mondragon: The Growth and Dynamics of the Worker Co-operative Complex*, ILR Press, Ithaca, NY.

Wilding, P. (ed.) 1986, *In Defence of the Welfare State*, Manchester University Press, London.

Wilding, P. 1982, *Professional Power and Social Welfare*, Routledge & Kegan Paul, London.

Wilensky, H. & Lebeaux, C. 1965, *Industrial Society and Social Welfare*, 2nd edn, The Free Press, New York.

Williams, F. 1989, *Social Policy, a Critical Introduction: Issues of Race, Gender and Class*, Polity Press, Cambridge.

Winter, T. (ed.) 2000, *Social Capital and Public Policy in Australia*, Australian Institute of Family Studies, Melbourne.

Wise, M. & Signal, L. 2000, 'Health promotion development in Australia and New Zealand', *Health Promotion International*, vol. 15, no. 3, pp. 237–48.

Woodcock, G. (ed.) 1977, *The Anarchist Reader*, Fontana/Collins, Glasgow.

Woodroofe, K. 1962, *From Charity to Social Work in England and the United States*, Routledge & Kegan Paul, London.

World Commission on Environment and Development 1987, *Our Common Future* (Brundtland Report), Oxford University Press, Oxford.

World Health Organization 2008, Closing the gap in a generation: Health equity through action on the social determinants of health, Commission on the Social Determinants of Health Final Report, World Health Organization, Geneva.

Wright, S. & Taylor, D. 1999, 'Success under Tokenism: Co-option of the Newcomer and the Prevention of Collective Protest', *British Journal of Social Psychology*, vol. 38, pp. 369–96.

Wronka, J. 1992, *Human Rights and Social Policy in the 21st Century: A History of the Idea of Human Rights and Comparison of the United Nations Universal Declaration of Human Rights with United States Federal and State Constitutions*, University Press of America, Lanham, MD.

Wynne, B. 1996, 'May the sheep graze safely? A reflexive view of the expert–lay knowledge divide', in S. Lash, B. Szerszynski & B. Wynne (eds), *Risk, Environment and Modernity: Towards a New Ecology*, Sage, London, pp. 26–43.

Young, I.M. 1990, *Justice and the Politics of Difference*, Princeton University Press, New Jersey.

Young, I. M. 1996 'Communication and the Other: Beyond Deliberative Democracy', in S. Benhabib (ed.), *Democracy and Difference: Contesting the Boundaries of the Political*, Princeton University Press, Princeton, NJ.

Index

C

E